Climate Governance in the Developing World

Climate Governance in the Developing World

Edited by
David Held, Charles Roger and Eva-Maria Nag

polity

First published in 2013 by Polity Press

Polity Press
65 Bridge Street
Cambridge CB2 1UR, UK

Polity Press
350 Main Street
Malden, MA 02148, USA

ISBN-13: 978-0-7456-6276-3
ISBN-13: 978-0-7456-6277-0(pb)

A catalogue record for this book is available from the British Library.

Typeset in 10.5 on 12 pt Swift Regular by
Servis Filmsetting Ltd, Stockport, Cheshire
Printed and bound in Great Britain by Clays Ltd, St Ives PLC

For further information on Polity, visit our website: www.politybooks.com

Contents

Contents

Contributors

Fitrian Ardiansyah has over fifteen years' experience in the fields of natural resource management, climate change and energy. At present, he is finalizing his doctoral research at the Crawford School of Public Policy at the Australian National University. He is also the Program Development Director for Pelangi Indonesia and Fellow at the International League of Conservation Writers. In previous years, he was a Program Director for Climate and Energy (WWF-Indonesia) and an expert member of the Indonesia Forest Climate Alliance and the Indonesian Official Delegates to the United Nations Framework Convention on Climate Change. He has received Australian Leadership and Allison Sudradjat Awards from the Government of Australia.

Aaron Atteridge is a Research Fellow at the Stockholm Environment Institute in Sweden. His work focuses on different aspects of climate policy, with a particular emphasis on understanding the interaction between international policy processes and the needs of developing countries. This includes analysis of climate politics in different countries and of climate finance, as well as the development of guidance on national adaptation planning and the examination of traditional biomass energy economies in developing countries. Among his previous roles, he has worked as a Senior Policy Officer on climate change and energy issues for the New South Wales government in Australia.

Jessica Blythe is a PhD candidate in the Department of Geography at the University of Victoria, Canada. She investigates the dynamics of change in social-ecological systems and has worked with fishing communities in southern Africa since 2004. Her current research explores how coastal communities respond to environmental change in Mozambique in order to contribute to the development of adaptive actions that promote human well-being and ecological health.

Robert Fletcher is Associate Professor of Natural Resources and Sustainable Development in the Department of Environment, Peace, and Security at the United Nations mandated University for Peace in Costa Rica. His research interests include climate change, conservation, development, ecotourism, environmental governance, globalization, and resistance and social movements. He has conducted field research concerning these topics in a number of sites in North, Central and South America.

Matías Franchini is a member of the Brazilian Research Network on International Relations and Climate Change at the University of Brasilia, and a member of the Department of Environment at the University of La Plata, Argentina. He is a PhD candidate and holds an MA in International Relations from the University of Brasilia. His main research interests are climate change, global environmental governance and Latin American studies. With Eduardo Viola and Thaís Ribeiro, he is co-author of *Sistema Internacional de Hegemonia Conservadora: Democracia e Governança Global na era da Crise Climática* (International System with Conservative Hegemony) (2012).

David Held is Master of University College, Durham, and Professor of Politics and International Relations at Durham University, UK. Among his most recent publications are *Gridlock: Why Global Cooperation is Failing When We Need It Most* (2013), *The Governance of Climate Change* (2011), *Cosmopolitanism: Ideals and Realities* (2010), *Globalisation/ Anti-Globalisation* (2007), *Models of Democracy* (2006), *Global Covenant* (2004), *Global Transformations: Politics, Economics and Culture* (1999) and *Democracy and the Global Order: From the Modern State to Cosmopolitan Governance* (1995). His main research interests include the study of globalization, changing forms of democracy and the prospects of regional and global governance. He is a Director of Polity Press, which he co-founded in 1984, and General Editor of *Global Policy*.

Angus Hervey is a PhD candidate and Ralph Miliband Scholar at the London School of Economics and Political Science, UK. He is an expert on environmental issues in southern Africa, and has published a number of articles on land use change, deforestation and the impacts of climate change in the region. With David Held and Marika Theros, he is co-editor of *The Governance of Climate Change: Science, Economics, Ethics and Politics* (2011).

Jae-Seung Lee is a Professor in the Division of International Studies, Korea University. He is currently an Editor-in-Chief of *Korea Review of International Studies* and Vice-Director of the Institute of Sustainable Development. He also serves as a member of the Policy Advisory Board of the Presidential Secretariat (Foreign and Security Affairs). During the year 2011–12, he joined the Walter H. Shorenstein Asia-Pacific Research Center and the Center for East Asian Studies of Stanford University as a visiting scholar. He holds a BA in political science from Seoul National University and an MA (1993) and PhD in political science from Yale University.

Lesley Masters is a Senior Researcher within the foreign policy and diplomacy programme of the Institute for Global Dialogue (IGD) at the University of South Africa. Her research focuses on environmental diplomacy, South Africa's foreign policy, the international politics of climate change and the governance of natural resources. She holds a PhD in International Relations from the University of Leicester, UK, and joined the IGD as a researcher in 2008 as part of its Multilateral Programme.

Eva-Maria Nag received her PhD on Indian political thought from the London School of Economics and Political Science (LSE), UK. She has taught undergraduate and postgraduate courses on political theory, ethics and public administration, and South and East Asian politics at the LSE, the School of Oriental and African Studies, King's College London and the American University in London, UK. She has also worked on global corporate issues with the Bertelsmann Foundation (Germany) and Tomorrow's Company (UK). She is one of the founding editors of *Global Policy*, an innovative and interdisciplinary journal bringing together world-class academics and leading practitioners to analyse both public and private solutions to global problems and issues. She is also a Visiting Fellow at the School of Government and International Affairs, Durham University, UK, where she works on comparative political thinking.

Lucentezza Napitupulu is an Affiliated Lecturer and Researcher in the Department of Economics, University of Indonesia. Having worked in climate change policy for the last eight years, she has provided consulting services for numerous stakeholders, including the Ministry of Environment and Ministry of Finance in Indonesia. She holds a Master's degree in Economics from North Carolina State University, USA, and is currently pursuing her PhD in Environmental Science at the Autonomous University of Barcelona, Spain. Her research interests are in environmental management and community governance.

Simone Pulver is Assistant Professor of Environmental Studies at the University of California (UC), Santa Barbara, USA. She received her doctorate in Sociology from UC Berkeley and also holds an MA in Energy and Resources from UC Berkeley, as well as a BA in Physics from Princeton University, USA. Her research investigates organizational responses to environmental challenges. She has been analysing international climate politics for the past fifteen years, with a particular focus on transnational corporations and developing economies. Before joining UC Santa Barbara in 2009, she was the Joukowsky Family Assistant Research Professor at Brown University's Watson Institute for International Studies, USA.

Budy P. Resosudarmo is an Associate Professor and Head of the Indonesia Project at the Arndt-Corden Department of Economics, Crawford School of Public Policy at the Australian National University. His research interests include determining the economy-wide impact of environmental policies and understanding the political economy of natural resource utilization. In 2005, he edited *The Politics and Economics of Indonesia's Natural Resources*, and in 2009, he co-edited *Working with Nature against Poverty: Development, Resources and the Environment in Eastern Indonesia*. He received his PhD in Development Economics from Cornell University, USA.

Charles Roger is a PhD student at the University of British Columbia and Liu Scholar at the Liu Institute for Global Issues, Canada. His research focuses on transnational governance, global environmental politics and international political economy. He holds a BA from Concordia University, in Montreal, Canada, and an MSc from the London School of Economics and Political Science, UK. His research has been supported by the Liu Institute for Global Issues, the Centre for International Governance Innovation, the Research Center for Chinese Politics and Business, and the Social Sciences and Humanities Research Council of Canada.

Jeannie Sowers is Associate Professor of Political Science at the University of New Hampshire, USA. Her research focuses on the politics of environment and development in the Middle East and North Africa. She is the author of *Environmental Politics in Egypt: Activists, Experts, and the State* (2013) and co-editor of *The Journey to Tahrir: Revolution, Protest, and Social Change in Egypt* (2012). She has published articles in *Climatic Change, Development and Change, Journal of Environment and Development* and *Middle East Report* and is on the editorial boards of *Global Environmental Politics* and *Middle East Report*.

Eduardo Viola is a Full Professor at the Institute of International Relations, University of Brasilia, Senior Researcher of the Brazilian Council for Scientific Research and Chair of the Brazilian Research Network on International Relations and Climate Change. He has published four books and more than one hundred journal articles and book chapters. He has been visiting professor at several international universities – Stanford, Colorado, Notre Dame and Texas, USA, and Amsterdam, Netherlands – and a consultant with Brazilian Ministries – Science and Technology, Education, Defence and Environment. He has also been a member of the Committee on Global Environmental Change of the Brazilian Academy of Science.

Preface

The problem of climate change cannot be overstated. It is an issue of global significance with far-reaching transnational as well as inter-generational consequences for the life chances of people across the world. The brute fact is that greenhouse gas emissions are rising at an alarming rate and we have done far too little to reverse this shocking trend. We seem to be racing towards a tipping point after which the risks of climate change become tragic, irreversible realities. Having said this, there have been many important efforts, locally, nationally and globally, to address this threat. Some have been more promising than others, but where there have been some successes it is important to understand how this has occurred and to try and build on these relative achievements. By understanding what works and what does not we shed light on a path to more effective climate governance.

The responsibility for addressing climate change has conventionally been placed on the shoulders of the industrialized world. Indeed, this notion is more or less enshrined in the United Nations Framework Convention on Climate Change and, especially, in the Kyoto Protocol. Since the dawn of industrialization, now-developed states have con-tributed immensely to global stocks of greenhouse gas, and they must take action to mitigate future climatic changes and reduce the effects of those already imminent. However, with the rapid development of Asia and many other regions of the world, developing countries are now becoming major contributors to climate change as well. China has become the largest single emitter of greenhouse gases; Brazil, India and Indonesia now produce more greenhouse gas emissions individually each year than Japan or Germany; and South Korea and Mexico's emissions outstrip those of France and Italy. As a result, the prospects for addressing climate change without major efforts by states in the developing world are rapidly diminishing. It is essential for them to shift their emissions trajectories downwards as they grow.

It is striking and encouraging that some developing countries have established sophisticated responses to climate change. This is a trend that warrants much greater attention. China, Brazil, South Korea, Mexico and others are increasingly on the frontline of climate policymaking and can be considered global leaders in a number of significant ways. Some of the actions they are taking are comparable to the finest efforts made by the wealthier, industrialized world.

Others, such as Argentina and South Africa, are clearly laggards, and most developing states probably come closer to their poorer record. Yet this observation gives rise to an important question: how are some developing countries becoming more ambitious and successful than others in responding to climate change? Since many – perhaps most – developing countries remain unprepared for climate change and face immense political and economic barriers, the answer to this question is not obvious. This book explores this issue by closely analysing the experiences of twelve different countries in three regions of the globe, in Asia, the Americas and Africa. By examining these countries, it offers the most comprehensive study thus far on climate governance in the developing world.

The research undertaken in this book initially developed as a result of a generous grant provided to the editors by L'Agence Française de Développement (AFD). We are very grateful to the AFD for having provided the resources to conduct this work, which was undertaken over a three-year period and involved extensive travel, interviews and data gathering in several countries. While the original AFD-funded research focused on only a subset of those countries covered in this book, it revealed empirical complexities that had gone largely unnoticed and, in our view, presented a number of interesting puzzles. Thus, we expanded the project's scale and scope by bringing a series of additional researchers on board in order to examine these new dimensions of climate policymaking across a wider range of countries.

The editors would like to thank the many people who have contributed to the development of this volume and the research that underpins it. Above all, the contributors have been more than generous in sharing their expertise for the benefit of this book. Working alongside them has been a learning experience in the best sense. Many more were involved in producing this book in other ways. For their support and/or for very helpful comments and discussion at various stages of research and writing, we would like to thank Richard Balme, Satishkumar Belliethathan, Jean-Marc Coicaud, Olivier Charnoz, Björn Conrad, Robert Falkner, Tony Giddens, Tom Hale, Jin Xiaoting, Vannina Pomonti, Eduardo Viola, Robert Wade, Anna Wishart, Zha Daojiong and Zhang Haibin. Angus Hervey and Kyle McNally are also to be thanked for providing important research support, as well as Aida Kowalska, Danielle Da Silva and Dave Steinbach. Finally, we would like to thank everyone at Polity for all they did to turn the manuscript into the book that is now in your hands.

David Held
Charles Roger
Eva-Maria Nag

5 November 2012

Abbreviations

AAP	Africa Adaptation Programme
ABD	Arab-British Dynamics Company
ADII	Association of Comprehensive Indigenous Development
AFE	average fuel economy
AIJ	activities implemented jointly
AMCEN	African Ministerial Conference on the Environment
ANC	African National Congress
AOI	Arab Organization for Industrialization
AOSIS	Alliance of Small Island States
AU	African Union
AusAID	Australian Agency for International Development
AWG-LCA	Ad Hoc Working Group on Long-Term Cooperative Action
BAPPENAS	National Development Planning Agency
BASIC	Brazil, South Africa, India, China
BAU	business-as-usual
BCCF	Brazilian Climate Change Forum
BRICS	Brazil, Russia, India, China, South Africa
C40	C40 Cities Climate Leadership Group
CAHOSCC	Conference of African Heads of State and Government on Climate Change
CANAECO	National Ecotourism Chamber of Commerce
CANE	Coalition Against Nuclear Energy
CAS	Chinese Academy of Sciences
CATIE	Centro Agronómico Tropical de Investigación y Enseñanza
CBD	Convention on Biological Diversity
CCA	Center for Atmospheric Sciences
CCGC	National Board for the Coordination of Disaster Management
CCS	carbon capture and sequestration
CDF	Clean Development Fund
CDM	Clean Development Mechanism
CER	certified emissions reduction
CFE	Comision Federal de Electricidad

Abbreviations

CFL	compact fluorescent lamp
CI	Conservation International
CICC	Inter-Ministerial Commission on Climate Change
CIM	Inter-Ministerial Committee for Climate Change
CIMGC	Inter-Ministerial Commission on Climate Change
CMA	China Meteorological Administration
CNA	National Environment Commission
CO_2e	carbon dioxide equivalent
COFEMA	Federal Council of the Environment
COMEGEI	Climate Change Office
CONCAMIN	Mexican Federation of Chambers of Commerce
COP	Conference of the Parties
CRE	Energy Regulation Commission
CRGE	climate-resilient green economy
CSE	Centre for Science and Environment (ch. 3); Conservation Strategy of Ethiopia (ch. 11)
CSP	Country Studies Program
CTGC	Technical Council for Disaster Management
CTL	coal-to-liquid
DANIDA	Danish International Development Agency
DEA	Department of Environment
DEAT	Department of Environment and Tourism
DME	Department of Minerals and Energy
DNPI	National Council on Climate Change
DOE	Department of Energy
EACP	East Asia Climate Partnership
EC	European Community
ED	Environmental Defense
EDRI	Ethiopian Development Research Institute
EEAA	Egyptian Environmental Affairs Agency
EECCHI	Energy Efficiency and Conservation Clearing House Indonesia
EIUG	Energy Intensive User Group
ENCC	National Strategy on Climate Change
EPA	Environmental Protection Authority
EPACC	Ethiopian Programme of Adaptation to Climate Change
ESCO	energy service company
EU	European Union
FCPF	Forest Carbon Partnership Facility
FDI	foreign direct investment
FONAFIFO	National Fund for Forestry Financing
FORESTA	Forest Resources for a Stable Environment
FRELIMO	Front for the Liberation of Mozambique

Abbreviations

FUNDECOR	Fundación para el Desarrollo de la Cordillera Volcánica Central
FYP	Five-Year Plan
G8	Group of 8
G20	Group of 20
G77	Group of 77
GDP	gross domestic product
GEF	Global Environment Facility
GGGI	Global Green Growth Institute
GHG	greenhouse gas
GIR	Greenhouse Gas Inventory and Research Center
GIZ	German Agency for International Cooperation
Gt	gigatonne
GTP	Growth and Transformation Plan
GW	gigawatt
GWh	gigawatt-hours
IBA	important bird area
IBAMA	Brazilian Institute of Environment and Renewable Natural Resources
IBSA	India, Brazil, South Africa
ICCSR	Indonesia Climate Change Sectoral Roadmap
IEA	International Energy Agency
IFCA	Indonesian Forest Climate Alliance
IFI	international financial institution
IGCCC	Intergovernmental Committee on Climate Change
IMCCC	Inter-Ministerial Committee on Climate Change
IMF	International Monetary Fund
INAM	National Meteorological Institute
INBio	National Biodiversity Institute
INC	Intergovernmental Negotiating Committee (ch. 9); Initial National Communication (ch. 12)
INE	National Ecology Institute
INGC	National Institute for Disaster Management
IPCC	Intergovernmental Panel on Climate Change
IPM	integrated pest management
IREP	Integrated Rural Energy Programme
JI	Joint Implementation
JICA	Japan International Cooperation Agency
KBIZ	Korean Federation of Small and Medium Business
KCCI	Korean Chamber of Commerce and Industry
KCER	Korea Certified Emissions Reduction
KEF	Korea Employers Federation
KITA	Korean International Trade Association

Abbreviations

KP	Kyoto Protocol
kWh	kilowatt-hour
LDC	least developed country
LED	low emissions development
LEDS	Low Emissions Development Strategy
LOI	letter of intent
LSE	London School of Economics and Political Science
LTMS	Long Term Mitigation Scenarios
LUCF	land use change and forestry
LULUCF	land use, land use change and forestry
MCT	Ministry of Science and Technology
MDM	Democratic Movement of Mozambique
MEMR	Ministry of Energy and Mineral Resources
MENA	Middle East and North Africa
MICOA	Ministry for the Coordination of Environmental Affairs
MINAG	Ministry of Agriculture
MINEAT	Ministry of Environment, Energy and Telecommunications
MMA	Ministry of the Environment
MME	Ministry of Mines and Energy
MOARD	Ministry of Agriculture and Rural Development
MoE	Ministry of Environment
MOFA	Ministry of Foreign Affairs
MOFED	Ministry of Finance and Economic Development
MOST	Ministry of Science and Technology
MOTC	Ministry of Transport and Communication
MOTI	Ministry of Trade and Industry
MOWE	Ministry of Water and Energy
MPD	Ministry of Planning and Development
MRV	measuring, reporting and verification
Mt	megatonne
MW	megawatt
NAMA	Nationally Appropriate Mitigation Action
NAPA	National Adaptation Programme of Action
NAPCC	National Action Plan on Climate Change
NBCI	National Biomass Cookstove Initiative
NCCCC	National Coordination Committee on Climate Change
NCCCLSG	National Climate Change Coordinating Leading Small Group
NCCS	National Climate Change Strategy
NDRC	National Development and Reform Commission
NEA	National Energy Administration
NEC	National Energy Commission
NEEDS	National Environment, Economic and Development Study

Abbreviations

NELG	National Energy Leading Group
NEPA	National Environmental Protection Agency
NGO	non-governmental organization
NLCCC	National Leading Committee on Climate Change
NMA	National Meteorology Agency
NRDC	Natural Resources Defense Council
NREA	New and Renewable Energy Authority
ODA	official development assistance
OECD	Organization for Economic Cooperation and Development
PARP	Poverty Reduction Action Plan
PASDEP	Plan for Accelerated and Sustained Development for Ending Poverty
PBMR	Pebble Bed Modular Reactor
PCA	Partnership for Climate Action
PCGG	Presidential Committee on Green Growth
PCN	Paz con la Naturaleza
PCSD	Presidential Commission on Sustainable Development
PECC	Special Climate Change Programme
PES	payment for environmental services
PND	National Development Plan
PNMC	National Policy on Climate Change
PPCR	Pilot Programme for Climate Resilience
PPP	purchasing power parity
PQG	Five-Year Plan
PRI	Institutional Revolutionary Party
PROALCOOL	National Alcohol Programme
PSA	Pago por Servicios Ambimentales (payment for environmental services)
PV	photovoltaic
R&D	research and development
RAN-GRK	National Action Plan for Greenhouse Gases Reduction
REDD	Reducing Emissions from Deforestation and Forest Degradation
REDD+	Reducing Emissions from Deforestation and Forest Degradation Plus
RENAMO	Mozambique National Resistance
Rs	Indian rupees
RWA	Rural Women's Assembly
SACP	South African Communist Party
SAGARPA	Ministry of Agriculture, Livestock and Rural Development
SANCO	South African National Civic Organization
SAP	structural adjustment programme

Abbreviations

SAPCC	State Action Plan on Climate Change
SCT	Ministry of Communications and Transport
SDPC	State Development Planning Commission
SEA	Strategic Environmental Assessment
SECOFI	Ministry of Commerce and Industrial Development
SEDESOL	Ministry of Social Development
SEDUE	Ministry of Ecology and Urban Development
SEMARNAP	Ministry of Environment
SEMARNAT	Ministry of Environment
SENER	Ministry of Energy
SEO	State Energy Office
SIDS	small island developing state
SINAC	National System of Protected Areas
SME	small and medium-sized enterprise
SRE	Ministry of Foreign Relations
SSTC	State Science and Technology Commission
SUP	Structural Adjustment Programme
SWEG	Elsewedy for Wind Energy Generation
TERI	The Energy and Resources Institute
TFCA	Tropical Forest Conservation Act
TNA	Technology Needs Assessment
TNC	The Nature Conservancy
TPES	total primary energy supply
UAE	United Arab Emirates
UK	United Kingdom
UKP4	President's Delivery Unit for Development Monitoring and Oversight
UN	United Nations
UNAM	Universidad Nacional Autónoma de México
UNCED	United Nations Conference on Environment and Development
UNDP	United Nations Development Programme
UNEP	United Nations Environment Programme
UN ESCAP	United Nations Economic and Social Commission for Asia and the Pacific
UNFCCC	United Nations Framework Convention on Climate Change
UN-REDD	United Nations collaborative initiative on Reducing Emissions from Deforestation and Forest Degradation
UNWTO	United Nations World Tourism Organization
US	United States (of America)
USAID	United States Agency for International Development
VA	voluntary agreement
VCO	voluntary carbon offset

Abbreviations

WBCSD	World Business Council for Sustainable Development
WRI	World Resources Institute
WWF	World Wide Fund for Nature

1

Editors' Introduction: Climate Governance in the Developing World

David Held, Charles Roger and Eva-Maria Nag

FOR most of the period since the early 1990s, the locus of action on climate change has largely been in the industrialized world. The 1997 Kyoto Protocol is, for example, the most ambitious international effort to establish quantitative limits on countries' greenhouse gas (GHG) emissions. During the first commitment period, it obliged a group of thirty-seven countries to reduce their emissions collectively to 5 per cent below 1990 levels by 2008–12. Yet this only applied to industrialized states, known as 'Annex I' countries in the United Nations Framework Convention on Climate Change (UNFCCC). Developing countries, known as 'non-Annex I states',[1] were effectively excluded from any binding obligations. Within the industrialized world, the European Union in particular has been at the forefront of efforts to govern climate change. The European Emissions Trading System, the world's first multinational emissions trading scheme, was launched in 2005, and a range of other Europe-wide climate policies have been enacted since then. Many European states, like the United Kingdom, Denmark and Germany, have also established policies to promote the adoption of renewable sources of energy, created policies to encourage energy efficiency, or implemented national carbon taxes designed to put a price on carbon and abate emissions.

Action in the industrialized world is, of course, not confined to the European continent and the British Isles. Outside of Europe, Japan has created a range of climate mitigation policies, New Zealand operates a mandatory emissions trading system, and Australia now plans to establish one as well. National policies in North America are much less developed and coherent, but individual states, provinces and municipalities in the United States and Canada have taken the lead and created their own climate change policies despite the dearth of action at the national level. California, for instance, has set a goal of reducing its emissions to 1990 levels by 2020 and has established a statewide cap-and-trade system to meet it; Quebec and British Columbia (in Canada) have implemented carbon taxes, while Alberta operates a baseline-and-credit emissions trading scheme;

David Held, Charles Roger and Eva-Maria Nag

and a number of cities in both the United States and Canada have established climate action plans. Finally, many sub-national governments in North America have also worked together through regional carbon trading schemes such as the Western Climate Initiative and the Regional Greenhouse Gas Initiative.

Even though the above developments in the industrialized world have been insufficient to meet the challenge of global warming, they have traditionally constituted the 'frontline' in the global battle against climate change. By contrast, developing countries since the early 1990s have consistently maintained that they have little obligation to take immediate action. In the international climate change negotiations, they have proven deeply reluctant to adopt binding mitigation targets similar to those adopted by industrialized states under Kyoto. Doing so, they have argued, would reduce the space for economic growth and development, which are viewed as overriding priorities. Further, since currently developed states did not have to curb emissions during their own industrialization experience, it would be patently unfair for developing countries to have to do so, even if this were for the 'global good'. They should be allowed to emit more in order to meet their legitimate socio-economic and developmental needs. Thus, the domestic climate change policies of most developing countries have traditionally been thought to be much less proactive than those in the industrialized world. While they occasionally took actions that had the side-effect of abating emissions (by reducing energy subsidies, for example; see Reid & Goldemberg 1998), one early review of climate change policies in low income countries by an analyst from the United Nations Development Programme (UNDP) summed up its findings by explaining that 'most developing countries are neither prepared to address nor interested in climate change' (Gómez-Echeverri 2000). Climate considerations have, for the most part, hardly figured in plans for economic development, policymaking has been limited, and those actions that have been taken have often been driven by multilateral and transnational actors from wealthier countries, with little domestic ownership (Olsen 2006).

To be sure, most developing states, especially least developed states, are still unprepared for, if not uninterested in, climate change. Yet, over the past several years, one of the most remarkable developments in the arena of climate change has been the growing number of non-Annex I states that have made unilateral commitments to mitigate emissions within their borders. China has recently pledged in its 12th Five-Year Plan to reduce the carbon intensity of its economy by 40–5 per cent from 2005 levels by 2020. Brazil, likewise, now aims to reduce national emissions by 36–9 per cent below its baseline emissions scenario by 2020. Mexico has announced that it intends to reduce emissions by up to 20 per cent from business-as-usual (BAU) by 2020, and plans to reduce emissions by 50 per cent by 2050. South Africa has set a goal of reducing emissions by 34 per cent below BAU by 2020 and by 42 per cent by 2025. Even Ethiopia, after playing a leading role rep-

2

resenting Africa in the climate negotiations, has established a target of becoming 'carbon free' by 2022. Beyond the elaboration of such targets, however, many developing states have also been creating a welter of more specific plans, programmes and policies for meeting them. These include, for instance, policies for encouraging the use of renewable sources of energy, improving energy efficiency, reducing rates of deforestation and land use change, and raising emissions standards in manufacturing, buildings and vehicles, to name just a few. Some, such as China and South Korea, have even announced plans to establish emissions trading schemes of their own.

Despite these growing commitments, most developing states have not yet adopted more conciliatory negotiating positions at the international level. Many continue to argue that they should not be obliged to adopt binding targets and timetables. Nonetheless, the commitments that developing countries have been making can be seen in the many declarations of Nationally Appropriate Mitigation Actions (NAMAs) that were submitted to the UNFCCC Secretariat after the signing of the Copenhagen Accord in 2009. By the end of 2012, a total of forty-four developing states had submitted NAMAs, in addition to commitments by forty-two industrialized countries.[2] NAMAs are, essentially, a set of targets or policies or actions that a country intends to undertake voluntarily in order to reduce their emissions. They do not establish binding international obligations and there are no legal requirements for states to follow through on their promises. Further, NAMAs vary considerably in their level of detail and ambition. Some set out precise quantitative emissions targets, such as those mentioned above, while others simply list actions without specifying their proposed scope and expected impact. Having said this, NAMAs do broadly offer a rough indicator of the growing scale of the commitments developing states have been making. Together, the commitments made by developed and developing countries cover more than 80 per cent of global emissions, and, if delivered, could reduce emissions from BAU by 6.7–7.7 billion tonnes (Stern & Taylor 2010). But, most interestingly, there now appears to be 'broad agreement' that the actions that have been proposed by developing countries may do more to reduce future global emissions than those pledged by industrialized states (Kartha & Erickson 2011).

Of course, not all plans are likely to be successful. Developing countries continue to face a number of challenges that make implementation especially difficult. In some countries, targets are also far less ambitious, meaningful and credible than elsewhere. Estimates of the stringency of seemingly ambitious plans have been questioned as well. Some, such as Fatih Birol, chief economist of the International Energy Agency, have optimistically estimated that China's recent commitment may reduce projected emissions by as much as one gigatonne or 25 per cent of the total world reduction needed to stabilize average global temperature rise at 2 °C (see AFP 2009). Critics of China's target argue, on the other hand, that its pledge represents nothing of the sort and, in fact, is little more than the continuation of current policies and measures. This is certainly an important matter for empirical investigation and debate. What is undeniable, however, is that there appears to be a new level of interest in climate change in certain parts of the developing world, a host of new unilateral commitments, and, in some places, seemingly ambitious domestic policies and programmes for achieving them. The locus of climate change policymaking appears to be shifting.

While the contexts within which developing and emerging economies are making their plans and commitments are different, as are their intentions and abilities to achieve them, we argue that there seems to be a new political dynamic underlying this remarkable set of developments that deserves careful scrutiny by both scholars and policymakers. Once considered perennial laggards, some developing countries are now widely regarded as climate policy leaders. Some commentators have even argued that a number of these countries are taking actions that are comparable to – or even more ambitious than – almost anything being done in the industrialized world. Our aim in this book is to explore such claims by closely examining the experiences of twelve important countries across three different regions: Asia, the Americas and Africa. In Asia we look at China, India, Indonesia and South Korea; in the Americas, Argentina, Brazil, Costa Rica and Mexico; and in Africa, Egypt, Ethiopia, Mozambique and South Africa. Together, these countries account for around 50 per cent of the world's population, about 25 per cent of global gross domestic product (GDP) and almost 40 per cent of the world's annual emissions of GHGs at present (when land use change is taken into account) (see table 1.1).

Four of the countries analysed in this book – Brazil, China, India and Indonesia – are 'major' emitters, accounting for almost 85 per cent of all the emissions produced by the countries we consider. They are all among the top ten annual emitters of GHGs globally, and account for over 50 per cent of the developing world's total emissions. These states are therefore intrinsically important from a normative or policy perspective, and have attracted a great deal of interest in scholarly and policymaking communities. Five of the countries – Argentina, Egypt, Mexico, South Africa and South Korea – are 'middle range' producers of GHGs. Their annual emissions are often comparable to those of many European states in absolute and, in some cases, per capita terms (South Korea, for instance). Although they are not individually decisive, the participation of a large number of such states in global mitigation efforts is essential, as they account for a significant share of emissions as a group. Together, the annual emissions produced by these five are similar to India's or Brazil's. Finally, we also consider several smaller 'minor' emitters – Costa Rica, Ethiopia and Mozambique – which are interesting precisely because they are not decisive, and yet (at least in the cases of Costa Rica and Ethiopia) have announced commitments to becoming 'carbon neutral' or 'carbon free' in the near future.

4

Table 1.1 Descriptive statistics: population, GDP and GHG emissions

	Population (billions) (2011)	GDP (trillion US$) (2011)	GHG emissions total (2005)[a]			GHG emissions per capita (2005)[a]	
			Mt CO_2e	Rank	Percentage of world total	Tonnes CO_2e	Rank
Asia							
China	1.3	7.3	7,194.8	1	16.7	5.5	94
India	1.2	1.9	1,865.0	7	4.3	1.7	152
Indonesia	.2	.8	2,035.5	5	4.7	9.0	58
South Korea	.1	1.1	567.8	14	1.3	11.8	35
Total	2.8	11.1	11,663.1		27.0		
Americas							
Argentina	.0	.4	361.4	27	.8	9.3	55
Brazil	.2	2.5	2,840.5	4	6.6	15.3	19
Costa Rica	.0	.0	9.9	135	.0	2.3	139
Mexico	.1	1.2	671.0	11	1.6	6.3	82
Total	.3	4.1	3,882.8		9.0		
Africa							
Egypt	.1	.2	227.2	33	.5	3.1	121
Ethiopia	.1	.0	73.5	68	.2	1.0	172
Mozambique	.0	.0	24.4	104	.1	1.2	164
South Africa	.0	.4	422.6	23	1.0	9.0	59
Total	.2	.6	747.7		1.8		

CO_2e = carbon dioxide equivalent. GDP = gross domestic product. GHG = greenhouse gas.
Mt = megatonne.
[a] Includes land use change.
Sources: World Bank (2012); WRI (2012).

The cases we have chosen are not of course representative of the total 'universe' of developing countries. Indeed, several lacunae should be immediately apparent. We do not analyse countries from West and Central Asia, some of which may fall into the category of 'middle range' emitters, nor do we consider small island developing states, some of which have made commitments to carbon neutrality (the Maldives and Tuvalu, for example). Exploring the dynamics of climate governance in such states offers an opportunity for future research and comparative analysis, but they are not dealt with in this study. Our cases were chosen primarily because they have submitted NAMAs or made unilateral commitments of various kinds to taking action on climate change. Overall, only 30 per cent of all non-Annex I countries have submitted NAMAs to the UNFCCC secretariat. Of the twelve analysed in this book, only Mozambique and Egypt have not developed NAMAs, though their experiences are interesting in other highly suggestive ways, discussed further below. These cases therefore constitute a unique group, but one which is intended to be broadly representative of the subset of developing countries that claim to be taking a more ambitious approach to the climate. The aim of each chapter is to examine the international and domestic contexts within which these commitments have been made, the interests at stake, the actors involved and the strategies and policies that have been developed.

In the rest of this introductory chapter, we first discuss why it is increasingly essential to understand the way climate governance is evolving in the developing world. We argue that it is important, above all, because developing countries are having a much greater effect on the climate than in previous decades. However, there are major theoretical issues at stake as well, as current theories of climate politics are not optimistic about the potential for effective climate governance in developing states. Thus, the finding that developing countries are taking action on the issue seems fundamentally to overturn some widely held assumptions about climate and environmental politics in the developing world. Having explored these issues, we then provide a brief overview of the individual cases, highlighting some of the most salient or interesting features and findings that they bring to light. Finally, we conclude by discussing some broad themes that appear across a number of the cases, and which bear upon the theoretical and policy-oriented questions that motivate this book.

What is at Stake?

Understanding how and why some developing countries have become more ambitious with respect to climate change is important, first of all, from a policy or normative perspective. Some developing countries are now major contributors to climate change on a number of measures. Indeed, the annual contributions of some developing states to total annual greenhouse gas emissions are comparable to or even greater than those of states in the developed world. China's share of total annual CO_2 emissions rose from 11 per cent in 1990 to nearly 24 per cent by 2006, and it is now the world's single largest emitter of GHGs. Individually, Brazil, India and Indonesia each now produce more GHGs each year than Japan or Germany, Asia's second largest and Europe's largest economy. South Korea produces more GHGs than France or Italy. Iran produces more GHG in absolute terms than all of Australia. Although many smaller developing countries are not yet major producers of GHGs, if we look at another measure – per capita emissions – it is clear that many are relatively large contributors on a per person basis. The list of top per capita emitters includes a great number of non-Annex I states, such as Belize, Guyana, Qatar and

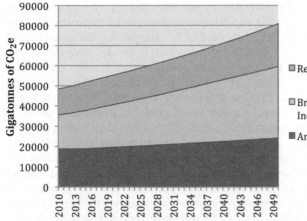

Figure 1.1 Projected global emissions, 2010–50

Source: Based on data from the figure 'GHG emissions: baseline, 2010–2050' from OECD Environmental Outlook Baseline; output from IMAGE/ ENV-Linkages.
CO_2e = carbon dioxide equivalent.

Malaysia. Among industrialized states, only Australia (the ninth largest per capita emitter in the world) makes the top ten.

In total, non-Annex I states currently account for just over half of all GHG emissions in absolute terms, with a few states like China, Brazil and India making up about half of that number in turn. Yet, as economies in the developing world grow, their contributions are only likely to get much larger if major changes do not take place today. As figure 1.1 shows, annual emissions from Annex I states are expected to be relatively stable between now and 2050. Emissions in the United States and Canada are rising and will continue to do so, while emissions in the European Union are expected to fall, though not nearly fast enough for the total level for all Annex I countries to decline. Annual emissions from non-Annex I states, on the other hand, are expected to grow by around 45 per cent. Emissions from Asia are likely to rise by about 53 per cent while those from Latin America and Africa will rise by about 26 per cent each, albeit from very different bases. Thus, developing states will naturally comprise a much larger share of total annual GHG emissions in a relatively short period of time, and their participation in mitigation efforts will be absolutely necessary if global levels of GHGs are to be stabilized at safe levels. In fact, emissions in the developing world are expected to grow so fast according to most 'business-as-usual' scenarios that, even if the industrialized world managed to reduce its emissions to zero by 2040, total global emissions will still be higher than they are today if no changes are made. At the very least, therefore, developing states will have to shift downward the trajectory of their emissions pathways, though many will need to make absolute reductions as well (for further discussion of required non-Annex I commitments see Elzen & Höhne 2008).

One of the best known and most often heard claims about climate change is that it is the historical emissions of industrialized countries that are largely responsible for triggering climate change. For this reason, the UNFCCC states that it is the now-developed world that 'should take the lead in combating climate change and the adverse effects thereof' (UN 1992, p. 4). Historical emissions in developing countries, it also states, are relatively low, and therefore their share of global emissions should be allowed to grow in line with their developmental needs. This picture of things constitutes the 'conventional wisdom' on climate change and undergirds the principle of common but differentiated responsibilities and respective capabilities that is enshrined in the UNFCCC: since developed countries have largely been responsible for the problem of climate change and developing states are expected to feel the worst effects, the former have a duty to mitigate and compensate for the harm to the latter by shouldering the main burden of abating emissions and providing funds for adaptation. Undoubtedly, there are important truths here. Yet this picture is swiftly becoming more complex and, in some places, outdated. Some developing states are already among the greatest contributors to global stocks of GHGs, and in upcoming years the historical contributions of many more will be on a par with industrialized states, as their emissions grow at unprecedented rates (Botzen et al. 2008). This is especially true when emissions arising from deforestation and land use change are taken into account, since they are primarily a phenomenon confined to the developing world (Baumert et al. 2005). Thus, many have come to argue that certain developing states have important ethical obligations to reduce their impact on the climate as well (Posner & Weisbach 2010; Harris 2011).

Given the burgeoning absolute, per capita and historical emissions of the developing world as a whole, proactive climate change policies by developing countries – and especially by several large developing states – are becoming increasingly urgent and, in some cases, ethically appropriate. The world can no longer afford the rigid division of responsibilities among Annex I and non-Annex I states that became entrenched in the UNFCCC and the Kyoto Protocol at the First Conference of the Parties (COP1) in Berlin in 1995. To some extent, this has begun to change after COP16 in 2011 in Durban, where developing countries agreed to negotiate an agreement with 'legal force' that will be applicable to all parties by 2015. The Durban Platform for Enhanced Action contains no mention of the terms 'Annex I' and 'non-Annex I', suggesting that this distinction may be on its way out. This is a promising step, but one that underlines the need to understand why some developing states are becoming climate leaders while others are remaining laggards. Gaining insights into how some developing countries have managed to shift towards, if not attain, a low carbon, climate-resilient development trajectory can help us to understand how climate laggards might become leaders in the future, as well as how to avoid some of the pitfalls along the way.

Understanding the evolution of climate governance in the developing world is also important from a theoretical perspective. The idea that some developing states may be becoming more committed to tackling climate change – and perhaps even doing more than some industrialized states – is something of an anomaly for many current theories of climate and environmental politics. Climate change is an inherently difficult problem to solve – a global 'tragedy of the commons' (Hardin 1968). All states have an incentive to 'free ride' on the efforts of others; their most favoured option is for others to mitigate their emissions while doing nothing and receiving a portion of the benefits others create. But since all have an incentive to pursue the same strategy, the ultimate outcome is suboptimal – a higher level of emissions will be produced than most desire. The 'tragedy of the commons' problem suggests that, other things being equal, states will not make the investments and changes needed to mitigate emissions unless they can be guaranteed that others will do so as well. Such a guarantee has not been possible thus far, largely because most emerging economies and the United States have proven reluctant to commit to binding obligations. However, other things are not always equal. As a number of studies have shown, some states have made the choice to limit their impact on the climate, despite the non-cooperation of many major emitters (Harrison & Sundstrom 2010; Rabe 2010; Selin & VanDeveer 2009; Hovi et al. 2003).

To understand why this is the case, scholars have focused on the underlying interests, ideas and institutions that have shaped states' decisions to take action. In the industrialized world, these have sometimes managed to spur efforts to abate the production of GHGs in some places. Yet the existing literature on climate politics is not optimistic about the possibility for effective climate governance in the developing world. Prevailing theories suggest, for instance, that the large proportion of autocracies in the developing world constitutes a major hindrance. Democracies have been found to be, on average, more likely to enact robust climate regulations, and they are simply more prevalent in the industrialized world (Dolšak 2009; Bättig & Bernauer 2009; Neumayer 2002). Lower levels of economic development are also likely to make economic growth a much more pressing concern than environmental issues. Achieving industrialization is, for many leaders in the developing world, simply a greater priority, and may even be tied to the perceived legitimacy of autocratic governments, as in China (Gómez-Echeverri 2000; Olsen 2006; Heggelund et al. 2010). Further, some have argued that individuals in developing countries are less likely to hold post-materialist 'green values' or may have limited access to credible information about climate change, and are correspondingly less motivated to take action, since the effects of global warming are primarily felt in the future or are poorly understood (Tjernström & Tietenberg 2008; Lahsen 2007; Inglehart

1995). A sense of historic injustice and mistrust in developing states may, in addition, contribute to lower cooperation on climate change (Roberts & Parks 2007). Finally, even if the 'political will' to take action on climate change is strong, residual problems of resources and governmental capacity are likely to impair efforts to do so.

All of this suggests that developing states should be perennial laggards on climate change and environmental issues more broadly. In many respects, these arguments also contain important elements of truth. Autocratic government, lower levels of economic development, and limited resources may raise important barriers across the developing world. But these barriers can be – and sometimes are – overcome, as our cases show. As such, existing theories do not help to explain why some developing states are more active than others, why the actions being taken have taken the shape they have, and why some developing countries may even be becoming more ambitious than their counterparts in the wealthier industrialized world. Further, the theories do not help to explain the timing of these developments. While some policies in the developing world, such as China's reduction of energy subsidies in the 1990s or Brazil's efforts to encourage the use of biofuels since the 1970s, have had important effects on emissions in the past (see Reid & Goldemberg 1998; Chandler et al. 2002), the scale and scope of climate policymaking in the developing world appear to have increased quite considerably in a very short period of time. Thus, there is an urgent need for more careful investigation of the factors and circumstances motivating the emergence of climate governance in parts of the developing world, as well as those that may be holding countries back.

The Cases

The countries that are examined in this book demonstrate that there is a wide range of experiences and levels of commitment across the developing world. Most of them, as noted above, have submitted NAMAs, or have committed to a 'headline' mitigation target of some kind. Although it is difficult to assess the likely impact that these commitments will have – and we do not try to assess this here – most studies suggest that, if they are followed up by real action, meeting them would represent a significant – though not sufficient – departure from 'business-as-usual' (Stern & Taylor 2010; Kartha & Erickson 2011). For each case, therefore, the extent of the efforts made to follow up is essential. Strategic planning, more detailed mid-range and sectoral targets, financing, monitoring arrangements, and adequate policies and programmes are needed. In these respects, the cases we look at exhibit greater variation at present. Often, detailed planning has been undertaken and governments have set additional mid-range and sectoral targets. Yet the implementation of policies and robust monitoring of commitments have been relatively slow or difficult in many of the cases. In what follows, we review the individual experiences of each of the countries covered in the book, drawing out some of the crucial points they bring to light and which bear upon the major themes of the book.

Some countries do suggest that planning has been coupled with large-scale implementation. The case of China, examined by David Held, Charles Roger and Eva-Maria Nag, may be a good example in this regard. Their chapter shows that China's 11th and 12th Five-Year Plans (FYPs) have been accompanied by a major effort to reform domestic climate and energy institutions and to develop energy efficiency and renewable energy policies and programmes, which are now framed in terms of an explicit 'carbon intensity' target. More specific targets have also been set in each of these areas, many of which seemed overly ambitious at first. However, evidence from China's experience under the 11th FYP suggests that the country has been relatively successful in meeting them. The evidence the authors review suggests that the country managed to fall just short of its target of reducing the energy intensity of its economy by 20 per cent and far surpassed some of its initial targets for renewable energy, especially with respect to wind turbine installation. Held, Roger and Nag argue that an increased perception of energy insecurity in the country, especially after 2002, was particularly important for spurring these efforts. Combined with international and domestic pressures (from individual bureaucracies, elites and civil society groups), this laid the basis for a more ambitious domestic climate change agenda. The authors also note, however, that China did in fact struggle to meet the targets set by the 11th FYP, and that there are important questions about the reality underneath China's seemingly impressive performance with regard to renewable energy trends that could prove problematic in the future.

The chapter by Aaron Atteridge explains that Indian climate policy, like that of China, has been developed via a 'top-down' process, motivated by a mix of domestic and international factors. India, Atteridge shows, was initially deeply reluctant about the possibility of binding emissions targets for developing countries at the international level – and, for the most part, continues to be so. This position has been the result of material challenges, such as the need to ensure energy equity and economic development, as well as normative commitments shared by government officials and civil society groups. In more recent years, though, there has been a growth of ambition. Breaking with past trends, the prime minister announced in 2007 that the country's emissions would never exceed those of industrialized states. Subsequently, in 2008, the National Action Plan on Climate Change was adopted, establishing eight 'National Missions' related to mitigation and adaptation. As Atteridge argues, these primarily build upon pre-existing objectives motivated by concerns about depleting resources, energy security and economic development. However, he notes that, as in China, there are major challenges involved in implementing policy, largely connected to doubts about the priorities and capacity of individual states and the structure of the industrial and agricultural sectors in the country.

Indonesia, examined by Budy P. Resosudarmo, Fitrian Ardiansyah and Lecentezza Napitupulu, is a case that clearly throws into sharp relief the problems that can hinder the implementation of seemingly ambitious climate change commitments by developing states. As announced by the president at the 2009 Group of 20 (G20) meeting in Pittsburgh, the country has committed to a major target of reducing emissions relative to a 'business-as-usual' baseline by 26 per cent by 2020. This is primarily to be achieved via Reducing Emissions from Deforestation and Forest Degradation Plus (REDD+) funding from industrialized countries. As a result, the climate strategy that the country has adopted is heavily geared towards forestry, and tends to neglect other important sources of emissions arising from fossil fuel consumption. Thus far, the country appears to be both unwilling and unable to remove the massive energy subsidies that distort prices and encourage inefficient use of fossil fuels. The forest-centric character of Indonesia's climate strategy is, in the main, a product of the country's agreement with Norway, which pledged to provide US$1 billion for implementation of a REDD+ programme. The large opportunities that this created in the arena of climate change have spurred competition among Indonesia's ministries for the leadership of the issue area, increasing the prominence of climate change in the government. But this has, as the authors argue, also made implementation difficult, as individual ministries have actively sought to undermine the efforts of others and closely guard their own climate change programmes, largely at the expense of necessary inter-ministerial cooperation.

Jae-Seung Lee's chapter on South Korea shows that major changes have been afoot in the country since the adoption of its low carbon green growth strategy in 2008. This plan is based on the premise that a comprehensive change is needed in order to meet the challenges of energy dependence and economic slow-down after the financial crisis, and in order to bolster future sources of 'qualitative' economic growth. The plan has involved a wide range of domestic institutional reforms, targets for renewable energy adoption and energy efficiency, major investments in 'green' projects, and the implementation of an Energy Goal Management Scheme, which makes a large number of companies responsible for lowering emissions and subject to penalties if they fail to meet their targets. A carbon trading system is currently under discussion as well. Though Lee's chapter is careful to note that there are underlying challenges that cast doubt upon certain aspects of the government's strategy, as well as doubts about the sustainability of the country's commitment after the change in government in 2012, it seems fair to say that South Korea is one of the more ambitious countries in our survey. Underlying the changes that have taken place, Lee argues, has been the country's motivation to pursue a leadership position in the UNFCCC and deflect pressure for it to adopt harder commitments, to spur investment in future sources of growth, and to mitigate the effects of price volatility and insecurity in the energy sector.

The chapter by Matías Franchini and Eduardo Viola considers the experience of Argentina. Argentina is an especially interesting case because it was one of the first countries to offer a voluntary commitment to reduce the growth of its emissions. At COP4, in 1998, Argentina put forward what has since been referred to as the 'Argentinian Proposal', which called for developing countries to make voluntary pledges as a sign of 'good will' and solidarity with industrial-ized states. This proposal was both innovative and controversial at the time, encountering significant resistance from the Group of 77 (G77). It clearly foreshadowed by more than ten years the NAMAs that many developing countries have now submitted. However, Argentina's period of leadership on climate change in the UNFCCC negotiations was a brief one. During the 2000s, as the country encountered eco-nomic crisis and political turmoil after 1999, climate change became a very low priority and has failed to become more important as the issue has risen up the global agenda. Despite the fact that the country has submitted a NAMA (which, it should be noted, only offers a list of actions rather than a precise target), Franchini and Viola argue that climate governance in the country is underdeveloped at best. Very little substantive planning has been undertaken and the policies and programmes that have been implemented are either very narrow in scope or largely ineffectual. The authors highlight, in particular, the adverse effects that domestic political instability has had on climate policymaking in the country, which results in short-term gains being prioritized over long-term planning.

The case of Argentina provides an interesting contrast with that of Brazil, which is examined by Held, Roger and Nag in chapter 7. In many respects, they show, Brazil already has elements of a low carbon economy thanks to the country's heavy use of hydropower and biofu-els. However, deforestation in the Amazon has made the country one of the world's largest emitters. The high rate of deforestation that prevailed throughout the 1990s and early 2000s was largely due to the government's limited ability and willingness to control legal and illegal economic activity in the Amazon. The relatively stringent laws that were in place were poorly enforced. Climate policymaking was therefore limited and deeply conservative. Yet, in the mid-2000s, this changed considerably, as the government began to reform existing forestry laws and made a greater effort to enforce them in response to several crises and policy activism within parts of the government. The rate of Amazonian deforestation began to decline, and this new development changed perceptions in the government while creating an opportunity for activists, policymakers and business groups to push for more stringent climate policies. After playing a decisive role at Copenhagen, Brazil put forward an ambitious target for curbing its emissions, and outlined specific goals for reducing deforestation.

The National Congress subsequently signed this voluntary pledge into law in December 2009. As a result, Brazil is now thought to be one of the more progressive countries in the climate regime, although this status remains fragile and contested, as an effort to revise parts of the Forest Code prior to Rio+20 revealed in 2012.

Other countries in the Americas that this book considers seem to have been relatively progressive on climate change issues as well. Like Brazil, Costa Rica has also been widely regarded as a climate leader, even a 'role model'. In Robert Fletcher's chapter, he shows that a dramatic reversal occurred in the country in the 1980s, when its rate of deforestation was the highest in the Western hemisphere. The country made considerable efforts to improve its reputation through the development of the national park system and the innovative payment for environmental services programme, which channels payments to private landowners for the positive environmental externalities their lands create, including carbon sequestration. These pre-existing governance mechanisms laid the basis for the country's pledge in 2007 to become the world's first carbon neutral country, a pledge that was submitted to the UNFCCC as the country's NAMA, along with a list of more specific measures. Fletcher notes, however, that there are likely to be major 'bumps on the road', as the country has taken few tangible steps towards this goal and the initiative remains highly reliant upon the successful mobilization of international resources that have yet to materialize.

Mexico aims to stand out as a climate leader as well, as Simone Pulver's chapter demonstrates. In 2010, the country made a commitment to reduce its emissions by 30 per cent relative to a 'business-as-usual' baseline by 2020 and, unusually for both developed and developing states, a 50 per cent reduction by 2050. These pledges, initially put forward in the country's NAMA, were formalized in the General Law on Climate Change, which passed through the Senate in 2011 and was signed into law in 2012. As such, Mexico became the first developing country in the world to have signed into law a long-term emissions reduction target. As with many developing states, the international negotiations provided the initial impetus for domestic climate initiatives in Mexico, helping crystallize a constituency of climate science and policy experts that has spearheaded domestic debates about the issue. Interestingly, as Pulver notes, this domestic discourse has consistently focused on both adaptation and mitigation. But only relatively recently have these and other factors paved the way for greater ambition under the Calderón administration, which made climate change a priority early on. Pulver nevertheless expresses concern about whether the government will remain committed to this climate change agenda under Calderón's successor, Enrique Peña Nieto, who was elected on a platform emphasizing economic growth and development of the energy sector.

Jeannie Sowers' chapter on climate change policies in Egypt takes as its starting point the country's extreme vulnerability to the effects of climatic changes and its negligible contribution to global GHG emissions. It is therefore surprising, she points out, that Egypt has largely chosen to focus its efforts on climate mitigation rather than climate adaptation programmes. Sowers notes that this particular emphasis has primarily been a result of financial incentives for developing countries offered by the UNFCCC, the Kyoto Protocol and specific international actors. Indeed, the major actors involved in fossil fuel extraction and distribution – Egypt's state-owned oil and gas firms and multinationals – have not yet made a serious commitment to renewable energy. Instead, concern for renewable energy is occasionally being driven by European actors interested in creating a new export infrastructure from the Middle East and North Africa to Europe based on large-scale wind energy and concentrated solar. This means that significant opportunities to focus on addressing domestic consumption among poor populations, in both rural and urban areas, via decentralized renewable energy technologies are not receiving the attention they deserve.

Climate policymaking in Ethiopia, which is the subject of chapter 11 by Held, Roger and Nag, has only developed relatively recently. For most of the period since the early 1990s, the issue was a very low priority; climate policies and programmes were severely underdeveloped. The country's participation in the UNFCCC negotiations was also relatively limited. However, this changed when, in 2009, the late prime minister, Meles Zenawi, was appointed as the chair of the Conference of African Heads of State and Government on Climate Change, a subcommittee of African Union leaders created in order to steer African participation in the UNFCCC prior to Copenhagen. His appointment dramatically changed the status of the climate change issue in Ethiopia, and helped to set in motion a policymaking process that eventually led to a national commitment to becoming 'carbon free' in the country's Growth and Transformation Plan and the articulation of a climate-resilient green economy (CRGE) strategy for meeting this objective. The authors argue that the CRGE strategy represents a dramatic change in Ethiopia's approach to climate change. But they also highlight how this plan represents more of a promise than a reality on the ground at present. Although some institutional reforms have taken place, many more need to occur in particular sectors before successful implementation is possible. Most worryingly, however, the plan relies heavily upon international climate finances that have not yet been supplied by the international community on the scale necessary for sustained long-term action.

The case study of Mozambique is one that paints a grim picture of the potential impact of climate change on one of the world's most vulnerable countries – one, furthermore, that barely produces meaningful levels of GHG emissions. In their chapter, Angus Hervey and Jessica Blythe discuss how the patterns and increasing intensity of flooding and drought in the country, which depends upon subsistence-level agriculture, have led to a political consensus on the need to establish policies for adapting to climate change. However, while agreement on the high level of crisis arising from climatic changes seems to have been reached within the domestic political arena, signs of innovative policies are clearly linked to bilateral and multilateral climate change preparedness and adaptation programmes, a fact which also helps explain the shape of climate change policymaking in the country. Key obstacles to implementation in Mozambique are a lack of policy coherence, a lack of domestic ownership over policies, inter-ministerial competition for resources, including resources meant for climate policy delivery, and widespread poverty. At the same time, the authors also offer pointers for hope arising from the mainstreaming of climate change policies in national poverty reduction programmes as well as apparent successes in the area of disaster risk reduction.

Finally, Lesley Masters' discussion of post-apartheid South Africa leaves open the direction of climate governance in the country. With some support from environmental activists, the government and political leaders, she explains, have thus far been the primary drivers of climate policies. As the country has sought to bolster its status as a leading member of the African Group, as part of the BASIC group (with Brazil, India and China), and as part of the G77 coalition, it has made a claim to being a 'responsible international citizen', and has tried to play a much larger role in the international diplomatic arena. In line with this, South Africa has offered ambitious mitigation targets, notably a recent commitment to reduce emissions by 34 per cent by 2020 and, furthermore, by 42 per cent by 2025. Yet, above all, the case highlights the challenges of setting such far-reaching targets and finding ways of implementing them in the face of other conflicting policy considerations. In particular, Masters' review demonstrates the major obstacles to effective implementation that have arisen as South Africa has embarked on a trajectory of largely fossil fuel-driven economic growth. While the government has sought to respond to the challenge with an array of 'green' policies and programmes that seek to create synergies between economic growth and environmental protection, Masters argues that the climate policies that have been developed fall far short of this goal, remain incoherent and conflicting, and have encountered strong resistance from the business community.

Overarching Themes Across the Cases

As the cases reviewed suggest, climate policymaking has grown in important respects across the developing world. In nearly all of the countries we have surveyed, the issue has become a much greater priority and policymakers seem to have become more ambitious than they were in the past. Yet the cases also clearly demonstrate the diversity of experiences and approaches that have emerged. Some countries, we believe, can clearly be characterized as climate leaders;

the targets they have set are meaningful and a wide range of policies has been created to meet them, leading to some successes in a relatively short period of time. In others, a variety of targets have been set, but implementation of the kinds of measures needed to achieve them has been relatively limited, and/or serious doubt can be cast on the adequacy of those policies that have been put in place. Piercing through this diversity, however, we argue that several key themes emerge, each of which has been relatively neglected in the theoretical literature at present.

First, new international pressures and opportunities have been very important for explaining the growth of unilateral commitments in the developing world. These include, first of all, international diplomatic pressures. As the first Kyoto period has come to an end, developing countries have been under much greater pressure to adopt climate change policies. Many industrialized states have now tied their future commitments to climate action by at least the more prosperous non-Annex I states. The US Senate's Byrd-Hagel Resolution of 1997, for example, obliged the US to refrain from signing any treaty that does not include climate policy commitments by developing states. Although officially condemned by other states at the time, such sentiments appear to have become widely shared. In recent years, the European Union, Japan and Canada, among others, have all stated that they will refuse to sign any further agreements that do not include commitments by at least the largest developing countries. Their calls have also recently been echoed by certain groups of developing states, such as the Alliance of Small Island States and the African Group of Negotiators, which have started to push for stringent commitments by countries such as China, India and Brazil. In response, some developing states within the international system have agreed to discuss more ambitious international measures. In this context, however, offering voluntary commitments occasionally appears to have been intended to deflect some of this diplomatic pressure. By doing so, developing states can argue that they are already doing their part to abate emissions, and that it is industrialized states which have not followed through on promises made at both the domestic and the international level. Making domestic commitments improves states' reputations and gives them a degree of leverage in the global negotiations on mitigation measures.

The changing landscape of global climate finance also seems to have been an important motivating factor in many cases. Recent years have seen industrialized states commit much greater – though still insufficient – resources to assist adaptation and mitigation of climate change across the developing world. Currently, around $32.5 billion of climate-related funding has been pledged to the developing world, and around $2 billion has already been disbursed (see CPI 2011). Much traditional official development assistance has also begun to include climate change considerations, raising concerns among many that funds badly needed for meeting other goals are being diverted towards projects and programmes that include climate 'co-benefits' (see Gupta & Van der Grip 2010). Private climate finance in the form of debt and direct equity investments in developing countries has grown as well. Indeed, it is currently nearly three times the size of public funding (CPI 2011). This includes, in particular, investment in renewable energy projects, energy saving technologies, and sustainable forestry and agriculture. Much of this involves the transfer of clean technology and know-how that is highly valued by developing states. As a result, many states are responding to these growing market and policy incentives by creating policies and contexts that are conducive to such investments and funding.

In addition, rising and increasingly volatile international and domestic energy prices have, in several cases, tended to shape commitments by developing states. The price of oil has, of course, increased considerably in the 2000s. The cost of extracting and transporting coal has also been growing, resulting in mounting pressure on several fast-developing states like China and India as attaining and transporting reliable supplies become increasingly problematic. At the same time, there has been a significant decrease in the costs of cleaner fuels, such as natural gas, and renewable energy technologies, making them more affordable and realistic options. All of these changes have been occurring at the same time as demand for energy and international competition for resources have been burgeoning across many parts of the developing world. Together, these factors appear to have made long-term energy investments in non-fossil fuel-based sources of energy increasingly attractive. They have made energy and climate change much more pressing concerns in the developing world than in the 1990s.

These three international pressures and opportunities are currently reconfiguring the environment in which developing states find themselves at present. However, the policies that are implemented in individual states and the extent of their commitments still appear to be highly dependent upon the balance of interests and power among the actors within them. Clearly, not all states have reacted to them in the same way. In each instance, supporters of more stringent climate policies must overcome sceptics and those opposed to more ambitious commitments. In this regard, a second theme that appears across a number of the cases considered in this book has been the importance of linkages between issues such as energy security, deforestation, and air pollution and climate policymaking. Climate change is a multi-dimensional issue, involving nearly all aspects of our economies. This contributes to the complexity of the problem. Managing it requires substantial changes in our basic infrastructure, from roads and buildings to the production of energy, and human behaviour, from the way we eat to the way we get to work. More often than not, though, it is precisely the connections between issues that may make action on climate change possible. Taking steps to solve certain local problems can create opportunities for addressing the global challenge of lowering emissions.

For example, for much of the 1990s and 2000s, the Brazilian government resisted attempts to lower emissions due to its inability or unwillingness to manage deforestation of the Amazon within its borders effectively. However, as a result of certain entirely home-grown political factors, especially crises and policy activism led by prominent figures such as Marina Silva and Carlos Minc, efforts to manage deforestation increased considerably after 2004. As deforestation declined, a climate policy 'blockage' was removed, perceptions of the policy trade-offs changed, and an opportunity was created for a coalition of civil society groups, businesses and policy entrepreneurs to agitate for more stringent climate policies at the domestic level. Concerns about domestic and international energy security can produce a similar effect, as the cases of South Korea, India and China demonstrate. In China, for example, current and projected energy demand is a source of considerable worry within the government, and has led to substantial efforts to increase the efficiency of energy use and the share of renewable sources of energy in the country's overall energy mix. These actions, in turn, created political space for the government to respond in a circumscribed fashion to international and domestic pressures for it to adopt a more robust climate change strategy. Thus, the efforts to solve one problem seem to have created crucial openings for governments to become more responsive to international and domestic actors calling for more proactive climate policies. Pre-existing commitments to action on particular issues with climate 'co-benefits' mean that local initiatives can be more readily translated and scaled up into unilateral commitments. The particular nature of the domestic problem and the government's response to it, moreover, may help to account for the shape and timing of climate policies in a given context.

A third, somewhat more speculative observation concerns the role of socialization processes and transnational actors in changing norms and calculations of costs and benefits. Socialization by scientific epistemic communities is one of the only sociological explanations that has been widely investigated in the literature on climate change. The role of scientific exchanges and the Intergovernmental Panel on Climate Change in putting climate change on the agendas of states has been well documented (Paterson 1996; Bodansky 2001; Bolin 2008; Schroeder 2008). However, a number of new socializing agents may be emerging and playing a more prominent part in the growth of domestic climate governance in the developing world. Numerous individual economists, international organizations (such as the OECD, EU and United Nations Environment Programme [UNEP]) and private consultancies (such as Korea's Global Green Growth Institute [GGGI] and McKinsey & Company) have become important advocates of the concept of 'green growth'. As a result of their activities and attempts to persuade states, the concept is becoming widely accepted, legitimized and increasingly included in serious policy discussions in developing states. This, we argue, may be changing perceptions of the trade-offs between economic growth and protection of the climate in developing states. The emergence of seemingly successful climate policies, and the embracing of the concept of 'green growth' in several prominent non-Annex I states, such as China, Brazil, South Korea and Mexico, have also arguably spurred emulation by others that look to these states as developmental leaders. This dynamic is evident in the case of Ethiopia. There, the government has been actively attempting to craft its climate policies using those in South Korea as a model, supported by transnational actors such as GGGI, McKinsey & Company and the UNDP. Moreover, it appears that information provided by such transnational actors has heavily influenced Ethiopian policymakers' evaluations of the cost and benefits of abating emissions.

Certain multilateral donors and norm entrepreneurs, such as non-governmental organizations (NGOs) and international actors like the World Bank, UNDP and EU, have similarly begun to support the connected idea of climate change 'mainstreaming' in development plans, moving the issue onto the agendas of ministries responsible for economic development (where once concern was largely confined to more peripheral ministries of environment and science). These actors have done so by, among other things, increasingly assessing the degree to which climate change and environmental issues have been mainstreamed in poverty reduction strategies and other development plans, and highlighting how and where particular development plans fall short of this goal. In many cases, this has also increasingly been tied to the distribution of aid, providing important material incentives as well. As a result, including specific goals related to climate change adaptation and mitigation in economic development plans may be becoming increasingly widely regarded as part of what an appropriate development plan should look like. Finally, several international organizations, especially UNDP, and many regional organizations have been prominent supporters of institutions dedicated to promoting climate governance in developing countries. They have provided capacity building services and helped to bolster bureaucracies aimed at meeting climate change objectives.

Multiple transnational agents, therefore, have been involved in promoting and making climate policy, and in spreading and legitimizing norms, such as climate mainstreaming, as well as related ideas like 'green growth'. Understanding the processes through which they affect climate policies across the developing world offers an important avenue for future research. However, we suspect that while forces of socialization may be important for explaining bureaucratic development, agenda setting, and the incorporation of green growth and climate change into development planning (especially at the early stages of institutionalization and climate policymaking), greater commitment to climate policy implementation in the developing world is still likely to be determined by material forces and domestic issue linkages in important ways.

Fourth, there are of course very significant barriers that appear to be hindering climate policymaking and the implementation of commitments across many of the countries that are surveyed here. Two barriers stand out, in particular, and deserve more careful investigation in the future. First, growing opportunities for financing climate projects and programmes have created incentives for some countries to adopt more ambitious climate change policies, but this has also, at times, led to negative effects upon implementation. Where the policies created are primarily geared towards attracting large-scale funding for implementation of commitments, such opportunities have simultaneously created incentives for domestic inter-ministerial competition for top leadership positions in order to capture funding channels and to become the authoritative distributor of climate finances. This process appears to increase the issue's priority domestically, as ministries seek to 'out-regulate' each other in the domain of climate change, but also creates disincentives for cooperation among relevant actors, thereby hindering cross-sectoral implementation of policies. The issues that such climate financing tends to address also seem to shape the kinds of climate policies that are created domestically and can encourage policies and programmes that may not reflect appropriate domestic priorities. The policy focus on mitigation in many parts of the developing world (Ethiopia and Egypt, for example) where adaptation is clearly an objective concern offers an example of this, but it can also been seen in Indonesia's narrow focus on deforestation at the expense of much-needed reforms in the energy sector.

Second, uneven domestic capacity and divergent interests among different institutions in the same country can seriously hinder domestic climate cooperation. In Ethiopia, for example, some ministries responsible for implementation of commitments appear to be relatively well positioned to do so, as is the case with the Ministry of Water and Energy, which has demonstrated a relatively high capacity for undertaking some of the kinds of projects that the country's climate strategy calls for. In other cases, institutional capacity is distinctly limited, as is the case with the Ministry of Agriculture and Rural Development. Ethiopia has yet to establish the kind of sustainable land management systems that are necessary for implementing REDD+ projects – one of the four initiatives designated for 'fast track implementation' in the country's climate strategy. The difficulties experienced setting up reforestation projects under the UNFCCC's Clean Development Mechanism serve as a potent reminder of the tremendous challenges that have been encountered in this field, even when financial incentives and significant international assistance are available.

India, China, South Africa and South Korea offer further examples. In these cases, central governments may be motivated to ensure the implementation of targets, but sub-national governments, where responsibility for implementation often ultimately rests, may have conflicting interests. With respect to energy efficiency, for instance, China has set sub-national energy targets through a bargaining process with local governments which are then responsible for meeting them. Yet, while these local governments collectively benefit from these measures, their individual inclinations are all too often to let others make the necessary investments and adjustments. Ensuring that goals are implemented requires adequate monitoring, but the delegation of responsibility in this manner can also create opportunities for shirking when monitoring policy implementation and the meeting of targets are difficult. Preliminary evidence of such problems may be found by looking at the conflicting estimates of carbon emissions at local and central levels of government, which appear to have diverged as China's commitment to action on climate change has increased over time (see Guan et al. 2012). In India, sub-national governments are also needed to implement national goals, but capacity is limited and there may be similar conflicting incentives between central and local governments, as Atteridge discusses in this volume. Finally, there may be divergent interests between the state and key elements of society, as the cases of South Africa and South Korea reveal. The governments in both countries have established ambitious targets and emphasized 'green growth' policies that are supposed to create economic opportunities while also limiting firms' impacts on the climate and environment. Yet such synergies may often be difficult to achieve in practice, giving rise to active resistance from business communities in response to the actual policies that are proposed.

Conclusion

Without the actions of developing countries, which now generate unprecedented volumes of GHGs, climate change cannot be stabilized or reversed. The developed world, irrespective of its greater contribution to the current stock of GHGs, cannot mitigate climate change on its own. Without the participation of developing countries the only agenda is adaptation; with the developing world mitigation remains a possibility.

The cases in this book show that this understanding is now becoming increasingly widely shared, North and South, East and West. For nearly all of the countries surveyed here, it is possible to document a substantial increase in concern about climate change. In most cases, explicit mitigation commitments have also been made, and in many, new institutions and policies for meeting these commitments have been put in place. One of the most remarkable aspects of these developments is that they have largely taken place since 2007. In a short period of time, countries in the developing world have advanced a number of major targets that could, if met, represent a significant departure from 'business-as-usual'. Further, some successes have already been achieved. In many places, of course, there are important questions about the reality beneath the commitments that have been made. Such considerations, which the individual chapters that follow bring to light, should lead to a circumspect view of the prospects for meeting these commitments in particular cases. Yet, as many climate initiatives have been put in place only recently, it is also probably unreasonable to expect full-scale implementation across all the cases at present. In some instances, it is clearly too soon for this. The chapters nevertheless suggest that success in several countries will be contingent on factors beyond their direct control. They depend, for instance, upon attaining access to adequate finances, technology and human resources. This underlines the fact that fulfilling the promises that industrialized states have made to the developing world – in terms of funding, technology and capacity building – is a necessary step.

The cases examined in this book show that each country is complex in its own right but there are some common factors in play that help to create the conditions for leadership on climate policies. Other factors, on the other hand, pose major obstacles. The distribution of these variables beyond the cases this book considers, we believe, will be an important determinant of the evolution of commitments and implementation across the developing world in the future. The objective of this book is to deepen our understanding of these variables and to see them as intimately linked to other critical processes – economic growth and development, resource management and consumption, international forces and domestic demands. The book shows that there has been remarkable progress in some places, and that, with concerted efforts, progress can be built upon. Whether such developments are extensive and effective enough to change the current trajectory of global GHG emissions is another question. On this matter the evidence does not look good, and much will depend upon our ability to reach an encompassing multilateral agreement in the near future. But without better knowledge of what works and what does not, the probability of success is certainly limited.

Notes

1 There are a number of countries in the 'non-Annex 1' group that are, in fact, quite rich and well developed. The group even includes a number of states that are a part of the club of rich countries known as the Organization for Economic Cooperation and Development (OECD). However, as a rule, just about all developing countries are a part of the non-Annex 1 group and the two terms are regarded as synonymous in this volume, except where noted.
2 This figure separates the European Union members. The voluntary commitments made by industrialized states are technically not NAMAs but quantified economy-wide emissions targets for 2020.

References

AFP (2009). *China's Climate Pledge to Meet a Quarter of Global Needs: IEA*. Agence France Presse. November 26. Available at: http://www.google.com/hosted-news/afp/article/ALeqM5i7xsOk388RHmUgVLC7jcxI7 KjarA.
Bättig, M. & T. Bernauer (2009). National institutions and global public goods:

are democracies more cooperative in climate change policy? *International Organization* 63(2)

Baumert, K., T. Herzog & J. Pershing (2005). *Navigating the Numbers: Greenhouse Gas Data and International Climate Policy*. World Resources Institute. Available at: http://pdf.wri.org/navigating_numbers.pdf.

Bodansky, D. (2001). The history of the global climate change regime. In U. Luterbacher and D. F. Sprinz (eds.) *International Relations and Global Climate Change*. Cambridge, MA: MIT Press.

Bolin, B. (2008). *A History of the Science and Politics of Climate Change: The Role of the Intergovernmental Panel on Climate Change*. Cambridge: Cambridge University Press.

Botzen, W., J. Gowdy & J. Van Den Bergh (2008). Cumulative CO_2 emissions: shifting international responsibilities for climate debt. *Climate Policy* 8.

Chandler, W., R. Shaeffer, Zhou D., P. R. Shukla, F. Tudela, O. Davidson & S. Alpan-Atamer (2002). *Climate Change Mitigation in Developing Countries: Brazil, China, India, Mexico, South Africa, and Turkey*. Pew Center on Global Climate Change. Available at: http://www.c2es.org/docUploads/dev_mitigation.pdf.

CPI (2011). *The Landscape of Climate Finance*. October. Available at: http://climatepolicyinitiative.org/wp-content/uploads/2011/10/The-Landscape-of-Climate-Finance-120120.pdf.

Dolšak, N. (2009). Climate change policy implementation: a cross-sectional analysis. *Review of Policy Research* 26(5).

Elzen, M. & N. Höhne (2008). Reductions of greenhouse gas emissions in Annex I and non-Annex I countries for meeting concentration stabilisation targets: an editorial comment. *Climate Change* 91.

Gómez-Echeverri, L. (2000). Developing countries are neither prepared to address nor interested in climate change. In L. Gómez-Echeverri (ed.) *Climate Change and Development: A Collaborative Project of the UNDP Regional Bureau for Latin America and Yale School of Forestry and Environmental Studies*. Available at: http://environment.research.yale.edu/publication-series/786.

Guan, D., Zhu L., Yong G., S. Lindner & K. Hubacek (2012). The gigotonne gap in China's carbon dioxide inventories. *Nature Climate Change* 2.

Gupta, J. & N. Van der Grip (2010). *Mainstreaming Climate Change in Development Cooperation: Theory, Practice and Implications for the European Union*. Cambridge: Cambridge University Press.

Hardin, G. (1968). The tragedy of the commons. *Science* 162 (3859).

Harris, P. (ed.) (2011). *China's Responsibility for Climate Change: Ethics, Fairness and Environmental Policy*. Bristol: Policy Press.

Harrison, K. & L. M. Sundstrom (eds.) (2010). *Global Commons, Domestic Decisions: The Comparative Politics of Climate Change*. London: MIT Press.

Heggelund, G., S. Anderson & I. F. Buan (2010). Chinese climate policy: domestic priorities, foreign policy and emerging implementation. In K. Harrison & L. M. Sundstrom (eds.) *Global Commons, Domestic Decisions: The Comparative Politics of Climate Change*. London: MIT Press.

Hovi, J., T. Skodvin & S. Andersen (2003). The persistence of the Kyoto Protocol: why other countries move on without the United States. *Global Environmental Politics* 3(4).

Inglehart, R. (1995). Public support for environmental protection: objective problems and subjective values in 43 societies. *PS: Political Science and Politics* 28(1).

Editors' Introduction

Kartha, S. & P. Erickson (2011). *Comparison of Annex 1 and Non-Annex 1 Pledges under the Cancun Agreements.* Stockholm Environment Institute Working Paper, WP-US-1107.

Lahsen, M. (2007). Trust through participation? Problems of knowledge in climate decision making. In M. E. Pettenger (ed.) *The Social Construction of Climate Change: Power, Knowledge, Norms, Discourses.* Aldershot: Ashgate.

Neumayer, E. (2002). Do democracies exhibit stronger international environmental commitment? A cross country analysis. *Journal of Peace Research* 39(2).

Olsen, K. H. (2006). National ownership in the implementation of global climate policy in Uganda. *Climate Policy* 5.

Paterson, M. (1996). *Global Warming and Global Politics.* New York, NY: Routledge.

Posner, E. & D. Weisbach (2010). *Climate Change Justice.* Princeton, NJ: Princeton University Press.

Rabe, B. (2010). *Greenhouse Governance: Addressing Climate Change in America.* Washington, DC: Brookings Institution Press.

Reid, W. V. & J. Goldemberg (1998). Developing countries are combating climate change. *Energy Policy* 26(3).

Roberts, J. T. & B. Parks (2007). Fueling injustice: globalization, ecologically, unequal exchange and climate change. *Globalizations* 4(2).

Schroeder, M. (2008). The construction of China's climate politics: transnational NGOs and the spiral model of international relations. *Cambridge Review of International Affairs* 21(4).

Selin, H. & S. VanDeveer (2009). *Changing Climates in North American Politics: Institutions, Policymaking and Multilevel Governance.* Cambridge, MA: MIT Press.

Stern, N. & C. Taylor (2010). *What do the Appendices to the Copenhagen Accord Tell Us about Global Greenhouse Gas Emissions and the Prospects for Avoiding a Rise in Global Average Temperature of More Than 2 °C?* Policy Paper, Centre for Climate Change Economics and Policy/Grantham Research Institute on Climate Change and the Environment, March.

Tjernström, E. & T. Tietenberg (2008). Do differences in attitudes explain differences in national climate change policies? *Ecological Economics* 65(2).

UN (1992). *United Nations Framework Convention on Climate Change.* Available at: http://unfccc.int/resource/docs/convkp/conveng.pdf.

World Bank (2012).*World Development Indicators.* Washington, DC: World Bank.

WRI (2012). *Climate Analysis Indicators Tool 2012.* Version 5.0. Washington, DC: World Resources Institute. Available at: http://cait.wri.org

PART I
ASIA

2

A Green Revolution: China's Governance of Energy and Climate Change

David Held, Charles Roger and Eva-Maria Nag

Introduction

CHINA is the world's largest emitter of greenhouse gases (GHGs). It is responsible for nearly 25 per cent of all CO_2 emissions and just under half of all the emissions of the developing world. Per person, its emissions now surpass even the global average, having grown by over 150 per cent between 1990 and 2008. Assuming its economy continues to expand at or near its current rate, and with it China's burgeoning appetite for fossil fuels, China's 'business-as-usual' emissions are expected to increase by between 57 and 75 per cent by 2025, depending on the projection used.[1] The policies China adopts to govern climate change, its domestic capacity for effective governance of its emissions and energy use, and any commitments that it makes are therefore of critical importance far beyond its own borders.

Thus, as the multilateral negotiations have turned towards the future design of a global climate regime, China has attracted growing attention. Reducing the country's emissions is necessary for limiting global GHG concentrations to sustainable levels, and it is increasingly thought to have an important ethical responsibility for reducing its impact on the climate as well (Harris 2011). But, as a developing country, it has steadfastly resisted any suggestion in the United Nations Framework Convention on Climate Change (UNFCCC) negotiations that it should adopt binding commitments to reduce its emissions. China's policymakers have consistently argued that industrialized states must take the lead on climate change, accepting the main burden of mitigation. Furthermore, any goals that China does adopt with respect to climate change should be fundamentally different from those for currently industrialized states. Unlike the latter, China's primary responsibility is to shift downwards the trajectory of its emissions relative to a 'business-as-usual' baseline – or, to reduce the 'carbon intensity' of its economy – and not to reduce its absolute levels of emissions. As a result, China has often been labelled a 'climate laggard' or 'hard-liner' by industrialized states, since it has taken a position that seems at odds with what others expect of it. Following Copenhagen, for example, Mark Lynas contended that China had 'wrecked efforts to reach a global deal', while Ed Miliband, then UK secretary of state for energy and climate change, accused China and other developing states of 'holding the world to ransom' (Lynas 2009; Vidal 2009).

Yet there has been a growing disjuncture between such views on China's position in the global climate change negotiations and what has been happening within its borders. Since the early 2000s, China has adopted a wide-ranging set of policies to tame its rapidly rising demand for energy by improving energy conservation and efficiency. It has also sought to raise the share of renewable sources of energy in its overall energy mix, and to increase the production and development of renewable energy technologies as well. In just under ten years, China has become one of the largest and fastest-growing markets for wind turbines and a leading producer of both turbines and solar photovoltaic panels (PV). Building on these accomplishments, China has recently offered new, ambitious energy targets and proposed a mandatory goal of reducing the carbon intensity of its economy by 40–5 per cent by 2020 that became a centrepiece of its 12th Five-Year Plan (FYP). By nearly any standard, China's domestic efforts have been impressive. Hu Angang, a prominent economist at Tsinghua University, has even gone so far as to characterize the changes that have recently taken place in China as a kind of 'green revolution' (Hu & Liang 2012).

In this chapter, we trace the evolution of China's energy and climate change policymaking. The first section focuses on China's initial institutional response to climate change, beginning with its preparations for the first international assessment of climate change science under the Intergovernmental Panel on Climate Change as well as for the United Nations Conference on Environment and Development, or 'Earth Summit', in Rio de Janeiro. During this early period, which lasted from 1988 to around 2002, the issue of climate change grew in importance in China, though the government's focus remained limited to obtaining specific outcomes in the international negotiations. Domestic climate policies were not developed to any considerable extent and were believed to be at odds with China's priorities as a developing country. The overriding concern of China's leaders during this period was – and largely continues to be – maintaining security and strong economic growth, which has been tightly intertwined with its burgeoning energy use and emissions of GHGs. At the turn of the millennium, however, China's rapidly growing demand for fossil fuels was itself becoming a worrying source of economic, environmental and political vulnerability. This realization stimulated efforts to reform the governance of energy in China and culminated in a range of ambitious policies that opened the space for China to adopt a carbon intensity target in response to new international and domestic pressures that appeared prior to Copenhagen. The initial period of domestic governance reform that began around 2002 is the subject of the second section, while the energy efficiency, renewable energy and climate change policies enacted under the 11th and 12th FYPs are the subject of the third section.

Of course, China's experience has not been without challenges. Provincial governments strained to meet, and collectively the country fell just short of, the energy intensity target set by the 11th FYP. Many have also raised concerns about the reality beneath China's seemingly impressive renewable energy trends. Going forward, there are worries about the sustainability of China's unprecedented plans to expand the use of renewable energy technologies and the central government's ability to enforce its various climate and energy policies as the number of stakeholders expands. These important concerns are discussed in the conclusion.

China's Early Engagement with Climate Change

China's domestic institutions for governing climate change were originally a response to needs that arose when the issue first appeared on the global agenda in the late 1980s. In anticipation of the global negotiations that would eventually culminate in the Earth Summit, in 1992, as well as the first international assessment of the science of climate change under the Intergovernmental Panel on Climate Change (IPCC), China needed to formulate its own position on climate change and the evaluation of its effects (Economy 1997). At the time, China had almost no history of research on climate change and had little domestic capacity for assessing the potential dangers it may pose to state and society. When Chinese policymakers were first prompted to ask scientists about the potential effects of rising average temperatures and sea level on China, shortly after the adoption of UN Resolution 43/53 in 1988, there was next to no existing data or analyses to provide an answer. The first task, then, was to coordinate a serious research undertaking to assess the science of climate change, what it meant for China and what could be done in response. An inter-agency group was established by the State Council's Environmental Protection Commission, which included the State Science and Technology Commission (SSTC), the National Environmental Protection Agency (NEPA), the China Meteorological Administration (CMA) and the Ministry of Foreign Affairs (MOFA). With significant international support, this early research effort laid the basis for subsequent research on climate change in China.

Coordination of Chinese climate policy soon followed in 1990, with the creation of the National Climate Change Coordinating Leading Small Group (NCCCLSG), which was originally stationed in and chaired by the CMA. The CMA would come to be a key player in the coordination of China's early climate change research by orchestrating China's participation in the IPCC and other international scientific programmes (Economy 1997). It was also responsible for implementing China's UNFCCC commitments after the treaty was ratified in 1992. After Rio, the CMA would continue to be one of the leading agencies, along with the Chinese Academy of Sciences (CAS), the SSTC and NEPA, especially in scientific debates about climate change within China. However, as a low ranking government body, it was increasingly sidelined by the more powerful State Development Planning Commission (SDPC) and MOFA in the actual climate policy-making process in subsequent years. Eventually, full responsibility for climate change policymaking was officially taken over by the SDPC in 1998, signalling a significant change in policy. The SDPC, which was reformed in 2003, and has since been known as the National Development and Reform Commission (NDRC), was (and, in its new form, continues to be) the most powerful comprehensive commission under the State Council, with overall responsibility for studying, developing and setting policies related to economic and social development, including the FYPs. Officially shifting responsibility for climate change to the SDPC therefore suggested that climate change was no longer being treated as a purely scientific question, but as a highly sensitive political and economic issue, especially after Kyoto in 1997 (Heggelund 2007).

Climate change was, however, still a largely international rather than domestic issue for China. Its focus was on ensuring that industrialized states took responsibility for climate change and implemented their UNFCCC commitments, while avoiding binding obligations for itself. Strict international commitments were thought to be at odds with China's political needs and priorities as a developing country. The government's legitimacy is typically thought to rest on the (at least) tacit support of several key industrial and commercial constituencies, the bureaucracies, the military and the mass public. Mainly, this has been achieved by maintaining the country's security and an economic growth rate above 7 or 8 per cent per year. Policies that threaten to restrict growth, such as binding commitments to reduce emissions, were therefore vigorously resisted. But Chinese negotiators also regularly argued, with the Group of 77 (G77), that developing countries had made a negligible contribution to global emissions in per capita and historic terms and should be allowed to increase their emissions as they develop. Thus, they have no moral obligation to make any commitments, voluntary or otherwise. However, while these principles largely remained enduring features of China's position in the UN negotiations in subsequent years, some changes began to occur in the late 1990s, coinciding with the shift in domestic authority towards the NDRC.

China's volte-face on the issue of flexibility mechanisms is one of the clearest ways in which its position changed during this time. In the early talks leading to the Earth Summit, Joint Implementation (JI) had been a particularly contentious issue for China, especially in so far as the concept was extended to include developing countries.

JI would, in theory, allow developed countries to earn credits for emissions reducing projects in other countries that could count towards their own emissions targets or could be sold to others. This would give them a degree of flexibility over how they would meet their emission reduction targets. However, at this early stage, China argued that JI was an unfair practice which would allow developed countries to shirk their responsibilities, and would involve a violation of sovereignty due to the invasive monitoring and verification measures that would be needed (Nielsen & McElroy 1998). Ultimately, against China's initial objections, provisions for JI were included in the UNFCCC, though only as a pilot phase without the possibility of credits – what became known as activities implemented jointly (AIJ).

Again, in the subsequent negotiations leading to Kyoto, the so-called 'Kyoto Flexibility Mechanisms' proved to be a key issue for China – the Clean Development Mechanism (CDM), in particular. The CDM, which originally stemmed from a Brazilian proposal, was designed to allow emission reduction projects in developing countries to earn certified emission reduction (CER) credits, which could be traded and used by industrialized states to meet a part of their emissions reduction targets under the Kyoto Protocol. In contrast to its generally negative position on JI in earlier negotiations, however, key Chinese officials in the NDRC came to see the CDM as a potential conduit for technologies and investments (Hatch 2003; Heggelund 2007; Heggelund et al. 2010). Participating in the CDM would also allow China to demonstrate its commitment to action on climate change, while remaining free of any binding obligations to specific emissions reduction targets. Chinese negotiators still expressed significant reservations about the CDM's institutions. They worried that the mechanism would primarily serve the interests of developed countries and would make it more difficult for developing countries to reduce emissions cheaply if and when they assumed some reduction commitments. China also objected to a US proposal suggesting that the resulting credits should be tradable in secondary markets, and preferred CDM projects to be arranged primarily through bilateral project-based institutional arrangements (Hatch 2003). But it became clear that China no longer objected to the CDM concept tout court as it had JI. At the Sixth Conference of the Parties (COP6), China called the CDM a 'win-win' mechanism for both developed and developing countries, and, at COP7, in Marrakech, China bolstered efforts to accelerate its launch (Bjorkum 2005). It would eventually come to be the most significant host of CDM projects (for a thorough discussion of China's CDM governance see Schroeder 2009b).

The evolution of China's early approach to the climate change negotiations suggests that while it initially resisted proposals asking it to adopt any commitments on ideological and political grounds, policymakers also gradually realized that certain kinds of commitments could be congruent with its domestic political and economic needs. Diplomats continued to argue that China had no obligation to

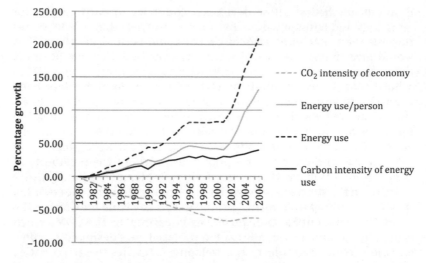

Figure 2.1   China's energy use, 1980–2006

Source: WRI (2011).

adopt overall binding mitigation targets, but became more flexible and pragmatic on a variety of other issues as time went on (for further discussion on the ways in which China's position in the UNFCCC has changed see Held et al. 2011 and Zhang 2006).

China's Evolving Energy Concerns and the Reform of Domestic Institutions

During the early period in its engagement with the UNFCCC negotiations, described above, China's economy had expanded tremendously. Between 1979 and 2002, from the time that domestic reform and the opening of its economy began to China's signing of the Kyoto Protocol, the country grew nearly sevenfold. Its annual rate of growth throughout this entire period averaged almost 10 per cent. At the same time, however, China's energy use had only tripled, and its energy use per capita increased by even less (see figure 2.1). This remarkable achievement was largely the result of domestic reforms in the ownership of state-owned enterprises, the closing or replacement of inefficient capital, and the removal of many energy subsidies in the mid-1980s (Reid & Goldemberg 1998; Garnaut et al. 2008). Further, due to these reforms, the carbon intensity of its economy had actually declined by nearly 70 per cent during this time. Between 1979 and 1996, China's aggregate emissions of GHGs had grown by around 135 per cent, but they managed to plateau for several years in the late 1990s, despite the country's high rate of economic growth. From 1992 to 2002, China's share of total global CO_2 emissions rose by only 3 per cent.

Yet, beginning in 2002, a shift occurred. After many of the opportunities for easy efficiency gains expired and as China's economic growth rate increased substantially at the start of the 2000s, its energy use in absolute and per capita terms began to rise, as did its emissions of GHGs. By 2008, the former had grown by roughly 90 and 75 per cent, respectively, while its emissions of CO_2 grew by an even greater amount. China's share of global CO_2 emissions rose from 15 to 22 per cent in just over five years. The change had a significant effect upon China's leaders. Above all, China's burgeoning energy use was increasingly seen as a major domestic and international security issue. Since 1993, China had become progressively more dependent upon foreign sources of oil to supply its growing economy, after decades of self-sufficiency. And demand was expected to skyrocket in the future. In combination with volatile and rising international prices, this state of affairs resulted in growing concerns amongst Chinese policymakers about the country's ability to acquire adequate, affordable and reliable supplies to feed its fast-growing industries (Downs 2006). Dependence upon the Strait of Malacca for around 80 per cent of China's oil imports and reliance upon the US Navy for ensuring the safety of the major sea-lanes of communication also resulted in significant strategic discomfort.

At the same time, the domestic determinants of China's energy security became a major worry too. With nearly 177 billion tonnes of proven reserves within its borders – approximately 14 per cent of the world total – China possessed enormous supplies of coal (EIA 2010). As such, the vast majority (roughly 70 per cent in 2003) of the country's energy supply was (and is) coal-based. Yet most of China's coal was located far from the coastal areas where demand for energy had been rising fastest. This made these areas highly vulnerable to shocks arising from China's weak long-distance energy transmission and transportation infrastructure. Such shocks would be especially burdensome to the country as a whole because coastal industries were responsible for producing most of China's gross domestic product (GDP). A number of severe energy shortages, bottlenecks and blackouts (in 2002–3, 2003–4 and 2005) were indeed produced by major imbalances in supply and demand, prompting coastal regions to begin importing coal from abroad, and making them relatively more reliant upon foreign sources of coal as well (Tu & Johnson-Reiser 2012).

Chinese anxiety about energy security pulled state policy in opposing directions. On the one hand, in order to expand energy supplies to meet demand, efforts were made to help national oil companies to secure trade and investment opportunities abroad and to acquire equity in foreign oil exploration and production. This facet of China's policy response attracted a great deal of attention (see, for instance, Downs 2000 and 2004; Currier & Dorraj 2011), since it meant China would become a much more significant player in global energy markets and could potentially change regional and global security dynamics. Domestically, expanding electrical generation capacity by bringing more and more power plants online was another dimension of this drive to meet demand. On the other hand, the government also increasingly sought to moderate consumption (Zha 2006; Kennedy 2010). Significant emphasis would, therefore, be placed on conserving energy and improving energy efficiency. Efforts would also be made to tame consumption of fossil fuels while boosting supply by increasing the use of renewable sources of energy. Pursuing these twin objectives drove China to undertake an ambitious effort to improve domestic energy governance and to implement a range of energy efficiency and renewable energy policies that would eventually undergird its approach to climate change. The latter are discussed more fully in the next section. In the remainder of this section, we look at attempts to reshape the institutions governing energy within China, as well as those directly related to climate change.

At the time that concerns about energy security began to grow at the start of the 2000s, there was next to no overarching governance structure in China's energy sector. Coordination of planning and investment among the major ministries, such as the Ministry of Petroleum Industry, the Ministry of Coal Industry, the Ministry of Nuclear Industry and the Ministry of Water Resources and Electric Power, along with the major national energy companies, was all but absent. However, following the severe energy shortages and black-outs that began in 2002, the Chinese government was shocked into an effort to improve its capacity in this area. In 2003, the National People's Congress made a first attempt by establishing an Energy Bureau under the NDRC. The Bureau was originally envisioned as an independent agency with a broad mandate to manage the energy sector. But real centralization of authority faced heavy resistance from entrenched interests within the state bureaucracy and the energy industry, and the final outcome represented a compromise solution between two distinct groups (Downs 2006). On the one side were the proponents of a centralized energy authority in the National People's Congress; on the other were the national energy companies as well as the NDRC, which wished to prevent the creation of any kind of body that might have real independent authority over their actions. As a result of this compromise, the Energy Bureau was established but it ultimately suffered from a lack of manpower, financial resources, autonomy and authority, which hindered its ability to coordinate energy policy. It proved unable to reconcile the multiple conflicts among the most important stakeholders.

Renewed energy crises in 2003 and 2004 highlighted the inadequacy of these initial institutional reforms. Thus, in a new effort to centralize energy policymaking, a National Energy Leading Group (NELG), headed by Premier Wen Jiabao, was created in 2005, along with a State Energy Office (SEO). Both were established by the State Council largely at the insistence of top officials from the NDRC, who had been dissatisfied with their ability to exert control over the energy sector through the Energy Bureau and saw the need to secure greater support from the top echelons of China's leadership (Downs 2006). The NELG acted as a high-level discussion and coordination body under the auspices of the State Council, while the SEO was subordinate to it. Overall, the creation of the NELG and SEO improved governance of the energy sector at the margin. Yet many of the persistent problems that had hindered effective governance remained, including bureaucratic fragmentation and poor institutional capacity (see Cunningham 2007). In many areas, the major administrative tasks continued to be managed by separate ministries, leading to poor coordination and resistance from influential constituencies to further centralization.

The most recent attempt to overcome the energy governance deficit in China involved the creation, in 2008, of a National Energy Commission (NEC), which would replace the NELG, and a National Energy Administration (NEA), which absorbed the SEO and a number of other agencies. Acting on behalf of the NEC, the NEA was tasked with managing the energy industry, drafting energy plans and policies, interacting with international organizations and authorizing foreign energy investments. At present, both the NEC and NEA continue to suffer from insufficient authority, autonomy and resources, making it difficult to undertake a coordinated effort to moderate energy demand on the scale needed (Downs 2008; Tsang & Kolk 2010). Many aspects of energy policymaking are still undertaken by a fragmented group of institutions. Nonetheless, while far from ideal, the NEC's and NEA's capabilities in each of the areas covered by their mandates have been greater than those possessed by the Energy Bureau as well as their direct predecessors, the NELG and the SEO. And, as the next section demonstrates, the major reforms that were undertaken clearly made possible the implementation of a wide range of important policies for improving energy efficiency and promoting renewable energy use.

At the same time as China's energy sector governance was being progressively reformed, China's domestic climate governance infrastructure underwent a similar shift. After China's approval of the Kyoto Protocol in 2002, the NCCCLSG was reorganized and became known as the National Coordination Committee on Climate Change (NCCCC). Established under the auspices of the State Council in 2003, it continued to be stationed in and chaired by the NDRC. For the most part, however, its actual policy outputs remained limited. The governance apparatus for managing CDM projects was created under its aegis and the first comprehensive review of climate change in China, the National Assessment Report on Climate Change, was published at the end of 2006 by the Ministry of Science and Technology (MOST, formerly the SSTC), the CMA and CAS. Nonetheless, the National Assessment did prove to be an important trigger for future policymaking as it forecast a range of negative trends in China arising from global warming, and received considerable attention from policymakers. Indeed, due to a growing perception of China's vulnerability following the National Assessment, as well as the greater salience of climate change in the international arena after COP13 in Bali, Indonesia, the NCCCC was replaced by the National Leading Committee on Climate Change (NLCCC). Headed by Premier Wen Jiabao, the mandate of the NLCCC, which coordinates twenty-seven different government agencies, would be much like that of its predecessors: to make major decisions and to coordinate national actions on climate change. However, the involvement of Premier Wen signalled the extent to which climate change, like energy, had risen up the government's agenda and attracted the attention of the country's top leadership.

Reform of China's energy and climate governance structures was not limited to changes in the central government. The creation of the NELG and NLCCC was also paralleled by the formation of similar leading groups and task forces designed to plan and coordinate action on energy efficiency and climate change in local governments (see discussion in Qi et al. 2008). Between June 2007 and March 2008, a number of provinces, provincial-level municipalities and autonomous regions established Leading Groups on Climate Change, Energy Saving and Pollution Reduction based on the central government's model. Many other provinces established Leading Groups on Energy Saving and Pollution Reduction that did not have 'climate change' in their titles, but nevertheless also had clear mandates to generate strategies and policies and to organize action on climate change as well as energy. Similar groups appeared at the prefectural and county levels too. Together, they were delegated responsibility for implementing the central government's energy and climate policies. And, subsequently, a number of these, including Xinjiang, Hubei, Fujian, Beijing, Liaoning, Shandong and Jianxi, developed their own climate change plans, while others even launched their own climate change research programmes (Tsang & Kolk 2010; Koehn 2008). Beijing, Shanghai and Hong Kong also became members of the C40 Cities Climate Leadership Group (C40) around this time, offering evidence of a new 'transnational' dimension to subnational governance of climate change in China (for more on this see Hale & Roger 2012).

Thus, after 2002, the entire structure of climate and energy governance in China changed quite considerably. The reform of institutions governing energy occurred primarily in response to growing concerns about China's energy security that were made all the more salient by periodic crises. Corresponding institutions for governing climate change were reformed mainly in response to international developments, but also as a result of the government's growing concern about the issue as the scale of the impacts became better understood following the National Assessment. As these changes took place, a range of new policies and programmes – discussed in the next section – were implemented. These initially focused on improving energy efficiency and promoting renewable energy use. But, since these had the additional 'co-benefit' of reducing China's carbon intensity as well, these created a political window for the government to adopt policies and targets more explicitly focused on climate change in response to international and domestic forces that mounted in the years leading up to Copenhagen.

Energy and Climate Change Policy Under the 11th and 12th Five-Year Plans

Despite the fact that the reform of institutions governing energy and climate change in China was only partial and piecemeal, the greater governance capacity that was achieved permitted a number of new climate and energy-focused programmes, policies and targets to be established. Taken together, these have amounted to a nearly unparalleled effort to promote energy efficiency and the adoption and production of renewable energy technologies. Largely through these initiatives, China managed to slow, to some extent, a number of the trends that worried China's leaders.[2] These accomplishments, in turn, created an opportunity for international and domestic actors to push successfully for the adoption of specific climate change policies and targets, which were eventually incorporated into the 12th FYP. Here, we consider the evolution of these policies.

Energy Efficiency Policies

China's first major step on the path towards a low carbon development trajectory was its target of reducing energy consumption per unit of GDP (its 'energy intensity') by 20 per cent. This was announced in the 11th FYP (2006–10). To meet this goal, energy conservation targets were set for each region, and for individual businesses noted for their inefficiency. The allocations for provincial governments were established through a process of negotiation: they were asked to propose an energy intensity target which then served as the basis for bargaining with the NDRC. Once a number was agreed upon, the provincial target was submitted to the National People's Congress for assessment and approval. Provincial governments then engaged in a similar process of bargaining with counties, municipalities and businesses, usually on the basis of a stricter provincial target as a hedge, since it was expected that a share of the targets set at lower levels might be missed (see Pan 2011). To support this national effort, a revised Energy Conservation Law was approved in 2007, which created a legal framework for promoting energy efficiency programmes. Among other things, the law made local governments accountable for implementing their shares of the national target. The State Council would periodically assess and report on the progress of local governments towards their energy intensity targets. And officials' adherence to their target was included as a key criterion in their performance evaluations.

National and sub-national policies and initiatives used to achieve these goals included:

- higher taxes on petroleum, coal and natural gas to encourage buyers to reduce consumption of, and diversify away from, such fuels;
- differentiated energy pricing, which raised the cost of energy on businesses that did not meet the government's energy efficiency standards;
- energy conservation and efficiency programmes focusing on public transport, alternative fuels, combined heat-and-power, surplus heat utilization, green lighting, high performance appliances and energy saving buildings;
- energy efficiency benchmarking in key sectors, such as construction and transportation; and,
- the Top-1,000 Enterprises Energy Conservation Programme, which encouraged key energy consuming businesses to engage in energy auditing and to establish energy conservation plans (see Worldwatch 2010).

The effects of these policies were felt across all levels of government. To meet local targets, provincial officials created incentives for local firms to comply through a process of 'log-rolling' with different groups, as described by Kostka and Hobbs (2012); they would, for example, bundle energy policies together with others that would produce benefits for local constituencies, such as the reduction of pollution, or they would set favourable policies for businesses in exchange for compliance. However, in many cases, these strategies were not sufficient on their own to meet the central government's targets. Officials also ordered the closure of more than 2,000 steel mills, cement works and factories as part of the efficiency drive (BBC 2010). And, towards the end of the FYP, some local authorities initiated ruthless energy rationing programmes, cutting electricity to homes, factories and even hospitals for much of the day on a regular basis (Li 2010). These actions raised a number of normative questions about the way in which energy efficiency goals were being pursued in China, and would affect the way that municipalities approached the new bargaining process that would set energy efficiency goals in the 12th FYP, as discussed below. But they testified to the determination with which the objective of energy efficiency was, and has been, pursued by the government. Indeed, a recent study of China's performance found that it had managed to achieve a 19 per cent reduction in its energy intensity, just short of its 20 per cent target and estimated to be equivalent to having avoided roughly 1,550 megatonnes (Mt) of CO_2 (CPI 2012). Other independent sources have also confirmed trends consistent with a near 20 per cent reduction (WRI 2012).

Renewable Energy Policies

Renewable energy policies proliferated in a similar fashion as China attempted to diversify supplies away from the use of fossil fuels, particularly coal and oil. Sensing, also, the major economic opportunities at hand in the markets for renewable energy products, as well as other benefits to be had in terms of reduced pollution and lower emissions, China became both a major producer and market for renewable energy products in a short period of time. China had, in fact, designated renewable energy technology as an area of potential growth as far back as the 1980s, investing a great deal of resources in research and development (R&D). Production of renewable energy products had also already begun to grow in the 1990s. But it was not until 2005 that China approved a Renewable Energy Law, which established a legal framework for enacting economy-wide renewable energy policies. This was then supplemented by the Medium and Long-Term Development Plan for Renewable Energy in 2007.

Together, these aimed to increase the use of non-fossil fuel energy sources in China's total energy consumption to 10 per cent by 2010 and 15 per cent by 2020, delegating certain responsibilities to local authorities and making the achievement of each target legally mandatory. Specific targets were set for each renewable energy source. By 2020, China aimed to have a total of 300 gigawatts (GW) of installed hydro capacity, 30 GW of wind capacity, 1.8 GW of solar PV capacity and 30 GW of biomass-based sources of energy production. Policies that were established by the Law and Plan to promote the development and use of renewables included:

- rules that required the operators of power grids to buy energy from renewable energy producers;
- feed-in tariffs, which obliged utilities to pay more for wind power than for other forms of electricity;
- concessional lending and the creation of a national fund to encourage renewable energy development;
- guidelines for renewable energy industries, and technical standards for renewable energy generation, technologies and products; and,
- rules designed to encourage the construction of renewable power generation facilities (see Worldwatch 2010).

This policymaking effort was supplemented by financial support from MOST for R&D on key renewable energy technologies, and by a host of policies, regulations, targets, subsidies and sectoral plans formulated and set by local governments as well, some of which also created low-carbon development zones which would focus on producing clean energy technologies (Gordon et al. 2010). In 2009, a special subsidy initiative known as the 'Golden Sun' programme were also launched specifically in order to foster solar

PV production, which had at this point lagged behind most other renewable technologies.

Efforts to promote the use and production of renewable energy showed significant results in a short period of time. Hydro, wind, biomass and solar PV energy use increased across the board, and China managed to become both a global market leader and the largest user of renewable energy (Gordon et al. 2010). Wind energy led the way, with capacity roughly doubling every year after 2004. By the end of 2009, China boasted installed capacity of nearly 26 GW, surpassing the United States to become the world's largest market for wind turbines (Fairley 2009). Its 2020 target of 30 GW of installed capacity was reached almost ten years ahead of schedule. Production of renewable energy technology improved dramatically as well. Wind, solar PV, solar heating, biomass, geothermal and ocean energy technologies all also saw significant gains. China became the third largest manufacturer of solar PV technology, producing around 30 per cent of the world total (Gordon et al. 2010), and a major manufacturer of wind turbines.

Climate Change Policy and the 12th Five-Year Plan

China's determination to manage its domestic energy issues, which had grown increasingly problematic at the start of the 2000s, made it possible for it to accumulate a number of very positive titles: the world's largest market for wind energy, the most installed renewable generation capacity, the third largest producer of solar PV, and so on. According to Worldwatch (2010, p. 11) its effort to increase energy efficiency and conservation 'has [had] few equals in other countries, developed or developing'. And while the carbon intensity of its GDP had risen between 2002 and 2005, China was able to reverse the trend, returning its economy to 2002 levels by the end of the decade. Despite these accomplishments, there were also a number of worrying developments that matched and in some respects overshadowed them. By 2009, China had indisputably become the world's largest emitter of GHGs, the world's largest consumer of coal, and the world's second largest producer and consumer of energy.

As China now possessed the potential to undermine any emissions reductions made by other countries, its cooperation was increasingly perceived to be essential to limiting global GHG emissions. Without strong action from China, any attempt to control global warming would be futile. Moreover, given China's central role in the world economy and persistent worries across the industrialized world about the eastward movement of business to Asia, policymakers in industrialized states were concerned about the competitiveness of their economies as well as the domestic political ramifications of adopting stringent climate regulations without a similar commitment by China. As a result, China came under renewed diplomatic pressure in multilateral and bilateral forums to adopt some kind of emissions target. Following the lead of the United States, the rest of the industrialized world demanded that China make a strong commitment to reducing its emissions before agreeing to any post-2012 targets. Its position on climate governance thus became a source of tension in nearly all its diplomatic relations.

These international forces were complemented at the domestic level by a host of new pressures from within the state. First, perceiving a new opportunity to expand their remit as a result of climate change's growing visibility and importance, a number of Chinese bureaucracies had begun to adopt the issue as their own and pushed for control over climate-related activities. As bureaucracies competed with one another for leadership positions this, in turn, created a new dynamic within the government that made serious policy change more likely (see Conrad 2010). Second, beginning around 2007, a more vocal and coherent set of civil society groups focusing on climate change issues appeared, and there were growing protests in relation to air and water pollution and related health problems across China, creating pressure for greater proactivity on environmental issues from below (Schröder 2011). Indeed, more than 50,000 disputes related to environmental pollution were reported from mid-2005 to mid-2006 (van Heuvelen 2007). The 2008 Beijing Olympics also provided a focal point for air pollution and environmental issues, compelling the government to grant the State Environmental Protection Agency greater scope for implementing clean air regulations in the years leading up to the games (Turner & Ellis 2007). Finally, a number of public intellectuals and scientific communities in China became vocal advocates of more rigorous climate change policies (see Schroeder 2009a). For example, Hu Angang, one of China's most widely known economists and a much-respected advisor to China's leadership, promoted the idea of 'green development' in China. He argued that China must not – and need not – pursue the high consumption and high pollution path of industrialization followed by the West. He criticized, too, the prevailing division of responsibility between developed and developing countries in the UNFCCC. With Su Wei, one of China's leading climate change negotiators, he pressed the government to adopt a strong carbon intensity target prior to Copenhagen.

These international and domestic attempts to pressure and persuade the Chinese government to adopt a more proactive approach proved to be substantial. Initially, in response, China agreed at COP13 – along with the rest of the G77 – to discuss taking Nationally Appropriate Mitigation Actions (NAMAs). This represented a notable departure from their long-held position of avoiding discussing commitments for developing states, voluntary or otherwise, though it did not immediately affect China's stance on the main issues. It agreed to 'discuss' NAMAs. Yet, in the subsequent negotiations of the Ad Hoc Working Group on Long-Term Cooperative Action of the UNFCCC, China continued to push to preserve Kyoto, demanded strong actions from developed countries, and continued to eschew any binding commitments for developing states. Chinese negotiators consistently called upon the principle of common but differentiated responsibility to justify the country's position. However, prior to Copenhagen, and in anticipation of the significant demands that would be placed on it there, China offered the international community a voluntary pledge to reduce its carbon intensity by 40–5 per cent from 2005 levels by 2020. Afterwards, the target was submitted to the UNFCCC secretariat as China's NAMA commitment under the Copenhagen Accord.

China was, at the time, widely accused of contributing to the failure of Copenhagen, and its voluntary commitment was deemed by some critics to be meaningless, representing little more than the continuation of current energy efficiency and conservation policies and measures. No doubt, China's pledge built upon the success of its previous energy efficiency and renewable energy policies. Yet others argued that it was significant, requiring a host of much more aggressive policies to meet it (Chandler & Wang 2009; Cohen-Tanugi 2010; Pan 2011). When the pledge was subsequently enshrined in China's 12th FYP, released in March 2011, it was indeed accompanied by a host of new goals.

The new FYP set a mandatory target of reducing energy intensity by 16 per cent by 2015, a figure which was arrived at by 'working backwards' from the carbon intensity target for 2020 (Liu 2012). This overall target was then used as the basis for allocating provincial energy intensity targets through negotiations with local governments that were similar to those which set intensity targets during the 11th FYP, discussed above. However, the central government is reported to have been much more cautious, as were local officials, who had been overly ambitious during the 11th FYP and struggled to meet their targets as a result (Feng & Yuan 2012). Greater thought was also given to local conditions, with politically sensitive regions in the west of China (Xinjiang and Tibet, for instance) generally given special treatment, as shown in table 2.1. One of the first efforts along the path towards meeting China's new energy intensity target was expansion of the Top-1,000 Enterprises Energy Conservation Programme, now widely considered to be a great success. The previous programme had achieved its goals ahead of schedule and has been estimated to have saved around 400 million tonnes of CO_2 (Lin et al. 2011). The expanded programme – the so-called Top 10,000 Programme – is now expected to involve 15,000–16,000 firms and could save as much as 610 million tonnes of CO_2.

Renewable energy, likewise, continued to be a major focus of China's energy strategy and industrial policy as elaborated in the 12th FYP. Prior to the plan's release, extremely ambitious renewable energy targets for 2020 had already been proposed. A new goal of reaching 150 GW of installed wind capacity had been set – a target nearly equal to the world's entire installed wind capacity of 157 GW at present. Overall, the government would aim to increase the share

44

Table 2.1 Regional energy intensity targets in China				
18% reduction	**17% reduction**	**16% reduction**	**15% reduction**	**10% reduction**
Guangdong	Beijing	Anhui	Gansu	Hainan
Jiangsu	Hebei	Chongqing	Guangxi	Tibet
Shanghai	Liaoning	Fujian	Guizhou	Qinghai
Tianjin	Shandon	Heilongjiang	Inner Mongolia	Xinjiang
Zhejiang		Henan	Ningxia	
		Hubei	Yunnan	
		Hunan		
		Jiangxi		
		Jilin		
		Shaanxi		
		Shanxi		
		Sichuan		

Sources: NDRC (2011); Fulton (2011).

Table 2.2 Current and targeted renewable energy production in China (gigawatts)					
	2006 (actual)	**2009 (actual)**	**12th FYP targets for 2015**	**Updated targets for 2015**	**Proposed 2020 targets**
Hydro power	130	197	250	260	300
Wind power	2.6	25.8	90	100	150
Biomass power	2.6	3.2	13	12	30
Solar power	0.08	0.4	5	10	20
Renewable energy share of final energy consumption	7%	9%	11.40%	N/A	15%

Sources: Climate Group (2011); NDRC (2011); Martinot (2010); Wang et al. (2010); Martinot & Li (2007).

of renewable energy sources in total energy consumption by 15 per cent. Once released, the FYP included targets that were broadly in line with these objectives for 2020. The plan revealed that China hoped to increase the use of non-fossil fuel-based energy to 11.4 per cent of total energy use by 2015. Individual figures for each technology were published later in the year, and are reported in table 2.2. These were, however, subsequently updated to include targets of 260 GW for hydropower, 100 GW for wind power and 10 GW for solar power, reflecting the NDRC's belief that actual trends were likely to 'outstrip' the original targets (Zhoa 2011). Production of renewable energy technologies was also given a boost in the new FYP. Both the wind energy and solar PV industries were identified as 'strategic industries' which would be the target of industrial policies. Other strategic industries that were identified included nuclear energy, hybrid and electric vehicles and energy saving and storage technologies.

Complementing these new energy intensity and renewable energy goals were several others focused explicitly on enhancing domestic climate change governance in other areas. Most notably, the 12th FYP proposed the gradual implementation of domestic carbon trading. In 2008, voluntary carbon exchanges had been established in Beijing, Tianjin and Shanghai, each with the support of networks of government agencies, businesses and experts. Some voluntary transactions had even taken place. The China Beijing Environmental Exchange, for example, held a sale in June 2011 for 210,000 tonnes of carbon to a group of customers that included Baidu, Air China, Merchants Bank and China Everbright Bank. The 12th FYP announced that China plans to build on these efforts, proposing that regional pilot projects be established to create the market infrastructure and experience required for successful carbon trading (NDRC 2011). The NDRC then followed up on this by asking seven provinces and cities to set overall emissions targets, prepare implementation plans and establish funds to set up the pilots. The provinces and cities include Hubei, Guangdong, Beijing, Tianjin, Shanghai, Chongqing and Shenzhen. The precise nature of these new schemes, their scale and scope, have yet to be elaborated in any detail. However, their evolution will be particularly interesting to follow as they potentially foreshadow a new stage of climate governance in China.

Conclusion

As the world's second largest producer and consumer of energy and the greatest emitter of GHGs in absolute terms, China occupies a critical position in the global governance of climate change. Significant efforts to limit its rising emissions over the upcoming years are essential for reducing global GHG concentrations to sustainable levels, and it has increasingly been argued that China has an important ethical responsibility to do so as well. In the UNFCCC negotiations, China has largely resisted demands from the international community for it to make binding commitments. But, domestically, it has adopted increasingly ambitious mandatory targets for energy and climate change in its 11th and 12th FYPs. The initial motivation to tackle China's burgeoning energy use arose, primarily, as a result of growing concerns about the country's energy security. Efforts were undertaken to improve governance capacity in the energy sector, and a range of policies were implemented to encourage energy efficiency and the deployment and production of renewable energy technologies. Yet these ambitious policies had the added 'co-benefit' of reducing China's carbon emissions per unit of GDP, and therefore opened a window for China to adopt an additional 'carbon intensity' target in response to international pressures as well as protests and persuasion by domestic actors. The shift that has occurred has been, in many ways, a remarkable one. Hu Angang, as noted in the introduction, has referred to the changes that have taken place as a kind of 'green revolution'. However, it is clear that a number of problems remain which have the potential to push the 'revolution' off course.

First, meeting the energy intensity target of the 11th FYP was very difficult for most local governments, and the challenge of meeting the new intensity target set out in the 12th FYP is likely to be even greater. During the 11th FYP, the central government mandated a rigid overall 20 per cent reduction, and was relatively inflexible in its regional allocation (Feng & Yuan 2012). Collectively, local authorities had an interest in lowering overall energy demand. But, individually, their incentives were shaped by the extent to which they could capture the benefits of implementation. This collective action problem meant that local government officials relied on a variety of log-rolling strategies to ensure that targets were met or even surpassed (Kostka & Hobbs 2012). Most provincial governments in China managed to meet their energy intensity targets (Feng & Yuan 2012). Yet they often strained to do so. This time around, local governments were far more cautious about the targets they agreed to, and the central government was more flexible in its allocation of targets as well. Still, the new 16 per cent energy intensity goal is regarded by many analysts as likely to be equally challenging, if not more so, since many of the low hanging fruits – large, energy inefficient power plants and businesses – have already been plucked (see Chandler & Wang 2009 and Pan 2011). From a global perspective, this is regarded as a good thing; with 'extended efforts', Cohen-Tanugi (2010) has estimated that China's 2020 commitment would be an important contribution to meeting global objectives. But the rising number of stakeholders that will need to be coerced or co-opted and the growing costs of abatement required to meet the new target are likely to complicate efforts greatly going forward. Very different – potentially more costly or draconian – strategies will be required on the part of local governments, and the extent to which these can be feasibly pursued is an open question.

Second, concerns have been voiced, likewise, about the reality underlying China's embrace of renewable energy. The rapid increase in deployment and production of renewable energy technologies has been one of the hallmarks of China's 'green revolution'. But obstacles have been encountered, especially with regard to the massive investments in wind. China suffers from inadequate long-distance transmission infrastructure, and most of the new wind farms that have been created are located in the north, far from China's rapidly growing coastal regions. Significant bottlenecks have been encountered as a result, a problem that has also plagued other forms of energy generation (particularly coal and hydropower), as previously discussed. In 2008, data from the China Electricity Council showed that as much as 28 per cent of China's wind capacity was left idle, unable to feed into the energy grid (Lu 2010). Poor construction also meant that 70–80 per cent of wind farms operated below capacity. Finally, the inherent intermittence of renewable energy sources such as wind has compounded bottlenecks due to the underdevelopment of energy management systems. Investment in wind farms by the major energy companies has continued, regardless, but as a result of these underlying challenges there are significant worries about the long-term sustainability of this trend. A lack of profitability and heavy reliance upon government-created incentives have led some, such as Shi Pengei, deputy chair of the China Wind Energy Association, to argue that the industry is now 'overheated', requiring significant investments in energy infrastructure and a much greater long-term commitment by the government in order to meet targets on time (see Lu 2010).

China's domestic governance of energy and climate change therefore faces an important set of challenges going forward. Chinese policymakers have so far shown great determination in their efforts to tackle climate change and burgeoning energy use. They have reformed institutions at an impressive rate and enacted new policies and programmes on a scale that is nearly unparalleled elsewhere in the world. Yet success in the future will depend upon further improvements in domestic governance capacity and the successful resolution of some of the key problems, outlined above, that threaten to stymie momentum. Ultimately, therefore, the ability of Chinese policymakers to match their new goals with adequate political, economic and technological capital remains to be seen, and will for some time remain a key question in considerations of China's ability to contribute to the governance of climate change.

Notes

An earlier version of this chapter was presented at the London School of Economics and Political Science's (LSE's) Department for International Development Workshop ('Tackling Climate Change: Are the Solutions Part of the Problem?') in 2011, kindly hosted by Robert H. Wade and Kate Meagher. The research upon which this study is based is primarily derived from semi-structured interviews with a range of stakeholders and observers in Beijing that were conducted in November 2010. Those interviewed included officials from several relevant bureaucracies, individuals from civil society groups that have closely followed climate change issues for some time, and a number of academics, journalists and diplomatic officials. All are to be thanked for contributing their time and energy, and, of course, none can be held responsible for any of the conclusions reached in this chapter. Finally, we would like to thank our colleagues who commented on the many iterations of this chapter.

1 See the World Resource Institute's CAIT database, http://cait.wri.org.
2 For instance, China managed to reverse the trend of rising energy intensity. The share of oil in China's total primary energy supply also steadily decreased after (roughly) 2004, as did the growth rates of oil imports, energy use and energy use per capita. The carbon intensity of China's economy also managed

to plateau after the uptick in 2002. Of course, in some cases these improvements reflect structural economic changes rather than policy changes, but evidence from CPI (2012) suggests that changes in policy under China's 11th FYP were a major factor underpinning these shifts. CPI calculate, for instance, that 87 per cent of the improvement in energy intensity was a result of improvements in energy efficiency, of which 69 per cent was due to (largely policy-induced) technological changes, while only 23 per cent was due to structural economic changes.

References

BBC (2010). *China Orders 2,000 Factory Closures over Energy Use*. Available at: http://www.bbc.co.uk/news/world-asia-pacific-10923214.

Bjorkum, I. (2005). *China in the International Politics of Climate Change: A Foreign Policy Analysis*. Fridtjof Nansen Institute (FNI) Report 12/2005. Available at: http://www.fni.no/doc&pdf/FNI-R1205.pdf.

Chandler, W. & Wang Y. (2009). *Memo to Copenhagen: Commentary is Misinformed – China's Commitment is Significant*. Carnegie Endowment for International Peace, Web Commentary. Available at: http://carnegieendowm ent.org/files/Memo_to_Copenhagen_edits_Revised_12-14-091.pdf.

Climate Group (2011). *Renewable Energy Development Targets in China's '12th Five Year Plan' Adjusted Upwards*. Briefing Note.

Cohen-Tanugi, D. (2010). *Putting it in Perspective: China's Energy Intensity Target*. NRDC White Paper, Natural Resources Defence Council, October. Available at: http://nrdcchina.net/phpcms/userfiles/download/201109/27/Putting%20 it%20into%20Perspective%20China's%20Carbon%20Intensity%20Target%20 2010%20Oct.pdf.

Conrad, B. (2010). Bureaucratic land rush: China's administrative battles in the arena of climate change policy. *Harvard Asia Quarterly*, Spring.

CPI (2012). *Annual Review of Low-Carbon Development in China (2011–2012): Climate Policy Initiative*. Available at: http://climatepolicyinitiative.org/beijing/ files/2011/11/China Low-Carbon Development-2011–2012.pdf.

Cunningham, E. (2007). *China's Energy Governance: Perception and Reality*. MIT Centre for International Studies. Available at: http://web.mit.edu/cis/pdf/ Audit_03_07_Cunningham.pdf.

Currier, C. & M. Dorraj (eds.) (2011). *China's Energy Relations with the Developing World*. New York, NY: Continuum.

Downs, E. (2000). *China's Quest for Energy Security*. Santa Monica, CA: RAND.

Downs, E. (2004). The Chinese energy security debate. *China Quarterly* 177.

Downs, E. (2006) *China*. Brookings Foreign Policy Studies, Energy Security Studies, Brookings Institute. Available at: http://www.brookings.edu/~/ media/Files/rc/reports/2006/12china/12china.pdf.

Downs, E. (2008). China's 'new' energy administration. *China Business Review* 35.

Economy, E. (1997). Chinese policy-making and global climate change: two-front diplomacy and the international community. In M. A. Schreurs & E. Economy (eds.) *The Internationalization of Environmental Protection*. Cambridge: Cambridge University Press.

EIA (2010). *International Energy Outlook 2020: Coal*. Available at: http://www.eia. doe.gov/oiaf/ieo/coal.html.

Fairley, P. (2009). *China's Potent Wind Potential.* Technology Review. Available at: http://www.technologyreview.com/energy/23460/?a=f.

Feng, J. & Yuan D. (2012). Behind China's green goals. In *China's Green Revolution: Energy, Environment and the 12th Five-Year Plan.* Available at: http://www.china dialogue.net/UserFiles/File/PDF_ebook001.pdf.

Fulton, M. (2011). *12th Five Year Plan – Chinese Leadership Towards a Low Carbon Economy.* Deutsche Bank Group: DB Climate Change Advisors. Available at: https://www.dbadvisors.com/content/_media/China_12th_Five_Year_Plan.pdf.

Garnaut, R., F. Jotzo & S. Howes (2008). China's rapidly growing emissions growth and global climate change policy. In L. Song & W. T. Woo (eds.) *China's Dilemma: Economic Growth, the Environment and Climate Change.* Canberra: ANU Press and Asia Pacific Press.

Gordon, K., J. Wong & J. McLain (2010). *Out of the Running: How Germany, Spain, and China Are Seizing the Energy Opportunity and Why the United States Risks Getting Left Behind.* Center for American Progress. Available at: http://www. americanprogress.org/issues/2010/03/pdf/out_of_running.pdf.

Hale, T. & C. Roger (2012). Chinese participation in transnational climate governance. In S. Kennedy & S. Cheng (eds.) *From Rule Takers to Rule Makers: The Growing Role of Chinese in Global Governance.* International Centre for Trade and Sustainable Development.

Harris, P. (ed.) (2011). *China's Responsibility for Climate Change: Ethics, Fairness and Environmental Policy.* Bristol: Policy Press.

Hatch, M. (2003). Chinese politics, energy policy, and the international climate change negotiations. In P. G. Harris (ed.) *Global Warming and East Asia: The Domestic and International Politics of Climate Change.* London and New York: Routledge.

Heggelund, G. (2007). China's climate change policy: domestic and international developments. *Asian Perspective* 21.

Heggelund, G., S. Andersen & I. F. Buan (2010). Chinese Climate policy: domestic priorities, foreign policy, and emerging implementation. In K. Harrison & L. M. Sundstrom (eds.) *Global Commons, Domestic Decisions: The Comparative Politics of Climate Change.* London: MIT Press.

Held, D., E. Nag & C. Roger (2011). *The Governance of Climate Change in China.* LSE Global Governance Working Paper 01/2011. Available at: http://www2.lse.ac.uk/globalGovernance/publications/workingPapers/climateChangeInChina.pdf.

Hu, A. & Liang J. (2012). China's green era begins. In *China's Green Revolution: Energy, Environment and the 12th Five-Year Plan.* Available at: http://www.china-dialogue.net/UserFiles/File/PDF_ebook001.pdf.

Kennedy, A. (2010). China's new energy security debate. *Survival* 52(3).

Koehn, P. (2008). Underneath Kyoto: emerging subnational government initiatives and incipient issue-bundling opportunities in China and the United States. *Global Environmental Politics* 8.

Kostka, G. & W. Hobbs (2012). Local energy efficiency policy implementation in China: bridging the gap between national priorities and local interests. *China Quarterly* 211.

Li, X. (2010). Power cuts call for energy efficiency. *China Daily.* Available at: http://www.chinadaily.com.cn/bizchina/2010–09/10/content_11286604.htm.

Lin, J., P. He et al. (2011). *The Race is On: China Kick-Starts Its Clean Economy.* ClimateWorks Network Knowledge Series, October. Available at: http://www.climateworks.org/download/?id=86f8db38–1272–41da-8fe94f9aa0021d13.

Liu, J. (2012). Reining in China's energy targets. In *China's Green Revolution: Energy, Environment and the 12th Five-Year Plan*. Available at: http://www.chinadialogue.net/UserFiles/File/PDF_ebook001.pdf.

Lu Z. (2010). *Hot Wind in the Desert*. Chinadialogue.com. Available at: http://www.chinadialogue.net/article/show/single/en/3616.

Lynas, M. (2009). How do I know China wrecked the Copenhagen deal? I was in the room. *Guardian* 22 December. Available at: http://www.guardian.co.uk/environment/2009/dec/22/copenhagen-climate-change-mark-lynas.

Martinot, E. (2010). Renewable energy power for China: past, present and future. *Frontiers of Energy and Power Engineering in China* 4(3).

Martinot, E. & J. Li (2007). *Powering China's Development: The Role of Renewable Energy*. Washington, DC: Worldwatch Institute.

NDRC (2011). *12th Five Year Plan*. English translation by the Delegation of the European Union to China. Available at: http://cbi.typepad.com/china_direct/2011/05/chinas-twelfth-five-new-plan-the-full-english-version.html.

Nielsen, C. P. & M. B. McElroy (1998). Introduction and overview. In M. B. McElroy, C. P. Nielsen & P. Lydon (eds.) *Energizing China: Reconciling Environmental Protection and Economic Growth*. Newton, MA: Harvard University Press.

Pan, J. (2011). Flexibility required to meet China's mandatory targets set in the 12th Five-Year Plan. *Advances in Climate Change Research* 2(3).

Qi, Y., L. Ma H. Zhang & H. Li (2008). Translating a global issue into local priority: China's local government response to climate change. *Journal of Environment and Development* 17.

Reid, W. & J. Goldemberg (1998). Developing countries are combating climate change: actions in developing countries that slow growth in carbon emissions. *Energy Policy* 26(3).

Schröder, P. (2011). *Civil Climate Change Activism in China: More than Meets the Eye*. Heinrich-Böll-Foundation. Available at: http://bocll.org/downloads/Climate_Change_Activism_in_China.pdf.

Schroeder, M. (2009a). The construction of China's climate politics: transnational NGOs and the spiral model of international relations. In P. Harris (ed.) *The Politics of Climate Change: Environmental Dynamics in International Affairs*. London: Routledge.

Schroeder, M. (2009b). Varieties of carbon governance: utilizing the clean development mechanism for Chinese priorities. *Journal of Environment and Development* 18(4).

Tsang, S. & A. Kolk (2010). The evolution of Chinese policies and governance structures on environment, energy and climate. *Environmental Policy and Governance* 20(3).

Tu, K. & S. Johnson-Reiser (2012). *Understanding China's Rising Coal Imports*. Policy Outlook, Carnegie Endowment for International Peace, 16 February.

Turner, J. & L. Ellis (2007). *China's Green Olympics: A Lasting Impact?* Available at: http://www.wilsoncenter.org/event/chinas-green-olympics-lasting-impact.

van Heuvelen, E. (2007). Unrest spurred by environmental health concern. In J. L. Turner (ed.) *China Environment Series 9*. Available at: http://www.wilsoncenter.org/sites/default/files/ces9.pdf.

Vidal, J. (2009). Ed Miliband: China tried to hijack Copenhagen climate deal. *Guardian* 20 December. Available at: http://www.guardian.co.uk/environment/2009/dec/20/ed-miliband-china-copenhagen-summit.

Wang, F., H. Yin & S. Li (2010). China's renewable energy policy: commitments and challenges. *Energy Policy* 38(4).

Worldwatch (2010). *Renewable Energy and Energy Efficiency in China: Current Status and Prospects for 2020*. Worldwatch Report 182. Available at: http://www.reeep. org/file_upload/7217_tmpphppGZ6Y0.pdf.

WRI (2011). *Climate Analysis Indicators Tool 2011*. Version 5.0. Washington, DC: World Resources Institute. Available at: http://cait.wri.org.

WRI (2012). *Atmospheric Changes Reveal China's Energy Trends*. ChinaFAQ. Available at: http://www.chinafaqs.org/files/chinainfo/ChinaFAQs_Atmospheric_Changes_ Reveal_Chinas_Energy_Trends.pdf.

Zha, D. (2006). China's energy security: domestic and international issues. *Survival* 48(1).

Zhang, H. (2006). China's position in international climate negotiations: continuities and changes. *World Economics and Politics* 2006–10.

Zhoa Y. (2011). Use of green power may outstrip Five Year Plan. *China Daily*. Available at: http://www.chinadaily.com.cn/business/201112/06/content_142 19227.htm.

3

The Evolution of Climate Policy in India: Poverty and Global Ambition in Tension

Aaron Atteridge

Introduction

CLIMATE policymakers in India face an inherently complex task. The rapid pace of economic development and expansion of the energy sector sits alongside persistent and widespread poverty. With respect to climate change, India is the fourth largest annual source of greenhouse gas (GHG) emissions in national aggregate terms, and thus subject to considerable international demands for it to join industrialized countries in taking action to cut emissions. Yet this is juxtaposed with the reality that in per capita terms the country is still a minor contributor to global emissions, on a par with some of the least developed countries (LDCs). An increasing desire to build international status, which requires positive engagement with questions of global governance – including climate change – competes with a domestic reality shaped by economic limitations and strong norms about sovereignty and equity that support the idea that action must come from others well before India. Meanwhile, it is clear that India is highly vulnerable to the impacts of climate change and thus has a very real stake in achieving a meaningful global agreement to tackle GHG emissions, which, in turn, is likely to require India to take some action domestically. The challenge for Indian policymakers, therefore, is to contribute to climate policy both domestically and internationally in a way that simultaneously protects and enhances its other domestic priorities while satisfying domestic norms as well as international pressures.

In the case of India, developments in domestic climate policy cannot be understood without also understanding trends in climate diplomacy within the United Nations Framework Convention on Climate Change (UNFCCC) negotiations, since the two have moved in parallel and both are arguably driven from the top down. For a long time India's approach to climate diplomacy consisted of a stable defensive stance that rebuffed calls for it to take action domestically to tackle GHG emissions or to link these to the developing international agreement. As a consequence, domestic action was thin on the ground. Recent years, however, have brought signs of India shifting behaviour internationally, as well as intensifying media coverage and parliamentary debate – and, in parallel, the proliferation of more advanced activity at the national and state levels on both mitigation and adaptation.

A noteworthy feature of the policy landscape at both the international and national levels is that it has, by and large, been the product of a small number of actors. Unusually for such a large and diverse country, climate change had until recently the appearance of a homogeneous, uncontested space. The bureaucracy, the Parliament and civil society, for the most part, shared norms and ideas about the onus for action, which meant that there were few debates about alternative courses of action, while most businesses appeared to be relatively disengaged. The same could be said of state governments, though many have now responded to calls by the prime minister for the preparation of state climate change action plans. As awareness about climate change grows and the domestic debate opens up, however, climate policy is becoming a more contested space.

This chapter describes the parallel development of Indian climate diplomacy and domestic climate policy. It gives an overview of the country's traditional approach to climate diplomacy, and describes the reasoning behind recent changes in order to explain the intensifying domestic policy landscape. The emerging strands of climate policy at the national and state levels are illuminated, as is the role that each has played in influencing policy at other levels. The chapter then concludes with some thoughts on the challenge that lies ahead for Indian policymakers.

India's Challenging Domestic and International Contexts

How India sees its contribution to the problem of rising atmospheric GHG concentrations, as well as its vulnerability to the impacts of climate change, partly helps explain how political leaders have responded to international calls for greater action to constrain emissions growth. The wider social, political and economic contexts in which the country's policymakers find themselves are relevant to the policymaking process as well.

India's contribution to global GHG emissions is challenging to represent simply and fairly, since portraits of the country's influence are usually heavily skewed by the sheer size of India's population. Most current estimates place it fourth in terms of nationally accounted annual emissions, after China, the US and the EU (and roughly equivalent to Russia). Some predict that annual emissions could exceed half those of the developed countries by 2040 (WRI 2009, in Vihma 2011). This part of the picture is commonly used by industrialized countries to label India a 'major emitter' and to argue that it has an important obligation to mitigate its GHGs. Yet in per person terms, India's contribution is much lower than these accounts suggest. Per capita emissions of around 1.7 tonnes of carbon dioxide equivalent (tCO_2e) are on a par with those of some of the LDCs and an order of magnitude below those of larger emitters like the US. This alternative part of the picture has guided the way the Indian public and policymakers have traditionally seen the onus for action and have reacted to being labelled a 'major emitter'.

Between 1994 and 2007, the Indian rate of annual emissions grew by 58 per cent, driven predominantly by a growing energy sector. More problematically from the atmosphere's perspective, The Energy and Resources Institute (TERI) in New Delhi projects that energy growth could expand by as much as 660 per cent between 2010 and 2030 (TERI 2008), with the majority expected to be met by fossil fuels, which already dominate primary energy production. Coal currently accounts for around 70 per cent of electricity generation, and a massive capacity expansion of new coal-fired plants is foreshadowed in the government's Approach Paper to the Twelfth Five-Year Plan (FYP), for 2012–17 (GOI 2011). Thus, India's impact on the climate is expected to grow considerably in upcoming decades. On the impacts side, India is highly vulnerable to the effects of climate change. The Fourth Assessment Report of the Intergovernmental Panel on Climate Change (IPCC 2007) describes potentially devastating impacts on, for instance, water availability and agricultural productivity, as well as threats from land inundation and important habitat loss, such as coastal wetlands.

In the wider picture, the fact that India is home to almost one fifth of the world's population means more than just high GHG figures. The sheer size and plurality of voices and interests represented in the world's largest democracy, along with unique social structures such as the caste system – which can powerfully shape political decisions, especially at the local level (Harriss-White 2003 in McCartney 2009) – mean that a very wide array of domestic norms can be brought to bear during any policy debate in the Parliament. Further, a very large number of India's nearly 1.2 billion people still face economic hardship, and poverty is widespread. India ranks 134th on the Human Development Index (UNDP 2011), with nearly 42 per cent of the population in 2005 living below the international poverty line (earning less than US$1.25 per day in purchasing power parity terms). According to the International Energy Agency (IEA 2012), nearly 300 million people lack access to electricity. As a result, domestic policy has understandably prioritized social and economic development, and in this regard the years since the early 1990s have witnessed a major transformation. Between independence in 1947 and the early 1990s, India had, in many important respects, a planned economy. This changed dramatically from 1991 onwards, when a crisis of depleted foreign currency reserves motivated the country's leaders to chart a new course emphasizing economic liberalization. The model for pursuing economic and social development has since been heavily predicated on attracting foreign direct investment (FDI). At the macro-level, economic growth rates of 7–8 per cent have been characteristic since the early 2000s, far eclipsing the growth rates of industrialized powers like the EU and US. In the context of these challenges, particularly the pressing needs to cut poverty levels, it is unsurprising that India has traditionally approached climate policy – both domestically and internationally – with some caution.

Early Engagement: India's 'Traditional' Climate Diplomacy

Since international negotiations on an agreement to tackle climate change began in the 1990s under the UNFCCC, India has generally rebuffed international pressure to accept obligations to curb its GHG emissions, along with any other suggestions for internationally imposed targets (such as for particular industrial sectors). Indeed, recent economic expansion tends to disguise the fact that India continues to identify itself as a developing country, and it follows that from the early days of international climate negotiations it has acted as an opinion leader within the Group of 77 (G77) bloc of developing countries. Indian arguments regarding a future international climate agreement have long been framed around a concept of 'equitable' burden sharing, guided by the UNFCCC's principles of 'common but differentiated responsibilities', 'historical responsibility' for emissions and 'respective capabilities'; Indian negotiators have in fact been credited with helping to craft the Convention's language around 'common but differentiated responsibilities' (Jakobsen 1999). India has also made strong demands for developing countries to receive financial and technological assistance from industrialized countries. This international position was a significant factor underpinning the absence of any major domestic Indian climate policy until around 2007, so it is important to understand the domestic norms and interests that were influential in shaping its stance.

Several norms and ideas have dominated the domestic debate and shaped how Indian actors view the issue of climate change. One is the notion that the country's social and economic development priorities would be compromised by taking on the burden of managing global environmental issues, accompanied by a sense of moral injustice at the stance taken by industrialized countries. These can be traced back at least as far as Prime Minister Indira Gandhi's speech to the United Nations Conference on the Human Environment in Stockholm in 1972. Another is the idea that India possesses limited financial and technical capacity, which features strongly in the domestic discourse and can be seen, for instance, in India's insistence on discussing intellectual property rights within the UNFCCC negotiations (to eternal frustration, since industrialized countries flatly refuse to do so). Climate diplomacy has also been influenced by a strong sense of national sovereignty and a desire to prevent outside intervention that has characterized India's political landscape since independence. The media and Parliament are particularly vociferous in response to any suggestion that the Indian government might have 'caved in' to demands imposed by Western countries or Western-dominated institutions. Sovereignty norms have also partly shaped India's response to a key question in the negotiations around how domestic action on climate change should be connected to an international agreement (i.e. what level of delegation of authority to the international level should be accepted by different parties).

Above all, the concept of equity has been central to the traditional Indian negotiating stance. As far back as 1991, a report by the Centre for Science and Environment (CSE) (Aggarwal & Narain 1991) triggered indignation at the way industrialized countries were seen to be framing responsibility for climate change and passing an unfair burden on to the world's poor (Jha 2009). The CSE report advocated a per capita approach to assessing a country's responsibility for taking action, and the government quickly adopted this idea, proposing that the Convention specify a convergence over time towards a common per capita emissions level for all countries (Vihma 2011). The framing of equity as 'equal per capita access to the atmosphere' has been so well institutionalized within Indian policy circles and the media that it essentially defines the way most domestic actors understand how, and upon whom, the burden for addressing climate change should be distributed. Although equity formulations for all countries, including India, share the materialist feature of maximizing their own future 'emissions space', to dismiss India's equity arguments as rhetoric only is to miss a critically important point: that equity convictions also derive from a strong sense of basic fairness. This is an important observation for understanding the relatively late emergence of domestic climate policy, because climate change was understood for a long time as an issue for other countries to deal with. India, it was believed, had more pressing priorities.

A further important feature of Indian climate diplomacy has been a lack of trust in international institutions generally and in the UNFCCC process specifically (Dubash 2009; Noronha 2009; Mathur & Varughese 2009). The trust deficit appears to manifest in three ways. The first is a lack of belief that industrialized countries are sincerely making efforts to negotiate a climate agreement. Here the intransigence of the US has often been cited as an example, as has the lack of political will amongst industrialized countries to agree to a second commitment period for the Kyoto Protocol, which fuelled suspicions that the major polluters were reinterpreting the Convention rather than operationalizing it (Vihma 2011). The second is a lack of trust that any agreement reached will be honoured. Often cited is the failure of most Kyoto Protocol signatories to meet their targets for the first commitment period, as an indication that there is no serious intention to fulfil previous obligations. The third is a suspicion that industrialized countries are using the climate regime to maintain their economic advantage over emerging economies such as India and China.

Beside this ideational platform, certain material factors have also worked against India agreeing internationally to shoulder any part of the global burden when it comes to GHG emission reductions. In particular, both energy security and energy access have been cited as reasons why India cannot afford to take on GHG constraints internationally. As already described, future growth in energy demand is projected to be met by a major expansion in fossil fuel capacity, while efforts to help poor rural communities shift from traditional biomass to more modern forms of energy will create further demand. Interestingly, energy security and energy access motivate a different response domestically, encouraging the government to adopt policies that improve energy efficiency and promote renewable energy. The 2008 National Action Plan on Climate Change, for instance, includes a number of key national missions focused on solar energy promotion and energy efficiency improvements.

Another major domestic challenge is the significant role played by small and medium-sized enterprises (SMEs) in the Indian economy. SMEs provide the largest chunk of industrial employment and hence represent a large 'voter' group in political terms. Indian SMEs are, for the most part, financially and technologically constrained, and this makes them highly sensitive to changes in energy prices. The fact that SME activity is also very heterogeneous acts as a potential constraint on the ability of the government to regulate environmental performance meaningfully, even if commitments to emission reductions were actually made (Bushan 2009; Stuligross 1999). Similarly, a majority of Indian livelihoods are supported by small-scale agriculture, which makes it politically difficult to address the large contribution to total GHG emissions coming from the agricultural sector (estimated to be around 17 per cent in official data for 2007 [Ministry of Environment and Forests 2010]), since those affected are numerous and poor.

One of the most interesting aspects of Indian climate diplomacy during this period is how consistent it remained, despite the 1990s and early 2000s being characterized by major economic transformation and some political change. Several factors help explain this continuity – and also the way domestic policy has developed. One is that India's stance in negotiations for most of the period has been shaped by bureaucrats, mainly from the environment ministry, and climate diplomacy has been conducted largely in isolation from other areas of foreign policy – a condition facilitated by the absence of any significant media coverage of climate issues prior to around 2007, and consequently a dearth of domestic debate (Jha 2009). This meant that few domestic actors became engaged with climate change as an issue. Another is that climate policy has generally been a top-down process, with very little pioneering by state governments and very little influence by non-governmental actors. Positioning in international negotiations does not appear to have been driven or even significantly influenced by industry, which on the whole has demonstrated little engagement with the process. It is quite probable that India's energy sector – which includes Coal India, the world's largest coal miner – sees future projections of domestic energy growth as so staggering that it perceives no commercial threats coming from developments in the international arena. Industry's contribution to the Indian positioning has thus far been rather narrowly confined to issues around the Clean Development Mechanism (CDM). These same features are visible in the formation of domestic climate policy.

The Seeds of Domestic Climate Policy

Despite its international rhetoric and positioning, India has a track record of domestic environmental legislation and of policies being influenced by international norms and experiences (Shrivastava 2007; Atteridge et al. 2012). It is therefore unsurprising that legislation and policies introduced by the middle of the 2000s had relevance for climate change outcomes – in particular, for the mitigation of GHG emissions – even if the policies themselves were more directly a response to other domestic priorities, such as energy security.

In the stationary energy sector, the 2001 Energy Conservation Act allowed the government to prescribe and ensure compliance with energy efficiency standards for residential, commercial and industrial consumers and producers. It also required major commercial energy users to conduct audits and cost–benefit analyses of actions to reduce consumption, overseen by the Bureau of Energy Efficiency established in 2002. The Ministry of New and Renewable Energy's Integrated Rural Energy Programme (IREP), introduced in 2003, aimed to improve domestic energy access in selected rural areas, with a focus on renewable energy. The 2005 Integrated Energy Policy encouraged the adoption of higher efficiency coal-fired plant during major new capacity expansions around the country, an effort to stimulate a shift from sub-critical to super-critical technology.

Domestic tax incentives, and to a lesser extent revenue from the CDM, had by 2007 stimulated a considerable number of renewable energy projects. The target of 3,075 megawatts (MW) of new grid-interactive renewables capacity included in the Tenth FYP, for 2002–7, was surpassed by more than 100 per cent. As a result, by 2007, India was already the world's fifth largest installer of wind capacity (MNRE 2008), which made up around 70 per cent of the more than 11,000 MW of grid-interactive renewables capacity. The Eleventh FYP, for 2007–12, adopted an ambitious target of installing a further 15,000 MW of renewable power, anticipating the bulk to be delivered by wind power. This expansion was to be supported by a combination of direct budgetary support (roughly Rs 105 billion, or €1.5 billion, was allocated in the FYP) and the introduction of feed-in tariffs.

In the transport sector, policies targeting cleaner fuels and vehicles and encouraging mode shifting were introduced. The government's 2001 Integrated Transport Policy promoted ethanol-blended petrol and biodiesel, and was followed in 2004 by a mandatory 5 per cent blending of petrol with ethanol. In 2003, the Planning Commission introduced a National Mission on Biodiesel aiming to establish large-scale jatropha plantations across twenty-six states in order eventually to support a target of 20 per cent blending by 2011–12 (though this proved unsuccessful). Also in 2003 the Auto Fuel Policy introduced an emissions standards 'roadmap' for new vehicles, and encouraged expansion of natural gas use in major cities, motivated particularly by regional air pollution concerns. The National Urban Transport Policy emphasized greater development and usage of public transport infrastructure, and a Working Group on Urban Transport including Mass Rapid Transport Systems under the Eleventh FYP, for 2007–12, was to evaluate future urban transport options. Finally, in the forestry sector, the 1999 National Forestry Action Programme introduced a twenty-year programme to curb deforestation and expand tree cover to encapsulate 33 per cent of India's total area.

Simply introducing ambitious policies does not guarantee all targets will be met, of course. Nonetheless, this array of policies and programmes indicates that despite the country's defensiveness in international negotiations, it had already by 2007 introduced domestic measures that would, if successfully implemented, constrain growth in GHG emissions. As will be later highlighted, this activity was subsequently ramped up in parallel with – and arguably as a result of – a significant shift in India's approach to international climate diplomacy. To understand why domestic climate policy intensified, it is first necessary to see the normative shift that took place amongst India's leadership, wherein climate diplomacy became part of a broader game.

A New Normative Perspective and a Shift in International Strategy

In 2007, Prime Minister Manmohan Singh announced at the World Economic Forum[1] in Heiligendamm, Germany, that India's per capita emissions would never exceed those of industrialized countries. This bold statement was met with sharp criticism from his domestic audience, who – despite the prime minister's efforts to downplay the event – were dismayed by the fact that for the first time a notional capping of India's emissions had been proposed internationally. Signs of change continued with the appointment in 2008 of a highly respected diplomat, Shyam Saran, as India's chief climate negotiator, and the following year that of Jairam Ramesh as the minister responsible for climate change. In September 2009 the prime minister was among the world leaders to sign the statement from the Major Economies Forum at L'Aquila endorsing a 2 °C target for limiting global warming.

Jairam Ramesh's foreign visits in the lead-up to the Fifteenth Conference of the Parties (COP15) in Copenhagen, meanwhile, were characterized by a softening of rhetoric and indications that India might be prepared to compromise on some aspects of its position in order to secure a meaningful international agreement. Just days before the Copenhagen meeting, India announced a voluntary emissions intensity target, pledging to cut the emissions intensity of its economy (carbon emissions per unit of gross domestic product [GDP]) by 20–5 per cent below 2005 levels by 2020. Over the following year, attempts to reframe India's traditional understanding of equity in per capita terms towards a new (albeit vague) 'per capita plus' approach resulted in India successfully introducing the concept of 'equal access to sustainable development' in the text of the Cancun Agreements at COP16 in 2010. Also at Cancun, Ramesh played an important role in helping to advance debate around the transparency of national actions, which eventually resulted in the concept of a differentiated form of transparency, called International Consultation and Analysis, for developing country mitigation actions.

To understand these changes and to appreciate their significance for domestic policy developments, it is important to see that the locus of influence over Indian climate diplomacy shifted during this period from the bureaucracy to the political sphere. With this came a change in the norms and material interests shaping Indian climate policy. A number of plausible external catalysts might be offered as reasons for this. The *Stern Review* (Stern 2006) brought the economic implications of climate change into sharp focus and would certainly have made an impact on India's economist prime minister. Then, in 2007, the IPCC's Fourth Assessment Report sent strong signals about the impacts that climate change would have globally and on India specifically. Also around this time, leading industrialized countries began to exert pressure on what they interchangeably called 'major emerging economies' or 'major emitters' to accept part of the burden for tackling GHG emissions. This pressure was exerted not only within the UNFCCC but also by extending climate discussions into other forums, particularly the Major Economies Forum and the Group of 8 plus 7 (G8 plus 7) meetings. Tellingly, it was outside the UNFCCC that Manmohan Singh's 2007 pledge about India's per capita emissions was offered.

As a result of greater political engagement inside India, the practice of climate diplomacy started being woven into the pursuit of broader foreign policy objectives. This meant, in short, that climate policy became a tool for pursuing objectives such as greater international status, enhancement of regional security and protection of national economic interests. Together, this combination of normative and realist motives encouraged greater alignment with the US and China, as strategically important international partners. Both the US and China would have a major influence over India's attempt to gain a long-sought-after permanent seat on the UN Security Council, while

US support was crucial for the realization of India's nuclear ambitions (culminating in the US–India Civil Nuclear Agreement in 2008). Both have relationships with India's neighbours, in particular Pakistan and Afghanistan, that have been perceived with some concern within India, while China and India are still engaged in active border conflict. Economically, both are key trading partners as well. While relations between the US and India have been cool in past decades, the nuclear deal seems to have helped engender a feeling of greater partnership, which the Indian prime minister has been keen to foster. Jairam Ramesh, for his part, has long promoted a reframing of India's relationship with China, even coining the term 'Chindia' in his book on the subject in 2005 (Ramesh 2005).

In climate diplomacy, the ambition of strategic partnership building manifests as more constructive Indian engagement on contentious issues for these two powers. Ramesh's offers on equity and transparency at Cancun, noted above, were received as 'positive' and 'constructive' by US negotiators, while in 2009 the signature of a 'Sino-Indian Memorandum of Understanding on Climate Change' preceded the announcement of more formal cooperation between India and China within the UNFCCC negotiations under the umbrella of the BASIC group (along with Brazil and South Africa). The latter offers further evidence of India's shifting approach to climate diplomacy, not least in that India is understood to have been a key player in actually bringing the group together (Hallding et al. 2011).

Within India, concerns were expressed about the country identifying itself outside the G77 and allying closely with a group that included the world's largest GHG emitter (China), one of the world's highest per capita emitters (South Africa) and countries that are for the most part further advanced on most social development indicators. Yet BASIC makes sense when seen through the prism of India's wider ambitions and motives, and follows a wider pattern of working with other major emerging economies, including through the India, Brazil, South Africa (IBSA) Dialogue Forum and the Brazil, Russia, India, China, South Africa (BRICS) forum. These are venues in which India can present itself at the high table of international politics, alongside other heavyweights. BASIC also has an interesting geopolitical dimension that links to concerns about energy security: India and China desperately need energy to maintain growth, while Brazil and South Africa are major sources.

In addition to building strategic international relationships, other factors have also played a role in the shifting Indian approach to climate diplomacy. One is a fear of isolation, following a fragmentation of G77 interests in 2009. When China announced an emissions intensity target just before Copenhagen, India broke from its stance of not pledging action internationally and followed immediately with its own intensity target. The promise of greater US action under Obama was higher in the lead-up to Copenhagen, and had the US shifted suddenly India could have been further isolated. Pressure from its traditional allies within the G77 group of developing countries also made its mark. Accusations of India 'hiding behind the poor' (Greenpeace 2007) have resonated both in relation to its own domestic poor, who share the country with a growing consuming class, and in relation to other poor countries within the G77, which share India's developing country status but not its economic capacity and dynamism. Politically, concerns emerged that vulnerable neighbours such as Bangladesh and small island states might begin to see India's recalcitrance as being as problematic as that of the US and other major emitters. Finally, on a more personal level, Minister Ramesh has been said to be acutely aware of the vulnerability of India to climate impacts. It has been suggested this personal sense of the importance for India of a meaningful international climate deal, coupled with recognition that India must do more to ensure such an agreement, partly explains Ramesh's approach.

Intensifying National Climate Policy

These developments at the international level, and the reasons behind them, are important to understand because they have kick-started more intense activity in the realm of domestic climate policy. In 2008, a National Action Plan on Climate Change (NAPCC) was released, in essence a strategy for tackling climate change while pursuing development. The NAPCC includes a target of reducing the emissions intensity of India's economy (per unit of GDP) by 20 per cent between 2007–8 and 2016–17, a target echoed in the Eleventh FYP, for 2007–12 – a slightly different formulation to the pledge offered internationally a year later, pre-Copenhagen. The NAPCC builds around eight National Missions that address both mitigation and adaptation objectives. The National Missions on Solar Energy and Enhanced Energy Efficiency, and to some extent those on Sustainable Habitat and Green India, focus strongly on mitigation (the latter two are a mix between mitigation and adaptation). Those on Water, Sustainable Agriculture, Sustaining the Himalayan Ecosystem and Strategic Knowledge on Climate Change are more closely aligned with adaptation.

While labelled with a stronger climate tag, recent policies linked to mitigation continue to be primarily motivated by material concerns over depleting resources. The rapid energy demand growth in both the stationary energy and transport sectors is occurring at a time when international competition for fossil based energy resources is intensifying, and, already a net energy importer, India faces the continued prospect of domestic energy resources being unable to keep pace with demand. With energy security firmly in mind, therefore, the National Solar Mission ambitiously targets the installation of 20,000 MW of solar generation capacity by 2020, of 100,000 MW by 2030 and of 200,000 MW by 2050.

In parallel, the National Mission on Enhanced Energy Efficiency follows in the footsteps of the earlier Energy Conservation Act of 2001. It identifies schemes to promote efficiency improvements among energy intensive industries, to support the emergence of energy service companies (ESCOs), which can help identify and implement energy savings measures across different sectors, and the introduction of fiscal signals (a peak electricity price) for industrial and commercial users to stimulate demand management initiatives further. The National Mission on Sustainable Habitat, likewise, continues an earlier policy focus on strengthening vehicle fuel economy standards, indicating that pricing measures will be used to encourage the purchase of efficient vehicles and greater use of public transportation.

Beyond the NAPCC, various other policies and processes are also increasingly relevant for mitigation objectives. The Bureau of Energy Efficiency has continued to lead various initiatives to, for example, develop energy efficiency manuals for some key energy intensive industrial sectors, as well as research and development (R&D) programmes for the commercial and household sectors. The Bachat Lamp Yojana was announced in 2009 with ambitions to use revenue from the CDM to replace 400 million incandescent household lights with energy saving compact fluorescent lamps (CFLs).

The National Policy on Biofuels, launched in 2009, proposed an 'indicative' target of 20 per cent blending of biofuels (biodiesel and bioethanol) by 2017. This policy has high level support, with a national Biofuel Coordination Committee headed by the prime minister and a Biofuel Steering Committee headed by the cabinet secretary. The National Biomass Cookstove Initiative (NBCI), also launched in 2009, aims to expand massively the uptake of more efficient household cookstoves among traditional biomass users and, if successful, could help reduce climate change-related emissions, particularly short-lived climate forcers such as black carbon (it could, on the other hand, increase GHG emissions if it ends up encouraging fuel switching from sustainable biomass to fossil fuels).

On the adaptation side, policies are, by and large, also driven by concerns about poverty, livelihood protection, vulnerability to climate risks and human security. The National Mission on Sustainable Habitat aims to protect key infrastructure from climate threats and improve disaster management. The National Water Mission focuses on resource conservation and waste minimization. The Green India Mission includes a focus on more effective utilization of land, as a key resource. The National Mission on Sustainable Agriculture focuses on food security, livelihoods and economic stability in rural India, where a large portion of the Indian population depends directly on the climate-vulnerable agriculture sector. The agriculture and water sectors are also prioritized in the National Mission for Sustaining the Himalayan Ecosystem, in response to potential threats to the flow of important perennial rivers. Finally, the National Mission on Strategic

Knowledge on Climate Change focuses on building India's scientific and technological capabilities to understand and predict the effects of climate change (Atteridge et al. 2012).

As already alluded to, domestic policy has been influenced heavily by India's approach to the international negotiations, and policy in both settings has been driven by a small number of actors. This terrain was first dominated by a narrow part of the national government bureaucracy, particularly the environment ministry, which crafted the traditional international negotiation stance. During this time, no major climate policies were initiated domestically – consistent with the idea that it was other countries, not India, that bore responsibility for action. As this changed, and the prime minister took a greater interest in using climate diplomacy to serve other ends, policymaking moved to a narrow section of the political sphere. Evidence that the political locus was narrow rather than a cross-government project can be seen in heavy parliamentary criticism, by representatives of both the government and opposition, for changes that the prime minister and Jairam Ramesh made to the Indian stance. Attempts to improve national coordination of climate policy are evident in the formation of the prime minister's Council on Climate Change, which is constituted by representatives from key ministries and external experts and which authored the NAPCC. Another increasingly critical institution is the Planning Commission, a powerful body with close links to the prime minister and, as the events described below illustrate, the potential to influence domestic climate policy. Pre-2007 engagement by the national Parliament appears to have been limited, with opposition parties considering climate change a job for the government and not a subject for important political debate. Although this has changed as greater media coverage has prompted more active debate, the Parliament appears overall to have had limited say over climate policy.

The engagement of Indian industry with climate policy, as previously noted, has been relatively low. For international negotiations it has contributed mainly technical advice to discussions about the CDM. The CDM was the original entry point to climate issues for most of the energy sector, and India has to date been a major host of CDM projects – by late 2012 it had received around a quarter of all CDM projects worldwide, second only to China.[2] There has been more engagement domestically, motivated by opportunities arising from policies targeting renewable energy and energy efficiency. The influence of major corporate entities such as Tata Power is difficult to observe directly, though it can be reasonably expected that they have well-established channels to the highest levels of government through which to express their particular needs and concerns. Other key industry actors that might be expected to feel threatened by climate policy, such as Coal India (mining) and National Thermal Power Corporation (electricity generation), are government owned companies, which could partly explain why they have not been highly visible in the policy debate or proactive in devising climate strategies (see, for example, Leggett 2010).

From the early 1990s onwards, most civil society organizations shared a common normative platform (centred on equity, as described above) and hence spoke with the same voice on climate change in support of the government's defensive international stance and without a major emphasis on developing domestic climate policy. However, different non-governmental organization (NGO) perspectives have emerged in recent years, particularly as domestic debate heated up following the IPCC's Fourth Assessment Report in 2007. Crudely, these might be divided into two categories. Local NGOs, by and large, continue to argue that the government should focus more on other pressing social and environmental issues rather than climate change. On the other hand, internationally affiliated NGOs, such as World Wide Fund for Nature (WWF) India and Greenpeace India, have pressed the government to become more ambitious in devising strategies to tackle GHG emissions. The influence of both groups is visible in different elements of policy. The former have been norm champions, exemplified most notably in the role played by CSE in introducing equity concerns to the domestic debate, which subsequently came to shape both India's international stance and its domestic response (or, for a long time, the lack thereof). The influence of the latter category has instead been more in the realm of policy substance. For instance, WWF India and Greenpeace India claim to have influenced the government in setting the Indian emissions reduction target offered before Copenhagen (suggesting it was based on modelling results they presented to the minister).

Sub-National Action on Climate Change: The States

In contrast to some countries where the seeds and substance of domestic climate policy emanated first from the sub-national level, from states or provinces rather than the national arena, Indian states have so far not been climate policy pioneers. Activity by the states has, primarily, been catalysed by policies and directions coming from the national government. The first State Action Plans on Climate Change (SAPCCs) emerged after the NAPCC was released in 2008, and especially after the prime minister's urging in 2009 for state policies to be developed to help implement the national policy. In the framework developed by the national government to guide preparation of state plans, emphasis has been placed on devising plans that fit with regional and local contexts and needs. As a result, the priorities visible in SAPCCs so far are clearly influenced by each state's vision for future economic development as well as its access to resources; in other words, by each state's sense of vulnerabilities and opportunities.

Gujarat, one of India's more industrialized states, set up India's first state climate change department and has announced policies to attract renewable energy investments. In doing so, it is likely to have been motivated by its potential wind and solar resources as well as the scent of economic opportunity associated with making itself a hub for the renewables industry (Atteridge et al. 2012). Gujarat also accounts for around 42 per cent of all certified emissions reductions (CERs) generated in India (Shah 2011), having established a CDM cell to coordinate the procurement of carbon credits. Kerala, on the other hand, has announced a green fund specifically for financing climate-related activities. Some states have also expanded the focus of their SAPCC beyond the scope of the NAPCC's National Missions; for instance, Rajasthan, whose plan prioritizes issues related to human health and desertification. In some cases, however, certain measures included in these SAPCCs appear to be at the expense of climate objectives, such as in Orissa, which articulated an aggressive expansion of coal-fired electricity generation capacity over the next decade (Atteridge et al. 2012).

It could be argued that the states which have been most ambitious in preparing climate plans, such as Orissa and Gujarat, are hoping to attract more resources from the national budget to fund what are essentially strategies for state development. Whatever the range of motivations, this need not diminish the fact that the NAPCC, coupled with increased domestic debate around climate change in the media and Parliament, has sparked a growing response at the state level. A major challenge going forward will be how well aligned the state and national policy landscape remains, given the diversity across states with respect to needs, interests and capacities.

Conclusion

Climate policy development in India has to a great extent been a 'top-down' process. Although earlier domestic initiatives – motivated by concerns about energy security – targeted energy efficiency and renewables, the first policies introduced specifically with a focus on climate change followed a decision by India's political leaders to change the country's engagement with the international process. The NAPCC came after the prime minister's announcement in 2007 that India's per capita emissions would never exceed those of industrialized countries, while the various state action plans developed to date have, in turn, been a direct response to the NAPCC.

What began this chain was arguably a shift in the lens through which the key political actors view climate diplomacy. Here, the focus has moved from one concerned only about domestic constraints to one that places an equal and sometimes greater emphasis on international opportunities, in particular by using climate diplomacy as a tool for achieving goals outside the climate realm. At the international level, India's traditional positioning of itself as a developing country is now in tension with the globalist ambitions of the country's leaders. The effect of a sense of globalism can be to compel policymakers to make normative choices 'empowering' India towards proactive commitment as opposed to 'passivity or paralysis'. In other words, as an ideology, it can override the effect of short-term political fluctuations which might otherwise interrupt a policy trajectory (Alamgir 2009).

To the extent that globalist ambitions and foreign policy priorities have motivated a shift in India's diplomatic response, these have also spurred domestic action to respond to climate change. However, there are vastly different priorities among actors in the domestic landscape, and the sheer scale and diversity of the country pose a major challenge when it comes to actual implementation. Action (or inaction) by the states will have a significant influence over the outcomes that are achieved, and to date there have been widely diverging priorities and levels of engagement across different states. A further challenge lies in the fact that both the industrial and agricultural sectors share structural features that make environmental regulation politically and/or technically difficult.

Internationally, India has shown signs of creativity and innovation over the last few years in appearing to reshape its positions while still holding on to key principles. While India feels unfairly labelled with terms such as 'major emitter', given its low per capita GHG emissions and widespread poverty, pressure by the US, EU and others signals international awareness of the country's growing economic might and reinforces that sense among political leaders, who are committed to enhancing the country's international status. India's leaders are therefore attempting to navigate between a deep sense that India has no moral obligation to reduce its GHG emissions – especially without strong action and financial support by industrialized countries – and sensing an opportunity to advance its place at the high table of global politics.

This continues to exert influence over domestic policy, too. An approach document to the Twelfth FYP (GOI 2011) prepared by the influential Planning Commission has generated some controversy by its inclusion of the idea that India should finance some of its own mitigation actions – a position that has been criticized by the Environment Ministry, in particular, for undermining India's international stance (Sethi 2012). The Planning Commission document outlines an emphasis on energy efficiency, accelerated renewables installation, and the adjustment of emissions intensive industrial sectors such as cement and steel manufacturing, possibly using an emissions cap-and-trade approach.

Although the new approach championed by Jairam Ramesh made some impression on the international stage, it was not well institutionalized domestically, as can be seen in the level of criticism directed at the minister throughout his tenure. To a large extent, the shift in India's stance was made possible by the charisma and entrepreneurship of the minister himself. Thus, although he had the backing of the prime minister's office, it was perhaps inevitable that the changes discussed in this chapter would be questioned when Ramesh left the portfolio, as he did in 2011. He was replaced by Jayanthi Natarajan as minister and head of India's negotiating team. Since then, India has perhaps taken a small step back in terms of engagement, maintaining a lower profile throughout the COP17 meeting in Durban in 2011 and for much of 2012, and has again received criticism from some quarters for being 'obstructionist'. This does not necessarily mean a shift back to old ways. There is an oscillation in behaviour at present which suggests the domestic push and pull of competing norms and interests is still settling the country's future approach to climate diplomacy.

The strong interplay between international and domestic arenas described here has so far been within a top-down framework, following a pattern of domestic policy bending to meet the norms and needs of India within the international arena. However, this may soon change, as a denser national and state policy landscape, coupled with greater domestic debate, will naturally encourage a wider array of actors to engage. This diversity is already evident, for instance, in the substance of different state action plans, and some states are now calling for greater state involvement in national and international climate policy. Seen from this angle, the challenge for India's climate policymakers may soon be even more daunting than it already is.

Notes

1 World Economic Forum, Gleneagles Dialogue on Climate Change – Third Meeting of the Energy and Environment Ministers, Heiligendamm, Berlin, September 2007.
2 See http://www.cdmpipeline.org.

References

Agarwal, A. & S. Narain (1991). *Global Warming in an Unequal World: A Case of Environmental Colonialism*. New Delhi: Centre for Science and Environment.
Alamgir, J. (2009). *India's Open-Economy Policy: Globalism, Rivalry, Continuity*. London: Routledge.
Atteridge, A., M. Shrivastava, N. Pahuja & H. Upadhyay (2012). Climate policy in India: what shapes international, national and state policy? *Ambio* 41.
Bushan, C. (2009). Indian industry and climate change: perceptions, policies and possibilities. In D. Michel & A. Pandya (eds.) *Indian Climate Policy: Choices and Challenges*. Washington, DC: Henry L. Stimson Centre.
Dubash, N. K. (2009). *Toward a Progressive Indian and Global Climate Politics*. Centre for Policy Research Climate Initiative, Working Paper 2009/1. New Delhi.
GOI (2011). *Faster, Sustainable and More Inclusive Growth: An Approach to the Twelfth Five Year Plan*. Planning Commission, India. Available at: http://planning commission.nic.in/plans/planrel/index.php?state=planbody.htm.
Greenpeace (2007). *Hiding Behind the Poor: A Report by Greenpeace on Climate Justice*. Available at: http://www.greenpeace.org/raw/content/india/press/reports/hiding-behind-the-poor.pdf.

Hallding, K., M. Olsson, A. Atteridge, A. Vihma, M. Carson & M. Roman (2011). *Together Alone: BASIC Countries and the Climate Change Conundrum*. Nordic Council of Ministers Publication Series.

Harriss-White, B. (2003). *India Working: Essays on Economy and Society*. Cambridge: Cambridge University Press.

IEA (2012). *World Energy Outlook 2012*. Paris: International Energy Agency.

IPCC (2007). *Climate Change 2007: Impacts, Adaptation and Vulnerability*. Contribution of Working Group II to the Fourth Assessment Report of the Intergovernmental Panel on Climate Change, eds. M. L. Parry, O. F. Canziani, J. P. Palutikof, P. J. van der Linden & C. E. Hanson. Cambridge: Cambridge University Press.

Jakobsen, S. (1999). *International Relations Theory and the Environment: A Study of Brazilian and Indian Policy-Making on Climate Change*. Copenhagen: Institute of Political Science, University of Copenhagen.

Jha, P. S. (2009). Indian public perceptions of the international climate change negotiations. In D. Michel & A. Pandya (eds.) *Indian Climate Policy: Choices and Challenges*. Washington, DC: Henry L. Stimson Centre.

Leggett, J. (2010). Coal India IPO shows the mountain we have to climb. *Guardian* 9 November. Available at: http://www.guardian.co.uk/sustainable-business/blog/coal-india-ipo-climate-change.

Mathur, U. & G. C. Varughese (2009). From 'obstructionist' to leading player: transforming India's international image. In D. Michel & A. Pandya (eds.) *Indian Climate Policy: Choices and Challenges*. Washington, DC: Henry L. Stimson Centre.

McCartney, M. (2009). *India: The Political Economy of Growth, Stagnation and the State, 1951–2007*. London: Routledge.

Ministry of Environment and Forests (2010). *India: Greenhouse Gas Emissions 2007*. Available at: moef.nic.in/downloads/public-information/Report_INCCA.pdf.

MNRE (2008). *Annual Report*. Available at: http://mnre.gov.in/file-manager/annual-report/2008–2009/EN/index.htm.

Noronha, L. (2009). Climate change and India's energy policy: challenges and choices. In D. Michel & A. Pandya (eds.) *Indian Climate Policy: Choices and Challenges*. Washington, DC: Henry L. Stimson Centre.

Ramesh, J. (2005). *Making Sense of Chindia: Reflections on China and India*. New Delhi: India Research Press.

Sethi, N. (2012). Plan panel seeks to rewrite India's climate change stance. *Times of India*, 21 August. Available at: http://articles.timesofindia.indiatimes.com/2012–08–21/developmental-issues/33301787_1_climate-change-greenhouse-gas-emissions-national-missions.

Shah, S. (2011). *Gujarat Clean Development Mechanism (CDM) cell: A State Level CDM Nodal Agency*. Available at: http://www.gujaratcmfellowship.org/document/Fellows/Carbon-Development-Mechanism-%28CDM%29–Cell-Shwetal-Shah-26Nov10.pdf.

Shrivastava, M. K. (2007). *Convergence in Climate Change Institutions and Consequences for Developing Countries: A Case Study of Supercritical Technology Adoption by NTPC*. MPhil dissertation, Centre for Studies in Science Policy, School of Social Sciences, Jawaharlal Nehru University, New Delhi, India.

Stern, N. (2006). *Stern Review on the Economics of Climate Change*. London: HM Treasury.

Stuligross, D. (1999). The political economy of environmental regulation in India. *Pacific Affairs* 72(3).

TERI (2008). *Mitigation Options for India: The Role of the International Community*. New Delhi: The Energy and Resources Institute.

UNDP (2011). *Human Development Index*. Available at: http://hdr.undp.org/en/statistics/hdi.

Vihma, A. (2011). India and the global climate governance: between principles and pragmatism. *Journal of Environment & Development* 20(1).

WRI (2009). *The Climate Analysis Indicators Tool (CAIT) Developed by the World Resources Institute*. Available at: http://cait.wri.org.

4

The Dynamics of Climate Change Governance in Indonesia

Budy P. Resosudarmo, Fitrian Ardiansyah and Lucentezza Napitupulu

Introduction

IN recent years, as described in other chapters in this book, the intention to mitigate greenhouse gas (GHG) emissions has been growing across a diverse range of non-Annex I countries. Often, these countries signal their intentions by announcing their commitments to Nationally Appropriate Mitigation Actions (NAMAs) in a list of policies and programmes that is submitted to the United Nations Framework Convention on Climate Change (UNFCCC) Secretariat. Indonesia is no exception in this regard. At the 2009 Group of 20 (G20) meeting in Pittsburgh, the president of Indonesia announced for the first time the country's national commitment to mitigating CO_2 emissions, particularly through the reduction of deforestation rates and forest degradation. It stated that Indonesia 'will reduce its annual emissions by 26 per cent by 2020 from BAU (Business As Usual)', and that, with international support, the country 'could reduce emissions by as much as 41 per cent' (Yudhoyono 2009). Indonesia was among the first non-Annex I countries to make such a commitment (Jotzo 2012), and it was subsequently submitted to the UNFCCC Secretariat as the country's NAMA on 30 January 2010. It was, nevertheless, a surprising move, and, domestically, was not well understood. Until that point, there had been important national discussions of Indonesia's contribution to global CO_2 emissions, but discussions of the kinds of programmes that should be adopted, if any, had been limited.

The international community embraced this commitment by promising funding and technical assistance to facilitate and encourage Indonesia's efforts. In May 2010, the government of Norway pledged to support Indonesia in its preparations for Reducing Emissions from Deforestation and Forest Degradation Plus (REDD+) by promising US\$1 billion conditional on Indonesia fulfilling certain tasks set out in a letter of intent (LOI) between the two countries. Within Indonesia, the commitment announced by the president was then translated into a national strategy for reducing CO_2 emissions as well as related sectoral commitments by various line ministries. In 2011, Presidential Decree No. 61/2011 on the National Action Plan for Greenhouse Gases Reduction (*Rencana Aksi Nasional Penurunan Emisi Gas Rumah Kaca*, or RAN-GRK) was enacted and was to lead to the production of a more detailed Indonesian NAMA commitment (Thamrin 2011).

Despite these promising commitments from both Indonesia and the international community, the development of climate change policies and the implementation of mitigation programmes in Indonesia has been challenging. Indeed, progress has been slow. In spite of the fact that there are over thirty REDD+ demonstrations throughout Indonesia at various stages of implementation, the implementation of a national REDD+ programme has been hampered by problems of unclear land tenure, other land-based short-term economic development projects, especially those related to mineral extraction and oil palm expansion, and weak forest governance in general (Resosudarmo et al. 2012). With respect to emissions arising from the energy sector, not only has Indonesia not started discussing the possibility of a carbon tax or a carbon market, although several research institutions have suggested the government initiate this, but it has so far proven unable or unwilling to eliminate the country's system of energy subsidies which has fostered inefficient use of fossil fuels (Nurdianto & Resosudarmo 2011). Support for reducing CO_2 emissions from fossil fuel combustion has been relatively weak both within Indonesian society and within the government.

This chapter is an attempt to explain why the Indonesian president made a major climate change commitment, although the issue of mitigation had not been widely discussed domestically. The chapter also offers an explanation as to why the implementation of this commitment has been relatively slow so far. Understanding the forces behind Indonesia's climate change commitment and the complexity of its implementation constitutes an important first step on the path towards resolving the challenges that have hindered progress. To achieve the first goal, this chapter will first review some of the major forces that led to and shaped Indonesia's climate change commitments, such as new information about Indonesia's status as a major emitter, and events, such as the Thirteenth Conference of the Parties (COP13) of the UNFCCC in Bali in 2007 and the G20 meeting in Pittsburgh in 2009. To achieve the second goal, this chapter will discuss the institutions that have been involved in the development of climate change policy in Indonesia: their roles, incentives, the strategies they have used to increase their authority, and the conflicts of interests that exist between them. The conclusion will then summarize the chapter's central arguments and draw out the main lessons for the future.

Explaining Indonesia's Climate Change Commitments

This section will describe in chronological order how climate change eventually emerged as one of the country's top national priorities, in order to explain Indonesia's commitment on this issue. In the 1980s and before, climate change was an issue that was discussed only within the Ministry of Environment (MoE) in a very limited way, and among climate scientists, of whom there were relatively few at the time in the country. Research on climate change issues in Indonesia started to become available to the public in the mid-1990s. However, significant work revealing Indonesia's contribution to global CO_2 stocks and reviews of existing climate change policies only emerged in the mid-2000s, especially around the time that Indonesia agreed to host COP13. Part of the reason for this more intensified and available research on climate change in the 2000s was that various environmental research centres (*Pusat Studi Lingkungan* or PSL) were established in major universities (Djajadiningrat 2010), influenced by international research communities that were also working on the issue of climate change.

One of the most widely cited and influential studies was published by PEACE (2007), which reviewed and summarized the existing literature on economic trends and future GHG emissions in Indonesia. This report showed, first, that Indonesia was among the top five global emitters and that almost 80 per cent of its CO_2 emissions came from deforestation and forest degradation. Figure 4.1 is, more or less, the same as that used by PEACE (2007). It shows that if emissions from land use, land use change and forestry are taken into account, Indonesia is one of the top emitters in the world. Second, the report also argued that the impact of climate change on Indonesia's ecology and society would be significant; particularly via sea level rise, ocean warming and coral bleaching. Finally, it argued that Indonesia had not done much to control its CO_2 emissions and ameliorate the impact of climate change thus far.

Several works followed the PEACE study that provided different estimates of Indonesia's CO_2 emissions, particularly from forestry-related sectors, but which reached broadly similar conclusions, namely that Indonesia was one of the largest CO_2 emitters and the main issue was deforestation, land use change and forest degradation (Ministry of Forestry 2008; Resosudarmo et al. 2009).[1] By focusing attention on these facts, these works managed to spur campaigns by international and national non-governmental organizations (NGOs), such as those by the World Wide Fund for Nature (WWF), Pelangi and Walhi (*Wahana Lingkungan Hidup Indonesia*), as well as donor organizations, for Indonesia to reduce its emissions. These campaigns were highlighted in the media and effectively put a great deal of pressure on the government to respond. They were particularly effective because, as the host of COP13, which was held in Bali in December 2007, Indonesia was under the world's spotlight. Indonesia's mitigation

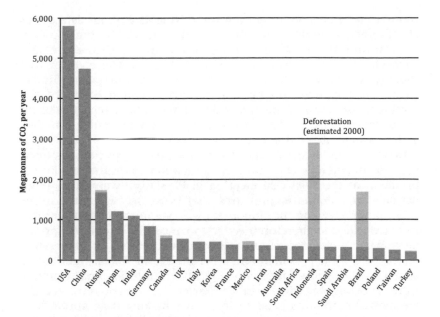

Figure 4.1   Top world CO_2 emitters, 2004

Source: Resosudarmo et al. (2009).

policies were regarded as relatively weak and its rate of deforestation was thought to be one of the highest in the world (Resosudarmo & Subiman 2006; Resosudarmo et al. 2012). Thus, Indonesia had little choice but to become more proactive and to display its willingness to participate in mitigating the GHG emissions arising from within its territory.[2] The participation of the Indonesian president in COP13 was, for instance, an initial attempt to demonstrate to the world that Indonesia was indeed concerned about the issue and willing to take action. Meanwhile, the international community, particularly aid agencies, also indicated that there were possibilities for establishing international sources of funding that Indonesia could reap if it was able to control its emissions, and these possibilities were certainly an attraction for Indonesia as well.

At the same time, at the end of the 2000s, the Indonesian economy was growing rapidly, despite the global financial crisis that began in 2007. The country's gross domestic product (GDP) was growing at an annual rate above 5 per cent. As the fourth most populated country in the world – and having demonstrated a strong ability to develop at a considerable rate – Indonesia was invited to become part of the G20. This seemed to acknowledge the fact that Indonesia was now one of the most important economies in the world. Yet this achievement also helped to convince the president of Indonesia that the country could do better than 'business-as-usual' in controlling the country's GHG emissions. In particular, it suggested to government officials that the country could take on mitigation commitments without deleterious effects upon economic growth. A report released by the National Council on Climate Change (DNPI) on Indonesia's GHG abatement curve, for instance (DNPI with McKinsey & Co. 2010), revealed that there were relatively cheap and easy options for mitigating climate change without jeopardizing the country's economy. Finally, the president also saw an opportunity for Indonesia to be seen as a leader among developing nations on the issue of climate change if it took action as a member of the G20.

Hence, it can be argued that the factors leading to the announcement of Indonesia's CO_2 emission mitigation commitments by the president at the 2009 G20 meeting in Pittsburgh were, first, international and domestic pressures that arose in response to new information showing that Indonesia was one of the largest emitters in the world, and therefore needed to control its emissions for any meaningful global reductions to take place; second, an expectation on the part of the president and other high level officials that taking action to mitigate emissions would attract international funding; third, growing confidence in the government as a result of the Indonesian economy's good performance, making it an appropriate time to couple economic and environmental policies; and, finally, the fact that the president was attracted to the idea that Indonesia could be seen as a developing country leader on the issue of climate change.

Climate Change Coordination and Institutional Competition for Climate Leadership

After COP13, it became clear that the president wanted to put the mitigation of Indonesia's GHG emissions at the top of the country's agenda, and the international community encouraged Indonesia to increase its efforts by offering promises of financial and technical support. This increased the incentives for the government to begin the elaboration and implementation of climate policies and programmes. But, notably, these same developments also created incentives for Indonesian institutions to vie for larger shares of climate change-related activities and funds. Their goal in doing so was clear: to achieve recognition as the leading institution conducting climate change programmes and therefore to control inflows of domestic and international funding for implementing climate change-related policies and programmes.

This tendency can be seen by briefly considering the experience of DNPI, although it is explored more fully in the following section. In 2008, the minister of environment at that time made a significant move to provide some overall direction to climate-related activities by persuading the president to establish DNPI, an institution that would develop national strategies, policies and programmes for mitigating and adapting to climate change, and which would coordinate their implementation across the country. The aim was for this council to become the leading institution for developing and implementing climate change programmes. In reality, however, DNPI was only partially successful at coordinating efforts on climate change. Seeing the growing opportunities at hand, line ministers subsequently developed their own programmes and sometimes even insisted that their ministries should be the leading institutions instead. Among these ministerial institutions, the ones directly competing with DNPI/MoE were the Ministry of Forestry and the National Development Planning Agency (BAPPENAS). Other related ministries, such as the Ministry of Energy and Mineral Resources and the Ministry of Finance, may not have been competing to be the leading national institution, but they did try to establish their own programmes and exert and maintain exclusive control over them.

Subsequent events exacerbated this tendency. At the end of 2009, for instance, a new minister of environment was appointed, yet the chairman of DNPI remained the previous minister of environment.[3] This situation created even more friction within the government since it meant that DNPI and the MoE were now competing for leadership in directing climate change programmes. Another institution that became involved in developing climate change policy around this time was the President's Delivery Unit for Development Monitoring and Oversight (UKP4), which is part of the President's Office. The president asked the UKP4 to oversee the implementation of the LOI with Norway in September 2010. The Norway pledge and the involvement of UKP4 precipitated the REDD+ national policy process and influenced the development of so-called 'REDD-readiness' programmes at the national level. It also led to the initiation of early actions in the form of Reducing Emissions from Deforestation and Forest Degradation (REDD) demonstration activities at sub-national levels (i.e. landscape or district levels) and the exploration of financing options. Demonstration activities for REDD+ have, as a result, burgeoned in Indonesia; in 2011, over thirty pilots associated with REDD+ were recorded (Forest Carbon Asia 2011; Forest Carbon Partnership 2011; Resosudarmo et al. 2012).

With these activities, the UKP4 became the pivotal institution for overseeing the most significant dimension of Indonesia's climate change strategy. This in turn increased its power considerably relative to the others that had been competing for the top leadership position. In May 2011, for instance, the UKP4 was able to convince the president to produce a Presidential Decree (No. 10/2011) on a forest moratorium as part of Indonesia's commitment with Norway. This moratorium impinged on the jurisdiction of a number of other ministries by ensuring that no new permits would be issued for forest clearance over the next two years and that there would be efforts to better manage primary forests and peat lands. Later in 2011, two other Presidential Decrees were issued, namely No. 25/2011, regarding the formulation of a REDD+ Task Force, and No. 61/2011, outlining more than seventy self-funded government programmes as part of the national action plan to mitigate GHG emissions (RAN-GRK). However, the good intentions behind establishing the UKP4 as the primary institution for leading REDD implementation has in reality had the effect of creating yet another institution competing to lead efforts to implement climate mitigation programmes.

Thus, as a number of ministries and institutions were brought in to manage the government's climate change strategy, this has had the unintended effect of further exacerbating the growing competition among the various ministries that were involved. And, most importantly, this competition has tended to limit progress in the implementation of climate change policies in the country. Despite the fact that 2020 is not far ahead, a national REDD+ programme has yet to be implemented, no comprehensive activities related to controlling the emissions from peat lands have been initiated, very little has been done to reform the energy sector to enable the large-scale adoption of renewable sources of energy in the country's energy mix; and finally, there has not been a major push to improve energy efficiency in industries and households. Competition among the various institutions that have separate mandates to take action on climate change has encouraged the production of various strategy documents and regulations related to climate change, as each institution has attempted to demonstrate leadership. But this competition has also meant that there is little incentive for any one institution to support documents and regulations initiated by others. Hence, the implementation of each of their programmes and regulations – which require cross-ministerial coordination for them to be successful – has so far been lagging.

The Institutional Setting of Climate Change Policymaking in Indonesia

This section considers the process of inter-ministerial competition in greater detail. In particular, it will describe the interests and actions of individual ministries, as well as past and potential conflicts with other institutions as related to the development and implementation of climate change policies. Almost all line ministerial institutions participate to varying degrees in the implementation of Indonesia's climate change programmes. However, this section will deal only with those with relatively significant roles in developing national climate change policies and implementing major climate change programmes, especially those related to the REDD+ programme. Finally, the section will turn to consider the role that the international community has played in all of this.

The Ministry of Environment (MoE)

Climate change issues have been part of the MoE's portfolio for a long time; long before any other institution became involved. Up until COP13, the MoE was Indonesia's focal point for the UNFCCC and was the Indonesian government's representative in various international forums to discuss and negotiate climate change issues. As such, the Ministry was an early champion of Indonesia's efforts to take action on climate change. It significantly contributed to the decision by the UNFCCC to allow Indonesia to host COP13 in Bali in 2007, where the minister of environment acted as president. It was therefore natural for the MoE to assume that, when other line ministers began to be involved in climate change matters around the time of COP13, it should take the lead in developing and overseeing the implementation of Indonesian climate policies.

After COP13, however, there were a number of challenges to the MoE's leadership. Examples include competition from BAPPENAS in developing the country's climate change strategy, competition from the MoE's offspring, DNPI, and, later on, the UKP4/REDD+ Task Force, to become the focal point for the UNFCCC. The MoE, nevertheless, made a number of attempts to resume its position. For example, the Ministry was a strong supporter of Law No. 32/2009, which explicitly stated it was responsible for conservation and management of CO_2 pollution in Indonesia, and for coordinating a CO_2 emissions inventory that would measure, report and verify activities related to the abatement of GHGs. The Ministry also engaged in a significant restructuring and reorganization of its own activities, creating a department explicitly dedicated to the management of activities related to climate change, in order to bolster its capacity for inter-ministerial coordination. Finally, it did its best to maintain a strong relationship with UNFCCC and to ensure that its minister could serve as the main focal point for the UNFCCC in Indonesia. It has used this relationship in order to bolster its own authority domestically. These efforts were relatively effective while Rachmat Witoelar was the minister of environment.

The challenge faced by the MoE was, however, its weakness compared to other ministries. For a long time, the MoE was not in the core of the Cabinet; it was effectively marginalized, and managed what were widely regarded as low priority issues. Furthermore, and relatedly, it was an institution with a relatively small budget and (frequently) poor quality human resources. Thus, it faced considerable difficulties in maintaining its hold on the leadership of climate change issues in the country. The toughest challenge for the MoE came when the president, as mentioned before, appointed a new minister of environment but kept the previous minister, Rachmat Witoelar, as the head of DNPI. As such, when he and his colleagues left the MoE and established DNPI to become the main focal point for UNFCCC, the MoE lost its most significant source of authority, and thereby its ability to lead climate change programmes in Indonesia.

The National Council on Climate Change (DNPI)

DNPI, discussed in greater detail above, is a specialized committee on climate change at Cabinet level. This institution was proposed by the then minister of environment to the president in order to strengthen the former's role in leading climate change initiatives in Indonesia. The president established DNPI in July 2008 with Presidential Decree (PerPres) No. 46/2008. Officially, DNPI is now the leading body managing the government's response to climate change, and it is more or less completely detached from the MoE. Its main responsibilities are to formulate national policies, strategies and programmes related to climate change, including adaptation, mitigation, technology transfer and financing. The head of DNPI was appointed as the president's special envoy for climate change and thus became the focal point for UNFCCC – on paper the most important person on climate change in the country. However, since its establishment, DNPI has never really been able to coordinate effectively all of the cross-cutting climate change programmes that have arisen across various line ministries and levels of government. A possible explanation for this could be the fact that DNPI neither has budgetary authority to derive its power from, nor is staffed with strong public servants linked with line ministries. The head of DNPI, although directly accountable to the president, also does not have ministerial status, which limits its authority considerably. Further, when the president decided to form the REDD+ Task Force as the main institution coordinating the implementation of REDD+ in Indonesia, DNPI effectively lost most of its power to coordinate the development of climate change policies and programmes.

The UKP4 and its REDD+ Task Force

The UKP4 is an institution within the President's Office that is widely respected for its role in evaluating and monitoring the performance of the Cabinet. It was, initially, not explicitly concerned with climate change issues. However, it became a key institution in this area after the president asked the UKP4 to lead the implementation of the arrangement with Norway. As mentioned in the previous section, the UKP4's first achievement in this regard was the orchestration of Presidential Decree No. 10/2011, passed in May 2011, which instated a two-year moratorium on new permits to clear primary forests and peat lands throughout Indonesia (Murdiyarso et al. 2011). In 2010, a REDD+ Task Force was established within UKP4 through Presidential Decree No. 19/2010, and the head of UKP4 also became the head of this new task force. When this occurred, the REDD+ Task Force effectively became the most powerful institution in the country for managing the implementation of REDD+, which gave it a significant degree of control over all climate policymaking due to the government's emphasis on REDD+ in its overall climate change strategy. Indeed, through the UKP4, the task force is theoretically able to control the activities of all other line ministries in this area. Further, the UKP4, or, to be precise, its current head, is very close to and has a direct link to the president, and regularly reports to the president on the performance of each ministry.

The challenges facing the REDD+ Task Force in leading the implementation of REDD+, however, have been more or less similar to those facing DNPI when it was more powerful. The UKP4/REDD+ Task Force has limited resources, in terms of both human capital and basic information. It many cases, it must rely on the human and informational resources of other ministries, effectively giving them a great degree of influence over its decisions. Further, despite its official powers, it has only a limited capability to enforce its programmes and goals vis-à-vis other line ministries and local governments. It seems that its main strategy has been to present other line ministries with a fait accompli by convincing the president to enact a Presidential Decree related to REDD+ or to announce programmes designed by the REDD+ Task Force in international forums. Since other ministries cannot challenge the president, they are obliged to comply with the decisions of the REDD+ Task Force, however reluctantly. Yet, as the current president's term will be up in 2014, it remains to be seen whether or not the newly elected president will support the UKP4/REDD+ Task Force as much as the current one has. If not, UKP4 and its REDD+ Task Force will be likely to lose the power to lead the implementation of REDD+ in the country, since its capacity for leadership ultimately rests on its presently close but ultimately tenuous relationship with the President's Office.

The Ministry of Forestry

The Ministry of Forestry has also become an important actor in the governance of climate change in Indonesia, and has tried to expand its authority over the issue area in recent years. Since the enactment of the Forestry Law in 1967 (Law No. 5/1967), the Ministry of Forestry has become a strong and lucrative department (Resosudarmo 2005), though it has also been strongly criticized by domestic and international observers for the way it manages Indonesia's forests. These criticisms have mainly been related to the fact that rates of deforestation in Indonesia have been among the highest in the world, releasing massive amounts of CO_2 (Hansen et al. 2009; Broich et al. 2011; FAO 2010), as well as evidence of rampant forestry-related corruption within the Ministry.

Around the time of COP13, however, the Ministry of Forestry took the initiative in leading the country's REDD programmes by establishing and leading the Indonesian Forest Climate Alliance (IFCA), which comprised various government departments, donor agencies, research institutions and NGOs. The main task of the IFCA was to outline key elements of REDD, including methodologies, land use policies, institutional arrangements and benefit distribution mechanisms (Ministry of Forestry 2008). It therefore became one of the key institutions in the arena of climate change as well. Yet, since the president created the REDD+ Task Force within UKP4 to manage the bilateral arrangement between Indonesia and Norway and to oversee REDD+ development at the national level, the Ministry's authority for leading the implementing of REDD/REDD+ has tended to wane. It has nevertheless remained an important ministry, as it has more data on forestry and forest coverage in the country than any other institution, which has given it a degree of leverage over the decision-making processes of other institutions, especially the REDD+ Task Force. Examples of its ongoing importance include its role in producing the indicative maps for the moratorium called for by the REDD+ Task Force, developing the Forest Resource Inventory System (part of the Indonesia National Carbon Accounting System, which is used for the monitoring, reporting and verification of GHG emissions reductions), and providing guidance for the development of REDD+ demonstration activities.

The National Development Planning Agency (BAPPENAS)

Like several of the other institutions described above, BAPPENAS has been a recent contender for the leadership position in the area of climate change. The advantage of BAPPENAS is that it has very strong human resources – indeed, its human resources are better than those of almost any other Indonesian government institution and it has considerable experience in coordinating the activities of other government agencies. On the issue of climate change, in particular, it has been able to demonstrate its leadership by producing several key strategic documents and reports on climate change policy in Indonesia which have helped to shape the government's overall approach. Most notably, in this regard, BAPPENAS produced the Indonesia Climate Change Sectoral Roadmap (ICCSR) in 2010, which elaborated sectoral commitments for achieving the emissions reduction target that was announced at the 2009 G20 summit in Pittsburgh. This report then served as the basis for Presidential Decree No. 61/2011, which established the RAN-GRK.

The production of the ICCSR was clearly an attempt by BAPPENAS to 'coordinate' other ministries in the context of climate change. It also overlapped with and undermined the role of DNPI to some extent. Despite this achievement, it remains unclear to what degree the implementation of the climate change programmes in Indonesia will take the form outlined in the RAN-GRK, and whether BAPPENAS will indeed have the capacity to coordinate them. Although it has been traditionally quite powerful, BAPPENAS is now a much weaker institution than it was in the past. Many of its mandates were transferred to the Ministry of Finance, for instance, by Law No. 17/2003 on government finance. Further, most line ministers still recall how dissatisfied they were when BAPPENAS was more powerful and able to control their activities effectively. They have, therefore, been extremely reluctant to cede any power to it yet again by having it coordinating national programmes related to climate change.

The Ministry of Finance

Adequate financing is, of course, required to sustain the implementation of all climate change-related programmes in Indonesia, and, as such, the Ministry of Finance – as the key ministry managing the government's budget – has become more crucial in the country's climate change activities over time. Together with the legislature, it has the primary authority over programme financing. Understanding its importance in this respect, Indonesia's finance minister initially facilitated parallel meetings at COP13 among finance and trade ministers which aimed at, among other things, reviewing the costs of damages from climate change, reviewing the policy instruments available for addressing the issue, setting objectives and common goals, and outlining steps to follow. These meetings drew dozens of trade and finance ministers, who, before COP13, had been largely silent in the climate debate. And, domestically, the Ministry of Finance has also strengthened its position relative to other ministries by forming a unit specializing in climate change finance.

In general, therefore, the Ministry of Finance has become more and more central to climate change policymaking, and it has actively attempted to expand its authority in the area (Resosudarmo & Abdurohman 2011). In contrast with several of the other institutions discussed here, however, its goals have been more limited. Its main intention has been to establish its leading position over the development of climate change financing policies and their implementation, including REDD+. At present, oversight of REDD+ financing continues to be coordinated under the REDD+ Task Force; in particular, under the Working Group on Funding Instruments. Although the Ministry of Finance is a member of the group, it has not yet come to play a leading role. It has, nevertheless, tried to leverage its authority in this area by emphasizing its strong knowledge of the country's finances and using its power to push for the implementation of policies related to climate finances. Its key disadvantage in doing so, however, has been that the Ministry has only limited knowledge of climate change issues. Thus, it must primarily assert itself in climate change policymaking processes as a collaborator rather than a leader. The Ministry, as noted above, actively sought to change this situation by building expertise in the area of climate finance, but this has not yet helped to bolster its authority over other institutions.

The Role of the International Community in Indonesia

On the issue of climate change, a number of international actors, such as bilateral aid donors, multilateral development agencies and private foundations, have worked together with the Indonesian government and various domestic institutions. Support from such actors increased dramatically in the lead-up to COP13 in Bali and prior to and after COP15 in Copenhagen. Together, these actors have shaped the development of climate change policymaking in Indonesia to a considerable extent. As discussed in the first part of this chapter, they have been extremely important for stimulating Indonesia's more ambitious approach to climate change. However, as we discuss below, they have also tended to exacerbate competition among Indonesia's ministries, thereby leading to poor implementation.

The most significant international actor that has influenced the development of climate change policymaking in Indonesia has, of course, been the government of Norway, which signed an agreement (an LOI) with the Indonesian government in late May of 2010, promising up to US$1 billion for supporting REDD+ development in Indonesia. This LOI has presented Indonesia with major opportunities, encouraging the groundswell of activities that has since taken place. Yet it has also presented challenges. Instead of utilizing existing institutions, for example, the LOI requires the establishment of new institutions to coordinate the implementation of REDD+ programmes; that is, not the REDD+ Task Force or DNPI or any other existing institution. The REDD+ National Strategy will be implemented by a new institution, the REDD+ Agency (REDD+ Task Force 2012) – and the head of this Agency will be directly responsible to the president. However, it remains to be seen whether or not this institution will be able to realize its mandate in view of the existing competition for authority in this area. Ultimately, therefore, progress on this collaboration has been slow. To date, only US$30 million has been disbursed.

With regard to the development of REDD+ institutions in Indonesia, a number of other bilateral aid and multilateral agencies have also supported the Ministry of Forestry in establishing a multi-stakeholder platform known as the IFCA, mentioned above, which has helped to develop REDD+ methodologies, strategies, financing and revenue distribution mechanisms (Ministry of Forestry 2008). At the sub-national level, likewise, the Australian Agency for International Development (AusAID) has helped to pilot REDD+ demonstration activities in Central Kalimantan province under the Kalimantan Forest Climate Partnership. Of the central multilateral development agencies, the World Bank's Forest Carbon Partnership Facility (FCPF) and the UN-REDD Programme are examples of two leading international organizations that focus on REDD+ development in Indonesia.

The influence of international actors, however, has not been confined to the domain of forestry. In the energy sector, bilateral donors and multilateral agencies have been working with Indonesia's government and other key actors to promote energy efficiency pro-grammes and renewable energy financing, and to address the issue of energy subsidies. These include the work carried out by the government of Denmark through the Danish International Development Agency (DANIDA). In collaboration with the Ministry of Energy and Mineral Resources (MEMR), DANIDA has helped establish the Energy Efficiency and Conservation Clearing House Indonesia (EECCHI), a service facility aiming to promote and enhance energy conservation (EECCHI 2012). Other transnational actors have also been helping to promote the use of renewable energy sources in the country's energy mix. The World Bank, the Japan International Cooperation Agency (JICA) and other aid agencies, for instance, have provided support for investments and have started initiatives aimed at reducing risks in geothermal energy development. These collaborative efforts in the areas of renewable energy development and energy efficiency, however, face continuous challenges, including significant up-front investments, subsidies for fossil fuels and electricity, and an opaque mix of political and multilevel regulatory authorities that generate uncertainty and high transaction costs for investors.

Finally, international agencies and bilateral donors have also played significant roles in the development of overall national level climate change policies. In particular, they have collaborated with the Indonesian government and relevant institutions in the production of strategic plans for achieving the government's overarching goal of reducing CO_2 emissions by 26 per cent by 2020. These include the Ministry of Finance's Green Paper (i.e. a joint work between the Ministry of Finance and the Australian government), the ICCSR (a joint project between BAPPENAS, line ministries and the German government), and Indonesia's Second National Communication under the UNFCCC (produced by the MoE in collaboration with the UNFCCC; Ministry of Environment 2010).

In general, therefore, a variety of international actors have been shaping Indonesia's approach to climate change to a considerable extent. Some, such as the government of Norway, have had a major impact. More than any other factor, its agreement with Indonesia has helped to raise the government's level of ambition, and its emphasis on REDD has defined the contours of its approach. Others have been less influential, although they have shaped the evolution of par-ticular programmes and helped draw the government's attention to particular issue areas. Nevertheless, it is also important to note that the activities and support of international actors have had negative side-effects. Indeed, international actors have stimulated competition amongst the various institutions involved in climate change policy-making. The promise of large-scale funds has been an important element in this regard, creating an incentive for institutions to com-pete for leadership. This is reinforced by the actual policies of certain donors and agencies; for the most part, they have tended to pick local counterparts without providing incentives for them to collaborate with other domestic institutions, further exacerbating the problem. This has led to greater attention being given to the issue of climate change within the government, but has also made it difficult for institutions to cooperate with each other as they seek to obstruct the leadership of others and vie for control of international funding at the expense of actual implementation.

Conclusion

This chapter attempts to account for the climate change commitment that was announced by the president of Indonesia at the 2009 G20 meeting, as well as Indonesia's strategy for achieving it. The chapter also attempts to explain why, despite the country's growing commitment to governing climate change and the elaboration of a climate change strategy, the implementation of climate change programmes has been lagging. On the factors leading to the announcement of Indonesia's CO_2 emissions mitigation commitments, this chapter has argued that international pressures for Indonesia to control its emissions, a growing perception on the part of the government of opportunities for attracting international funds for REDD programmes, growing confidence in the economy's performance, and the president's interest in being known as a leader among developing nations on the issue of climate change have been the key variables influencing the country's growing ambition. The strong emphasis on the part of the international community on REDD, and the provision of international funding for REDD projects in the country, have also shaped the government's climate change strategy significantly, raising the importance of mitigating emissions from forestry in its overall approach and sidelining other issues such as emissions in the energy sector by comparison.

On the question of why the implementation of climate change programmes has been relatively weak, this chapter has argued that the main reasons are as follows. First, there is no clear hierarchy of authority among the various institutions involved in the country's climate change policymaking process. This is, at base, due to a tug of war among Indonesia's ministries over whether climate change should be regarded as a sectoral or inter-sectoral issue. Although, in general, climate change is widely thought to be an inter-sectoral issue – a view held by the Indonesian president – sectoral ministries in Indonesia continue to argue that climate change is a sectoral issue, and that they should develop and lead particular programmes on climate change fitted to their sector. The Ministry of Forestry, for example, persists in thinking of REDD+ as a purely sectoral programme, and argues that it alone should design and lead the implementation of the programme. A similar situation exists with regard to MEMR and energy use and efficiency policies, as well as with the Ministry of Finance and the financing of climate change programmes. Meanwhile, BAPPENAS has argued that climate change is an inter-sectoral developmental issue which, as such, falls within its remit.

Second, there seems to be little consensus among governmental institutions on who should take the lead in developing climate policies in the country and implementing climate change programmes. Currently, there are at least three institutions with mandates to lead climate change policymaking in the country. Since the end of the 1960s, BAPPENAS has had a mandate to coordinate medium-term development planning, and, as mentioned above, it has argued that climate change should be treated no differently from any other development issue. It therefore has a strong claim to be the leading institution on the issue of climate change. Nevertheless, other institutions also have presidential mandates to lead policy development on climate change. DNPI is one, and another – though it is much more specifically focused on REDD+ – is the REDD+ Task Force. All three are competing to capture the authority to coordinate climate change-related activities across the country, and this comes at the cost of reducing incentives for them to cooperate with each other, ultimately resulting in ineffective policy implementation. Third, overlapping tasks and conflicting policies among institutions on climate-related issues are quite common. This is the case with BAPPENAS, DNPI and the REDD+ Task Force, as described above, and it holds true for many other ministries and institutions as well. The MoE's activities in many cases overlap with those of MEMR, the Ministry of Forestry and other line ministries, and agreement among them over the terms of cooperation and the distribution of responsibilities has proven difficult to achieve.

Fourth, there are cases in which some government institutions view climate change programmes negatively. For instance, when it comes to REDD+, governmental ministries with programmes to develop industrial timber plantations, agricultural crops and mining activities have vested interests in being able to use the remaining forest and peat land areas (Resosudarmo et al. 2012), and would thus perceive themselves as losers in the promotion of climate change programmes. In addition, it is also worth noting that international donor policy in Indonesia generally seems to exacerbate the problem. So far, there has not been any coordination among international donor activities related to climate change. The donors develop their own programmes, bring in their own experts to run or coordinate Indonesian climate change programmes, and pick different institutions in the country to be their partners in implementing them. These activities then empower their partner institution to compete against other institutions to capture a larger share of climate change programmes. International donors have therefore not provided any incentive for their partners to collaborate with other local institutions.

What direction should Indonesia now take to develop its climate change programme better in the near future? There are not many environment programmes that could be considered to have been successful, so lessons from previous programmes are rather limited. Furthermore, the scale and complexity of the climate change problem limit their relevance. However, the implementation of the integrated pest management (IPM) programme to reduce the use of toxic pesticides during the early 1990s may hold some lessons (Resosudarmo 2010). The IPM programme was successful because of (1) solid local research on the topic providing the government with accurate information on the issue; (2) national political will to implement the programme, meaning all institutions were willing to support it; (3) the president clearing an institutional bottleneck, that is, removing resistance to the IPM programme by some institutions; (4) international institutions providing proper support; and, finally, (5) instant benefits provided to the people implementing the programme.

In the case of climate change, the key to successfully implementing climate change programmes, including REDD+, might be different from those relevant to IPM. Nevertheless, we would like to argue that, first of all, strong political will and leadership are needed. Currently it is not clear whether the Indonesian people actually do care about the issue of climate change. National and local Parliaments as representatives of the people have not said much regarding climate change so far. On the leadership issue, first, the Indonesian president should choose one of the existing institutions as a lead institution, be consistent with this choice, and explicitly instruct the other governmental bodies to follow its directives. Second, clear job descriptions should be defined for each institution involved in the development of climate change policies and implementation. A kind of institutional breakthrough is needed to resolve the conflict of interest among the institutions involved. In the case of IPM, initially the Ministry of Agriculture resisted implementing the programme, so the president decided to bypass the Ministry and asked BAPPENAS to implement the programme instead. Once the programme was up and running, the Ministry of Agriculture was asked to join in, and was delegated clear tasks as a condition for involvement. Third, coordination among international institutions is needed so that coherent support can be delivered, limiting domestic institutional fragmentation and providing sufficient resources for implementation. Fourth, people affected by the climate change programmes should benefit from these early on, or should at least understand how they might benefit. Finally, we would argue that local research on climate change is essential. Currently, domestic research is relatively weak, so it needs support and also has to be linked to efforts undertaken by international research communities. International donors and research institutions could contribute to this as well.

Given that there are many challenges, serious doubts remain as to whether or not Indonesia will be able to control its CO_2 emissions in line with its broad agreements and commitments. The signs for hope are not quite there yet and there will be a long way to go before Indonesia can truly become a climate policy leader.

Notes

1 Drafts of these papers were circulated in 2007, though their actual publication came later.
2 As the global warming potential is expressed as a factor of CO_2, this paper uses 'CO_2' and 'GHG' interchangeably.
3 Indicating the ambition of the previous minister of environment to be able to lead climate change activities in the country.

References

BAPPENAS (2010), *Indonesia Climate Change Sectoral Roadmap: Synthesis Report*. Jakarta: BAPPENAS.

Broich, M., M. Hansen, F. Stolle, P. Potapov, B. A. Margono & B. Adusei (2011). Remotely sensed forest cover loss shows high spatial and temporal variation across Sumatera and Kalimantan, Indonesia 2000–2008. *Environmental Research Letters* 6(1).

Djajadiningrat, S. T. (2010). Internalisasi kebijakan pembangunan berkelanjutan ke dalam kebijakan pemerintah. In I. J. Azis, L. M. Napitupulu, A. A. Patunru & B. P. Resosudarmo (eds.) *Pembangunan Berkelanjutan: Peran dan Kontribusi Emil Salim*. Jakarta: Kepustakaan Populer Gramedia.

DNPI with McKinsey & Co. (2010). *Indonesian GHG Abatement Cost Curve*. Jakarta: DNPI.

DNPI and UNFCCC (2009). *National Economic, Environment and Development Study (NEEDS) for Climate Change: Indonesia Country Study*. Jakarta: DNPI.

EECCHI (2012). *About EECCHI*. Available at: http://www.energyefficiencyindonesia.info/eecchi.

FAO (2010). *Global Forest Resources Assessment: Global Tables*. Rome: FAO.

Forest Carbon Asia (2011). Global Comparison of Forest Carbon (FC) Projects: Forest Carbon Projects/Pilots in Asia – FC Updates: Projects on the Ground. 13 July. Available at: http://www.forestcarbonasia.org/fc-updates/projects-on-the-ground.

Forest Carbon Partnership (2011). *REDD Readiness Progress Factsheet: Indonesia*. February. Available at: http://www.forestcarbonpartnership.org/fcp/sites/forestcarbonpartnership.org/files/Documents/PDF/Mar2011/Indonesia%20Progress%20Sheet%20030111.pdf.

Hansen, M. C., S. V. Stehman, P. V. Potapov, B. Arunarwati, F. Stolle & K. Pittman (2009). Quantifying changes in the rates of forest clearing in Indonesia from 1990 to 2005 using remotely sensed data sets. *Environmental Research Letters* 4(3).

Jotzo, F. (2012). Can Indonesia lead climate change? In A. J. S. Reid (ed.) *Indonesia Rising: The Repositioning of Asia's Third Giant*. Singapore: Institute of Southeast Asian Studies.

Ministry of Environment (2010). *Summary for Policy Makers: Indonesia Second National Communication under the UNFCCC*. Jakarta: Ministry of Environment.

Ministry of Forestry (2008). *IFCA 2007 Consolidation Report: Reducing Emissions from Deforestation and Forest Degradation in Indonesia*. Jakarta: Forestry Research and Development Agency.

Murdiyarso, D., S. Dewi, D. Lawrence & F. Seymour (2011). *Indonesia's Forest Moratorium: A Stepping Stone to Better Forest Governance?* Working Paper 76,

CIFOR, Bogor. Available at: http://www.cifor.org/publications/pdf_files/W Papers/WP-76Murdiyarso.pdf.

Nurdianto, D. A. & B. P. Resosudarmo (2011). Prospects and challenges for an ASEAN energy integration policy. *Environmental Economics and Policy Studies* 13(2).

PEACE (2007). *Indonesia and Climate Change: Working Paper on Current Status and Policies.* Jakarta: PEACE.

REDD+ Task Force (2012). *REDD+ National Strategy.* Jakarta: Indonesia REDD+ Task Force.

Resosudarmo, B. P. (ed.) (2005). *The Politics and Economics of Indonesia's Natural Resources.* Singapore: Institute of Southeast Asian Studies.

Resosudarmo, B. P. (2010). *Understanding the Success of an Environmental Policy: The Case of the 1989–1999 Integrated Pest Management Program in Indonesia.* Working Papers in Trade and Development No. 2010/09, Arndt-Corden Department of Economics, Crawford School of Economics and Government, Australian National University.

Resosudarmo, B. P. & Abdurohman (2011). *Green Fiscal Policy and Climate Change Mitigation in Indonesia.* CCEP Working Paper No. 1109, Centre for Climate Economics and Policy, Crawford School of Economics and Government, Australian National University.

Resosudarmo, B. P. & N. L. Subiman (2006). The link between firm characteristics, bribery, and illegal logging in Indonesian wood-based industries. *ASEAN Economic Bulletin* 23(3).

Resosudarmo, B. P., D. A. Nurdianto & A. A. Yusuf (2009). Greenhouse gas emission in Indonesia: the significance of fossil fuel combustion. In B. Robiani, B. P. Resosudarmo, A. A. Alisjahbana & A. Rosa (eds.) *Regional Development, Energy and the Environment in Indonesia.* Palembang: Indonesian Regional Science Association.

Resosudarmo, B. P., A. A. Nawir, I. A. P. Resosudarmo & N. L. Subiman (2012). Forest land use dynamics in Indonesia. In A. Booth, C. Manning & T. K. Wie (eds.) *Land, Livelihood, the Economy and the Environment in Indonesia.* Jakarta: Yayasan Obor.

Thamrin, S. (2011). *Indonesia's National Mitigation Actions: Paving the Way towards NAMAs.* Paper presented at the CCXG/Global Forum on Environment Seminar on MRV and Carbon Markets, 28–9 March, Paris.

Yudhoyono, S. B. (2009). *Intervention by H.E. Dr. Susilo Bambang Yudhoyono President of the Republic of Indonesia on Climate Change at the G-20 Leaders Summit 25 September 2009, Pittsburgh, PA [13:00 – Working Lunch].* Available at: http://forest climatecenter.org/files/2009–09–25%20Intervention%20by%20President%20 SBY%20on%20Climate%20Change%20at%20the%20G-20%20Leaders%20 Summit.pdf

5

Low Carbon Green Growth and Climate Change Governance in South Korea

Jae-Seung Lee

Introduction

On the issue of climate change, South Korea straddles the industrialized and developing worlds. It is an Organization for Economic Cooperation and Development (OECD) country, with the fourteenth largest gross domestic product (GDP) in the world, yet it is classed as a non-Annex I party under the United Nations Framework Convention on Climate Change (UNFCCC) with the status of a developing country. As an 'advanced developing state', South Korea has been under strong pressure from the international community to participate more actively in global efforts to mitigate emissions. In response, its system of climate change governance has evolved with the advancement of the global climate change regime since 1992. Initially, South Korea began to develop measures to cope with climate change largely as a follower rather than a leader in the global regime. However, its response to the climate change agenda has rapidly accelerated after 2008, when it began to take a much more proactive stance. South Korea is now widely regarded as a role model among developing countries, particularly following the announcement and implementation of its low carbon green growth strategy (hereafter 'green growth') announced in 2008.

Korea faces a number of challenges in relation to climate change. Its greenhouse gas (GHG) emissions accounted for 1.3 per cent of the world's total in 2005, making it the fifteenth largest emitter in the world and the ninth largest in the OECD (Jones & Yoo 2011). Between 1990 and 2005, the country's emissions almost doubled. This large increase was primarily a result of the rapid economic growth that Korea has experienced, with emissions from the energy sector contributing the most substantial portion in the overall total (Jones & Yoo 2011). Though the pace of this increase in emissions has slowed down since 2000,[1] South Korea still confronts many obstacles in relation to the mitigation of GHGs within its territory. The effects of climate change in Korea have also been observed in many areas, presenting

91

similarly enduring challenges. The average temperature in Korea has risen by 1.5 °C over the last 100 years, which is more than double the global average. This has resulted in a reduction in the length of the winter season by one month, while summers have lengthened by 20 days compared to the 1920s. There has also been a marked increase in the frequency of typhoons and torrential rainfall, which can have costly effects upon the country's infrastructure and agricultural sector (Han 2005, 2006; Lee 2010a). As a result of these changes, the need for comprehensive adaptation measures at the national level has also intensified in recent years.

Of course, Korea ratified the Kyoto Protocol of the UNFCCC in 2002 as a non-Annex I country. Thus, it had no multilateral obligation to set a specific GHG reduction target during the initial commitment period (2008–12). Nevertheless, as required by all parties under the Framework Convention, Korea implemented policies to cope with climate change by enhancing voluntary measures and building relevant institutions. Various means for improving energy efficiency, institutions related to the Clean Development Mechanism (CDM) and energy demand management policies have been introduced and implemented in order to reduce GHG emissions since 1992. In the international climate change negotiations, South Korea also argued for voluntary and flexible mechanisms, though these suggestions did not resonate widely within international society (Lee 2010a). However, climate change governance in South Korea reached a major turning point in 2008 when the government announced its green growth strategy to deal proactively with climate change and clean energy development.

The objective of this chapter is to examine the causes, achievements and challenges of climate change governance in South Korea by exploring the evolution of its climate change policies. The next section covers the initial evolution of South Korea's climate change policy over the period 1992–2008, which saw a number of climate change plans and institutions developed, largely in response to developments in the international climate regime. The third section will address the paradigm shift towards low carbon green growth after 2008, showing how the government's green growth policies and related institutions for their implementation have evolved since then. The fourth part will discuss international and domestic variables that have shaped South Korea's approach to climate change governance. The conclusion will then address the remaining internal and external challenges that may arise in the process of responding to the climate change in South Korea in view of its more ambitious agenda, as well as the task of consolidating climate change governance in response to them.

The Evolution of South Korea's Climate Change Policies, 1992–2008

South Korea's response to climate change was first initiated in reaction to the Rio Earth Summit in 1992. The Ministerial Committee for the Global Environment was established in 1992 to cover climate change issues as part of a diverse global environmental agenda. However, at the time, this Committee did not receive sufficient attention and had only limited authority, since environmental and climate change issues did not appear to be sufficiently urgent to be dealt with within inter-ministerial meetings. The Kyoto Protocol, signed in 1997, led to the introduction of specific targets and implementation mechanisms for GHG reductions, such as the CDM and Joint Implementation (JI). Even though South Korea was not listed in Annex I of the Protocol, which mandated numeric reduction targets for a group of thirty-seven industrialized states, the adoption of the Kyoto Protocol highlighted the need to recognize the environmental and economic implications of climate change. South Korea's efforts to cope with climate change then began to take a more concrete shape in April 1998, when the Korean government set up the Pan-Governmental Organization on the Climate Change Convention under the Prime Minister's Office in order to devise a more systematic response.[2] Soon after, the First Comprehensive Action Plan for the Climate Change Convention, 1999–2001 (Office for Government Policy Coordination 1998), was released in December 1998. It introduced thirty-six tasks, including voluntary agreements (VAs) and 111 detailed measures, such as support for energy service companies and the expansion of forestation projects (Government of the Republic of Korea 2003).

The Presidential Commission on Sustainable Development (PCSD), a standing presidential advisory body, was then established in 2000. Its aim was to balance the objectives of continuous economic development, environmental protection and responses to international environmental issues in general. The PCSD reviewed the nation's major policies and plans related to economic development and environmental protection, as well as the 'Agenda 21' measures adopted at the 1992 United Nations Conference on Environment and Development (UNCED). Overall, it had a broader scope and function beyond just the climate change regime (IGES 2008). The Special Committee on Climate Change was, however, established by the National Assembly the following year, in March 2001, and quickly began to draw attention to climate change issues at the legislative level. The Committee on the Climate Change Convention, headed by the prime minister, was also established soon after, in September 2001. The Committee was essentially an expansion and modification of the Pan-Governmental Organization on Climate Change Convention (Government of the Republic of Korea 2003).[3]

The Second Comprehensive Plan on the Climate Change Convention, 2002–4, was then adopted on 5 March 2002. It contained a detailed outline of projects and programmes designed to reduce GHG emissions in Korea in three relevant areas: (1) through the promotion of GHG reducing technologies and the development of environment friendly energy; (2) through the strengthening of related policies and measures for supporting GHG reductions; and (3) through the promotion of public participation and international cooperation. The plan resulted in the adoption of eighty-four tasks on five major agendas of capacity building. Subsequently, the Third Comprehensive Plan on Climate Change Convention, 2005–7, was introduced on 3 February 2005. The Third Comprehensive Plan outlined ninety tasks designed to establish (1) a basis for implementing the convention on climate change, (2) sectoral GHG emissions reduction projects, and (3) the means for facilitating adaptation to climate change. A total of nineteen government departments and other related organizations participated in the implementation of the Third Comprehensive Plan (Lee 2010a). The Fourth Comprehensive Plan on Combating Climate Change, 2008–12, was then adopted on 17 December 2007. It elaborated a series of means for minimizing the impact of climate change through reinforced mitigation and adaptation measures (PMO 2007; Yoo 2008).[4] Also, in the Fourth Plan, the period for implementation was extended from three to five years.

While the First and Second Comprehensive Plans were largely a response to developments in the international climate change regime, the Third and Fourth Comprehensive Plans offered more substantial policy packages. Energy conservation and efficiency measures have constituted an important pillar of GHG reductions in all of these periods, as the biggest portion of GHG emissions in Korea has traditionally come from the energy sector. The National Committee on Energy Conservation, for example, launched a VA system in 1998 in order to encourage energy efficiency in the business sector. Allegedly, this programme managed to save a cumulative total of 19 million tonnes of energy by 2008 (de Serres et al. 2010). Over the years, South Korea has also introduced three energy efficiency programmes aimed specifically at electronics and appliances. These were (1) mandatory energy efficiency standards and labelling, established in 1992; (2) high efficiency appliance certification, established in 1996; and (3) the standby electricity reduction programme, established in 1999 (Lee 2010b). In addition, the government launched several average fuel economy (AFE) regulations in January 2006 in order to save fuel and reduce emissions from vehicles (Jones & Yoo 2011).

Thus, the system of governance designed to respond to climate change in South Korea has been evolving continuously since the 1990s. Throughout this period, the importance of GHG mitigation and measures to counter climate change began to be more widely recognized both by the government and by the public. The series of Comprehensive Plans put forward policy measures in order to cope with the climate change problem. However, these earlier measures had a number of significant drawbacks. First, political momentum behind these climate change policies was not strong enough to make a more ambitious approach possible; in general, they were not very stringent and did not have a major effect on the country's emissions trajectory. Climate change issues were often sidelined as a result of the primacy of economic growth and an industrialization agenda within the government. Second, various actors within the government were often divided over the issue. The different stances of relevant ministries – in particular, the Ministry of Environment and the Ministry of Commerce and Industry (which became the Ministry of Knowledge Economy in 2008) – often led to stalemate in the policymaking process. As GHG mitigation measures were thought to undermine industrial competitiveness, any far-reaching climate change policies that were proposed also encountered strong objections from the commercial and industrial sectors. While a number of climate change plans were adopted and implemented throughout this period, then, the overall response to climate change in Korea was passive and incremental.

Low Carbon Green Growth: The New Paradigm in Climate Change Policy, 2008–2012

The system of climate change governance in South Korea, described in the previous section, was considerably reshaped with the launching of the 'low carbon green growth' strategy (PCGG 2010, p. 7),[5] which was announced by President Myung Bak Lee on the sixtieth anniversary of Liberation Day, 15 August 2008. This part of the chapter addresses the introduction and evolution of the green growth paradigm and reviews its most important elements.

The Green Growth Policy Shift

The green growth strategy articulated a new national vision for the future. The president's vision aimed to shift Korea's development model from one that was 'quantity-oriented' and 'fossil-fuel dependent' to one that focused on 'quality-oriented' growth and used a greater share of renewable sources of energy (STI Policy Review 2010, p. 112). At its core, it was based on the recognition that a fundamental and comprehensive change was needed for South Korea to overcome successfully the challenges arising from an economic slow-down, energy import dependency and climate change (PCGG 2011). Green growth focused not just on balancing development and environmental (and climate) protection, but on promoting investment in environment protection in order to foster economic growth. Economic growth based on these dynamics would realize qualitative growth by facilitating a mutually beneficial relationship between the economy and the environment (UNEP 2010). New ideas, innovations and leading technologies would constitute essential elements of this new paradigm (UNEP 2010). Thus, the green growth strategy was much more than a new approach to climate change and environmental issues; it was a new, overarching development framework that had implications for nearly all areas of the nation's economy.

Following the initial announcement of the president's vision of green growth, the Korean government adopted a master plan that would serve as a roadmap for implementing the strategy. The National Strategy for Green Growth had mid-term (2009–13) and long-term (2009–50) targets, with specific objectives and action plans for each. The government set out these policy targets to ensure that South Korea would become the world's seventh largest 'green economic power' by 2020 and the fifth largest one by 2050. In addition, it specified three 'pillars' of green growth: (1) mitigation of climate change and energy independence, (2) the creation of new engines for economic growth, and (3) the improvement of quality of life and enhanced international standing (Jung & Ahn 2010).

Towards these ends, the National Strategy for Green Growth established a target of increasing the share of renewable energy sources in Korea's total primary energy supply (TPES) from the current 2.4 per cent to 6 per cent by 2020, 11 per cent by 2030, and 30 per cent by 2050. The government also planned to increase the use of nuclear power, which had lower operating costs than oil- and gas-based power plants in Korea and produced fewer GHGs. Nuclear energy's share of total electricity generation capacity was targeted to increase from 26 per cent in 2007 to 41 per cent by 2030. Overall, the government proposed 111.4 trillion won of investment by 2030, including research and development (R&D) subsidies of 11.5 trillion won, in order to achieve Korea's green growth objectives. Table 5.1 shows the key policy targets of the green growth strategy that was set by the Lee administration. Their elaboration, it should be noted, was also paralleled by the adoption of the Green New Deal, the government's stimulus package in response to the 2008 financial crisis, which was introduced on 6 January 2009 as an effort to kick-start the country's green growth strategy. The Green New Deal was, essentially, an investment plan of 50 trillion won (US$38.5 billion) for the 2009–12 period and included nine key green projects and spill-over projects that aimed to create 956,000 new jobs in the green sector (PCGG 2010).

The subsequent Five-Year Green Growth Plan then absorbed the Green New Deal strategy for 2009–12. It was formulated in order to implement green growth in a much more systematic fashion. It incorporated policy measures for the reduction of GHG emissions, for the development and production of renewable energy sources and for climate change adaptation, as well as measures related to the 'greening' of buildings, cities, transport and lifestyles. Under the First Five-Year Plan, the South Korean government was to invest 107 trillion won in order to meet these goals, equivalent to roughly 2 per cent of the annual GDP growth forecast for the target period. The government budget, with respect to green growth, would be spent on, amongst

Table 5.1	Key policy targets in Korea's green growth strategy		
	Key indicators	**2007**	**2012**
Green industries	Share of renewable energy	2.24%[a]	>11%[b]
	Solar power (global market share)	0.3%	5%
	Green car related jobs (thousand workers)	260	300
	Green homes (households)	14,500	>100,000
	Share of LED lighting	<1%	30%[c]
	Share of nuclear energy (in terms of electricity capacity)	26%	41%[b]
	Fuel economy for vehicles (<1,600 cc)	12.4km/l	14.55km/l
Enhanced quality of life	Co-generation facilities	47	78
	Energy efficiency certifications for buildings	Public buildings	All buildings
	Hybrid vehicles	1,386	30,000
	Waste regeneration	1.8%	31%
	Expansion of carbon sinks	625 million m²	779 million m²
	Public participation on climate action	23.6%	60%
Global leadership	GHG emission	591.1 tonnes CO_2	−30%[d] (BAU)
	Climate change plans by local government	<10%	100%
	Share of ODA on green growth	11%	18%

BAU = business-as-usual. ODA = official development assistance.
[a] In 2006. [b] By 2030. [c] By 2015. [d] By 2020.

Source: PCGG (2008).

other things, the major Four Rivers Restoration Project, R&D in green technology, and green transport. Twenty-seven green technologies, in particular, were identified as strategic investment priorities (STI Policy Review 2010).

South Korea announced its official GHG mitigation goal on 17 November 2009, just before the Fifteenth Conference of the Parties (COP15) in Copenhagen. The Korean government decided to aim to cut the country's GHG emissions by 30 per cent relative to the 'business-as-usual' (BAU) scenario by 2020, which implied an absolute cut of 4 per cent relative to 2005 levels (PCGG 2011, p. 32).[6] The target set by the Korean government assumed the highest level of mitigation recommended by the Intergovernmental Panel on Climate Change (IPCC) for developing countries in order to limit global temperature rise to under 2 °C (Jones & Yoo 2010).[7] Ultimately, of course, its target was a voluntary and unilateral action. It was submitted as the country's Nationally Appropriate Mitigation Action (NAMA) to the UNFCCC Secretariat on 25 January 2010. However, in contrast to many other voluntary mitigation commitments made by non-Annex I states, Korea's commitment was not conditional on international agreements and support.[8] It was hoped that by taking this stance its commitment would contribute to a more conducive atmosphere for other developing countries as well as further commitments from the industrialized world (PCGG 2010).

Nevertheless, concerns about the stringency and appropriateness of this reduction goal were immediately voiced, particularly by the business community. Many businesses regarded the 30 per cent reduction goal as an overly ambitious target for South Korea. As mentioned, Korea's GHG emission had almost doubled between 1990 and 2005, and its economy was still heavily dependent on energy intensive industries, such as steel and petrochemicals. Despite the rhetoric of green growth and a slight deceleration of GHG emissions growth in the 2000s, the business community worried that a drastic curbing of GHG emissions would still be a heavy burden for the Korean economy. Yet, in spite of such criticisms, the 30 per cent mitigation goal had been based on the Korean government's firm commitment to an ambitious climate and energy agenda. The goals it had elaborated were reinforced by strong political support from the President's and Prime Minister's Offices. And, under Korea's strong presidential system, ministries and other public institutions had to follow the guideline set by the top executives.

The Development of Institutions for Green Growth

The green growth policies elaborated by the government were followed by the establishment of relevant institutions for overseeing their implementation. This process began with the creation of the Presidential Committee on Green Growth (PCGG) in 2009, a coordinating body under the direct control of the president that would manage the green growth strategy. The PCGG integrated the National Energy Committee (within the Ministry of Knowledge Economy), the National Commission on Sustainable Development (within the Ministry of Environment) and the Task Force on Climate Change (within the Prime Minister's Office). The rationale behind this move was that, by becoming a single entity, they could pursue the goal of low carbon green growth and GHG reductions in a much more systematic and concerted manner.

Under the Committee, three Councils were installed: the Green Growth and Industry Council, the Climate Change and Energy Council, and the Green Life and Sustainable Development Council. A Green Financial System Council was then added in the second year. In each ministry, a chief green officer, generally at the director-general level, was also designated as the official focal point for interacting with the Committee. The Committee was itself composed of approximately fifty members, including two co-chairpersons, one from within the government and one from the private sector. As of March 2012, the Committee had thirty-three non-governmental and thirteen governmental members (PCGG 2011).

Table 5.2 Korean sectoral GHG reduction target by 2020 (%)							
Industry	Transport	Power generation	Buildings	Agriculture	Waste	Public	National
18.2	26.7	34.3	26.9	5.2	12.3	25	30

Sources: Greenhouse Gas Inventory and Research Center database, www.gir.go.kr; Lee & Yu (2012).

Following its launch in February 2009, the PCGG worked to establish regulations related to the implementation of green growth through the formulation of the National Strategy for Green Growth and the Five-Year Green Growth Plan in July 2009, mentioned above. The Framework Act on Low Carbon, Green Growth, which provided the legal foundation for implementing the green growth strategy, was passed on 29 December 2009, and signed into law on 13 January 2010 (Government of the Republic of Korea 2010a, 2010b).[9] Finally, the pre-existing Comprehensive Plan on Combating Climate Change, the National Energy Plan, and the Sustainable Development Act were incorporated into the Framework Act on Low Carbon, Green Growth.

In addition to the PCGG, a number of other new institutions and schemes were also introduced after the government announced the country's target for the reduction of GHGs in 2008. In June 2010, for example, the Greenhouse Gas Inventory and Research Center (GIR) was established under the Ministry of Environment as a national GHG inventory hub and mitigation think-tank. Shortly after, the GIR announced sectoral national greenhouse gas reduction targets in July 2011. To meet the national objective of a 30 per cent reduction, each sector was assigned a specific reduction target of between 5.2 per cent and 34.3 per cent, relative to an established baseline (Lee & Yu 2012).[10] Table 5.2 shows the assignment of sectoral reduction targets established by the GIR.

On the basis of the Framework Act, the Korean government adopted two major GHG reduction schemes: the Energy Goal Management Scheme and the Carbon Cap and Trade Scheme. The Energy Goal Management Scheme replaced a pilot project of negotiated agreements on energy use that the government had launched in 2010.[11] The new scheme would require companies responsible for CO_2 emissions above 25,000 tonnes per annum to set individual mandatory emission reduction targets. Under the new scheme, companies in power generation, manufacturing, construction, waste management and transport have had to negotiate targets with the government, and would be subject to penalties if they failed to meet these (Jones & Yoo 2010). Four hundred and seventy-three sites – including industrial plants, power generation facilities and large buildings, which together account for around 61 per cent of the country's total GHG emissions – have been subject to this policy as of 28 March 2011, and the government plans to extend the coverage of this scheme gradually to entities with lower annual GHG emissions as well (Lee & Yu 2012).

Penalties for non-compliance can run up to 10 million won (approximately US$10,000), and emissions reductions that exceed the target cannot be credited for the next period. However, these penalties are actually quite low, and the absence of strong regulatory mechanisms has been regarded as a major weakness of the Energy Goal Management Scheme. And, despite these low penalties, the Scheme has still been strongly opposed by much of the business community in Korea.

Since 2005, the South Korean government has also been operating a carbon trading scheme, known as Korea Certified Emissions Reductions (KCERs), which has been open to firms that have reduced CO_2 emissions by more than 500 tonnes a year through various energy efficiency measures and through investments in renewable energy. At the time of writing, the Emission Trading Scheme Act – a major expansion of this initiative – is waiting for a congressional endorsement in order to be phased in by 2015. In practice, however, the government has purchased most KCERs so far in order to promote and compensate for this GHG reduction scheme. Active carbon trading in the private market has not been firmly established yet. The introduction of a comprehensive carbon market and trading scheme has also been delayed due to internal objections from participating sectors (Lee & Yu 2012). In sum, then, these two GHG reduction schemes have made limited progress so far and their full implementation will require more time and the establishment of concrete penalties and incentives for ensuring compliance and participation.

Explaining South Korea's Climate Change Governance

As the preceding sections of this chapter have shown, South Korea's system of climate governance has evolved considerably during the past two decades. Progress has been made in establishing institutions designed to oversee and achieve the government's policy objectives. The overarching concept of green growth, introduced in 2008, provided a firm basis for the pursuit of a climate change agenda that is compatible with other policy priorities, such as economic growth and continued improvements in quality of life. This evolution can be understood as an ongoing response to various external and internal challenges. South Korea's policies have been, first, a product of external pressures arising from the global climate change regime, especially from other OECD states which insist that Korea should participate in global mitigation efforts. Second, these policies have been part of the political leadership's response to a number of domestic interests and strategic priorities, as well as its own ideas about the best developmental path for the country in the future. Both are discussed in turn in the rest of this section.

Coping with the Global Climate Change Regime

The initiation of a system of climate change governance in South Korea grew, first of all, in reaction to developments in the global climate change regime. The establishment of the Ministerial Committee in 1992, for example, was a direct response to the outcomes of the Rio Summit in 1992. Much of the subsequent institutional evolution, from the enactment of the Kyoto Protocol until the introduction of the green growth policy concept in 2008, also occurred alongside important changes at the international level – the Kyoto Protocol, the establishment of the CDM, and so on. The climate change policies that appeared in response to these developments during this period were, however, modest in scope and passive in nature. South Korea was, of course, not listed in Annex I of the UNFCCC and was not required to make mandatory GHG reductions. But South Korea was not altogether free from international pressure to participate in the climate change regime in subsequent years. Together with the US and Mexico, South Korea was one of the few OECD countries that remained outside of the Kyoto Protocol. Further, as a major GHG emitter, South Korea's participation was crucial to the success of global mitigation efforts. Other Annex I countries, therefore, insisted that Korea join the Kyoto Protocol for the second commitment period, running from 2013 onwards.

The domestic shift that took place in Korea came about partially due to the realization that South Korea could no longer avoid this pressure from Annex I states to become a more responsible participant in the global climate change regime. Taking a more proactive approach was a better way of positioning the country in the ongoing negotiations. And by occupying a distinct position balanced between those of developed and developing countries, rather than taking sides as part of one or the other grouping, Korea could assume a 'bridging role'. It could offer a green growth model while actively participating in technology transfer and the provision of environment-related official development assistance (ODA). By developing a green growth strategy, it could provide a model for developing countries to combine economic growth, GHG reductions and other environmental concerns effectively, which could promote greater cooperation in the global negotiations (Yun et al. 2011). This would allow Korea to take on a leadership role, which would increase its reputation on the issue of climate change. But it would also help to deflect pressure for Korea to adopt the same kinds of commitments as its OECD peers. Korea argued that flexible and voluntary mechanisms, such as unilateral CDM projects, a voluntary CO_2 reduction target and a range of dynamic unilateral schemes, would better reflect its own circumstances as an export driven economy.

Since the launch of its green growth strategy, therefore, Korea has become much more active in high level discussions on global climate change governance, seeking to project its vision of green growth as a 'middle way' on the issue of climate change. In the UNCCC negotiations, for example, South Korea proposed the NAMA Registry in September 2009 at the UN Climate Change Summit, which was subsequently embraced in Durban in December 2012. The potential for shifting developed and developing economies towards a green growth strategy was also emphasized at Group of 8/Group of 20 (G8/G20) meetings in Japan (Toyama) and in Italy (L'Aquila) in 2008 and 2009, for instance. Korea has, similarly, sought to increase international awareness of the green growth concept by establishing the Global Green Growth Institute (GGGI) in June 2010. GGGI would aim to systematize theories of green growth and disseminate green growth models around the world (for more on this, see chapter 11 on Ethiopia by Held, Roger and Nag in this volume, for example). South Korea also signed a Green Growth Partnership with Denmark during a bilateral summit in March 2010. And, finally, the government has supported green growth in developing countries through the East Asia Climate Partnership (EACP). By doing so, the South Korean government has tried to enhance its international image by positioning itself as an 'early mover' in the transition towards a green economy and as a 'mediator' between developing and developed nations in the area of climate change and sustainable development.

Building Domestic Momentum for Climate Change Governance

Nevertheless, the recent developments in Korea have not simply been a function of international pressures and opportunities; they have also been a product of Korea's political leadership's response to key domestic interests and strategic priorities, as well as its own ideas about the best approach to development in the future. Indeed, Korea's political leadership has proven to be the most important variable influencing the evolution of climate change governance in South Korea. It has been motivated by multiple factors that reflect the specific policy context within which Korea found itself in the late 2000s. Particularly after 2007–8, there was an urgent need to deal with economic slowdown with a new kind of economic stimulus that would put Korea on a surer economic footing. Energy crises – and the security of Korea's energy supply, which is heavily reliant on fossil fuels and almost entirely reliant on imported fuel sources – had also been a major worry since the mid-2000s because of the growing volatility of the global energy market and regional security concerns. Based on these considerations, as well as those related to the international regime (discussed above), the green growth strategy was devised as a flagship policy initiative and rapidly grew in scope. Indeed, it absorbed a number of related policy agenda items — environment, river management, energy, construction, etc. The president and policy executives also quickly found a number of vested interests who supported the green growth initiative and began to allocate more resources to this multi-purpose policy package. The green growth strategy contained a number of 'no-regret policies' such as clean energy, new lifestyle initiatives, and measures related to emissions mitigation. In a sense, then, the government's green growth policy was an interesting *mélange* of political will, long-term political interests and short-term responses to a number of urgent issues.

Political consensus on green growth, however, has not always been harmonious. Most opposition parties criticized the unilateral approach of the government. They claimed, for instance, that the overestimated budget and attention placed on the Four Rivers Restoration Project, which occupied a big portion of the green growth strategy, had distorted the green growth initiative and were poorly justified. But these opposition parties did not provide a clear alternative to the existing climate change and green growth policies, which resonated quite widely in Korean society. Furthermore, most local governments, regardless of political orientation, welcomed the green growth budget as it would increase fiscal stimulus in the middle of the economic slow-down. Climate change governance, therefore, was based on a relatively stable political equilibrium between the strong policy drives of the Presidential Office and lukewarm political opposition.

The lack of consensus is also evident in the reaction of nongovernmental organizations (NGOs) and various businesses to the government's green growth agenda. NGO activities related to climate change have increased in recent years, and their influence on policy-making has grown over time. Environmental NGOs used to focus on energy conservation, opposing nuclear power generation, and renewable energies; yet climate change issues quickly became a major focus based on their earlier efforts. For example, the Centre for Energy Alternative and the Korean NGO community's Energy Network picked up climate change issues as their main activities. Big environmental NGOs, such as the Korea Foundation for Environment Movement and Green Korea United, established climate change units in their organizations as well. The Green Start Movement, a national campaign, was also launched in October 2008 to reduce GHGs, and has been supported by the Ministry of Environment. Utilizing Local Agenda 21, this movement encompasses 206 nation-wide networks and around 5,000 participating agencies from the public, business and civil sectors.

NGOs have been particularly active in educating the public about the government's approach to climate change through various campaigns, presentations and hearings. For the most part, therefore, they have welcomed and supported the government's approach. However, many of the same NGOs have also occasionally had disagreements with the government led green growth strategy as well. Some have argued, in particular, that the central government did not listen to the voice of civil society in the elaboration of its green growth policies. Others have been sceptical about the effectiveness of the Four Rivers Restoration Project, or they have advocated a more 'preservation oriented' green growth policy. Furthermore, many NGOs have been critical of the heavy emphasis on nuclear energy as a strategy for the mitigation of GHGs. But, in spite of their increased influence and visibility, South Korea's environmental NGOs have faced a few internal problems that have dulled the effects of these critiques. In particular, they have often lacked the large budgets needed for effective political campaigning, adequate organizational abilities have sometimes been missing, and they have frequently relied on the government's support for their activities.

South Korea's invigorated climate change policy has grown to become a crucial issue in various business sectors as well. The low carbon green growth strategy in South Korea, of course, involves a major industrial policy dimension with a strong focus on the development of clean technology industries, job creation and new business opportunities. Such policies have increased business opportunities, and are relatively widely supported as such. But the government's policies have also had negative implications for some businesses, primarily as a result of the greater costs stemming from compulsory reduction targets. Further, even though the business sector recognized the principle of low carbon green growth, many businesses have claimed that a rapid implementation of GHG mitigation targets as well as the Korean emissions trading scheme would entail negative impacts which would compound the already difficult economic circumstances that have prevailed as a result of the global financial crisis. The four major business associations in Korea – the Korean Chamber of Commerce and Industry (KCCI), the Korean International Trade Association (KITA), the Korean Federation of Small and Medium Business (KBIZ) and the Korea Employers Federation (KEF) – have, for example, submitted a joint proposal to the government that expressed concerns about the government's proposed emissions trading scheme. And, while a few large companies have been optimistic about the government's new low carbon and clean energy strategies, many small- and medium-sized enterprises, particularly in the manufacturing sector, are sceptical about the benefits of green growth.

The shift towards proactive climate change governance in Korea has nevertheless produced an ideational transition, which has helped to blunt these criticisms. The idea of green growth has quickly become a 'sacrosanct' political doctrine, and low carbon schemes as well as the promotion of clean energy have become widely accepted as 'appropriate' policymaking or 'best' practice in the government, business community and civil society. The concept's ability to tap into economic interests as well as its affinity with many existing institutions – namely strong industrial policies – has proven instrumental in this respect. It also builds upon the considerable public concern about climate change that has grown since the early 1990s. Over the years, climate change has attracted increasing attention from civil society and the wider public, and therefore the South Korean government's green growth initiative helped to mobilize widespread support across Korean society for more ambitious policymaking. All of this has contributed to the subsequent reinforcement of government policies.

Conclusion

South Korea's efforts to govern climate change have evolved in response to two factors. On the one hand, they have been part of an effort to cope with pressures emanating from the global climate change regime and to take domestic actions that would put the country in a strategic position balanced between developed and developing country coalitions. On the other hand, they have increasingly been a product of homegrown domestic interests and the ideas promoted by the country's political leadership. Whereas the country's system of domestic climate governance initially evolved solely in response to developments in the international regime, the country has now become much more proactive as a result. The key shift took place after the elaboration of the green growth strategy in 2008. The strategy elaborated by the government put forward a new vision for development in the country; he identified measures for reducing both GHG emissions and dependence on fossil fuels, while at the same time connecting these goals with the task of creating new sources of economic growth (PCGG 2010).

South Korea's climate change governance, however, still confronts a number of challenges that could derail the progress that has been made so far. First of all, the ongoing UNFCCC negotiations suffer from considerable uncertainties, and the lack of any global framework for governing emissions reductions could have negative effects upon the trajectory of South Korea's climate change policymaking. In recent years, the cleavages both within and between groups of developed and developing countries have become all too apparent, and these fractures could undermine efforts to establish international policies on mitigation and adaptation. Ongoing failure in the international negotiations could also then undermine domestic support in Korea, shattering the public's growing consensus on the idea of green growth.

Second, in view of its energy intensive and export oriented industrial sectors, the structure of South Korea's economy remains unfavourable in many respects. There are no 'easy' mitigation measures in South Korea, and the costs of transitioning to a low carbon economy could be much higher than expected. Moreover, these costs are not likely be shared equally by all stakeholders. Big businesses and affluent classes could get on a smooth track to a low carbon society, since they are likely to be the primary beneficiaries of green growth industrial and renewable energy policies. But small- and medium-sized companies as well as less affluent parts of the population could be exposed to tougher burdens in relation to the reduction of GHG emissions (Lee 2010a). If the cost of mitigating GHG emissions begins to be felt unequally among different emitters, the legitimacy of 'green growth' could be seriously undermined.

Finally, the 2011 Fukushima nuclear accident has added another question to the climate change debate, since Korea's growth strategy currently emphasizes the development of nuclear energy as a low carbon source of energy. While replacing traditional fossil fuels domestically, the export of nuclear technology for global use was also expected to be a major means of stimulating South Korea's economic growth.[12] However, as a result of global scepticism about the safety of nuclear technologies, this agenda has become one of the most controversial dimensions of South Korea's green growth strategy. Although the South Korean government remains strongly committed to pro-nuclear strategies of green growth, the speed and modes of implementation could be negatively affected by global developments in this area.

In sum, climate change governance cannot simply be regarded as solely an environmental issue. Its implications extend to key policy areas, including energy, industry, agriculture, transport and international relations, among others. Given the multi-layered nature of the problem, South Korea's approach to climate governance must be equally multi-faceted, and it still needs to be carefully consolidated by bringing a broader range of stakeholders into the policymaking process in forthcoming years. Incorporating grassroots efforts, particularly within civil society and the private sector, will be an important task in this process. The consensus on the low carbon green growth principle seems irrevocable at this stage, yet the specific modalities of its implementation during the next administration could be modified with a different focus and institutional scheme.

Notes

1 Eighty-three per cent of the increase in GHGs had occurred by 2000.

2 Its organization consisted of three levels of regular meetings, five task forces and a pool of experts. Ministerial level meetings, chaired by the prime minister, and meetings at a vice-ministerial level, chaired by the deputy minister of government policy coordination, were held frequently when needed; a working session for director-generals was also held once a month, chaired by the economic policy coordinator of the Office for Government Policy Coordination. The five task forces were set up for each major field in the negotiations: energy, industry, environment, agriculture and forestry. Finally, these meetings were supported by a pool of experts from government-affiliated institutes and academia (Office for Government Policy Coordination 1998).

3 The Committee consisted of a vice-ministerial level working group, chaired by the deputy minister of government policy coordination, a coordination working group of director-generals chaired by the economic policy coordinator of the Office for Government Policy Coordination, five task forces for each major field, and five research teams staffed with relevant specialists.

4 The title of the Plan was changed slightly, from 'Comprehensive Plan on Climate Change Convention' to 'Comprehensive Plan on Combating Climate Change'.

5 The term 'green growth' was first promoted by the United Nations Economic and Social Commission for Asia and the Pacific (UN ESCAP) in order to

introduce a new development paradigm for fast developing Asian countries. Some countries adopted a similar concept called 'eco-modernization' or, the more widely used term, 'sustainable development'. However, 'green growth' in South Korea contains THE stronger concept that economic growth will not be compromised by the goal of environmental protection – a concept that is much better embraced in countries with strong development needs.

6 On the basis of a study of its mitigation potential, the government considered three mitigation scenario options of 21, 27 and 30 per cent reductions from BAU in August 2009. The government itself conducted extensive consultations involving the Presidential Committee on Green Growth (PCGG), other relevant government bodies, industries, the financial sector and other private sector stakeholders. National Assembly hearings and over eighty different public opinion surveys were conducted to help determine the target that should be set (PCGG 2011, p. 32).

7 The 2020 targets for Japan, the United States and the EU still called for larger emission reductions of approximately 30 per cent, 17 per cent and 13 per cent respectively, relative to the 2005 level.

8 For example, Mexico also pledged to reduce emissions by up to 30 per cent relative to its BAU baseline by 2020. However, the Mexican reduction target was based on the condition of adequate financial and technology transfer mechanisms from developed countries.

9 The main purpose behind the enactment of the Framework Act on Low Carbon, Green Growth was to (1) implement measures to address climate change and energy issues effectively and promote sustainable development, (2) build the implementation system for green growth to implement low carbon green growth strategies in an efficient and systematic matter, and (3) devise a variety of institutional systems to promote low carbon green growth in the region (Jung & Ahn 2010, p. 6).

10 The industrial sector accounts for 31 per cent of the total GHG emissions of Korea. If emissions from generation are distributed to the end use sector, its share becomes larger (Lee & Yu 2012, pp. 11–12).

11 The pilot project included thirty-eight firms, covering 41 per cent of total energy consumption in the industrial sector. The negotiations resulted in agreements to reduce energy use by 3.7 per cent (relative to the average of 2007–9) between 2010 and 2012.

12 South Korea signed its first export agreement for nuclear power plants with the United Arab Emirates in 2010.

References

De Serres, A., F. Murtin & G. Nicoletti (2010). *A Framework for Assessing Green Growth Policies*. OECD Economics Department Working Papers, No. 774. Paris: OECD.

GIR (2011). *Roadmap for Realization of 2020 Low Carbon, Green Society*. Available at: http://www.mltm.go.kr/portal/common/download/DownloadMltm2.jsp?File Path=/upload/portal/DextUpload/201107/20110712_093924_677.hwp&FileNa me=110712(%C8%AD_10%BD%C3%C0%CC%C8%C4)_2020%B3%E2_%C0%FA% C5%BA%BC%D2_%B3%EC%BB%F6%BB%E7%C8%B8_%B1%B8%C7%F6%C0%BB _%C0%A7%C7%D1_%B7%CE%B5%E5%B8%CA_%C8%AE%C1%A4(%BA%CE%C3 %B3%C7%D5%B5%BF).hwp. [in Korean]

Government of the Republic of Korea (2003). *Second National Communication of the Republic of Korea under the United Nations Framework Convention on Climate Change*. Available at: http://unfccc.int/resource/docs/natc/kornc02.pdf.

Government of the Republic of Korea (2010a). *Enforcement Decree of the Framework Act on Low Carbon, Green Growth*. Available at: www.moleg.go.kr/FileDownload. mo?flSeq=38102.

Government of the Republic of Korea (2010b). *Framework Act on Low Carbon, Green Growth*. Available at: http://www.uncsd2012.org/content/documents/South% 20Korea%20Framework%20Act%20on%20Low%20Carbon%20Green%20Grow th%202010.pdf.

Han, W. J. (2005). *Climate Change Impact Assessment and Development of Adaptation Strategies in Korea (I)*. Seoul: Korea Environment Institute. [in Korean]

Han, W. J. (2006). *Climate Change Impact Assessment and Development of Adaptation Strategies in Korea (II)*. Seoul: Korea Environment Institute. [in Korean]

IGES (2008). *Climate Change Policies in the Asia-Pacific: Re-Uniting Climate Change and Sustainable Development*. IGES White Paper. Hayama: Institute for Global Environmental Strategies.

Jones, R. S. & B. Yoo (2011). *Korea's Green Growth Strategy: Mitigating Climate Change and Developing New Growth Engines*. OECD Economics Department Working Papers, No. 798. Paris: OECD.

Jung, T. Y. & J. E. Ahn (2010). *Domestic Policies for Climate Change: Republic of Korea*. Paper presented at the Asia Climate Change Policy Forum, Australian National University, 26–7 October, Canberra.

Lee, J. (2010a). Coping with climate change: a Korean perspective. In A. Marquina (ed.) *Global Warming and Climate Change: Prospects and Policies in Asia and Europe*. London: Palgrave Macmillan.

Lee, J. (2010b). Energy conservation in South Korea. In E. Thomson, Y. Chang & J. Lee (eds.) *Energy Conservation in East Asia: Towards Greater Energy Security*. Singapore: World Scientific.

Lee, J. & Yu, J. (2012). The economic opportunities and constraints of green growth: the case of South Korea. *Asie. Visions* 50.

Office for Government Policy Coordination (1998). *First Comprehensive Action Plan for Climate Change Convention*. Available at: http://contents.archives.go.kr/next/ content/listSubjectDescription.do?id=006577.

PCGG (2008). *Green Growth: A New Path for Korea*. Seoul: PCGG. Available at: http:// www.google.ca/url?sa=t&rct=j&q=green%20growth%3A%20a%20new%20 path%20for%20korea&source=web&cd=1&cad=rja&ved=0CC4QFjAA&url=ht tp%3A%2F%2Fwww.mofat.go.kr%2Fwebmodule%2Fcommon%2Fdownload. jsp%3Fboardid%3D8120%26tablename%3DTYPE_ENGLISH%26seqno%3D02 0fa9010046fc2fa403903c%26fileseq%3D006fa2f8105a031041032fbb&ei=p8f 0UJPbFsvMigKhioCAAg&usg=AFQjCNFbSMHdLDrNYgrmV-HruRGM5Jqapw&- bvm=bv.41018144,d.cGE.

PCGG (2009). *Road to Our Future: Green Growth, National Strategy and the Five-Year Plan (2009–2013)*. Available at: http://www.koreanconsulate.on.ca/en/down- load.php?id=395&from=board.

PCGG (2010). *2008–2009 Progress Report*. Available at: http://www.greengrowth. go.kr/?p=42561.

PCGG (2011). *Growth in Motion: Sharing Korea's Experience*. Available at: http:// www.gggi.org/sites/www.gggi.org/files/research/GreenGrowthInMotion.pdf.

PMO (2007). *The Fourth Comprehensive Plan on Combating Climate Change*. Available at: http://contents.archives.go.kr/next/content/listSubjectDescription.do?id =006577.

STI Policy Review (2010). In focus: Korean national strategy and five year plan (2009–2013) for green growth. *STI Policy Review* 1(1).

UNEP (2010). *Overview of the Republic of Korea's National Strategy for Green Growth.* Available at: http://www.unep.org/PDF/PressReleases/201004_unep_national_ strategy.pdf.

Yoo, S. J. (2008). *Climate Change Policies in Korea.* Available at: http://www.esri. go.jp/jp/workshop/080225/02_country1_Korea.pdf.

Yun, S., M. Cho & D. von Hippel (2011). The current status of green growth in Korea: energy and urban security. *Asia-Pacific Journal* 9(4).

PART II

AMERICAS

6

Discounting the Future: The Politics of Climate Change in Argentina

Matías Franchini and Eduardo Viola

ARGENTINA is the second largest economy in South America. It is the third most populous country in the region (41 million in 2010) and the second largest in terms of territory (2.8 million km²). It is also one of the largest emitters of greenhouse gases (GHGs) among South American states, behind only Brazil. In 2011 the country was responsible for producing approximately 450 million tonnes of carbon dioxide equivalent (CO_2e), or roughly 1 per cent of the global total.[1] Per person, almost 11 tonnes of CO_2e were emitted. As this suggests, the carbon intensity of Argentina's economy is very high. Nearly 1.03 tonnes of CO_2e were produced per US$1000 of gross domestic product (GDP) measured in exchange rate terms; it is 0.63 tonnes if measured in purchasing power parity (PPP) terms. The country is, therefore, a fairly large contributor to global GHG concentrations by world standards. It is not in the same league as countries like China, Brazil or the United States. But, on average, it produces more GHGs per capita than France, Italy or Spain. In absolute terms, it annually produces more GHGs than the Netherlands and more than twice as much as Belgium. Further, in contrast with these states, its emissions are expected to rise considerably as the country's economy grows.

At the same time, the current and expected consequences of climate change for Argentina's natural and human environment are wide in scope and profound in intensity. Climate variability – especially variations in inter-annual rainfall patterns – has the potential to alter the socio-economic dynamics in the country significantly, especially in agricultural production and exports. It may also damage infrastructure and threaten the health and security of a large share of the population (Secretary of the Environment and Sustainable Development of Argentina 2007). Another element that enhances Argentina's vulnerability is the fact that several major cities are located close to the shorelines of rivers, a fact which is expected to increase the risks of severe flooding. The lack of adaptive capacity

113

is itself yet another relevant source of vulnerability, since resources required for adapting to climate change are expected to compete with those earmarked for other developmental needs.

In this chapter, we analyse Argentina's efforts both to reduce emissions and to adapt to climate change. We have two main aims. First, we examine Argentina's climate policies since the early 1990s or so. We do so by conducting a comprehensive overview of the stance it has taken in the international negotiations under the United Nations Framework Convention on Climate Change (UNFCCC), and of the governance structures, policies and programmes that it has established for governing climate change domestically. From this analysis, we conclude that Argentina is a climate laggard at present, both internationally and domestically. It is a society that, despite growing evidence of a global climate crisis, has not been able to articulate a significant response to the process, in terms of either mitigation or adaptation. Paradoxically, Argentina seemed to have taken on a strong leadership role within the UNFCCC negotiations around 1998–9, when the government announced a voluntary commitment to reduce the growth of GHGs between 2008 and 2012. However, this leadership was only superficial and brief. The so-called 'Argentinian Proposal' was quickly abandoned by Argentine authorities after the Fourth Conference of the Parties (COP4), which took place in Buenos Aires. The proposal itself was, we argue, driven by opportunistic behaviour rather than more profound economic and social forces. As we explain further below, even when the national economy in the 1990s was going through a modernization process that could have made a more proactive approach to climate change a feasible objective, the main driver of the voluntary commitment was the predisposition of the Carlos Menem administration (1989–99) to align its position with US foreign policy aims.

The second objective of this chapter is to explain why Argentina remained a climate laggard. This is an especially interesting task because, at first glance, Argentina appears to have many characteristics that might lead us to expect it to have been more ambitious than it has been: an upper middle income country with a high level of human development, a well educated population, high vulnerability, and good opportunities for investing in renewable energy. It even, as just noted, appeared to take a more forward looking position at certain points in the global negotiations. Nevertheless, it has systematically failed to articulate an effective response. We argue that this is due to the very low priority given to climate issues within Argentine society; the existence of very high discount rates in politics, amplified by a number of factors which can together be conceptualized as a 'heritage of decadence'; growing nationalist and isolationist tendencies; and persistent factious behaviour among political forces. To achieve these objectives, the chapter is divided into three sections and a conclusion. In the first section we analyse Argentina's emissions profile: its GHG production, the emissions profiles of major sectors and the carbon intensity of GDP. Next, we characterize Argentina as a climate laggard, after considering its record on climate politics and policies since the early 1990s. In the third section we present the key domestic variables underpinning its climate laggardness. We conclude by highlighting the particular challenges Argentina faces in responding effectively to climate change, which demands a long-term approach to public policymaking.

Argentina's Emissions Profile

Three sources of data are used in this section to analyse Argentina's evolving emissions profile between 1990 and 2011. For the period 1990–2000, the main source is Argentina's second national communication to the UNFCCC (Secretary of the Environment and Sustainable Development of Argentina 2007); for the period 2000–5, the main source is Fundación Bariloche's 2008 report;[2] and finally, for the post-2005 period, we have used our own estimates based on the trajectories of the main GHG-producing sectors.

Argentina's emissions expanded by almost 40 per cent between 1990 and 2005 at an annual average rate of almost 2.7 per cent. Since 2000, however, the rate has almost doubled relative to the rate that prevailed throughout the previous decade, placing the level of emissions in 2005 at 25 per cent above the year 2000 levels. Per capita emissions, likewise, reached almost 8 tonnes of CO_2e in 2005, representing a 20 per cent increase above 1990 levels and an annual growth rate of 1.3 per cent. It is again worth noting the path of the index between 2000 and 2005: per capita emissions grew by 25 per cent throughout the whole period and 5 per cent annually. Table 6.1 shows the values for five key years in both absolute and per capita terms.

The major change that took place between the pre- and post-2000 periods is closely connected to a shift in the carbon intensity of Argentina's economy. The carbon intensity of Argentine GDP was 0.84 tonnes of CO_2e per US$1,000 in 2000 and 0.95 in 2005, roughly 12 per cent above 2000 levels (see table 6.2). This was a dramatic departure from past trends. Indeed, by 2000 there had actually been a reduction in carbon intensity of approximately 15 per cent relative

Table 6.1 Total and per capita emissions in Argentina, 1990–2011

Year	1990	1997	2000	2005	2011
Total emissions (million tonnes of CO_2e, including LULUCF)	216.3	242.0	238.7	298.0	450
Per capita emissions (tonnes of CO_2e/population)	6.6	6.9	6.3	7.9	11

CO_2e = carbon dioxide equivalent. LULUCF = land use, land use change and forestry.

Sources: Fundación Bariloche (2008); authors' estimates based on Fundación Bariloche data.

Table 6.2 Carbon intensity of GDP in Argentina, 1990–2011 (tonnes CO$_2$e per US$1,000).

Year	1990	1997	2000	2005	2011
Carbon intensity of GDP (PPP)	1.23	0.75	0.70	0.71	0.63
Carbon intensity of GDP (exchange rate)	1.18	0.85	0.84	0.95	1.03

CO$_2$e = carbon dioxide equivalent. GDP = gross domestic product. PPP = purchasing power parity.

Sources: Fundación Bariloche (2008); authors' estimates based on Fundación Bariloche data.

to 1990 levels. During the 1990s, therefore, carbon intensity had been falling, but the trend reversed in the years after 2000. In spite of that expansion, the country's carbon intensity did not reach 1990 levels. But if we use a PPP measure of GDP, the trajectory is quite different: 1.23 tonnes in 1990, 0.70 in 2000, 0.71 in 2005 and 0.63 in 2011. This difference is primarily due to the fact that until 2001 Argentina maintained a rigid parity between the dollar and the peso, and therefore we should not interpret the absolute number as an indication that Argentina's carbon intensity trajectory had in fact stabilized.

Looking at the emissions produced by each sector (table 6.3), the most notable characteristic of Argentina's profile is the large weight of the energy and agricultural sectors, which together were responsible for over 90 per cent of the country's emissions between 1990 and 2005. In the case of the energy sector, its share grew from 1990 until 2000 to comprise almost 60 per cent of all emissions. They peaked in 2000, and then stabilized at around a 50 per cent share in subsequent years. In contrast, the agricultural sector's share decreased throughout the period 1990–2005, from 46 to 42 per cent. The waste and industry sectors, by contrast, each increased their shares in total emissions between 1990 and 2005. However, they maintained relatively low shares overall, amounting only to a combined 13 per cent share of total emissions in 2005. The land use, land use change and forestry

Table 6.3 Emissions by sector in Argentina 1990–2005 (percentage of total, including LULUCF emissions)

	1990	1997	2000	2005
Energy	48	54	59	50
Industry	4	4	5	6
Agriculture	46	44	50	42
LULUCF	−2	−8	−20	−5
Waste	4	6	6	7

LULUCF = land use, land use change and forestry.

Source: Fundación Bariloche (2008).

(LULUCF) sector displayed a dramatic increasing capacity for CO_2 absorption between 1990 and 2000, but then declined between 2000 and 2005 due to an extreme expansion of agricultural production in previously abandoned lands and government incentives for reforestation and afforestation.

Argentina Post-2005

In order to examine Argentina's emissions trajectory in the post-2005 period we use updated data on the main emissions producing sectors from 2005 onwards. In the energy sector, for example, carbon intensity continued to rise: electricity produced by thermoelectric power plants grew from 47 to 57 per cent between 2003 and 2010, while nuclear and hydroelectric sources contributed less to total energy generation, with shares falling from 9 to 6 per cent and 43 to 35 per cent respectively. Interestingly, in contrast with trends throughout the world during this period, natural gas also lost ground relative to other 'dirtier' fossil fuels, such as gas and diesel oil, in total electricity generation. In 2003, natural gas accounted for 98 per cent of all fossil fuels used in electricity generation, and in 2010, its share fell to 70 per cent (IAE 2011). These trends have primarily been the result of the low energy prices made possible by federal policies in Argentina which have encouraged wasteful patterns of consumption and discouraged investments and supply expansion. Energy demand grew by 44 per cent between 2003 and 2010, but energy supply expanded by only 22 per cent (IAE 2011). Between 2003 and 2010, furthermore, oil and natural gas production fell by 8 and 18 per cent respectively, a unique occurrence in Latin America. As a result, fossil fuel imports rose from US$550 million in 2003 to US$4.4 billion in 2010. Discoveries in 2011 and 2012 of vast shale gas reserves in the country – close to 22 trillion cubic meters (IEA 2011) – have opened a window of opportunity to reverse this situation, making a reduction in both carbon intensity and energy shortages possible. However, the great financial resources needed to explore these reserves, combined with the poor investment environment created by the government's energy policies, make this scenario highly improbable.

Summary: Argentina as GHG Emitter

If 1990 is regarded as the base year, Argentina's emissions have grown intensively in both absolute and per capita terms. But the trend is even worse if the post-2000 period is compared with the 1990–2000 period: the rate of emissions growth has accelerated since 2000, doubling the pace of the preceding decade. The carbon intensity of Argentina's economy – which had been falling prior to 2000 – increased as well. These trends urgently need to be reversed if Argentina's per capita emissions are to be reduced to the levels recommended by the Intergovernmental Panel on Climate Change (IPCC 2007). The best

GHG reduction possibilities for Argentina are in the energy sector, which, as noted, is the primary source of emissions. Improving energy efficiency and the development of clean alternative energy sources are the most affordable strategies. The potential for solar, wind and hydroelectric energy is especially significant (De la Torre et al. 2009). The transport subsector also offers some potential, since it is heavily road based and inefficient at present. Emissions reductions may be possible in the LULUCF (carbon capture in soils and vegetation) and waste management sectors, too. However, as we show below, Argentina has so far proven unwilling or unable to create the kinds of policies that might allow it to take advantage of these opportunities.

Argentina as a Laggard on Climate Change: Politics and Policies

In this section we focus on the political dimension of climate change in Argentina in order to assess whether the country is acting as a leader or a laggard in the global governance of climate change. We do so by covering both domestic and foreign climate policies since the early 1990s: the legal framework, governance structures, policies and programmes, and the stance taken by Argentina in the international negotiations under the UNFCCC. From this analysis, we conclude that the country has remained as a climate laggard over the considered period, given the lack of ambition underlying the climate policies we review.

There is, however, a paradox we would like to discuss before entering this section. At COP4, in 1998, Argentina submitted an innovative and controversial proposal in relation to climate change mitigation, apparently moving away from its previous position as well as that taken by most of the developing world. President Carlos Menem announced that his administration was ready to adopt a voluntary emissions reduction target for the period 2008–12 that would lower Argentina's emissions trajectory relative to a benchmark level. The Argentine government argued that the proposal was designed to facilitate discussions with the industrialized world regarding the Kyoto Protocol. The stance was broadly aligned with the position of the US administration, which also managed to convince South Korea of the benefits of the proposal. But it was heavily opposed by the Group of 77 (G77) and China.

Regarding Argentina's proposal, a series of considerations are in order. First, it was indeed an ambitious proposal that would have involved a more profound commitment by developing states in terms of emission reductions. It presaged, by nearly ten years, the Nationally Appropriate Mitigation Actions (NAMAs) which would eventually become an important component of the post-Bali negotiations, that is, after 2007. Second, it implied a major break between Argentina and its traditional allies in the G77/China coalition and Mercosur. The contradiction was especially apparent with Brazil, which had taken a very conservative position in the negotiations at the time due to its serious concerns about the sovereignty of the Amazon region (Viola & Franchini 2012). Third, in the domestic public sphere, the proposal focused the attention and efforts of local political authorities as never before: public speeches regarding climate change were made, a group of specialists was called upon to undertake a viability study, and a public servant corps was summoned to establish the emissions target. Fourth, and finally, the decision to make the proposal was made at the highest levels of the federal government, without the participation of other political or societal actors, and without any open debate about its potential ramifications.

In the end, however, the 'Argentinian Proposal' proved to be nothing more than an anomaly in its climate change policy. The proposed target of reducing Argentina's emissions trajectory from 2 to 10 per cent relative to the 2008–12 business-as-usual (BAU) scenario was presented at COP5 in Bonn, but it was never implemented. Why was the proposal made in the first place? The explanation can be traced to Argentina's international stance during the Menem administration, namely to align automatically with US interests. Hence, the announcement of voluntary targets had nothing to do with growing climate awareness. It was primarily guided by an opportunistic political calculus. The proposal was not based on domestic factors, though the 1990s macroeconomic trend in Argentina was consistent with a carbon intensity reduction, as noted above. Menem's economic reforms prioritized foreign investments and energy efficiency, and by doing so they triggered a process of modernization that reduced the rhythm of GHG production. Political and economic elites were also more open to greater involvement at the international level at the time. But domestic political factors – electoral incentives, business interests and so on – were not behind the proposal. Further, over the subsequent decade, Argentina would return to a nationalistic and mercantilist conception of economic development which would discourage foreign investment and economic efficiency. As a result, the carbon intensity of Argentina's economy grew, and the government made no effort to prevent or slow this trend, as we demonstrate in the following section.

Climate Change in the Domestic Realm

In Argentina, the main legal framework for addressing climate change is limited to the UNFCCC and Kyoto Protocol (KP); some executive orders establishing an Argentine Carbon Fund or dealing with some of the KP flexibility mechanisms; and, finally, a series of resolutions from the secretary of the environment and the Ministry of Sustainable Development. But no significant national legislation focused on establishing the minimal institutional premises for dealing with climate change has been enacted thus far. The government has created some specific bureaucratic structures for managing climate change. These include the Directorship of Climate Change and the Argentine Office for the Clean Development Mechanism (CDM). However, they lack any real political power and are very peripheral within the state bureaucracy. Consequently, they have had little or no effect upon the design and implementation of any major policies related to climate change in the energy, environmental, industrial or agricultural sectors.

The specific climate policies that do exist in Argentina so far have never had a significant impact on the country's emissions trajectory. On the one hand, many of them have never actually been implemented. This has been the case, for example, with the 1999 emissions trajectory reduction proposal and the National Strategy on Climate Change created in 2009. The latter proposal, which attempts to create a national framework to stimulate a transition to a low carbon economy, has only produced a few documents with rather vague general guidelines and has not been considered at all by core decision-makers. On the other hand, many of the efforts so far undertaken have focused on research and impact assessment, with no impact on GHG emissions.

To get a clearer understanding of the current state of climate policies in Argentina, we present a brief report on the set of NAMAs that the government submitted to the UNFCCC under the Copenhagen Accord (Government of Argentina 2010). The individual measures in the country's NAMA proposal are listed in table 6.4. According to Argentine authorities, these measures are consistent with climate change mitigation, although their likely impact on GHG production is not quantified or demonstrated. This is, nevertheless, the closest thing to a climate mitigation commitment stemming from the government at present, and given the context of Argentine governance it should be considered only as a formal paper, with a remote probability of being implemented. We consider each of the measures in turn.

On the subject of energy efficiency (item 1), doubts regarding the actual outcomes of national programmes, like PIEEP, coexist with high federal subsidies to residential electricity and fossil fuel consumption in the area of transport. On the supply side (item 2), and according to the last national energy balances (Government of Argentina 2012), clean energy sources are becoming a smaller part of Argentina's energy matrix. Their share of total energy generation decreased from 9 per cent in 1990 to 7 per cent in 2008, while 'dirtier' fossil fuels are replacing natural gas in electricity production. The situation is somewhat better in the area of biofuels (item 3), since the country has become one of the major exporters of biodiesel, and because it has become mandatory for diesel and gasoline to contain at least 5 per cent biomass mixture since 2010. Nevertheless, there are also doubts about the sustainability of the future expansion of biofuels that this entails, especially due to the pressure that biodiesel production puts on the agricultural frontier.

Table 6.4 Argentine mitigation actions, 2009
1. Energy efficiency Executive order 140/07: creates the electricity and natural gas rational use programme, giving incentives for consumption reduction.
Law no. 26,473: bans imports of incandescent light bulbs.
Other programmes: Programa de incremento de la eficiencia energética y productiva de la PyME Argentina (energy efficiency programme for small and medium firms); Programa de calidad de artefactos energéticos (electric artefacts quality standards); Programa de ahorro y eficiencia energética en edificios públicos (energy efficiency in public buildings).
2. Renewable energy Law no. 26,190: grants benefits to renewable energy production.
Renewable energy programme in rural markets.
Law no. 26,123: promotes hydrogen as fuel and energy vector.
3. Biofuels National biofuels programme.
Law no. 26,093: establishes a 5 per cent minimum of bioethanol and biodiesel in fossil gasoline and diesel in 2010; awards fiscal benefits.
Law no. 26,344: promotes ethanol in sugar-cane productive chain.
4. Forest management Law no. 26,331: promotes sustainable use of native forests.
Law no. 26,342: grants incentives to forestry enterprises.
5. Urban waste management National plan for integral urban solid waste management: biogas capture and construction of waste disposal sites.
Source: Authors' elaboration based on Government of Argentina (2010)

In relation to forest management (item 4), some consensus exists regarding the quality of the legal framework, which introduced the concept of environmental services and created a special fund to pay for them. Further, since the creation of the law in 2007, deforestation has fallen by about 60 per cent (FARN 2009). However, this reduction has been primarily a result of the depletion of forested areas on the agricultural frontier rather than a consequence of the new law. In fact, there has been little progress in terms of actual implementation of the law, especially with regard to the forest fund and forest zoning at the state level. In any case, emissions coming from deforestation are almost irrelevant in Argentina, since LULUCF emissions constitute such a small portion of total GHG emissions. Public policies in the area of waste management (item 5) are confronted with a similar situation as a result of poor implementation of the law and limited coordination among the relevant subnational entities within the Federal Council of the Environment (COFEMA).

Climate Change in the International Realm: Warming Climate, Frozen Policy

Like its domestic climate change policies, Argentina's stance on climate change in the international arena has been a conservative one.

Since the early 1990s, the country has held to a radical interpretation of the common but differentiated responsibilities principle. And, with the brief exception of the period 1998–9, this has not changed. To support this statement, we first discuss several long-standing features of Argentina's international position on climate governance. We then summarize the country's current negotiating position in the UNFCCC.

With respect to Argentina's stance in the international negotiations, certain positions have been systematically defended over the past twenty or so years. First, the multilateral level, specifically the United Nations, has been regarded as the appropriate sphere for responding to the climate crisis. Second, national development is held to be an inalienable imperative. Third, the principle of common but differentiated responsibilities should be the guiding principle for allocating responsibilities in the international regime. Industrialized states should adopt quantitative emission targets while developing states should take only nationally appropriate mitigation actions. Fourth, there is a major need for technology and financing from the industrialized world for undertaking appropriate mitigation and adaptation measures. Fifth, the Kyoto Protocol's flexibility mechanisms, specifically the CDM, should be safeguarded. Sixth, and finally, Reducing Emissions from Deforestation and Forest Degradation (REDD) should be adopted as a central component of the climate change regime. These positions have usually been influenced by Argentina's membership in the G77/China coalition – the most important negotiating group for developing countries, which traditionally has low ambitions in the mitigation arena. Overall, however, it should also be noted that climate change has always been a peripheral issue on the international agenda for Argentina.

The current features of Argentina's official stance on climate change in the international negotiations can be summarized as follows: it recognizes the seriousness of the climate problem in accordance with the scientific evidence compiled in the fourth IPCC report and declares that it is wholly committed to the principles laid out in the convention (UNFCCC 2008a, 2008b, 2009a, 2009b, 2009c, 2010). The country also states that the problem of climate change requires a cooperative effort and must involve every actor in the international community. However, at the same time, Argentina rejects the possibility of establishing quantitative emission reduction targets for developing countries and defends the idea that only the developed world must make mandatory commitments. The only circumstances in which Argentina would agree to deepen mitigation actions would be if this were connected to substantial financial and technological support from industrialized states. One of the main concerns on the part of Argentine negotiators, further, has been to block international regulations that could impose trade barriers to local exports. The so-called 'just transition' – minimizing the negative effects of the low carbon economy on the labour world – has also entered the country's agenda in the last few years. And, finally, it is worth noting the inclusion of sovereignty claims over the Falklands/Malvinas Islands in the submissions made to the UNFCCC.

Regarding the flexibility mechanisms created under Kyoto, Argentina's official stance has been one of systematic defence. It has highlighted not only their contribution to the convention's overall purpose, but also their favourable effects upon national development. In terms of the country's position on NAMAs, Argentina did not agree with the Copenhagen Accord. However, in February 2010, the country answered the invitation to submit a NAMA proposal. As we saw, in that submission Argentina listed a set of public policies that are supposedly consistent with the mitigation of climate change, although with no quantitative references. In further statements, the government has also highlighted some of the advances made in Copenhagen, such as the 2° C limit, and it has recognized the need for the international community to reduce 85 per cent of its emissions by the year 2050.

Overall, we therefore argue that Argentina offered a rigid interpretation of the principle of common but differentiated responsibilities, mainly because it does not recognize the possibility of adopting emissions reduction targets and subordinates any mitigation commitment to the financial and technological support of developed countries. This vision of international climate politics has been more or less frozen in place since the signing of the UNFCCC in 1992. And this frozen stance is inconsistent with two of the main developments in the international system: the acceleration of the climate crisis and growing evidence of the need for middle income countries to adopt mitigation measures (Viola et al. 2013).

Conclusion

Up until now, the efforts that Argentina has undertaken to deal with its climate vulnerability and growing emissions have been minimal and unorganized. Climate change has not been internalized into the country's legal system; the government structures created to manage the issue are peripheral within the state bureaucracy; climate policies have been unambitious or never fully implemented; and Argentina's stance in international negotiations has been frozen. Only between 1998 and 1999 was Argentina willing to accept a quantified voluntary commitment to reduce its emissions trajectory relative to a benchmark level, suggesting that it might take unilateral actions. However, that proposal was never implemented. Since then, Argentina has remained as a climate laggard, unwilling to propose quantified targets. As we saw, the NAMA proposed within the Copenhagen framework is a very light commitment, and given the context of Argentine governance the policies it elaborates have only a remote probability of being implemented. In the next section, we explore the reasons for this climate 'laggardness' in greater detail.

Explaining Climate Policymaking in Argentina

In the first part of this chapter we have focused on describing Argentina as a climate laggard in the global governance of climate change. This section now turns towards explaining why this has been the case. Argentina's conservatism is surprising, to some extent, since many characteristics of the country's socio-economic situation – middle to high per capita incomes, very high human development levels, high education levels, high vulnerability and a number of good opportunities for investing in renewable energy sources – might lead us to expect a more ambitious approach. However, a combination of domestic and international factors, both material and social, imprisons Argentina in the conservative field, with few prospects for major changes in the medium term. In what follows, we analyse these factors, emphasizing how high discount rates among the main actors in domestic politics as well as what we refer to as the 'heritage of decadence' – a socio-cultural worldview that strongly shapes political behaviour – are probably the key factors underpinning Argentina's policies, or the lack thereof. Nationalist and isolationist tendencies, and low levels of climate awareness within the society, are also relevant factors. We begin by discussing the low levels of climate awareness in Argentina, which signal the fact that there are few electoral incentives for politicians to take a more ambitious approach.

Low Awareness of Climate Change in Argentine Society

Many factors support the conclusion that the climate issue remains a low priority for the population and the Argentine elite. In 2005, the research firm Poliarquia Consultores conducted a broad survey of public attitudes towards environmental issues (FVSA 2005). The results were indicative of the fact that the issue of climate change was low on the public agenda. Only 7.5 per cent of the sample considered climate change to be the main environmental problem in Argentina. Indeed, it was rated far below problems like flooding or local pollution. Another survey conducted in 2006 by Ipsos-Mora y Araujo (2006) pointed to similar conclusions: only 1 per cent of the sample considered climate change to be the most pressing environmental problem. It was rated far behind local pollution at 82 per cent.

The way in which the press deals with climate change can also be regarded as an indicator of low climate awareness. Two works are referred to here. First, a study produced in 2008 by Konrad Adenauer Stiftung on the prevalence of climate change issues in the Latin American press shows what little attention the main Argentine newspapers give to the problem. From a sample of 4,100 articles in the newspaper El Clarín – the most important publication in Argentina – only 11 (0.27 per cent) mentioned the matter. The performance of the second most important newspaper, La Nación, was only marginally better: 18 of 3,900 (or 0.46 per cent) (FARN 2010). A second study arrived at similar conclusions (FARN 2010). It analysed all articles related to the environment that were published in 2009 in the three largest Argentine newspapers (*El Clarín*, *La Nación* and *Página/12*) and found that only 0.3 per cent of the total mentioned climate change. Furthermore, almost all climate change news appeared in the days surrounding COP15 (7–18 December 2009), with a daily average of three articles in each newspaper.

In the business sector, similarly, no significant movements have appeared to take a position on the Argentine government's approach to climate change as has happened in Brazil (see chapter 7 in this volume, by Held, Roger and Nag). Indeed, the major economic sectors in Argentina have mainly taken a conservative stance, if they have taken any position at all. In the energy industry, for example, fossil fuel sectors remain dominant, leaving little space for more reformist agents, such as those related to nuclear, hydroelectric, solar and wind energy. The transport subsector is also a conservative bunker, since it is heavily road based, is inefficient and benefits from subsidized fuel prices. The agribusiness sector, which is very important in terms of GDP, exports and technological modernization, can again be regarded as deeply conservative, with generally high carbon intensity levels and a traditional insensitivity to environmental concerns. Only the forestry sector has taken a more ambiguous stance, with some conservative forces related to deforestation coexisting with more progressive sectors associated with a relevant (although under-explored) forest industry.

As a result of the low priority given to the climate change issue among the electorate and the business sector, it has not appeared on the platform of any relevant Argentine political party, nor has it generally been a part of the discourses of any central political figures. It is currently not a topic on the legislative agenda, and it was not an important matter in the 2007, 2009 or 2011 political campaigns. Sub-national political dynamics reflect the lack of electoral incentives as well, as there have been no relevant measures or reactions from Argentine provinces regarding global warming and no significant climate policies have been adopted at the municipal level. The only partial exception is Mendoza, a western province that has developed long-term planning and a rational approach to the use of natural resources, largely due to problems of water scarcity and local production that relies heavily on the climate. Ultimately, therefore, high degrees of climate awareness in Argentina seem to be confined to academia, specialized state bureaucracies – despite their limited political clout in the government – and certain non-governmental organizations (NGOs).

Discounting the Future and the Heritage of Decadence

One of the central factors leading to Argentina's low level of climate proactivity – and perhaps the most important one from our perspective – has been the presence of high discount rates among those involved in politics. This has primarily been a product of the uncertain political and economic environment in Argentina and a long tradition of violating contracts and the rule of law which has fostered low levels of trust, low ability to make credible commitments, and high uncertainty about future behaviour. As a result, extreme short-term considerations are prioritized in political and economic calculations; only the most immediate considerations of economic, political and social well-being are highly valued, while long-term concerns are heavily discounted. This limited vision of political dynamics is not confined to political leaders and policymakers, but is pervasive in society as well.

This extreme myopia is also amplified, we argue, by a number of factors which can together be conceptualized as a 'heritage of decadence', a socio-cultural worldview which has been a product of the repeated social, economic and political crises that Argentina has suffered since the early 1930s and a distinctly romanticized perception of the past that foretold progress and relevance, but instead turned out to be a frustrating experience. The effects of an environment of chronic political instability (institutional or dramatic political changes in 1930, 1943, 1946, 1955, 1962, 1966, 1969, 1973, 1976, 1983, 1989, 2001 and 2003) and economic unrest (in 1975, 1982, 1989–90, 2001–2 and 2012) have, in short, been augmented by the perception of past decadence. The worldview that this experience has fostered also leads social and political actors to secure immediate material gains over all else and to contribute little to the production of enduring public goods. This short-sighted approach, further, is closely related to other two key features of Argentina's political culture: resentment and *movimentismo*[3] (Leis & Viola 2008). Resentment operates by stimulating the need for quick and low-cost economic outcomes within society as a way to a rapid revival of the utopian past, while *movimentismo* explores those sentiments by offering easily understandable yet utopian solutions. As a consequence, both Argentina's society and its political leadership have tended to focus on short-term benefits, with the former choosing candidates that present quick and easy ways out of the country's present predicament and the latter being forced to demonstrate instantaneous results.

Within this context it is therefore not surprising that climate change has not been a prominent issue in Argentina. If an opportunity existed for a significant expansion of climate awareness in the country, this would have been during the time in which economic and political stability was apparently consolidated in the 1990s. But even during this decade two major vulnerabilities remained: the severe fiscal deficits of the provinces and the Argentine economy's declining international competitiveness due to the pegging of its national currency to the US dollar. As a consequence, at the beginning of the new century, Argentina found itself immersed in the worst crisis in generations,[4] a crisis which has resulted in the deepening of 'short-termism'.

Even after the surprising economic recovery that began in 2003, it is clear that the political system has suffered deep impacts, many of them inconsistent with a more substantial climate commitment. These include the decline of the traditional bipartisan system and the chaotic transition to a more fragmented and weak political structure; the awakening and consolidation of social movements with greater capacity to alter the political agenda; and the almost daily need for the federal government to affirm its authority over those actors. The outcome of these impacts has been the consolidation of a deeply fragmented public arena, with many influential agents demanding immediate solutions from the national government, which in turn has had to concentrate its political capital on satisfying the most urgent of those demands in order to maintain some level of political and social stability.

Factious Political Behaviour

The 2001–2 crisis in Argentina was, at the same time, new evidence of – and tended to reinforce – another long-term feature of Argentine civic culture: factious political behaviour. Irremediable divisions and polarization in the public sphere have been a constant since the country's independence in the second decade of the nineteenth century. On many occasions, those differences were expressed in a violent fashion, galvanizing their protagonists to kill and die for different interpretations of social organization and for personal rewards. As the latest democratization process began in the early 1980s, the use of violence as a legitimate way to express political disagreements seems to have ended, creating minimal conditions for the development of a more pluralistic and tolerant approach to domestic political relations. However, even in the absence of a violent component, Argentina's sectarianism not only survived, but managed to stimulate other crises, two of which ended in the rupture of the normal functioning of democratic institutions: 1989 and 2001.

The 2001 crisis was an extreme example of Argentina's leadership's inability to arrive at consensual solutions to difficult situations. At the same time, it tended to reinforce the country's inclination towards factious political behaviour. After the episode, the general understanding has been that the country lives within an unstable and unpredictable system, even when the economy expands. In this context, weakness is the one vulnerability the national authorities cannot afford to show. The frustrating experience of the Alianza[5] has had such a strong impact that even the most inconsistent political behaviour can be forgiven by most voters if it is not perceived as softness. The political leadership that came after the crisis – President Nestor Kirchner (2003–7) and his wife Cristina Fernandez (2007–15) – understood as did no other the need for strong, assertive leadership in Argentina, and translated that need into a Manichaean vision of public affairs, where every competitor is an enemy and any divergent opinion is evidence of a conspiracy.

This sectarian approach to public affairs is, at the same time, both a cause and an effect of the limited rule of law. Unable and unwilling to translate competing interests into coherent policies, Argentina's political institutions have been dominated by the narrow individual interests of corporations and unions, resulting in underinvestment in public goods. And since the quality of political institutions is crucial to an effective response to climate change, this is a major obstacle in Argentina.

International Isolationism

Finally, the 2001–2 crisis has had yet another profound impact upon Argentina's capacity to manage climate change within its borders: the crisis strengthened nationalist and isolationist tendencies. In the 1990s, Argentina went through a deep transformation in terms of its international stance, establishing an alliance with Western democracies and giving more visibility and priority to foreign affairs. In the next decade, however, first as a consequence of the crisis – especially the debt default – and later as a deliberate political choice, Argentina developed a low international profile, and scarcely participated in global and regional governance structures. Indeed, it even began to resist some basic facets of globalization, such as international finance and trade.

The progressive closing of Argentina's economy is one of the most significant manifestations of this process. Successive protectionist measures increased restrictions on imports, even on imports from Argentina's close partners in Mercosur, while export taxes were elevated. Hostile measures against private investment created a negative environment for foreign direct investment, and have led to capital flight over the last few years. The country only managed to navigate through subsequent macroeconomic troubles – fiscal deficits, relative price distortions and high inflation – without falling into a new crisis because of high commodity prices, especially food prices, which softened the blow. The economy was able to expand the nominal value of its exports without any significant increase in production or gains in productivity. Thus, the recent features of the global economy ironically operated as enabling conditions for Argentina's isolationism and nationalist practices.

This negligence in dealing with international affairs is explained by the absolute priority given by the government to domestic politics. Foreign policy became entirely subject to short-term domestic priorities and every course of action was defined according to its capacity to feed the hegemonic political project of the Kirchner faction within the Peronist group. Thus, international relations are, in general, considered to be an even lower priority than they are in most countries, and specific issues only really garner attention when they are convergent with or impinge upon short-term domestic goals.

Conclusion

Argentina is not a central agent of climate governance because of its self-imposed outlier position in the international system and its lack of significant technological resources to stimulate the transition to a low carbon economy. In addition to this lack of capacity, the country has not been willing to take any action to preserve the stability of the climate system or to make any effort to facilitate the construction of a global climate deal. Emissions since the early 2000s have grown faster than the global average, which was around 3 per cent annually, and the outlook for the main emissions-producing sectors is highly pessimistic, especially in energy, where inadequate policies have stimulated wasteful patterns of consumption and growing carbon intensity.

At the same time, climate awareness in Argentine society is extremely low and, consequently, climate change is a low priority for the government as well. As a result, domestic climate policies are underdeveloped and, with respect to the country's foreign policy, Argentina is locked into a radical interpretation of the common but differentiated responsibilities principle that has not changed considerably since the Rio Earth Summit in 1992. For these reasons, we have categorized Argentina as a climate laggard. The country is far from implementing a strong voluntary mitigation commitment, and given the very low probability of any significant breakthrough in the international negotiations, the most likely outcome for Argentina is more of the same. The rapidly deteriorating domestic situation – growing inflation, economic stagnation and social unrest – is yet another obstacle to almost any Argentine policy consistent with climate leadership.

There are, nevertheless, elements that should stimulate a more ambitious climate commitment in Argentine society. In the first place, Argentina is highly vulnerable to the impacts of climate change, in terms both of exposure, especially in the agricultural sector, and of its lack of adaptive capacities. In the second place, the country has some low cost mitigation options, meaning that it would not be overly problematic to find viable ways to reduce its emissions trajectory. Alternative sources of energy, shale gas and REDD are sectors that could become winners in a transition to a low carbon economy. These potentialities are, however, blocked by factors shaping the conduct of public affairs in Argentina. Indeed, there are certain minimal conditions that societies and political leadership must meet in order to generate enough consciousness and will to create and implement concrete climate policies: political and economic stability, sensitivity to developments at the international level, some engagement with global governance mechanisms, awareness of climate vulnerability, and a willingness to take action on long-term problems. As we saw in previous pages, Argentina has a negative record in all of these categories.

Above all, the myopic vision of Argentine political culture makes the policymaking required for successful climate governance difficult. Global warming is a long-term problem. GHGs remain in the atmosphere for anywhere from a few decades to thousands of years and the effects of climatic changes are cumulative, becoming evident only with time. At the same time, while the most appropriate response to the problem must be quickly executed and globally planned, the actions undertaken will have visible results only in the long run. Climate change politics and policies have to do with the future, with risk management, with uncertainties and the legacies of future generations. But these are all areas where Argentine governments have been sorely wanting.

Giddens (2009, p. 2) considers the basic problem of climate change to be a high rate of future discounting, a concept that draws attention to the difficulty humans have with attributing the 'same level of reality to the future as they do to the present'. A minor reward in the present is often chosen over a major prize in the future. The British author recognizes that even European societies, which may be more advanced in terms of their civic cultures, their ability to manage future risks, and their commitment to global governance mechanisms, are not prepared to deal with the task, and that much time will pass before climate change becomes a central political issue. We argue that Argentine society and its political leadership face even greater obstacles in this regard.

Long-term considerations are closely linked to the idea of sustainability. In a way, it is a behaviour that can be stimulated by rules. Yet, at root, it is basically a value, a principle that inspires responsibility for the future consequences of our actions in spite of our eventual absence. Sustainable values and actions are rare in Argentina's society and government precisely because they require overcoming short-term considerations. So far, Argentina has been able to assimilate neither a demand from the international scientific community (the need for emerging countries to embrace the climate problem as their own) nor the brute reality of an educated, middle income society producing 1 per cent of all global GHGs, and with per capita emissions above the average for the European Union.

In the end, it is difficult to imagine a more demanding challenge for Argentine political sensibilities than the current climate crisis. A more ambitious approach to climate governance would require Argentina to abandon deep-rooted social patterns, such as the prevalence of a worldview that prioritizes short-term considerations in public matters; the factious character of political behaviour, fuelled by notions of resentment and *movimentismo*; and the low sensitivity to and concern for international developments, grounded in nationalist and isolationist tendencies. Unfortunately, the first years of the second Kirchner administration have only tended to reinforce this already deeply engrained pattern.

Notes

1 Given the lack of government data since 2000, we made our own estimations regarding 2011 GHG emissions, based on two sources: (1) a 2008 report from Fundación Bariloche that indicates that emissions grew by 5 per cent annually between 2000 and 2005, and (2) the trajectory of major emissions sectors – energy and agriculture – between 2006 and 2011. As a result we estimate that Argentina's GHG emissions expanded by approximately 7 per cent annually since 2006. This is an unusual case of emission growth by global standards, but economic growth in Argentina between 2006 and 2011 was unusual too: 7.5 per cent annually with no major improvement in carbon intensity.

2 Fundación Bariloche is a fifty-year-old scientific non-governmental organization (NGO) that has been helping the national government in the construction of national communications.

3 This refers to a specific kind of Latin American populism in Argentina and constitutes a core dimension of *peronismo* as a political party and union-based social movement. It describes a political behaviour that fights political parties and representative democracy in the name of a 'pure' relationship between the leader and the people. This kind of political attitude has borrowed many things from Italian fascism.

4 GDP fell almost a quarter between 1998 and 2003, leaving millions in unemployment (20 per cent in 2002) and poverty (55 per cent in 2002). Economic crisis led to social unrest, which forced the resignation of President De la Rúa in December 2001, two years before the end of the constitutionally established term. The socio-political situation gained some stability only in 2003.

5 A coalition of two parties – the Unión Cívica Radical and Frente País Solidario – that led Fernando De la Rúa (1999–2001) to the presidency, which he abandoned amidst strong social unrest.

References

De la Torre, A., P. Fajnzylber & J. Nash (2009). *Low Carbon, High Growth: Latin American Responses to Climate Change*. World Bank. Available at: http://siteresources.worldbank.org/BRAZILEXTN/Resources/LowCarbonClimateChangeReport.pdf.

FARN (2009). *Informe Ambiental Anual 2009*. Fundación Ambiente y recursos Naturales. Available at: http://www.farn.org.ar.

FARN (2010). *Informe Ambiental Anual 2010*. Fundación Ambiente y recursos Naturales. Available at: http://www.farn.org.ar.

Fundación Bariloche (2008). *Argentina: Diagnósticos, Perspectivas y Lineamientos para Definir Estrategias Posibles ante el Cambio Climático*. Available at: http://www.endesacemsa.com.

FVSA (2005). *La Situación Ambiental Argentina en 2005*. Fundación Vida Silvestre Argentina. Available at: http://www.fvsa.org.ar/situacionambiental/navegador.html.

Giddens, A. (2009). *The Politics of Climate Change*. Cambridge: Polity.

Government of Argentina (2010). *Communication regarding Copenhagen Accord*. 15 February. Available at: http://unfccc.int/files/meetings/cop_15/copenhagen_accord/application/pdf/agentinacphaccord_english.pdf.

Government of Argentina (2012). *National Energy Balance 2010*. November. Available at: http://www.energia.gov.ar/contenidos/verpagina.php?idpagina=3366.

IAE (2011). *Sector Energético Argentino: Balance de la Gestión de Gobierno 2003–2010*. Instituto Argentino de Energía General Mosconi. Available at: http://iae.org.ar.

IEA (2011). *World Energy Outlook 2011: Are We Entering a Golden Age of Gas?* International Energy Agency. Available at: http://www.iea.org.

IPCC (2007). *Cambio Climático 2007: Informe de Síntesis*. Available at: http://www.ipcc.ch/pdf/assessment-report/ar4/syr/ar4_syr_sp.pdf.

Ipsos-Mora y Araujo (2006). *Las actitudes hacia el consumo sustentable*. Available at: http://www.ambiente.gov.ar/archivos/web/CIPLyCS/File/IPSOS%20cuantitativo.pdf.

Leis, R. & E. Viola (2008). *América del Sur en el mundo de las democracias de mercado*. Rosario: Homo Sapiens and CADAL.

Secretary of the Environment and Sustainable Development of Argentina (2007). 'Segunda Comunicación Nacional de la República Argentina a la Convención Marco de las Naciones Unidas sobre Cambio Climático'. Available at: http://www.ambiente.gov.ar/archivos/web/File/home_documentos/Informe_Final_2CN.pdf.

UNFCCC (2008a). *Views on Elements for the Terms of Reference for the Review and Assessment of the Effectiveness of the Implementation of Article 4, Paragraphs 1(c) and 5, of the Convention*. Subsidiary body for implementation, United Nations Framework Convention on Climate Change. Available at: http://unfccc.int/resource/docs/2008/sbi/eng/misc01.pdf.

UNFCCC (2008b). *Ideas and Proposals on the Elements Contained in Paragraph 1 of the Bali Action Plan*. Ad Hoc Working Group on Long-Term Cooperative Action under the Convention, United Nations Framework Convention on Climate Change. Available at: http://unfccc.int/resource/docs/2008/awglca4/eng/misc05.pdf.

UNFCCC (2009a). *Ideas and Proposals on the Elements Contained in Paragraph 1 of the Bali Action Plan*. Ad Hoc Working Group on Long-Term Cooperative Action under the Convention, United Nations Framework Convention on Climate Change. Available at: http://unfccc.int/resource/docs/2009/awglca5/eng/misc01.pdf.

UNFCCC (2009b). *Ideas and Proposals on the Elements Contained in Paragraph 1 of the Bali Action Plan*. Ad Hoc Working Group on Long-Term Cooperative Action under the Convention, United Nations Framework Convention on Climate Change. Available at: http://unfccc.int/resource/docs/2009/awglca6/eng/misc04p01.pdf.

UNFCCC (2009c). *Ideas and Proposals on the Elements Contained in Paragraph 1 of the Bali Action Plan*. Ad Hoc Working Group on Long-Term Cooperative Action under the Convention, United Nations Framework Convention on Climate Change. Available at: http://unfccc.int/resource/docs/2009/awglca7/eng/misc06.pdf.

UNFCCC (2010). *Additional Views on which the Chair May Draw in Preparing Text to Facilitate Negotiations among Parties*. Ad Hoc Working Group on Long-Term Cooperative Action under the Convention, United Nations Framework Convention on Climate Change. Available at: http://unfccc.int/resource/docs/2010/awglca10/eng/misc02.pdf.

Viola, E. & M. Franchini (2012). Climate policy in Brazil. Public awareness, social transformations and emission reductions. In I. Bailey & H. Compston (eds.) *Feeling the Heat: The Politics of Climate Policy in Rapidly Industrializing Countries*. Houndmills: Palgrave Macmillan.

Viola, E., M. Franchini & T. Lemos Ribeiro (2013). *Sistema Internacional de Hegemonia Conservadora: Governança Global e Democracia na Era da Crise Climática*. São Paulo: Annablume.

7

Controlling the Amazon: Brazil's Evolving Response to Climate Change

David Held, Charles Roger and Eva-Maria Nag

Introduction

B RAZIL is a unique country in the global climate change regime. Thanks to its large size and impressive rate of economic growth in recent years, it is regarded as one of the major emerging economies that will play an increasingly influential role in global politics in upcoming decades. It is one of the members of the BASIC group (with South Africa, India and China) that made its mark on the global climate change negotiations at Copenhagen in 2009. Yet the challenges it faces are very different from those of its BASIC counterparts. Unlike the other BASIC countries, Brazil is not a major producer of fossil fuel-based emissions. Due to the already large share of renewable energy sources in its overall energy mix, its fossil fuel-based emissions amounted to only 1.9 tonnes of CO_2 per capita in 2005. By comparison, China, with a much larger population, produced 5.1 tonnes of CO_2 per capita and neighbouring Argentina, with a nearly equivalent level of gross domestic product (GDP) per capita, emitted more than twice as much (about 4 tonnes of CO_2 per capita). In many respects, therefore, Brazil already has a low carbon economy, a result of important decisions and investments in hydropower and biofuels in previous decades. Without these, the World Bank has said, 'Brazil's current energy matrix would be far more carbon intensive' (2010, p. xv).

Despite its impressive use of renewable sources of energy and low fossil fuel-based emissions, however, Brazil is one of the major net producers of greenhouse gases (GHGs) amongst both developing and industrialized countries. This is because the tremendous rate of deforestation in the Amazon contributes significantly to overall global GHG levels, swamping the low emissions from the rest of its economy. In 1990, shortly after the Amazon first began to attract global attention, the World Resources Institute (WRI) estimated that the GHGs produced by deforestation in Brazil were greater than those stemming from the annual use of fossil fuels in the United States (WRI 1990, p. 346). This turned out to be an exaggeration; a subsequent report by the WRI dramatically reduced its previous estimate (WRI 1992, p. 348). Nevertheless, according to the most recent figures available, when emissions from land use change and forestry (LUCF) are taken into account, Brazil emits more CO_2 per person than Germany, Europe's largest economy, and nearly three times as much in absolute terms (WRI 2011).

For many years, the Amazon has been a sensitive topic for Brazilian policymakers, who have historically regarded the rainforest as a major economic and strategic asset. Efforts to control deforestation have frequently been frustrated by the deeply entrenched interests, both licit and illicit, that have benefited from Amazonian deforestation and poorly enforced laws. And, largely due to these same forces, the country has long taken a broadly conservative position on climate change. The 1997 'Brazilian Proposal', for example, suggested that international responsibilities for reducing carbon should be allocated according to historical emissions. This supported the argument that the country had little need to take action, despite its large contribution to global GHG levels at present, and should not be required to make binding emissions commitments to lower its emissions of GHGs. In 1998, at the Fourth Conference of the Parties (COP4) in Buenos Aires, the country's negotiators even steadfastly resisted an Argentine proposal for voluntary emissions commitments (see chapter 6 in this volume, by Franchini and Viola, for more on this).

But, in recent years, there have been some notable changes in Brazil's domestic approach to climate change governance, as well as its stance in the United Nations Framework Convention on Climate Change (UNFCCC) negotiations. In 2008, the Brazilian Inter-ministerial Committee on Climate Change released its National Plan on Climate Change, announcing the country's intention to take action domestically, regardless of developments in the international arena. Calling climate change a 'strategic issue for both the present and the future of national development', the Plan outlined the actions that Brazil would undertake to curb emissions and adapt to climatic changes in its territory. These included commitments to improving energy efficiency, maintaining the high share of renewable energy sources in the country's energy mix, further encouraging the sustainable use of biofuels, and – most significantly – reducing deforestation rates and eliminating net loss of forest coverage by 2015. The targets set out in the plan were then offered as a voluntary commitment under the Copenhagen Accord and signed into national law in 2009. According to the government, the measures would reduce Brazil's national emissions by 36–9 per cent below its baseline emissions scenario by 2020.

While this new, ambitious approach to climate change governance in Brazil reflects a number of new domestic political dynamics at work, it rests on a number of critical decisions that have been made over the past century – particularly, to invest in hydropower and support the production and use of biofuels. These investments form the background against which climate politics in Brazil is now playing out, and are discussed in the first part of this chapter. Despite Brazil's substantial advantages in its energy profile, however, we argue that the inability to control the Amazon effectively held it back from taking a more robust domestic approach to climate change and heavily influenced the government's position early on in the international negotiations. Changes began to occur only as Brazil achieved greater success in controlling deforestation, primarily as a result of factors only partially or indirectly connected to climate change: repeated deforestation crises, violence in the Amazon, and politics within the ruling Worker's Party. The government's greater ability to limit deforestation opened space for other actors to advocate successfully for a more robust commitment to climate change. Towards the end of the decade, greater public concern and attention to the issue, pressure from prominent environmental activists and political figures, and growing support from the Brazilian business community compelled the government to adopt quite significant climate targets. This shift is explored in greater detail in the second half of the chapter.

The Background to Brazil's Current Approach

In many ways, Brazil is an anomaly amongst the major emerging economies. In China, India and South Africa, for example, energy use accounts for over 90 per cent of all GHG emissions. In Brazil, on the other hand, it accounts for only 15 per cent. The relatively small contribution of Brazil's energy sector to its yearly emissions arises from the fact that much of its energy use is not carbon intensive by world standards. In 2007, the country produced only 1.59 tonnes of CO_2 per tonne of oil equivalent. Primarily, this is thanks to the dominance of renewable energy sources in its energy matrix. As figure 7.1 shows, while fossil fuels (coal, natural gas and petroleum) account for 52 per cent of Brazil's total primary energy supply, 46 per cent is provided by renewable energy sources, with biomass and hydropower constituting 32 per cent and 14 per cent of the total respectively.

This unique energy mix is primarily a result of a number of key public and private decisions, reaching as far back as the end of the nineteenth century, to invest heavily in renewable energy sources, especially hydropower and biofuels. Without this history of investment, the World Bank (2010) has estimated that Brazil's energy sector emissions would be twice as high and that its total national emissions would be at least 17 per cent higher, assuming that its energy mix was similar to the prevailing global average. The political and economic decisions that influenced the evolution of Brazil's energy sector – the majority of which were made before climate change became an important international and domestic issue – have, as a result, been an important influence on Brazil's present approach to climate governance. Without them, Brazil's LUCF emissions would

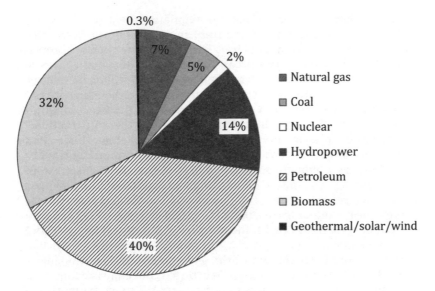

Figure 7.1 Brazil, total primary energy supply, 2009

Source: IEA (2012)

only be one part of a larger problem, and the government's ability to reduce deforestation would not have opened a political window for more robust climate policies in quite the same way that it has. In this section, therefore, we begin by clarifying how and why the Brazilian energy sector has evolved as it has by looking closely at its experience with hydropower and biofuels. We then turn to consider the main source of Brazil's GHG emissions: deforestation and land use change.

Hydropower in Brazil

Hydroelectricity is the cornerstone of Brazil's electric power system, accounting for approximately 85 per cent of all power generation and over 77 per cent of total installed capacity. Investment in hydropower began around the start of the twentieth century, driven by the favourable Brazilian landscape and climate and the scarcity of high-quality coal reserves. Nearly all investment at this early stage was undertaken by small private companies which signed a variety of different service contracts with state and municipal governments. The most significant of these early energy providers was Brazilian Traction, Light and Power Company, known as 'Light'. Light was a Toronto-based company (now Brookfield Asset Management) established in the 1890s and it served Rio de Janeiro and São Paulo. Other players, such as the American firm AMFORP, also became important investors in Brazil, obtaining several large concessions. And, by 1910, 86 per cent of all electricity in Brazil was being generated from hydroelectric sources.

Nevertheless, no overall federal regulations existed to govern hydropower generation until the implementation of the Water Code by the Vargas government in 1934. The Water Code clarified property rights related to water resources, established a national concession system, and set corresponding regulations that would be overseen by the National Council for Water and Power, established in 1939. Following the Water Code, the creation of a public company to construct the Furnas Hydropower Project, and the construction of the first transmission lines to connect the São Paulo, Minas Gerais and Rio de Janeiro electricity grids, Brazil then gradually began to move towards a publicly owned system (de Oliveira 2007; Leite 2009). Electrobras was created in 1961 in order to act as a holding company for all the regional supply companies and the federal government's energy investments. Increasingly, it would oversee development of the power system along with the Ministry of Mines and Energy (MME), created in 1960.

The growing participation of the government, which deepened as the military took power in 1964, did little to reduce the predominance of hydropower in the country's energy matrix; in fact, between 1965 and the mid-1990s, when the Brazilian power sector was partially reformed, hydropower's share of total energy generation increased from around 73 to nearly 90 per cent. Previously, as noted, hydropower projects had been built without any effort to coordinate investments by the different power companies. But, beginning in the 1960s, the government developed a long-term power sector strategy with the assistance of CANAMBRA, a Canadian–American engineering consultancy, that gave a prominent role to hydropower. The plan produced by CANAMBRA emphasized that other forms of power generation continued to be costly in Brazil and should be limited to an ancillary role. Hydropower should continue to serve as the basis for industrial development, a view which was subsequently reinforced among policymakers after the oil crises of the 1970s, which made hydropower even more attractive compared to fossil fuel-based sources.

Coordinated planning of the system, therefore, encouraged a massive expansion of hydroelectric capacity, highlighted above all by the construction of the Itaipu dam on the Paraná River on the border with Paraguay. The dam, which would be jointly managed by Paraguay and Brazil, began operation in 1984 and remains the largest hydroelectric power plant in the world in terms of the annual amount of energy generated. It aimed to meet nearly 20 per cent of Brazil's total energy consumption. However, problems began to occur as large dams became a central target of contestation because of the large numbers of people affected by their construction. Indigenous groups and environmental activists challenged the government's approach and received strong support from the Catholic church. The centralized planning system also met problems in the 1980s as a result of the country's macroeconomic crisis and the related financial difficulties encountered by the federal government and a number of the larger states. The crisis in the power sector itself culminated in a partial privatization of many assets in the mid-1990s. The reform was 'partial' primarily because privatization was largely limited to the major distribution companies. Prominent interests linked to the hydropower construction industry, which aimed to avoid any risk of a major shift towards thermal generation, resisted further efforts to privatize energy generation.

Fossil fuels did become a more important component of Brazil's energy mix after the reforms, increasing their share of generation capacity to just under 23 per cent by 2005. However, the actions of the pro-hydropower interests in Brazil ensured Brazilian dependence on hydropower (de Oliveira 2007). Indeed, the emphasis on hydropower would persist despite a severe energy crisis in 2001 as a major drought took hold. The crisis, induced largely by underinvestment in thermal power and a corresponding high dependence on hydroelectricity, contributed to Lula's victory in the 2002 presidential elections. Blaming privatization, he promised to return the country to a centralized energy planning system. Yet hydropower, the new government emphasized, would remain the cornerstone of the Brazilian electricity sector. Indeed, as of 2011, at least fifteen to twenty major dams were being planned in the Amazon Basin alone, including the Belo Monte dam on the Xingu River, which is expected to be the third largest dam in the world once completed. The government's support for large-scale hydroelectric projects has also, thus far, persisted despite heavy resistance from environmental and indigenous groups. It has survived the resignations of several prominent environmentalists – Marina Silva, minister of the environment (in 2008), and Abelardo Azevedo, head of the Brazilian Institute of Environment and Renewable Natural Resources (IBAMA) (in 2011) – from important government positions due, wholly or in part, to pressure from MME and other vested interests in the government determined to attain approvals for dam projects in the Amazon.

Biofuels in Brazil

In addition to hydropower, biofuels, especially ethanol, have played an important role in Brazil's energy matrix, particularly in its transport sector. Ethanol in Brazil is made primarily out of sugarcane, which is considered to be more energy efficient and economical than other bioethanol feedstocks such as corn or rapeseed. It also, according to many studies, produces fewer GHGs than petroleum substitutes. According to the IEA (2007), for example, the 'well-to-wheel' CO_2 emissions from sugarcane-based ethanol can be as much as 90 per cent lower than conventional gasoline. Its widespread use has, therefore, been thought to have a significant impact on the country's emissions. While disagreements remain, at least one study estimates that Brazil's ethanol programme has resulted in the avoidance of as much as 110 megatonnes (Mt) of CO_2 each year between 1975 and

2000, making it 'probably one of the most efficient GHG mitigation efforts ever executed' (Roman 2007, p. 78).

Of course, the mitigation of emissions was not the original purpose behind biofuels. Brazil's efforts to regulate the domestic sugar industry and promote ethanol date back as far as the 1930s. The year 1931 saw the creation of the Institute for Sugar and Alcohol, which aimed to regulate the industry, set prices and support growers at a time when prices had collapsed as a result of the Great Depression. The country's poor balance of payments due to heavy dependence on imported oil had also motivated the Vargas government to encourage the use of ethanol as a substitute. But this early effort was, generally, unsuccessful – both in reducing oil imports and in promoting the use of ethanol in gasoline (Nass et al. 2007). Attempts to promote ethanol production and use were then renewed in the 1970s when the international price of oil reached record highs and the price of sugar collapsed, creating a crisis in Brazil. Brazil was, at the time, importing roughly 80 per cent of its petroleum, and the jump in prices doubled the cost of meeting national demand. Sugar, on the other hand, was a key industry and source of foreign exchange for the country; its growers and processors constituted a powerful political coalition. Worried about dissipating valuable foreign exchange on oil imports, the economic impacts of high cost petroleum and the extremely harmful effects of price volatility on the sugar industry, the military government of Ernesto Geisel responded by creating the National Alcohol Programme (PROALCOOL) in 1975.

Originally intended as a temporary expedient, PROALCOOL rapidly grew with the support of Geisel, the Ministry of Industry and Commerce and powerful sugar interest groups (Hira & de Oliveira 2009). Together, they overcame considerable opposition from a coalition comprised of the MME, Petrobras, the Ministry of Finance and the central bank. Their efforts were, crucially, reinforced by the second oil shock in 1979 and technological advances that allowed combustion engines to run entirely on alcohol. Supported by PROALCOOL's regime of tax incentives and subsidies, sales of alcohol-fuelled cars reached 645,551 units in 1985, compared to gasoline-fuelled car sales of 26,675, and production of ethanol rose to nearly 12 billion litres (Dias de Moraes 2007; Hira & de Oliveira 2009).

After 1985, however, the programme encountered significant problems as the price of oil declined to historic lows and the price of sugar increased, making ethanol relatively more expensive. Facing a burdensome macroeconomic crisis as well, the government slowly began to remove the system of tax incentives, subsidies and price supports that undergirded the ethanol industry. As these were removed, production of ethanol dropped from its peak in 1985 and sales of alcohol-fuelled cars saw a marked decline, reaching as low as 40,707 vehicles in 1995 (Dias de Moraes 2007; Hira & de Oliveira 2009). Gasoline-fuelled car sales climbed to 1,234,254 automobiles. Along with the privatization of many Brazilian industries that occurred at the time, PROALCOOL was officially ended in 1991, and, for most of the 1990s, the ethanol industry stagnated. Sales of alcohol-fuelled cars reached a low of 1,120 vehicles in 1997.

Only in 2003, with the introduction of flex-fuel engines that could run on varying mixtures of gas and alcohol, was the industry re-energized. With flex-fuel vehicles, consumers could easily switch fuels and would be able to respond quickly to changing prices in both the ethanol and gasoline markets. Again, the government intervened to assist with the adoption of flex-fuel vehicles by making them eligible for tax breaks, as it had for entirely alcohol-based cars. And as flex-fuel vehicles became popular with consumers, dominating new car sales, production of ethanol grew to nearly 18,000 litres per year, buoyed by the high cost of oil. Foreign and domestic investment likewise increased as the industry proved it was viable without government support in the new economic climate of high oil prices. At present, the use of biofuels in transport has expanded to such an extent that around 80 per cent of all cars now use a flexible mixture of gasoline and ethanol.

Deforestation and Land Use Change in Brazil

Brazil's strong investments in hydropower and biofuels have helped to make the country's energy sector much less carbon intensive than it otherwise would be. Its fossil fuel-based emissions are low by global standards. As a result, the challenge of governing climate change in Brazil is quite unique among emerging economies. Whereas China, South Africa and India have tended to focus on energy use, the main issue in Brazil is related to controlling emissions arising from deforestation and land use change. As figure 7.2 shows, between 1988 and 2004 just over 18,000 km^2 were deforested each year in Legal Amazônia, on average – equivalent to an area roughly the same size as Slovenia or Kuwait. The emissions produced by deforestation on such a scale were enormous. In 2005, for example, LUCF accounted for 1,830 Mt of CO_2 emissions, or 84 per cent of Brazil's total emissions of CO_2 for the entire year. This is roughly equivalent to the total annual CO_2 emissions of Indonesia, greater than the total emissions of India, more than twice as great as the annual emissions produced by Germany, and nearly three times the annual emissions produced by Canada.

The origins of large-scale deforestation in Brazil lie in policies and actions first undertaken by the military government in the 1960s and 1970s. Motivated by geopolitical concerns about the security of the Amazon borders and the need to ensure control of its vast natural resources, the government set about populating the empty, unguarded region and integrating it into the core economy (Foresta 1992). The goal of settling the Amazonian frontier was pursued, initially, through major highway construction projects and large agricultural settlement schemes, and by providing a variety of tax breaks for attracting investment into Amazonian industries and agriculture, all of which were crucial determinants of deforestation during this

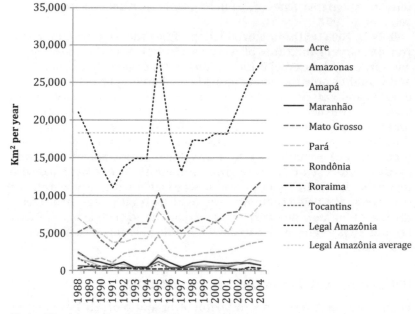

Figure 7.2 Amazonian deforestation, 1988–2004

Source: MMA/INPE (2010)

time (Binswanger 1991). This continued as the government's strategy in the Amazon shifted in the later 1970s away from 'top-down' settlement of the frontier and the building of major highways. In response to the rise in oil prices and the greater need for foreign exchange, the government's policies started to focus on encouraging exports from a number of critical development zones through its POLAMAZONIA programme. Started in 1974, POLAMAZONIA facilitated, in particular, projects related to agriculture and mining in the Amazon by constructing critical infrastructure and encouraging exports and investment through a system of taxes and special subsidies. By comparison to its previous approach, POLAMAZONIA was less concentrated on populating the Amazon – though 'bottom-up' settlement of the Amazon continued apace – but it contributed to deforestation via its facilitation of large-scale capital-intensive agriculture and forestry projects.

Legislation to control deforestation did exist; the Forest Code of 1965 required that rural properties maintain at least 50 per cent of the native forest, as well as all forests in environmentally sensitive areas, such as alongside bodies of water and on steep terrain. However, the capacity of the state to enforce these rules was generally unable to match the immense incentives for clearing land. Furthermore, by the 1990s, the dominant drivers of deforestation in Brazil were increasingly market forces rather than the ostensibly government-controlled factors (i.e. infrastructure projects and settlement schemes) which had initiated the deforestation process (Andersen 1996; Margulis 2004). According to Andersen (1996), population growth and the level of economic activity became the leading determinants of deforestation in the late 1980s and 1990s. Margulis (2004), likewise, found that deforestation was primarily caused by prevailing economic conditions and the profitability of medium- and small-scale cattle ranching, although soy bean farming had become an increasingly important factor as well (Hecht 2005). Da Silva and Kis-Katos (2010), for example, identify meat and soy bean prices as well as rural financial conditions as the leading drivers of land use change. Thus, for many years, Brazil's largest source of emissions appeared to be beyond the control of the federal government. Instead, the Amazon was being governed by powerful farmers and loggers, both licit and illicit, as well as poorer rural populations whose activities contributed to deforestation in remote areas.

The Evolution of Climate Change Governance in Brazil

Initially, climate change was regarded by the Brazilian government as a technical, scientific and foreign policy issue. It was not a major domestic political concern, except perhaps in certain states and municipalities.[1] Climate policymaking was, therefore, largely the preserve of the highly regarded Ministry of External Relations, known as Itamaraty, and the Ministry of Science and Technology (MCT). During the early years of the UNFCCC negotiations, Brazil's position largely reflected domestic ambivalence about making stringent commitments. This was most apparent in the 'Brazilian Proposal' of 1997 (see Cole 2012). The proposal stated that responsibility for mitigating emissions in the international climate change regime should be tied to historical or cumulative rather than present-day per capita emissions (which are quite high in Brazil), and that therefore the country should have few international obligations. The proposal also argued in favour of a Clean Development Fund (CDF) designed to channel fines levied on Annex I countries that exceeded their emissions targets to countries in the developing world. Notably, the proposal for the CDF laid the basis for what eventually emerged as the Clean Development Mechanism (CDM). But the position taken in the proposal was, essentially, a conservative one, and served to bolster Itamaraty's argument that Brazil had no responsibility to take actions domestically.

Brazil's conservative approach to the international negotiations was primarily a product of the various domestic interests in the National Congress that were arrayed against any ambitious stance on deforestation. States with economies closely connected to Amazonian industries were relatively powerful in the National Congress and most opposed any policies that would place limits on deforestation. Their opposition hamstrung the government's ability to control deforestation effectively in the 1990s, despite relatively strong forestry legislation. And since any attempt to reduce Brazil's impact on the climate would mean reducing deforestation – the main source of emissions – international mitigation commitments were regarded as a political and economic threat. They would be vigorously resisted in the UNFCCC. Nevertheless, as the politics surrounding deforestation of the Amazon began to change in the late 1990s and early 2000s, political space began to open for environmental groups, scientists, politicians and businesses concerned about climate change to assert themselves more effectively. In combination with pressure from the international community, especially in the years prior to the high-stakes and high-profile Copenhagen negotiations, these factors managed to produce a major shift in Brazil's approach to climate governance.

A New Approach to Climate Change

Brazil's current climate governance structures began to take shape during Cardoso's second term. Internationally, political investment in the creation of the CDM ensured that the country would push for ratification of the Kyoto Protocol, especially after the United States (the other main supporter of the CDM) withdrew its support in 2001. Brazil played an important part in helping to bring together the coalition of states that made subsequent agreements at Marrakesh and after possible. Domestically, this effort in the international negotiations was supported by the creation of the Inter-Ministerial Commission on Climate Change (CIMGC) in July 1999. Composed of representatives from nine different ministries as well as the Office of the President, and jointly chaired by the MCT and Ministry of the Environment (MMA), the CIMGC was designed to coordinate action on the issue of climate change across ministries and provide inputs into the government's position in the UNFCCC. The following year, it was supplemented by the creation of the Brazilian Climate Change Forum (BCCF). Designed to enhance the articulation and exchange of ideas about climate change policies, the Forum was comprised of federal, state and municipal government officials, as well as non-governmental organizations (NGOs), academics and businesses, with President Cardoso as its first chairman. Though the BCCF did not have any official power over government policymaking, it provided an important arena for members of civil society and the business community to engage openly with government officials on the issue of climate change.

The CIMGC and BCCF institutionalized the issue of climate change in the Brazilian government for the first time, though their appearance did not immediately translate into strong domestic climate change policies. Primarily, they were created as a result of a desire to develop stronger positions in the UNFCCC negotiations. Around the same time, however, a number of important events coincided to produce a more effective system for forest and land management, and this would eventually have an important effect on climate change policymaking as well (see Banerjee et al. 2008). First among them were major deforestation crises (in 1995 and 1996), which attracted considerable public attention and galvanized Brazil's Congress to modify the Forest Code of 1965. The reform increased the area that needed to remain forested on land in the Amazon from 50 to 80 per cent. This was then followed by the creation of the National Forest Program and the National Conservation Area System, in 2000, which increased the share of sustainably managed private and public forest land and established a framework for the creation and management of national conservation areas.

Together, these changes significantly improved forestry legislation in Brazil and raised the number of protected areas. But they were not enough on their own. Deforestation again escalated to crisis levels in 2004, attracting public condemnation of lax enforcement. Violence related to deforestation in the Amazon also erupted. An American missionary, Dorothy Stang, was murdered in 2005, as were a number of landless workers and activists in various conflicts over land. The intense political fallout from these crises helped to pave the way for further reforms, such as the 2006 Public Forest Management Law. They also made it possible for the MMA to step up enforcement of forestry laws and regulations. The MMA's capacity had been greatly enhanced around this time by the introduction of the Real Time Deforestation Detection System, which provided much more frequent satellite data on deforestation and allowed for more timely enforcement operations. Yet the leadership of Marina Silva (a globally respected socio-environmentalist, associate of the late Chico Mendes, and minister of the environment from 2003 to 2008) and Carlos Minc (minister of the environment after Silva, and a founding member of Brazil's Green Party) proved to be decisive for translating the deforestation crisis into greater MMA authority as well (see Banerjee et al. 2008; Hochstetler & Viola 2012). Silva and Minc had both been given their positions as heads of the MMA largely in order to boost the Lula administration's environmental credentials. Both had had distinguished careers as environmentalists, and, along with growing international and domestic pressure from NGOs and governments, they were able to bolster, at the margin, its ability to carry out its mission in the Amazon more effectively.

The cumulative impact of these changes became apparent to policymakers only towards the end of the decade. On paper, the number of protected areas grew substantially, from just over 20 in 1984 to over 100 in 2002. By 2009 there were 150 protected areas, totalling 700,000 km^2, an amount roughly equivalent to 8–11 per cent of Brazil's total land area. The number of fines levied for violation of forestry laws and regulations increased as well, while a large number of law enforcement operations were undertaken in order to interdict illegal logging. As a result of these changes, deforestation rates in Brazil gradually

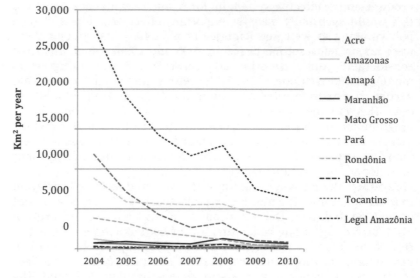

Figure 7.3 Amazonian deforestation, 2004–10

Source: MMA/INPE (2010)

began to decline across all states from the high levels that prevailed in 2004. The deforestation rate in Legal Amazônia reached its lowest recorded level in 2010 – just over 6,000 km² per year (see figure 7.3). This was all the more significant because the decline occurred while Brazil was experiencing high GDP growth rates throughout the period. To the government, therefore, it became increasingly clear that the Amazon could be governed effectively without overly detrimental effects on economic growth.

The change in worldview that this precipitated created a window for groups to push for more robust deforestation and climate policies, as subsequent events showed. Since the election of Lula in 2002, climate change had more or less moved to a back-burner on the national agenda. Engagement continued, but mainly in terms of developing Brazil's scientific understanding of the issue and how it affected the national economy, health and natural environment. A significant initiative was undertaken, for example, to develop Brazil's Initial National Communication to the UNFCCC, released in 2004, which provided a comprehensive assessment of the current state of affairs and decisive issues for Brazil as related to climate change. It made especially clear to policymakers the major challenges that Brazil would encounter as global temperatures rose, as well as the potential range of options and opportunities for taking action domestically. The most significant change in Brazil's domestic governance framework during this period was the creation of Brazil's CDM-related institutions, with the MCT becoming the Designated National Authority (see Friberg 2009). However, beginning around 2007, as climate change gained in worldwide political significance, climate policymaking again began to take shape – this time in a very different manner.

Growing electoral interests played a key role, as Hochstetler & Viola (2012) have emphasized. By mid-decade, politicians in Brazil faced new incentives to shift their approach on global warming as a result of changes in the attitudes of Brazilian voters. According to the Pew Global Attitude Surveys, for example, the number of Brazilian respondents expressing concern about environmental problems grew from 20 per cent to 49 per cent between 2002 and 2007 – the largest rise among the forty-seven countries included in the sample during this period. With respect to climate change, in particular, the Pew Research Center (2009) found that 90 per cent of those surveyed reported that global warming was a very serious problem – the highest share among all those countries surveyed. By comparison, in next-door Argentina – with the second highest share – only 69 per cent of the population thought so. Other polls reveal similar levels of concern. According to a poll conducted by Gallup in 2007 and 2008, 76 per cent of Brazilians considered climate change to be a very serious threat, while 63 per cent thought that less wealthy countries should be expected to limit their emissions (Gallup 2008). Thus, the public became broadly more supportive of greater action on climate change in the years leading up to Copenhagen.

This high level of awareness and support amongst Brazilians could be attributed to a number of factors. First, several extreme weather events became focal points for worries about the impacts of climate change in Brazil. For example, reporting on Hurricane Catarina in 2004, the first to have formed in the South Atlantic since records had been kept, created an opportunity for prominent climate scientists to make their voices heard (Rohter 2007). A drought in the Amazon the following year, which resulted in substantial losses of crops, forest fires and related economic damage, was, similarly, an important catalyst of public awareness. Second, coverage of climate change in the media increased considerably following the release of the Stern Review, Al Gore's *An Inconvenient Truth* and the IPCC's Fourth Assessment Report. One study by ANDI (2009) that documented climate change reporting across fifty national and regional newspapers between 2005 and 2008 found that there was a significant increase in the number of articles, reports and editorials on global warming. During the first half of 2007 alone, the number of articles increased by nearly 200 per cent. Importantly, the study also found that in 80 per cent of these publications the veracity of the science of climate change was taken for granted. Only 9.5 per cent offered a contrarian perspective.

Second, a major cross-section of large and small businesses became important advocates of proactive climate change policies in the second half of the 2000s. Growing support from businesses initially occurred in response to the business community's dissatisfaction with the government's international position on LUCF in the UNFCCC. Its conservative stance, many argued, had blocked possible avenues for international investment in environmental services in Amazonian states. Then, in 2009, as Hochstetler & Viola (2012) have noted, three broad business coalitions – from a range of high carbon emitting/energy intensive sectors, such as agribusiness and the mining industry – became advocates of strong climate policies (see also Viola & Franchini 2012). Each of them made a number of powerful public statements in favour of Brazilian leadership. Led by Vale, one group of twenty-two large corporations released an 'Open Letter to Brazil about Climate Change', calling for declines in deforestation and a reduction of emissions from energy and cattle ranching. A second advocacy group, the Brazilian Climate Alliance, consisted mainly of agribusiness industry associations and also called for strong climate policies and control of deforestation. Finally, a third, the Coalition of Corporations for the Climate, demanded mandatory climate policies and 'peaking' of emissions between 2015 and 2020. Such strong statements from the private sector served further to bolster advocacy by environmental activists, both inside and outside of the government, as well as the more broad-based support from the general public.

A third factor was the growing number of environmental activists occupying key positions within the government, which made it possible to exert much greater pressure over climate policy sceptics than might have otherwise been the case. Building on the national and transnational alliances that had been established during the Earth Summit, environmental activists had increasingly shifted away from confrontational tactics towards a more professional, collaborative – and more influential – kind of relationship with state officials, especially in the 2000s (Alonso & Maciel 2010). Former activists (e.g. Marina Silva, Carlos Minc, etc.) penetrated the state and, in the 2000s, took on important positions in state bureaucracies that allowed them to influence government policymaking more effectively. Despite countervailing pressure from elements in the National Congress and certain ministries, such as Itamaraty and the MCT, they were increasingly able to put climate change on the government's agenda – especially after successes had been achieved in controlling deforestation without concomitant negative effects on economic growth. This could be seen most vividly when climate change unexpectedly became a key dimension of the 2010 presidential election after the former minister of the environment, Marina Silva, renounced her membership in Lula's Workers' Party and joined the race as a Green Party presidential candidate. Silva proved to be very appealing to middle income voters – as a result of her strong positions on corruption, social and environmental issues – as well as with low income voters – as a result of her strong Christian faith and her past history as a rubber tapper. The announcement of her candidacy had a strong effect on the election's trajectory. After garnering 19 per cent of the votes, she managed to force a second round of voting after drawing votes from Dilma Rousseff. Yet, more importantly for our purposes here, her campaign managed to shift public debate towards topics such as climate change, deforestation and sustainable development. Silva's opponents, Rouseff and José Serra, were forced to place greater emphasis on these issues in their campaigns as well. Although Silva would ultimately lose in the first round of voting, her strong performance demonstrated the appeal these issues had for voters.

In response to this changing domestic situation, the government started to become more proactive. Though the key shift in policy occurred later in 2009, Lula initially called for the elaboration of a national plan for restructuring the government's activities and policies related to climate change in April 2007. In November 2007, the Inter-Ministerial Committee for Climate Change (CIM) was created under the Office of the Presidency to replace the CIMGC, and was given the task of preparing a National Policy on Climate Change through a Presidential Decree. Subsequently, after an extended consultation process among the ministries and regulatory agencies involved, the CIM released the National Plan on Climate Change in December 2008, outlining an ambitious strategy for lowering emissions which marked a significant departure from the government's previous approach to climate change. The plan identified seven major targets:

1. stimulating energy efficiency in the economy;
2. keeping Brazil's high share of renewable energy in its electric matrix;
3. encouraging the sustainable increase in the share of biofuels in the national transport matrix and working towards the structuring of an international market of sustainable biofuels;
4. seeking sustained reduction in deforestation rates, in all Brazilian biomass, in order to reach zero illegal deforestation;
5. eliminating the net loss of forest coverage in Brazil by 2015;
6. strengthening inter-sector actions concerned with the reduction of the vulnerabilities of populations; and
7. identifying environmental impacts resulting from climate change and stimulating scientific research that could trace out a strategy to minimize the socio-economic costs of the country's adaptation. (adapted from Government of Brazil 2008)

Several of these targets, of course, merely signalled the government's intention to continue or enhance policies which were already prominent in national policymaking. For instance, the expansion of biofuels and the creation of greater opportunities for exporting to international markets had already become an important dimension of national policy. The Plan, nevertheless, recast them specifically as climate mitigation actions. Under each target a number of individual actions were elaborated, calling not only for the implementation of already existing policies and laws but, frequently, for the establishment of altogether new ones as well. Targets 4 and 5 were, by far, the newest and most ambitious. They marked the first occasion on which the Brazilian government established specific macro-goals for tackling LUCF as part of a comprehensive approach to climate change. Again, the Plan specified the objectives of each target. Target 4, for instance, called for reducing the average deforestation rates for 2006–9 by 40 per cent compared to the average rate that had prevailed in Brazil from 1996 to 2005, as well as for 30 per cent reductions (in relation to the preceding period) for the following two four-year periods.

The Plan was not altogether free from criticism. In late 2008, a group of prominent national and international civil society organizations expressed their dissatisfaction with the government's consultation process, the Plan's incompleteness and its lack of overall targets for reducing GHG emissions. A 'manifesto' coordinated by the Climate Observatory was presented to Carlos Minc, the minister of the environment. It contained a number of important criticisms of the Brazilian Plan and called for the establishment of a comprehensive legal framework for tackling climate change. But, in 2009, the government took two actions that partially addressed several of the concerns expressed in the manifesto, largely as a result of the assertive advocacy of Carlos Minc and other pro-environment representatives in the National Congress (Marina Silva – at this point a presidential candidate – among them), who had taken on other, more conservative groups and bureaucracies, such as Itamaraty and the MCT. First, taking a leadership role in the negotiations, the government submitted its Plan as a voluntary commitment under the Copenhagen Accord and announced that it would aim to reduce national emissions by 36–9 per cent below its baseline emissions scenario by 2020. Second, the government took the unprecedented action of making the National Policy on Climate Change (the Política Nacional sobre Mudança do Clima, or PNMC), which now included the overall emissions reduction target presented to the world at Copenhagen, legally binding with the passing of Federal Law No. 12.187. This law would still leave much of the legal framework and mechanisms for reaching the Plan's goals to be established. Individual mandatory targets would require other federal decrees to specify the actions that needed to be taken in order to meet them (Crawford et al. 2010). However, the law would require all government policies and programmes to take account of the PNMC in their elaboration and implementation, and a National Fund for Climate Change was created to help implement it.

Conclusion

Brazil's approach to climate change has, therefore, altered quite dramatically in recent years. Since the start of the UNFCCC negotiations, the country has had a very strong position with respect to its energy emissions. In contrast to many emerging economies, its energy sector was not very carbon intensive. However, deforestation effectively made Brazil one of the most notable contributors to global emissions in the developing world. Effective control was hindered by the absence of the rule of law; poor monitoring and enforcement capacity, as a result of the Amazon's size and the poorly resourced, understaffed, undertrained and sometimes corrupt enforcement agencies; and active resistance from many Brazilian politicians, who feared the potentially dire economic consequences of hard limits on land use change and deforestation. The country's inability to govern Amazonian deforestation effectively shaped Brazil's conservative position in the multilateral negotiations to a considerable extent. Domestically, it was not feasible for the government to set targets on emissions if it could not effectively control the market forces that produced huge cycles of deforestation.

Between 1996 and 2006, however, the Brazilian government changed course on the Amazon as a result of repeated deforestation crises, growing violence, greater institutional capacity and political dynamics within Lula's Workers' Party. Deforestation rates began to decline across all states after 2004 because of improved legislation and better enforcement of laws and regulations by the MMA and IBAMA. Importantly, this occurred while the Brazilian economy was expanding significantly, and this strengthened the government's confidence in its ability to set and meet deforestation targets without sacrificing economic growth. Internationally, Brazil continued to be something of a climate 'laggard', refusing, along with other developing states, to sign up to compulsory emission reductions. It continued to insist, rightly, that developed countries take responsibility for their historical role in creating the problem. Yet, at the domestic level, changes in Brazil's ability to control deforestation created an opportunity for domestic actors to push for a more proactive approach to climate change. Awareness and support among Brazilian voters increased and created new incentives for politicians, environmental activists occupying important positions within the state were able to put pressure on the government and shape political debate, and many businesses advocated for more ambitious policies as well.

These new forces in Brazilian politics have underpinned an important shift in the government's approach to climate change. Brazil is now thought to be one of the more progressive non-Annex I countries in the climate change regime (see World Bank 2010; Abramovay 2010). However, it is important to note by way of conclusion the many challenges that remain and which could place this status at risk. Vested interests within the government continue to oppose strong enforcement of forestry laws in Brazil and hope to repeal existing legislation. Prior to the Rio+20 Summit, in 2012, the Lower House of Brazil's National Congress managed to pass a revised Forest Code that would have reduced the area of land that needs to remain forested on private property and created an amnesty for past violations. Ultimately, many of the most worrying revisions were vetoed by Dilma Rousseff in order to pre-empt the international and domestic outcry that would have occurred had the changes passed unaltered while Brazil hosted the Rio+20 Summit. But the attempt clearly demonstrated that strong opposition forces could threaten the gains achieved thus far. Going forward, a number of new trends in Brazil are also likely to put renewed pressure on the Amazon in upcoming years. The government is pushing for roughly US$120 billion of public and private sector investment in the Amazon by 2020, including new roads, electricity transmission systems, mines and industrial farms. Many also worry that its strong emphasis on biofuels and hydropower may have unintended effects on LUCF emissions. The planned flooding of large swathes of the Amazon for the new Belo Monte dam, for example, has been heavily criticized for underestimating its potential impact on the climate. Finally, the government's emphasis on the development of the 'Pre-Salt' oil fields, including industrial policies favourable to the automotive and other oil-related sectors, may also prove counterproductive and could create tensions with other 'pro-climate' forces. Thus, while the changes that have taken place have led to a major turn-around in Brazil's domestic approach, the successes that have been achieved ultimately remain fragile.

Notes

The research upon which this study is based is primarily derived from semi-structured interviews with a range of stakeholders and observers in Brasilia and Rio de Janeiro that were conducted in May 2011. Those interviewed included officials from several relevant bureaucracies, individuals from civil society groups that have closely followed climate change issues for some time, as well as a number of academics, journalists and diplomatic officials. All are to be thanked for contributing their time, and, of course, none can be held responsible for any of the conclusions reached in this chapter. We would also like to thank our colleagues who read through and commented on various iterations of this chapter, especially Eduardo Viola, whose insights added great value.

1 See, for example, the discussion of climate change politics in the state and city of São Paulo in Hochstetler & Keck (2007), Abramovay (2010) and Lucon & Goldemberg (2010).

References

Abramovay, R. (2010). Decarbonizing the growth model of Brazil: addressing both carbon and energy intensity. *Journal of Environment & Development* 19(3).

Alonso, A. & D. Maciel (2010). From protest to professionalization: Brazilian environmental activism after Rio-92. *Journal of Environment & Development* 19(3).

Andersen, L. E. (1996). The causes of deforestation in the Brazilian Amazon. *Journal of Environment & Development* 5(3).

ANDI (2009). *Mudanças Climáticas na Imprensa Brasileira. Uma Análise Comparativa de 50 Jornais nos Períodos: Julho de 2005 a junho de 2007, Julho de 2007 a dezembro de 2008.* Available at: http://migre.me/3aK8k.

Banerjee, O., A. J. Macpherson & J. Alavalapati (2008). Toward a policy of sustainable forest management in Brazil: a historical analysis. *Journal of Environment & Development* 18(2).

Binswanger, H. P. (1991). Brazilian policies that encourage deforestation. *World Development* 19(7).

Cole, J. C. (2012). Genesis of the CDM: the original policy making goals of the 1997 Brazilian Proposal and their evolution in the Kyoto Protocol negotiations into the CDM. *International Environmental Agreements* 12(1).

Crawford, C., S. Teles da Silva & K. Morris (2010). South/North exchange of 2009. The challenges of climate change and regulation for governments on the political left: a comparison of Brazilian and United States promises and actions. *Pace International Law Review Online Companion* September.

Da Silva, J. H. G. & K. Kis-Katos (2010). Economic causes of deforestation in the Brazilian Amazon: a panel data analysis for 2000s. *Proceedings of the German Development Economics Conference, Hannover 2010* (34).

de Oliveira, A. (2007). Political economy of the Brazilian power industry reform. In D. Victor (ed.) *The Political Economy of Power Sector Reform: The Experiences of Five Major Developing Countries.* Stanford, CA: Stanford University Press.

Dias de Moraes, M. A. F. (2007). *Reflections on Brazil's Ethanol Industry.* MRE Report. Available at: http://www.dc.mre.gov.br/imagens-e-textos/Biocombustiveis-08 ing-consideracoesetanol.pdf.

Foresta, R. (1992). Amazonia and the politics of geopolitics. *Geographical Review* 82(2).

Friberg, L. (2009). Varieties of carbon governance. The Clean Development Mechanism in Brazil: a success story challenged. *Journal of Environment & Development* 18(4).

Gallup (2008). *Top-Emitting Countries Differ on Climate Change Threat.* Available at: http://www.gallup.com/poll/124595/Top-Emitting-Countries-Differ-Climate-Change-Threat.aspx.

Government of Brazil (2008). *National Plan on Climate Change: Executive Summary.* Available at: http://www.mma.gov.br/estruturas/imprensa/_arquivos/96_1112 2008040728.pdf.

Hecht, S. (2005). Soybeans, development and conservation on the Amazon frontier. *Development and Change* 36(2).

Hira, A. & L. G. de Oliveira (2009). No substitute for oil? How Brazil developed its ethanol industry. *Energy Policy* 37.

Hochstetler, K. & M. Keck (2007). *Greening Brazil: Environmental Activism in State and Society.* Durham, NC: Duke University Press.

Hochstetler, K. & E. Viola (2012). Brazil and the politics of climate change: beyond the global commons. *Environmental Politics* 19(1).

IEA (2007). *Biofuel Production.* IEA Energy Technology Essentials. Available at: http://www.iea.org/techno/essentials2.pdf.

IEA (2012). *2009 Energy Balance for Brazil.* IEA Energy Statistics. Available at: http://www.iea.org/stats/balancetable.asp?COUNTRY_CODE=BR.

Leite, A. D. (2009). *Energy in Brazil: Towards a Renewable Energy Dominated System.* London: Earthscan.

Lucon, O. & J. Goldemberg (2010). São Paulo – the 'other' Brazil: different pathways on climate change for state and federal governments. *Journal of Environment & Development* 19(3).

Margulis, S. (2004). *Causes of Deforestation of the Brazilian Amazon.* World Bank Working Paper No. 22.

MMA/INPE (2010). *PRODES Database.* Available at: http://www.obt.inpe.br/prodes/seminario2010/index.html.

Nass, L.L., P. A. Pereira & D. D. Ellis (2007). Biofuels in Brazil: an overview. *Crop Science* 47.

Pew Research Center (2009). *Pew Global Attitudes Project.* Available at: http://pewglobal.org/files/pdf/264.pdf.

Rohter, L. (2007). Brazil, alarmed, reconsiders policy on climate change. *New York Times* 31 July.

Roman, M. (2007). *What Order in Progress? Brazilian Energy Policies and Climate Change in the Beginning of the 21st Century.* Centre for Climate Science and Policy Research, Report 07:02. Available at: http://liu.diva-portal.org/smash/get/diva2:241999/FULLTEXT01.

Viola, E. & M. Franchini (2012). Climate politics in Brazil: public awareness, social transformations and emissions reduction. In I. Bailey & H. Compston (eds.) *Feeling the Heat: The Politics of Climate Policy in Rapidly Industrializing Countries.* Basingstoke: Palgrave Macmillan.

World Bank (2010). *Brazil: Low Carbon Country Case Study.* Washington, DC: World Bank.

WRI (1990). *World Resources, 1990–91.* Oxford: Oxford University Press.

WRI (1992). *World Resources, 1992–93.* Oxford: Oxford University Press.

WRI (2011). *Climate Analysis Indicators Tool 2011.* Version 5.0. Washington, DC: World Resources Institute. Available at: http://cait.wri.org.

8

Making 'Peace with Nature': Costa Rica's Campaign for Climate Neutrality

Robert Fletcher

Introduction

O N 7 June 2007, the then president and Nobel Peace Prize laureate Oscar Arias Sánchez made international headlines by announcing Costa Rica's intention to become the world's first carbon neutral country by 2021, the nation's bicentennial.[1] In the following months this announcement was propagated by news agencies around the world, further cementing Costa Rica's long-standing reputation as a global leader in progressive environmental initiatives (see e.g. Evans 1999; NRDC 2007). Heralding Arias' pledge, for instance, the watchdog organization Climate Action Tracker praised Costa Rica as a 'role model' for the world (cited in Hermwille 2011, p. 10), while Hermwille (2011, p. 10) more recently asserted that '[b]y accepting such a demanding challenge' the nation has advanced 'to the forefront of climate protection and set an example for developing and developed countries alike'.

This inclusion of Costa Rica in 'the vanguard' (Hermwille 2011, p. 10) of climate change policymakers is a dramatic reversal of fortune from the 1980s, when the country, on the contrary, boasted the highest deforestation rate in the Western hemisphere (Evans 1999), resulting in some scathing international criticism for poor environmental stewardship (e.g. Hunter 1994). In this chapter, I chart Costa Rica's dramatic transformation in the global spotlight from environmental 'laggard to leader', particularly in terms of the country's ambitious and innovative measures to address the effects of anthropogenic climate change. Climate governance in the country is highly complex and dynamic, involving numerous stakeholders at different scales, both domestic and international. Rather than a comprehensive assessment, therefore, I can provide only an overview of some of the regime's most significant highlights. The analysis is based on my long-term ongoing research investigating strategies of environmental governance throughout the country. This research, involving interviews and participant observation with natural resource managers and users in a number of locations, has examined various dimensions of environmental governance, including ecotourism and protected area conservation (Fletcher 2012a), watershed management and hydroelectric power development (Fletcher 2010), and payment for environmental services (Fletcher & Breitling 2012).

I begin by describing the drivers behind the country's largely successful effort to reverse deforestation, documenting this effort's increasing incorporation into climate change concerns via an innovative payment for environmental services (PES) programme. I then discuss the development of the carbon neutrality initiative and its evolution through the end of the Arias administration. I suggest that all of this can best be understood by situating it within the overarching context of Costa Rica's evolving approach to governance generally, a trend towards increasing neoliberalization throughout the society over the past several decades expressed in the environmental arena in an increasing emphasis on so-called 'market-based mechanisms' such as ecotourism, PES and Reducing Emissions from Deforestation and Forest Degradation (REDD). On the other hand, as with all neoliberalization efforts, this process has been partial and piecemeal, with the state retaining a strong hand in aspects of environmental governance as well as other political arenas. This hybrid neoliberal–welfare state structure, I contend, largely defines Costa Rica's climate governance strategy at present. After developing this framework, I outline some of the significant obstacles in this face of actualizing this ambitious neutrality proposal and describe how these are being addressed.

Making 'Peace with Nature'

In the 1950s, a full 50 per cent of Costa Rica's territory was covered in forest (Evans 1999). Diffusion of the chainsaw in that period, however, dramatically transformed this picture, allowing the agricultural frontier to expand much more quickly than before (Cole-Christensen 1997; Evans 1999). This was encouraged by a national forestry policy decreeing that title to new land could be claimed only by 'improving' (i.e. clearing) it. In the 1970s, deforestation accelerated because of the growth of the global fast food industry, whose demand for beef compelled increased clearing of forest for pastureland (Edelman 1999; Evans 1999). By the end of the 1980s, indeed, Costa Rica had become the foremost supplier of beef to the North American fast food market while its deforestation rate, as noted above, was among the highest in the world.

The alarming pace and impacts of this deforestation were recognized early, first by the biologists, mostly European and North American, who had been busy documenting Costa Rica's impressive biodiversity since the end of World War II (Evans 1999; Chornook & Guindon 2008). They and others began to campaign for protection of the remaining rainforest in the face of agricultural expansion,

156

appealing to private landholders as well as the national government. Both efforts found sympathetic audiences. Campaigning on the private front resulted in the establishment, in 1973, of the famous Monteverde Cloud Forest Reserve, owned by an immigrant community of Quakers from the United States and managed by the Tropical Sciences Center, a research institute based in San José (Vivanco 2006). Meanwhile, political lobbying had led to enactment in 1969 of a new Forestry Law that established a National Park Service, under the direction of legendary conservationists Mario Boza and Alvaro Ugalde, which quickly set about expropriating representative parcels of forest throughout the country's numerous eco-zones and placing them under federal protection. The result was a frenetic contest between the forces of expansion and preservation, each encouraged by its own arm of the government, each striving to claim as much remaining unclaimed land as possible before the other could gain hold of it.

Despite the nascent Park Service's efforts, however, Costa Rica's forests continued to disappear at an impressive rate, such that by 1990 the percentage of land under forest cover had diminished by half to under 25 per cent total (Evans 1999). By this time, the Park Service's enclosure campaign had begun to wane, with most of the land capable of expropriation already acquired, such that over one quarter of the country was eventually included in the national protected area system. Despite continued issues of illegal logging and other forms of encroachment in the national parks, most of the remaining deforestation at this time was occurring on private land (as well as government land with less stringent regulation and oversight).

Hence, mechanisms were needed to discourage deforestation on these lands in the absence of formal, state-centred, command-and-control regulation. In 1991, the United States Agency for International Development (USAID) took an initial step in this effort with a US$7.5 million grant to create an incentive structure to address deforestation in the particularly affected Sarapiquí province in the northeast of the country (Borges-Mendéz 2008). Out of this initiative grew the non-governmental organization (NGO) Fundación para el Desarrollo de la Cordillera Volcánica Central (FUNDECOR), created jointly by USAID and the Costa Rican state. Its programme, Forest Resources for a Stable Environment (FORESTA), became the pilot project for a national system of payment for environmental services (called Pago por Servicios Ambimentales, or PSA), initiated in 1997 via a renovated Forestry Law (Ley no. 7575) enacted the previous year.

Under the PSA programme, funds are provided to the private owners of forest parcels for the environmental services their lands are seen to confer (see Pagiola 2008; Daniels et al. 2010). The programme encompasses four distinct services – watershed maintenance, biodiversity preservation, carbon sequestration and scenic beauty – that are bundled together in a single payment which varies with the specific modality in which a given parcel is enrolled. The programme comprises a number of such modalities, including conservation of existing forests, planned reforestation, natural regeneration, agroforestry and sustainable forest management (this last modality was briefly excluded from the programme in 2000, then subsequently reintroduced), each with its own specific requirements and payment structure (for details see Daniels et al. 2010).

While PSA encompasses several other environmental services in addition to carbon sequestration, the programme was Costa Rica's first concerted effort to conjoin forest policy with the growing global effort to address anthropogenic climate change. The programme was complemented by the creation of a national joint implementation office intended to link PSA with the emerging Kyoto Protocol of the United Nations Framework Convention on Climate Change (UNFCCC), particularly the flexibility mechanisms under discussion at the time, so that Costa Rica would be able to fund PSA through the sale of carbon credits on the international market expected to develop out of Kyoto. To help jumpstart this initiative, Norway provided an initial payment of US$2 million in 1997 for 200 million tonnes of CO_2 equivalent offsets (Sánchez-Azofeifa et al. 2007, p. 1167). In the years since its inception the PSA programme has proven very popular and expanded substantially, such that by 2008 it had encompassed nearly 700,000 hectares nationwide (Daniels et al. 2010) while continuing to receive five times the applications it was able to support (Sierra & Russman 2006). As a result, PSA has become quite well known internationally and widely celebrated as a model of best practice for the development of PES programmes elsewhere (see e.g. Pagiola 2008; Daniels et al. 2010). The most recent assessments suggest that as a result of this and other efforts Costa Rica's forests have now recovered to 1950s levels, encompassing 52.38 per cent of the country (FONAFIFO 2012).

The carbon neutrality initiative launched in 2007 by President Arias (and codified in Decree No. 33487–MP) therefore represented merely an intensification of Costa Rica's long-standing effort to link domestic environmental protection to climate action, both at home and internationally. Titled 'Paz con la Naturaleza' ('Peace with Nature', or PCN), the initiative was a skilful and self-conscious effort to capitalize on the two attributes for which Costa Rica is most known in the international arena: its ostensibly non-violent nature (represented, foremost, by the abolition of its formal military in 1948 and Arias' receipt of the Nobel Peace Prize in 1987); and its aggressive environmental protection (symbolized, as noted above, by its extensive system of protected areas and global reputation as 'ecotourism's poster child' [Honey 2008, p. 160]). The initiative built on a more general *Peace with Nature* manifesto presented by Arias the previous year, in which he called on 'all the countries of the world to unite in a joint effort to strengthen their actions and political commitment in order to reverse the trends of environmental degradation caused by the impact of human activities on the planet's ecosystems' (Arias Sánchez 2006, p. 5). Towards this end, Arias committed Costa Rica to 'lead an initiative by the developing countries that transcends the requirements of international agreements and obligations' as well as 'to promote a form of national administration that will allow our nation to aspire to an economic and social development that is environmentally sustainable' (ibid.).

The mechanisms for accomplishing these aims, however, were not clearly specified. In relation to the international agenda, Arias called for 'a new ethic and a new vision of international cooperation' and formation of 'an alliance between developing countries and developed countries, with a view to achieving the common objective of reversing environmental degradation and maintaining and restoring the planet's vital ecosystems', in pursuit of 'an active and enduring Peace with Nature' (Arias Sánchez 2006, pp. 8, 9). On the national front, the president promised, Costa Rica would pursue a number of vaguely defined goals, including a 'Focus on solutions', a 'Search for partners outside the public sector', 'Designing solid and coherent frameworks for environmental management in the executing units' and 'The "greening" of Public Administration' (Arias Sánchez 2006, pp. 11–12).

The climate neutrality campaign initiated the following year thus constituted the first tangible crystallization of these aims. It was quickly followed by the development of a National Climate Change Strategy (NCCS) under the direction of the minister of environment and energy, Roberto Dobles (Dobles 2008), and the establishment of a new governmental office, led by biologist Pedro Leon, to direct and coordinate climate action across the public sector. Alvaro Umaña, former minister of environment under Arias' first administration in the 1980s, was designated climate change ambassador to represent Costa Rica during UNFCCC negotiations.

The National Strategy guiding all of these efforts comprises both mitigation and adaptation measures (Dobles 2008). Mitigation entails carbon capture and storage through protected area management and a national tree planting campaign, as well as greenhouse gas (GHG) emissions reductions in eight sectors: (1) energy, (2) transport, (3) agriculture and livestock, (4) industry, (5) solid waste, (6) tourism, (7) water resources and (8) land use change. Adaptation calls for risk and vulnerability reduction in seven areas – (1) water resources, (2) agriculture and livestock, (3) fishing, (4) health, (5) infrastructure, (6) coastal areas and (7) biodiversity – as well as 'research and monitoring, early warning systems, [and] strengthening of capacity to improve in an integrated way the country's economic, social, environmental and biophysical capacity to adapt' (Dobles 2008, p. 15).

While the Arias administration was concerned to ensure that the PCN initiative survived the end of its four-year term, the proposed law drafted towards this end was never enacted. As it turned out, there was indeed reason for concern. When Laura Chinchilla, one of Arias' vice-presidents, was elected to succeed him in 2010, funding for PCN ceased and the office was disbanded. It was replaced, however, with a new Direccion de Cambio Climático (Climate Change

Department), headed by William Alpízar, within the Ministry of Environment, Energy and Telecommunications (MINAET), which has assumed responsibility for the climate neutrality campaign and NCCS implementation, as well as the nation's commitment to pursue low emissions development (LED) generally by executing Nationally Appropriate Mitigation Actions (NAMAs) consistent with recent UNFCCC negotiations (see this volume's introduction).

A Green Neoliberal Republic?

These activities are situated within the history of Costa Rica's changing approach to environmental governance generally, characterized by a process of progressive neoliberalization over the past several decades (Edelman 1999). While the term 'neoliberalism' has been employed in diverse ways within academic analyses (see Flew 2012), most precisely defined it refers to the economic philosophy promoting principles of decentralization, deregulation (or more commonly reregulation from states to non-state actors), marketization, privatization and commodification in political and economic affairs (see Harvey 2005; Castree 2008). This philosophy, advanced in the postwar period as a challenge to the popularity of the welfare state in that era, gained prominence in the 1980s with its adoption as the basis of the Reagan and Thatcher administrations in the US and UK, respectively, and subsequent promotion throughout the less developed world by international financial institutions (IFIs) such as the World Bank and International Monetary Fund (IMF) as a component of so-called 'structural adjustment' programmes (SAPs) (see esp. Harvey 2005).

Consonant with this history, prior to the 1980s Costa Rica was characterized by a pervasive welfare state presence in virtually all sectors of society (Edelman 1999). This state-centred approach characterized governance within the environmental sector as well, as represented by the command-and-control 'fortress conservation' model (Brockington 2002; Igoe 2004) dominant within the national park system (Evans 1999). Beginning with Costa Rica's involvement in the 1980s debt crisis, however, this situation transformed dramatically. Three rounds of structural adjustment under supervision by the World Bank and IMF over the next decade spurred pronounced neoliberalization in a variety of sectors, with state agencies downsized or privatized and dramatic cutbacks demanded in welfare provisions, and NGOs offering independent social services increasingly promoted to fill the 'governance gap' left vacant by the retreat of the state (Edelman 1999).[2] This trend quickly manifested within the environmental governance arena as well. In 1991, the consolidated National Park Service was replaced by a far more decentralized National System of Protected Areas (SINAC), which divided the country into eleven distinct 'conservation areas' administered in semi-autonomous fashion. Decreased funding for park management as a component of structural adjustment (Evans 1999) led to an environmental govern-ance gap of sorts that has been increasingly filled by NGOs, both domestic and international, which developed independent conserva-tion policies espousing a variety of market-based strategies, including several well-known debt-for-nature swaps negotiated with the Costa Rican state. In addition, a substantial percentage of the nation's conservation began to be undertaken through an extensive network of private nature reserves, owned by both NGOs and discrete individu-als (Langholz 2003), facilitated by a newfound liberalization of Costa Rica's domestic ownership regulations in order to stimulate foreign direct investment as a novel development strategy (Edelman 1999).

The PSA programme, introduced in the wake of a third SAP under the supervision of the World Bank, which demanded an end to state subsidies for forest management as a condition for a new series of loans, signified an intensification of this neoliberalization within the environmental sector. Explicitly described by many advocates as a 'market-based mechanism' (see e.g. Heindrichs 1997; Pagiola et al. 2002; Brandon 2004), the programme was self-consciously designed to move forest policy 'away from deficit-plagued, subsidized opera-tions that are only able to survive with the aid of state "alms" and toward a form of profitable, competitive land use based on sound business principles' (Heindrichs 1997, p. 23). In quintessential neo-liberal fashion, the programme was also designed to shift the locus of resource control and financing from the state towards non-state actors – particularly the 'private forestry sector' – in order to 'put into practice ideas such as administrative decentralization' and 'mixed public and private financing' (Heindrichs 1997, pp. 11, xi). The struc-ture of the Fondo Nacional de Financiamiento Forestal (National Fund for Forestry Financing, or FONAFIFO), the 'parastatal' agency charged with programme administration, reflects this aim, with two of its five managing directors drawn from the private sector (Heindrichs 1997). In an explicit strategy to achieve 'maximum decentralization' (Heindrichs 1997, p. 43), moreover, FONAFIFO was made largely autonomous in its design and administration and would receive its funding directly from the payments it brokers in order to provide managers with 'a vital interest in identifying and developing new sources of funding' (Heindrichs 1997, p. 43).

Costa Rica's NCCS continues this neoliberal emphasis. The princi-pal means of financing the plan, stated explicitly at several points, is building on the current PSA programme to access international carbon markets. As the Strategy explains, 'carbon markets are the opportunity to establish links between climate change and the competitiveness of national strategies', while '[a]ppropriate financial instruments and carbon markets provide effective incentives for developing countries' (Dobles 2008, p. 20). In conjunction with this, the national carbon neutrality initiative is intended as a branding mechanism to leverage 'C-Neutral' products and services through 'the sustained creation of value for target customers in the market or segment of interests, which proves to be superior to the value offered by the competition' (Dobles 2008, p. 14). In this effort, 'industries and all commercial activities should use carbon neutrality as a business tool, improving competitiveness, profitability, management and customer service quality' (Dobles 2008, p. 22).

On the other hand, Costa Rica in general has long resisted the extreme neoliberalization implemented in other places and retains a strong state presence in many sectors of society (Edelman 1999). In terms of environmental governance, this is evidenced by continued reliance on the state-centred 'fortress' model for managing the majority of protected areas (Fletcher 2012a). Within climate policy specifically, despite common official rhetoric pronouncing PSA a paradigmatic market-based mechanism, in reality the state directly regulates the programme in a number of ways, most significantly in that a large portion of the programme's funding (about 40 per cent) is generated through a national fuel tax and water taxes while only about 1 per cent is actually financed through the voluntary market exchanges intended to form the programme's basis (Daniels et al. 2010; Fletcher & Breitling 2012). Both the NCCS and carbon neutrality initiative appear to reinforce this dynamic, placing the national government at the centre of activity, even in terms of efforts to harness international markets for climate change funding. Hence, Costa Rica's climate governance regime displays the same hybrid neoliberal–welfare state structure evidenced throughout the society at present (Fletcher 2012a; Fletcher & Breitling 2012).

All of this occurs within the context of a global environmental governance system that has itself become increasingly neoliberalized over time, characteristically promoting the quintessential neoliberal tenets outlined above with respect to natural resource management in countless locations around the world, as a rapidly growing body of research documents (see e.g. Heynen et al. 2007; Igoe & Brockington 2007; Brockington et al. 2008; Brockington & Duffy 2010; Arsel & Büscher 2012; Roth & Dressler 2012). As in the case of Costa Rica, however, this neoliberalization is invariably partial and context-specific, involving articulation and accommodation with pre-existing local socio-economic institutions (see Harvey 2005; Dressler & Roth 2010; Büscher & Dressler 2012).

In line with this analysis, researchers have highlighted an increasing neoliberalization within global climate change discourse and policy in particular (see Fletcher 2012b). Oels (2005) for instance, observes that global discourse concerning climate change underwent a decisive shift in the 1980s and 1990s, particularly following the 1997 Kyoto Summit, towards increasing neoliberalization (or 'advanced liberal government', as she, following Rose [1999], labels it). Expanding upon this analysis, While and colleagues (2009) describe a multi-stage shift in climate change discourse consonant with changing environmental policy in general. Like Oels, the authors describe climate change discussion as centred on a state-led 'prevention and control' approach in the 1970s (While et al. 2009, p. 5). In the 1980s, however, concern over climate change became incorporated into the emerging sustainable development discourse, in terms of which the issue became fused with concerns to sustain economic growth within a neoliberal framework 'characterized by flexibility, ambiguity and a lack of prescription in target-setting' (While et al. 2009, p. 7). The authors then identify a further wave of neoliberalization in the 1990s 'characterized by experimentation with market-based "new environmental policy instruments"' (ibid.) such as carbon trading and PES – a process that has intensified in recent years as climate change has become 'the new "master concept" of environmental regulation' generally (While et al. 2009, p. 2).

Neoliberalization within climate change policy is demonstrated most starkly, perhaps, by the Kyoto Protocol (Oels 2005), which has promoted: (1) an emphasis on the creation of markets for trade in environmental services (Bumpus & Liverman 2008); (2) commodification of resources in order to 'price nature's services' (Bumpus & Liverman 2008, p. 132); (3) privatization through assigning individual property rights for emissions production; (4) a decentralized governance structure involving loose coordination by transnational institutions; (5) reliance, by and large, on voluntary mitigation measures adopted by discrete nation-states or 'sub-national units' (regions, cities, etc.) (While et al. 2009); and finally, (6) the increasing influence of 'non-nation state actors' (e.g. NGOs and businesses) within climate politics (Okereke et al. 2009).

Beyond the State

In relation to this last dynamic, while the national state, as noted above, remains central to climate change policy, climate governance in Costa Rica has increasingly included a variety of non-state actors too. This is due, in large part, to the fact that, consistent with neoliberal policy in general (Levine 2002), funds for climate action administered by IFIs as well as private donors are increasingly directed specifically towards non-state actors as an ostensibly more efficient and flexible alternative to cumbersome and bureaucratic state agencies (Okereke et al. 2009). Prominent non-state players in Costa Rica include, of course, FUNDECOR, the NGO mentioned above as responsible for administering PSA in the Sarapiquí region. As noted earlier, Costa Rican conservation has long been strongly influenced by a number of prominent international NGOs, including such powerhouses as Conservation International (CI), The Nature Conservancy (TNC), World Wide Fund for Nature (WWF) and the Natural Resources Defense Council (NRDC), as well as others less well known outside the country, and many of these have become involved in climate mitigation and adaptation projects as the global emphasis in environmental governance (and funding) becomes increasingly focused on climate change specifically (While et al. 2009). The internationally renowned agricultural research institute Centro Agronómico Tropical de Investigación y Enseñanza (CATIE) is also involved in a number of initiatives, including a reforestation project developed jointly with NRDC and an innovative effort to reduce emissions from milk and beef production by capturing methane and engaging in other energy saving measures vis-à-vis cattle raising. A domestic civil society group called 'co2Neutral2021' composed of self-styled 'young professionals' has established itself as a watchdog of sorts to monitor the government's progress towards carbon neutrality and promote their own initiatives in this effort.

Elements of the private sector have entered the climate arena as well. The recently formed National Ecotourism Chamber of Commerce (CANAECO), composed of prominent domestic tourism operators, has established an agreement with FONAFIFO to promote 'Climate Conscious Travel' by urging operators to compensate for their clients' emissions both en route to and within the country through paying into the PSA programme. CANAECO's board of directors includes representatives of Nature Air, a domestic carrier claiming to be the 'world's first certified carbon neutral airline' on the basis of their offsetting of emissions through PSA, in addition to Mapache, a car rental agency that pursues a similar strategy. Such initiatives make up the small portion of the PSA programme funded through voluntary payments by domestic businesses, including a number of private hydroelectric dams as well as several beverage manufacturers with an interest in securing clean water sources (Blackman & Woodward 2010). There are also innumerable independent conservation and reforestation projects implemented on privately held land throughout the country.

In addition to this work by non-state actors at the domestic level, Costa Rican climate policy is strongly shaped by various international interests. The World Bank has long been particularly influential, having helped to establish the PSA programme, as noted above, and continuing to mould it both through research and advising (see e.g. Pagiola 2008) and through finance; currently about 40 per cent of PSA funding comes from World Bank loans and grants from the Global Environment Facility (GEF), an institution created by the World Bank in conjunction with the United Nations Environment and Development Programmes (Daniels et al. 2010). The German International Development Bank (Kreditanstalt für Wiederaufbau) funds approximately 10 per cent of PSA for carbon sequestration in the north of the country as well (Blackman & Woodward 2010).

The US government has also been quite influential in climate change policy (and many other aspects of Costa Rican politics) for some time. As previously noted, USAID helped spur PSA development through the FORESTA project that created FUNDECOR, and the organization has recently renewed involvement through the Tropical Forest Conservation Act (TFCA), which provides funds for forest protection in less developed countries specifically linked to carbon sequestration via a new generation of debt-for-nature swaps. Costa Rica has been targeted twice by this programme thus far, first in 2007 with a pledge of US$26 million in debt forgiveness over sixteen years, then again in 2010 with a second commitment of US$27 million more (USAID 2012). All of this money is to be administered as part of the Costa Rica Por Siempre (Costa Rica Forever) fund for domestic conservation enhancement jointly managed by CI, TNC and the Costa Rican National Biodiversity Institute (INBio), another 'parastatal' entity responsible for inventorying the nation's natural resources (see Evans 1999). The US government is also promoting a Low Emissions Development Strategy (LEDS) through its State Department presence in San José with a modest (US$1.5 million) fund primarily directed towards energy efficiency improvements in the agriculture and transport sectors responsible for the majority of the country's emissions.

The Promise of REDD+

As in much of the rest of the (particularly less developed) world, stakeholders throughout Costa Rica are placing much of their faith for future climate action in the emerging Reducing Emissions from Deforestation and Forest Degradation Plus (REDD+) initiative. Costa Rica was, in fact, one of the original architects of this initiative, having first proposed in conjunction with Papua New Guinea a simpler RED plan focused only on avoiding emissions from deforestation before the Eleventh Conference of the Parties (COP11) in 2005 in Montreal (Governments of Papua New Guinea and Costa Rica 2005). This proposal urged the UNFCCC 'to take note of present rates of deforestation within developing nations, acknowledge the resulting carbon emissions, and consequently open dialogue to develop scientific, technical, policy and capacity responses to address such emissions resulting from tropical deforestation' (Governments of Papua New Guinea and Costa Rica 2005, p. 2). It concluded by highlighting 'the climatic importance of deforestation and facilitat[ing] meaningful discussion by suggesting some possible approaches. Parties must effectively address the significant emissions resulting from deforestation and the associated implications relative to lasting climatic stability. Time is of the essence' (Governments of Papua New Guinea and Costa Rica 2005, p. 10). In subsequent meetings this proposal was expanded to include issues of land degradation (the second D) as well as conservation and enhancement of existing forest stocks (the +) and was thus eventually promoted as an expanded REDD+ initiative, endorsed by the UNFCCC in 2007 at COP13 in Bali and finally adopted as policy at COP16 in Cancun. In terms of global governance the initiative is supported both by the UN through its collaborative initiative on Reducing Emissions from Deforestation and Forest Degradation (UN-REDD Programme) (http://www.un-redd.org) and by the World Bank through the Forest Carbon Partnership Facility (FCPF). Commonly cited World Bank estimates suggest that global financing for REDD+ will reach at least US$30 billion by 2020 (see e.g. Phelps et al. 2010).

Hence, Costa Rica along with many other less developed nations around the world is hoping to tap this greatly anticipated new source of funds for its climate change initiatives. While the specific architecture of the REDD+ mechanism remains under discussion, Costa Rica is among a number of countries awarded funding (in this case US$3.4 million) though the FCPF's 'REDD Readiness' initiative to develop the rigorous measuring, reporting and verification (MRV) procedures requisite to programme implementation. As Daniels et al. (2010, p. 2124) observe, REDD+ 'will undoubtedly include using PES as a mechanism to address deforestation', and this is particularly true with respect to Costa Rica, whose Readiness Plan states quite explicitly that the PSA programme 'will act as a basis of Costa Rica's REDD+ Strategy' (Government of Costa Rica 2010, p. 9). Hence, the majority of REDD+ funds are likely to be managed by FONAFIFO, which hopes to use this money to address the perennial excess demand by landowners for inclusion in PSA. FUNDECOR is also hoping to access REDD funds for its PSA projects in Sarapiquí through an agreement with another NGO called Pax Natura (which, despite its similar name, appears to have no relation to Arias' Peace with Nature initiative) to broker avoided deforestation credits on the voluntary carbon offset (VCO) market (see Bumpus & Liverman 2008).

Programme officials claim, however, that the majority of REDD funds will be directed towards indigenous communities, which are able to register much larger parcels than individual landowners and which have been largely excluded from the benefits of many development initiatives in the past. Costa Rica's REDD Readiness Plan, consonant with World Bank requirements, was in fact drafted with indigenous consultation and calls for creation of a REDD+ board of directors comprising FONAFIFO's current board and two additional members, one drawn from 'civil society' and the other representing the Association of Comprehensive Indigenous Development (ADII). Hence, indigenous peoples, long marginalized within national politics (see Evans 1999), may be able to harness REDD+ to gain a more central position within environmental governance discussions. On the other hand, significant concerns have been raised internationally concerning the potentially negative impacts of REDD+ development on indigenous communities generally (e.g. Newswire 2011).

As Phelps and colleagues (2010) observe, the emphasis on national-level accounting in most REDD+ discussions may have important ramifications for the future of environmental governance generally, possibly functioning to reverse the dominant neoliberal trend towards decentralization, noted above, increasingly promoted over the past several decades, by recentralizing forest governance in the hands of the state institutions responsible for MRV implementation. This, indeed, seems likely to occur in Costa Rica, where, as noted above, REDD policy is intended to be directed primarily by the national government via FONAFIFO.

Still, most authorities continue to envision REDD as an intensification of neoliberal policies. As the Costa Rican REDD Readiness Plan states, while some stakeholders, including indigenous groups and civil society representatives, demand that REDD policy 'would not exclusively target global carbon markets for the reward of avoided deforestation and enhancement in forest carbon stocks', the majority of stakeholders apparently 'agree that the compensation for the reduction of emissions or improvement of stocks in privately owned forests is more viable through local and global market mechanisms' (Government of Costa Rica 2010, p. 9).

Bumps on the Road

Notwithstanding all of the ambitious national plans and concrete local actions detailed above, it is apparent that the Costa Rican government has taken few tangible steps thus far actually to implement its carbon neutrality proposal. The civil society group co2neutral2012 in fact claims that since the plan's introduction the country's emissions have risen substantially, declaring in 2009:

> [W]e believe that few effective measures have been implemented to reduce carbon emissions since the Peace with Nature declaration. Indeed, Costa Rica's greenhouse gas emissions have continued to grow at alarming rates. If the country continues on its current unsustainable development path, its emissions will increase by at least 33% by 2021. (Roberto Jimenez, press release, 9 August 2009)

While no comprehensive assessment of Costa Rica's carbon footprint has been undertaken since, this trend does not appear to have reversed in subsequent years (Long 2011). Hence, the nation's status as global role model for climate change action pegged to its neutrality pledge remains a largely unrealized potential at present. There are a number of significant obstacles, indeed, to actualizing this potential. The first and foremost of these concerns money. Direccion de Cambio Climático officials claim that neutrality could in fact be realistically achieved by as early as 2014 if sufficient funding were available. Costs estimates vary but they are all quite high. According to an evaluation conducted by the prestigious business school INCAE, attaining neutrality would cost in the order of US$7.8 billion (Long 2011, p. 22). Pedro Leon, former head of the PCN office, has cited even larger figures: around US$10 billion for investment in clean energy production with an equivalent amount needed to build an efficient system of mass public transport.

Such funds are clearly far beyond anything that the Costa Rican state could possibly hope to mobilize on its own (Long 2011). From the outset, indeed, the government has been quite candid that carbon neutrality cannot be achieved without substantial financial assistance from international donors. The NCCS states bluntly that 'the totality of the cost' for implementing the Strategy 'cannot be covered domestically' (Dobles 2008, p. 23). Hence, the Strategy seeks, as one of its key components, to 'Exert international influence and Attract financial resources', explaining, 'In order to implement the strategy, an access to new and additional financial resources is required, including official funds, concessions toward developing countries, and carbon markets' (Dobles 2008, pp. 18, 20).

In effect, while proclaiming the goal of carbon neutrality, the initiative has from the beginning left itself a face-saving way out of sorts, in that failure to achieve its aim could always be blamed on the international community's unwillingness to support the effort with sufficient financial backing. Hence, some civil society groups contend that 'the pledge was less about emissions and more about public relations' (Long 2011, p. 23). Meanwhile, in 2012 Climate Action Tracker downgraded its evaluation of Costa Rica's performance to merely 'Sufficient' because the nation has made its carbon neutrality initiative 'conditional to external support'.

Second, there are important questions of measurement with respect to neutrality calculations. As Gössling (2009) observes, this is a central issue in any carbon neutrality initiative. In Costa Rica's case, perhaps the most significant measurement issue concerns energy production. The nation is widely viewed as 'a world leader in renewable energy use' (NRDC 2007, p. 1) because most (currently 93 per cent) of its domestic energy is produced without fossil fuels, the majority of this (about 80 per cent of the total) generated by hydroelectric dams (ICE 2009). Hydropower, especially, is generally considered 'clean' energy with zero GHG emissions (Fletcher 2010). Yet in reality hydroelectric dams, particularly in tropical environments, tend to produce substantial emissions, primarily from the methane produced by submerged vegetation released during reservoir drawdown or spill-over (see Mäkinen & Khan 2010). These emissions, however, are neither measured nor taken into account in calculating Costa Rica's carbon balance (Fletcher 2010). Given that the nation's electricity demand is projected to increase by 6 per cent per year for the foreseeable future, and that the majority of this is to be met with increased hydroelectricity production (ICE 2009), including such emissions in neutrality calculations would probably make it quite difficult for the country ever to achieve its goals (Fletcher 2010).

What is taken into account in neutrality calculations depends as well upon how entities 'define their system boundaries' (Gössling 2009, p. 21). The Kyoto Protocol, for example, does not require any specific parties to assume responsibility for emissions from international air transport, while the UN World Tourism Organization's (UNWTO) more recent Davos Declaration, intended to address the tourism industry's climate implications (see UNWTO 2007), demands 'that destinations would only be responsible for emissions released during the tourists' stay' (Gössling 2009, p. 21). Yet revenue generated through international tourism arrivals constitutes one of Costa Rica's most important revenue streams (Honey 2008). Hence, groups such as CANAECO believe that international air transport should be included in Costa Rica's carbon assessment if it is to constitute a meaningful measure.

A third significant issue concerns the extent to which PSA, the main instrument of carbon mitigation at present and the foundation upon which future REDD+ policy is to be based, is in fact responsible for the reduction in deforestation rates commonly attributed to it. Sánchez-Azofeifa et al., for instance, contend that this reduction is actually more due to

> previous forest conservation policies in Costa Rica, including a 199[6] legal restriction on forest clearing ... All of the prior policies, including the creation of national parks and biological reserves and the 199[6] law, have very effectively lowered deforestation ... The success of these previous programs subsequently left the PSA program with little forest clearing to prevent. (2007, p. 1172)

Hence, Daniels and colleagues (2010, p. 2124) conclude that while PSA may have some impact on deforestation in particular locations, 'At the national level, PES had virtually no additional impact on lowering deforestation because forest would have been conserved on PES sites even without payments.' If such assessments are correct, future expansion of the programme in relation to REDD+ funding may be less impactful than anticipated.

Fourth, Costa Rica may have difficulty accessing REDD+ funds even if they materialize on a global scale. PSA, as previously noted, has long been intended to capitalize on international carbon markets by attracting foreign buyers for its carbon offset credits. Yet in reality such buyers have largely failed to appear; the only significant contribution to the programme thus far was from Norway in 1997 (Sánchez-Azofeifa et al. 2007). Overall, as mentioned above, only about 1 per cent of the programme is actually financed by the voluntary transactions envisioned to form its main foundation (Blackman & Woodward 2010). As a result, the programme has been forced to increase reliance on the state-mandated taxes and IFI grants or loans that were eventually to be superseded by self-sustaining markets (Fletcher & Breitling 2012).

REDD+ markets may be even more difficult for Costa Rica to access. The nation's forests are relatively small by world standards, not even appearing in the global 'top ten' (Mollicone et al. 2007, p. 2). Limited REDD+ funds, therefore, are likely to be prioritized elsewhere where they can achieve greater impact. This is compounded by the fact, noted at the outset, that Costa Rica's deforestation rate is currently zero or even negative in some estimates, calling into question the additionality that can be claimed for REDD+ initiatives. In response to this concern, the government asserts that 'the perception that there is no deforestation in Costa Rica is wrong. Despite the fact that in Costa Rica forest coverage is being recovered (net deforestation is negative), forests are still being lost (there is gross deforestation)' (Government of Costa Rica 2010, p. 10). This means that even if forest is expanding overall it is still being lost in certain areas. Hence, avoided deforestation within the country is calculated with respect to specific regions rather than the nation as a whole. In this way, it is hoped that a case can be made for additionality. It remains to be seen, however, whether the international community will find this argument sufficiently convincing.

Conclusion

In the above, I have outlined the current state of the climate change governance regime in Costa Rica, centred on the government's ground-breaking pledge to achieve carbon neutrality to coincide with the nation's bicentennial celebration. I described the origins of this campaign in Costa Rica's long-standing efforts to address environmental degradation, through such measures as the development of the national park system and PSA programmes, resulting in the reversal of the serious deforestation previously rampant throughout the country. I contextualized these environmental initiatives within the nation's evolving governance structure, which has generally moved towards increasing neoliberalization in line with SAPs promoted by influential IFIs, yet also balanced by the state's continued pervasive presence in many societal sectors. Finally, I outlined various obstacles in the path to carbon neutrality and how stakeholders are addressing these.

From its long track record of proactive environmental action, it is clear that Costa Rica possesses the political will to organize a substantial climate response if authorities commit themselves to this goal. Whether the nation will be able to achieve carbon neutrality in any meaningful sense, however, is a far more difficult question. It is apparent that significant action in whatever form will depend, fundamentally, on mobilization of substantial international financial resources which, given the glacial movement of recent UNFCCC negotiations, appear less and less likely to materialize. Hence, as with the international climate governance regime as a whole, the future remains uncertain for this erstwhile global leader of progressive climate action.

Notes

1 This claim was subsequently pre-empted by the Maldives' vow to achieve carbon neutrality by 2020.
2 While NGOs are commonly considered advocates of civil society autonomous from both national states and capitalist markets, critics increasingly contend

that NGOs' dramatic rise over the last several decades has been part and parcel of neoliberalization, helping to promote the principles of decentralization and devolution central to neoliberal doctrine (see e.g. Chapin 2004; Levine 2002).

References

Arias Sánchez, O. (2006). *Conceptual Document: Peace with Nature*. Available at: http://www.costaricasingapore.com/pdf/7b%20Paz%20conceptual%20copy.pdf.

Arsel, M. & B. Büscher (eds.) (2012). *Development and Change* 43(1). Special issue on 'Nature™ Inc.'.

Blackman, A. & R. T. Woodward (2010). User financing in a national payments for environmental services program: Costa Rican hydropower. *Ecological Economics* 69.

Borges-Méndez, R. (2008). Sustainable development and participatory practices in community forestry: the case of FUNDECOR in Costa Rica. *Local Environment* 13(4).

Brandon, K. (2004). The policy context for conservation in Costa Rica: model or muddle? In G. W. Frankie, A. Mata & S. B. Vinson (eds.) *Biodiversity Conservation in Costa Rica*. Berkeley, CA: University of California Press.

Brockington, D. (2002). *Fortress Conservation: The Preservation of the Mkomazi Game Reserve, Tanzania*. Oxford: James Currey.

Brockington, D. & R. Duffy (eds.) (2010). *Antipode* 42(3). Special issue on 'Capitalism and Conservation'.

Brockington, D., R. Duffy & J. Igoe (2008). *Nature Unbound: Conservation, Capitalism and the Future of Protected Areas*. London: Earthscan.

Bumpus, A. & D. Liverman (2008). Accumulation by decarbonisation and the governance of carbon offsets. *Economic Geography* 84.

Büscher, B. & W. Dressler (2012). Commodity conservation: the restructuring of community conservation in South Africa and the Philippines. *Geoforum* 34(3).

Castree, N. (2008). Neoliberalising nature: the logics of deregulation and reregulation. *Environment and Planning A* 40.

Chapin, M. (2004). A challenge to conservationists. *WorldWatch* 17(6).

Chornook, K. & W. Guindon (2008). *Walking with Wolf*. Hamilton, Ontario: Wandering Woods Press.

Cole-Christensen, D. (1997). *A Place in the Rainforest*. Austin, TX: University of Texas Press.

Daniels, A., V. Esposito, K. J. Bagstad, A. Moulaert & C. M. Rodriguez (2010). Understanding the impacts of Costa Rica's PES: are we asking all the right questions? *Ecological Economics* 69.

Dobles, R. (2008). *Summary of the National Climate Change Strategy*. San José: Ministry of Environment and Energy.

Dressler, W. & R. Roth (2010). The good, the bad, and the contradictory: neoliberal conservation governance in rural Southeast Asia. *World Development* 39(5).

Edelman, M. (1999). *Peasants against Globalization: Rural Social Movements in Costa Rica*. Stanford, CA: Stanford University Press.

Evans, S. (1999). *The Green Republic: A Conservation History of Costa Rica*. Austin, TX: University of Texas Press.

Fletcher, R. (2010). When environmental issues collide: climate change and the shifting political ecology of hydroelectric power. *Peace & Conflict Review* 5(1).

Fletcher, R. (2012a). Using the master's tools? Neoliberal conservation and the evasion of inequality. *Development and Change* 43(1).

Fletcher, R. (2012b). Capitalizing on chaos: climate change and disaster capitalism. *Ephemera* 12(1/2).

Fletcher, R. & J. Breitling (2012). Market mechanism or subsidy in disguise? Governing payment for environmental services in Costa Rica. *Geoforum* 43(3).

Flew, T. (2012). Michel Foucault's *The Birth of Biopolitics* and contemporary neoliberalism debates. *Thesis Eleven* 108(1).

FONAFIFO (2012). *Estudio de Cobertura Forestal de Costa Rica*. San José: FONAFIFO.

Gössling, S. (2009). Carbon neutral destinations: a conceptual analysis. *Journal of Sustainable Tourism* 17(1).

Government of Costa Rica (2010). *REDD Readiness Preparation Proposal (R-PP)*. Available at: http://www.forestcarbonpartnership.org/fcp/sites/forestcarbon partnership.org/files/Documents/PDF/Sep2010/R-PP_Costa_Rica_English_08 -19-10.pdf.

Governments of Papua New Guinea and Costa Rica (2005). *Reducing Emissions from Deforestation in Developing Countries: Approaches to Stimulate Action*. Available at: http://unfccc.int/resource/docs/2005/cop11/eng/misc01.pdf.

Harvey, D. (2005). *A Brief History of Neoliberalism*. Oxford: Oxford University Press.

Heindrichs, T. (1997). *Innovative Financing Instruments in the Forestry and Nature Conservation Sector of Costa Rica*. Eschborn: Deutsche Gesellschaft für Technische Zusammenarbeit.

Hermwille, L. (2011). *The Race to Low-Carbon Economies has Started: Developing Countries Leading Low-Carbon Development (Briefing Summary)*. Berlin: Germanwatch.

Heynen, N., J. McCarthy, P. Robbins & S. Prudham (eds.) (2007). *Neoliberal Environments: False Promises and Unnatural Consequences*. New York, NY: Routledge.

Honey, M. (2008). *Ecotourism and Sustainable Development: Who Owns Paradise?* 2nd edn. Washington, DC: Island Press.

Hunter, J. R. (1994). Is Costa Rica truly conservation-minded? *Conservation Biology* 8(2).

ICE (2009). *Plan de Expansión de la Generación Eléctrica 2010–2021*. San José: Instituto Costarricense de Electricidad.

Igoe, J. (2004). *Conservation and Globalization: A Study of National Parks and Indigenous Communities from East Africa to South Dakota*. Belmont, CA: Wadsworth/Thomson.

Igoe, J. & D. Brockington (eds.) (2007). *Conservation and Society* 5(4). Special issue on 'Neoliberal Conservation'.

Langholz, J. A. (2003). Privatizing conservation. In S. Brechin, P. Wilshusen, C. Fortwangler & P. West (eds.) *Contested Nature*. Albany, NY: State University of New York Press.

Levine, A. (2002). Convergence or convenience? International conservation NGOs and development assistance in Tanzania. *World Development* 30(6).

Long, C. (2011). Costa Rica's challenge. *Latin Trade* 19(2).

Mäkinen, K. & S. Khan (2010). Policy considerations for greenhouse gas emissions from freshwater reservoirs. *Water Alternatives* 3(2).

Mollicone, D., A. Freibauer, E. D. Schulze, S. Braatz, G. Grassi & S. Federici (2007). Elements for the expected mechanisms on 'Reduced Emissions from

Deforestation and Degradation, REDD' under UNFCCC. *Environmental Research Letters* 2.

Newswire (2011). *Declaration of the Indigenous Peoples of the World at COP 17.* Newswire, 7 December. Available at: http://intercontinentalcry.org/newswire/declaration-of-the-indigenous-peoples-of-the-world-at-cop-17.

NRDC (2007). *Costa Rica: Setting the Pace for Reducing Global Warming Pollution and Phasing Out Oil.* Washington, DC: Natural Resources Defense Council.

Oels, A. (2005). Rendering climate change governable: from biopower to advanced liberal government? *Journal of Environmental Policy & Planning* 7.

Okereke, C., H. Bulkeley & H. Schroeder (2009). Conceptualizing climate governance beyond the international regime. *Global Environmental Politics* 9(1).

Pagiola, S. (2002). Paying for water services in Central America: learning from Costa Rica. In S. Pagiola, J. Bishop & N. Landell-Mills (eds.) *Selling Forest Environmental Services: Market-Based Mechanisms for Conservation.* London: Earthscan.

Pagiola, S. (2008). Payments for environmental services in Costa Rica. *Ecological Economics* 65.

Pagiola, S., J. Bishop & N. Landell-Mills (2002). Market-based mechanisms for forest conservation and development. In S. Pagiola, J. Bishop & N. Landell-Mills (eds.) *Selling Forest Environmental Services: Market-Based Mechanisms for Conservation.* London: Earthscan.

Phelps, J., E. L. Webb & A. Agrawal (2010). Does REDD+ threaten to recentralize forest governance? *Science* 328.

Rose, N. (1999). *Powers of Liberty.* Cambridge: Cambridge University Press.

Roth, R. & W. Dressler (eds.) (2012). *Geoforum* 34(3). Special issue on 'The Global Rise and Local Implications of Market-Oriented Conservation Governance'.

Sánchez-Azofeifa, G. A., A. Pfaff, J. A. Robalino & J. P. Boomhower (2007). Costa Rica's payment for environmental services program: intention, implementation, and impact. *Conservation Biology* 21.

Sierra, R. & E. Russman (2006). On the efficiency of environmental service payments: a forest conservation assessment in the Osa Peninsula, Costa Rica. *Ecological Economics* 59.

UNWTO (2007). *Davos Declaration: Climate Change and Tourism; Responding to Global Challenges.* Available at: http://www.unwto.org/pdf/pr071046.pdf.

USAID (2012). *Tropical Forest Conservation Act (TFCA) Program Descriptions: Costa Rica.* Available at: http://www.usaid.gov/our_work/environment/forestry/tfca_descs.html#Costa_Rica.

Vivanco, L. A. (2006). *Green Encounters: Shaping and Contesting Environmentalism in Rural Costa Rica.* New York, NY: Berghahn.

While, A., A. E. G. Jonas & D. Gibbs (2009). From sustainable development to carbon control: eco-state restructuring and the politics of urban and regional development. *Transactions of the Institute of British Geographers* NS 2009.

9

A Climate Leader? The Politics and Practice of Climate Governance in Mexico

Simone Pulver

Introduction

MEXICO stands out among emerging economies as a leader on climate policy. In line with the pledges of other developing countries, in 2010 the Mexican government committed to reducing its greenhouse gas (GHG) emissions by 30 per cent from a business-as-usual (BAU) scenario by 2020. However, unlike the rest of the world, Mexico has also pledged a 50 per cent reduction in GHG emissions by 2050 (CAT 2012). Moreover, both pledges were formalized in Mexico's General Law on Climate Change (Ley General de Cambio Climático), which was passed by the Mexican Senate in December 2011 and signed into law by President Felipe Calderón in June 2012 (Black 2012). With this legislation, Mexico became the only developing country and one of only two countries in the world to have legislated long-term GHG emissions reduction targets (Vance 2012). The implementation of the General Law on Climate Change is left to Calderón's successor, President Enrique Peña Nieto, who assumed the presidency in December 2012. The prospects of the new climate change law are uncertain under the Peña Nieto administration, which was elected on a platform pledging economic growth and increased oil and natural gas production (Teixeira 2012). Nevertheless, simply the legislation's passage showcases the dynamism of climate governance in the developing world and Mexico's climate leadership.

This chapter examines the history and evolution of climate policy in Mexico. Like other emerging economies, Mexico is both a significant contributor to global GHG emissions and vulnerable to the impacts of climate change. From the early 1990s, Mexico's GHG emissions (excluding land use and forestry emissions) have increased from 425 to 640 million tonnes of CO_2 equivalent, reflecting both economic development and population growth. In terms of annual CO_2 emissions, Mexico ranks eleventh overall and fifth among developing countries (UNFCCC 2012a). In terms of cumulative GHG emissions, Mexico ranks fourth among developing countries, behind China,

India and South Africa (World Bank 2012). Mexico's 2009 per capita GHG emissions were 3.72, compared to 16.9 for the United States, 5.13 for China and 1.37 for India (World Bank 2012). The major emissions sectors are energy production and transformation (43 per cent), transport (18 per cent), and land use change and agriculture (21 per cent) (Government of Mexico 2006). In terms of climate-related vulnerabilities, drought and desertification pose threats to food production and livelihoods in the northern and central regions of the country. Coastal areas are threatened by rising sea levels and increased tropical storms. Mexico is also home to biodiverse ecosystems that are vulnerable to climate change (SEMARNAP 1998).

As in many developing countries, the initial impetus for action on climate change in Mexico came from the international arena. In the 1990s, climate change activities in Mexico were structured primarily around the international climate change negotiations and the domestic reporting requirements imposed by the 1992 UN Framework Convention on Climate Change (UNFCCC). Over time, the structures of the international climate regime helped to coalesce a constituency of climate science and policy experts in Mexico, who then used the international process to foster a domestic climate policy debate. Unusually for an emerging economy, domestic climate policy discussions emphasized not only impacts and adaptation but also mitigation responsibilities. In most developing countries, responsibility for mitigating climate change is ascribed to the industrialized countries of the Global North. For example, this has been the consistent negotiating stance of the Group of 77 (G77) and China negotiating bloc in the international climate negotiations. In Mexico, the narrative of international responsibility is complemented by federal government initiatives delineating a domestic climate strategy for Mexico, focused both on adaptation and on mitigation. On the adaptation side, concerns about climate impacts have focused on the link between climate change and extreme weather events and consequent effects on agriculture and public health. On the mitigation side, the modernization and transformation of the energy sector and sustainable forest management are at the centre of debates about GHG emissions reductions.

The chapter has a three part structure. The first section details Mexico's participation in the international climate regime, beginning in 1991 through Mexico's hosting the international climate negotiations in Cancun in 2010. Second, I trace the history of domestic climate policy activities in Mexico, starting with the Salinas and Zedillo presidential administrations and concluding with an assessment of likely action under the present Peña Nieto administration. The third section presents a content analysis of climate change news coverage on Mexico from 1996 to 2009, highlighting the particular issues that have animated public debate about climate change in Mexico.

Mexico in the International Climate Change Regime

Mexico has been a consistent and active participant in the international climate regime. Mexico's participation can be tracked via its delegation to the international climate negotiations, leadership in negotiating groups and its contribution of text to the negotiations process. Mexico was among the hundred countries that sent a delegation to the first round of the international climate negotiations (Intergovernmental Negotiating Committee, INC 1) in February 1991, and a Mexican delegation has been in attendance at all subsequent rounds of negotiation, most recently the Eighteenth Conference of the Parties (COP18) to the UNFCCC held in Doha, Qatar, in December 2012. The size of Mexico's delegation has ranged from two government representatives to over a hundred representatives of federal, state and local government as well as industry and civil society, and peaked at 118 delegates in 2010, when the negotiations were held in Cancun. Delegation size can serve as one indicator of the level of domestic interest in climate issues. Figure 9.1 suggests limited interest in the climate issue from 1991 to 1999, although the Mexican delegation grew steadily along with the growth in total number of state delegates. Between 2000 and 2006, interest increased with an average delegation of around thirty individuals. Compared to other countries, Mexico was underrepresented at COP15 but overrepresented at COP16.

Mexican delegates have held leadership roles in various rounds of the climate negotiations. For example at INC 1, the head of Mexico's delegation, Edmundo de Alba, was elected as co-chair, along with a delegate from Japan, of the negotiating group on binding GHG reduction commitments. Mexico used its leadership position to promote the status quo. In negotiating the 1992 UNFCCC, Mexico sided with countries like the United States, Japan, Canada, Australia and New

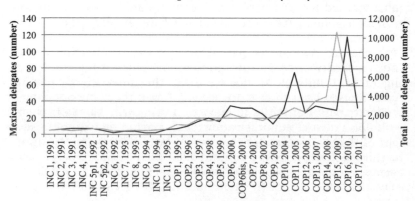

Figure 9.1   Participation in UNFCCC negotiations, 1991–2011

176

Zealand which were opposed to binding national GHG reduction targets (Mintzer & Leonard 1994). These countries prevailed: the text of the UNFCCC did not mandate binding reductions in GHG emissions. At subsequent rounds of negotiation, Mexico changed allegiances and joined the negotiating bloc that favoured binding GHG emissions reductions for industrialized countries. Mexican delegates also shifted focus to issues of particular concern to the nation. For example, at COP6 in 2000, Mexico's environmental minister, Julia Carabias Lillo, served as co-facilitator of the informal consultation process on the role of land use, land use change and forestry in meeting Kyoto targets. Lillo's background as a conservation biologist was useful in guiding negotiations about forest management. COP6 also marked the establishment of the Environmental Integrity negotiating group, constituted by Mexico, South Korea and Switzerland. The creation of this small negotiating group reflects Mexico's desire both to have an independent voice in the negotiations and to highlight its perceived differences from other country clusters. Unlike other developing countries, Mexico is a member of the Organization for Economic Cooperation and Development (OECD); unlike industrialized countries, Mexico has not committed to binding GHG reductions at the international level.

A second metric of Mexico's participation in the international climate negotiations is its formal submissions to the UNFCCC process. Country submissions may take the form of draft negotiating text, overarching proposals laying out a framework for negotiations, expressions of support for a particular policy or methodological approach, and general technical background. Submissions range in length from a single sentence to several pages. Country submissions on specific topics may be solicited by the UN Climate Change Secretariat or submitted at the initiative of national delegations. Submissions may be made by individual countries, by groups of countries agreeing on a proposal, or on behalf of negotiating groups, such as the Alliance of Small Island States (AOSIS), G77 and China, and the European Community (EC). Between 1991 and 1997, Mexico submitted only three documents to the Climate Change Secretariat, a low number when compared to active submitters such as the EC (46 submissions), Australia (28 submissions) and the United States (23 submissions). However, from 1999 onwards, Mexico became more active in contributing written submissions to the negotiations process. To date, Mexico has submitted text on 52 occasions, mostly as an individual contributor but at times as part of a group of Latin American countries. An analysis of the content of Mexico's submissions shows a clear interest in issues of deforestation and afforestation both under the Clean Development Mechanism (CDM) and within the UNFCCC regime more broadly (eleven submissions), the modalities of the CDM (eight submissions), vulnerability and adaption (eight submissions), and, more recently, technology transfer (two submissions).

The highpoint of Mexico's participation in the international climate negotiations came in 2010, when it hosted COP16 of the UNFCCC in Cancun. COP16 was led by Ambassador Patricia Espinoza, the Mexican secretary of foreign affairs, and was attended by 12,000 individuals, divided evenly between government delegations and representatives of non-governmental organizations (NGOs) and international organizations (Government of Mexico 2010). COP16 was particularly important because of the collapse of COP15 negotiations in Copenhagen in 2009. The international community had set itself a 2009 deadline to negotiate a follow-up agreement to the Kyoto Protocol, which would include binding GHG reduction commitments for both industrialized and developing countries. Despite record attendance of both civil society delegates and heads of state at the negotiations, agreement was not reached. This both reduced expectations for COP16 and shifted the burden of rescuing the international negotiations process onto Mexico, as the host country for COP16.

The Cancun Accords, the outcome of COP16, reaffirmed the two-track international negotiations process focused on a second commitment period for the Kyoto Protocol and longer-term cooperative action under the UNFCCC. It also provided an opportunity to review progress on the voluntary climate pledges for 2020 that were an element of the COP15 Copenhagen Accord. The pledge framework provided an opportunity for Mexico to spotlight its leadership on mitigation in the developing world (table 9.1). Compared to other large developing countries, Mexico pledged both aggressive mid-term GHG reductions (30 per cent from BAU by 2020) as well as long-term commitments (50 per cent by 2050). The Cancun Accords also brought to fruition the proposal for the Green Climate Fund (Fondo Verde). President Felipe Calderón had proposed the Fondo Verde, as a means to consolidate and activate funding for mitigation, adaptation and technology transfer activities around the globe (EU 2010). The financial goal was

Table 9.1 National GHG emissions reductions pledges, 2010	
Country	**GHG emissions reductions pledge**
Brazil	*Own effort*: reduction of 36.1–38.9% compared to BAU in 2020
China	*Own effort*: reduction of 8.5% compared to BAU in 2020
India	*Own effort*: reduction of 20–5% of gross domestic product (GDP) in the emissions intensity by 2020 in comparison to the 2005 level
Indonesia	*Own effort*: reduction of 26% in 2020 based on a deviation from BAU scenario in 2020 *With international finance*: reduction of 41% in 2020 based on a deviation from BAU scenario in 2020
Mexico	*Own effort*: reduction of 30% in 2020 and reduction of 50% in 2050 based on a deviation from BAU scenario in 2020
South Korea	*Own effort*: reduction of 30% in 2020 based on a deviation from BAU scenario in 2020

Source: UNEP (2010)

to start with funding of US$10 billion and to expand to US$100 billion annually to fund sustainability projects. Payments to the fund would be based on quotas, with developed countries contributing a higher percentage. Developing countries would contribute as well, but lesser amounts, and would have greater access to funding. The Green Fund proposal was advanced in various international venues and officially submitted to the UNFCCC negotiations at an August meeting in Accra (Government of Mexico 2008). The idea of the Green Climate Fund had been adopted at COP15, but was ratified at COP16, with implementation details deferred to COP17.

Domestic Climate Policy Initiatives

The UNFCCC negotiations provided the venue for Mexico to participate in international decision-making about climate change.[1] However, equally important, they served as an impetus for (and at times an obstacle to) domestic climate initiatives. Mexico's domestic climate policy developments reflect the interplay between the domestic and international arenas. The following section catalogues domestic climate policy initiatives during presidential administrations from 1988 to the present day. Presidential politics has had a significant effect on climate policy because most initiatives have been spearheaded by the federal government. Mexican presidents have also tended to wait until the end of their six-year terms to introduce climate programmes. The exception to this rule was President Calderón (2006–12), who made climate change a policy issue from his first year in office. However, even Calderón's General Law on Climate Change was not passed until 2012 and was left to his successor to implement.

The Salinas and Zedillo Administrations, 1988–1994 and 1994–2000

Climate change first emerged as an issue in Mexico in the early 1990s during the Salinas administration. In 1991, at the beginning of the international negotiations process, interest in the climate issue was limited to a few key individuals in Mexico's ministries of foreign relations and environment. For example, at INC 1 in 1991, Mexico was represented by a five-person delegation, including representatives from the Ministries of Foreign Relations (Secretaría de Relaciones Exteriores, SRE), of Ecology and Urban Development (Sub-Secretaría de Desarollo Urbano y Ecología, SEDUE)[2] and of Energy (Secretaría de Energia, SENER). At subsequent INCs, the delegations were limited to diplomats from ministries of foreign affairs and environment. However, six years later, a more formalized inter-ministerial dialogue became the forum in which Mexico's stance in the international negotiations was coordinated. The group of ministries participating in the formal inter-ministerial dialogue included

SRE, SENER and the Ministries of Environment (SEMARNAT), of Commerce and Industrial Development (Secretaría de Comercio y Fomento Industrial, SECOFI), of Agriculture, Livestock and Rural Development (Secretaría de Agricultura, Ganadería, Desarrollo Rural, Pesca y Alimentación, SAGARPA), of Communications and Transport (Secretaría de Comunicaciones y Transportes, SCT) and of Social Development (Secretaría de Desarrollo Social, SEDESOL) (see Belausteguigoitia & Lopez-Bassols 1999; SEMARNAP 1998).

The emergent institutionalization of the climate change issue within Mexico's federal government between 1991 and 1998 traces back to three causes. First, the development of scientific expertise in Mexico centred on climate research helped consolidate a climate policy community. After the adoption of the UNFCCC in June 1992, a group of scientists and environmental bureaucrats at the Center for Atmospheric Sciences (Centro de Ciencias Atmósphera, CCA) at Mexico's national university (Universidad Nacional Autónoma de México, UNAM) and at the National Ecology Institute (Instituto Nacional de Ecología, INE), the research arm of SEMARNAT, established a national scientific programme on global climate change (Programa Nacional Científico sobre Cambio Climático Global) (Gay Garcia 1994). This effort was led by Carlos Gay Garcia, based at UNAM's CCA, and received support from the US Country Studies Program (CSP), which provided financial and technical assistance to developing countries to support efforts to address climate change. Mexico's application for support was funded during the first round of applications in October 1993. The country study process helped coalesce a group of scientists and bureaucrats working on climate change in Mexico. These individuals then became the central nodes in the network of Mexican scientists working on climate change. Over a third of the thirty-five contributors to the first CSP workshop remain leading experts in Mexico on climate change science and policy.

Second, the 1994 Mexican presidential election that replaced Carlos Salinas with Ernesto Zedillo led to a change in the environmental leadership in federal government. In appointing his new Cabinet, the president named research scientist Carlos Gay Garcia as the lead technical negotiator for Mexico's UNFCCC delegation and as head of the delegation at meetings of the UNFCCC's scientific subsidiary bodies. In that capacity, Gay convened an ad hoc group for inter-ministerial dialogue on climate change, including SRE, SEMARNAT, SENER and SECOFI. Third, the UNFCCC itself fostered institutionalization. Under the convention, countries are required to submit national GHG inventories and national communications about domestic climate activities. Mexico's first official national GHG inventory was published in December 1995 (Di Sbroiavacca & Girardin 2000) and its first National Communication under the UNFCCC was completed in 1996 and submitted in November 1997 (Government of Mexico 1997). Both documents were based on data collected via the country studies research effort (Ramos-Mane & Benioff 1995; Benioff et al. 1997).

The research emphasis that characterized Mexico's early domestic climate change initiatives continued until 1997, when the successful negotiation of the Kyoto Protocol led to a politicization of climate policy. In Mexico, Zedillo appointed Julia Carabias Lillo, head of SEMARNAT, as lead coordinator of the Mexican climate policymaking process, replacing research scientist Gay. At the same time, the ad hoc group for inter-ministerial dialogue was converted into a formal Inter-Ministerial Committee on Climate Change (Comité Intersecretarial de Cambio Climático), with an expanded list of seven participating ministries. In particular, SENER began to take a much more active interest in the climate issue. Unlike the ecologists and atmospheric scientists that populated the halls of UNAM, INE and SEMARNAT, and whose focus was on Mexico's ecological vulnerability to climate change, SENER staff were concerned about the impact of international GHG regulations on Mexico's oil economy. They opposed binding international GHG reductions, in line with other oil-exporting countries that vocally opposed action on climate change (SENER 1998).

The divergence between SEMARNAT and SENER intensified in 2000, when the Mexican Senate was considering ratification of the Kyoto Protocol. On one side of the issue, SENER and SECOFI emphasized the potential negative consequences of international GHG regulations on Mexico's economy. In contrast, staff at SEMARNAT and diplomats in SRE pushed for ratification. They argued that the decision to ratify had low costs and high benefits. As a developing country, ratification would not obligate Mexico to a GHG reduction commitment. Rather, ratification would increase Mexico's standing in the international community and would gain it access to the Kyoto mechanisms, particularly the CDM. The CDM finances low carbon projects by creating a market for GHG emissions reductions credits generated in developing countries, and CDM financing was attractive to a range of stakeholders in Mexico, from city officials working to reduce air pollution in Mexico City (West et al. 2004) to corporations in the cement, steel and petrochemical sectors. Some of the most vocal support for the CDM came from Mexico's national oil company (Petroleos Mexicanos, or Pemex). Pemex executives saw the CDM as a way to channel foreign investment into company operations (Pulver 2007). On 29 April 2000, the 128–member Mexican Senate voted unanimously to ratify the Kyoto Protocol, but only after a late night session at which envoys from both SEMARNAT and SENER were invited to the presidential residence at Los Pinos. Following presidential advice, the Senate ratified the Kyoto Protocol, and Mexico's instrument of ratification was deposited at the UN headquarters in New York in September 2000. Mexico was the twenty-ninth country to ratify the Kyoto Protocol (UNFCCC 2012b).

Ratification signalled a victory for SEMARNAT and briefly re-energized efforts to create a domestic climate policy framework for Mexico. In line with the renewed momentum, SEMARNAT and INE drafted a national programme on climate change, concurrent with their preparation of Mexico's Second National Communication under the UNFCCC (Government of Mexico 2001). However, the national programme was received critically during the public review period and was downgraded to a national strategy. Moreover, the document was drafted in the final year of Zedillo's term, and newly elected President Vicente Fox chose not to continue the activities of the previous administration.

The Fox Administration, 2000–2006

Under the Fox administration, climate policy became a secondary priority. Appointing his new cabinet, Fox opted for Victor Lichtinger, trained as an agricultural and natural resource economist, to replace ecologist Carabias as minister of the environment. Although Lichtinger had attended five rounds of the international climate negotiations in 1991 and 1992, he did not make climate change a high profile issue at SEMARNAT. Fox also constrained the scope of INE's climate programmes, retasking it as a research institute, limited to preparing Mexico's GHG inventory and national communications to the UNFCCC (Tudela et al. 2003). Finally, Fox looked to international dynamics to set his domestic climate policy agenda.

The first setback to climate policy in Mexico was the decision in March 2001 by President George W. Bush to withdraw the United States from the Kyoto Protocol. While US ratification of the Kyoto Protocol had always been unlikely, the US had adopted and signed the text of the treaty. President's Bush's decision signalled to the international community that his administration was not at all interested in the climate issue. The US withdrawal undermined the Kyoto Protocol's prospects for entry into force, the effectiveness of the international climate regime, and the robustness of the newly emergent carbon markets. For example, Mexican analysts estimated a carbon price of US$10–20 per tonne, based on likely US demand for carbon credits (Quadri 2000), and hoped that the US would look to its North American Free Trade Agreement partner for CDM opportunities (CCA/ CEC 2001). When the United States pulled out of the Kyoto Protocol in 2001, the projected price of carbon credits under the CDM declined substantially.

A presidential visit to Europe in the spring of 2002 reinvigorated domestic interest in climate change. At the time, European governments were pushing for ratification of the Kyoto Protocol. The European Union's decision to ratify was announced in May 2002, followed by those of Japan and Canada. These international developments inspired some domestic action in Mexico. In 2003, the federal government established a Climate Change Office (Comité Mexicano para Proyectos de Reducción de Emissiones y de Captura de Gases de Efecto Invernadero, COMEGEI), tasked with vetting Mexico's CDM projects. The COMEGEI is housed within SEMARNAT, although SENER was equally interested in controlling CDM decisions (SEMARNAT 2006).

The office ramped up CDM activities in 2005, when the Kyoto Protocol entered into force. That same year, the Fox administration also created a permanent Inter-Ministerial Commission on Climate Change (Comisión Intersecretarial de Cambio Climático, CICC) to coordinate Mexico's climate initiatives. In the final year of Fox's presidency, the CICC developed a national climate strategy for Mexico, and Mexico submitted its Third National Communication on Climate Change to the UNFCCC (CICC 2006; Government of Mexico 2006).

The Calderón Administration, 2006–2012

Felipe Calderón was elected to the Mexican presidency in July 2006 and assumed the office in December. His administration became a turning point in Mexico's domestic climate policy activities. Unlike his predecessors, who waited until the end of their six-year terms to tackle the climate issue, Calderón made climate change a focus at the beginning of his presidency. At the centre of his efforts was the development of a National Strategy on Climate Change (Estrategia Nacional de Cambio Climático, ENCC), which was presented in May 2007 (CICC 2007). Drafted under the new administration, the document builds on the work the CICC produced in 2006.

The ENCC outlined GHG mitigation options in the energy generation, energy use, and vegetation and land use sectors, projecting total emissions reductions of 124 million tonnes of CO_2 equivalent by 2014. The strategy is wide-ranging in its goals, affecting thirty-two federal programmes, including Pemex and the state-owned electric utility (Comision Federal de Electricidad, CFE). The ENCC also specified a climate change adaptation strategy, identified future research priorities, and contained plans for the central government to assist Mexico's thirty-one states in developing state-specific climate programmes. The Calderón administration also coordinated the ENCC with the National Development Plan, 2007–12 (Plan Nacional de Desarrollo, PND). The PND is the key planning document the federal government publishes each term, and for the first time it included climate change-related actions (Office of the President of the Government of Mexico 2007).

Critics were sceptical of the ENCC's voluntary status and thought it unlikely that Mexico would meet the 2014 target (CCC Newsdesk 2007). However, Calderón remained committed to the strategy. In 2008, he presented for public review the Special Climate Change Programme (Programa Especial de Cambio Climático, PECC), which elaborated on the ENCC and set concrete mitigation and adaptation goals for 2009–12 and 2020–50. The PECC is divided into four sections. The first details adaptation measures to be taken, and the second deals with mitigation actions. The third explains the variety of efforts in communication, education, economic actions and political coordination needed to achieve the goals outlined in the first sections. The final section explains Mexico's stance in the international climate negotiations. The PECC also includes the long-term mitigation goal of a 50 per cent reduction in GHG emissions by 2050 that Juan Elvira Quesada, Mexico's minister of environment under Calderón, announced to the international community in December 2008, at COP14 in Poland (Wynn 2008).

The revised version of the PECC was published in June 2009 (CICC 2009). Its public launch was accompanied by publication of *The Economics of Climate Change in Mexico*, a study led by UNAM economist Luis Galindo in the spirit of the Stern Review on the Economics of Climate Change (Government of Mexico 2009b). The report argues that by 2100, the cost of climate impacts will be at least three times the costs associated with cutting Mexico's GHG emissions by 50 per cent. Finally, the Mexican Congress approved US$200 million for greenhouse mitigation projects specified in the PECC via the Fund for Sustainable Development and Energy Transition (Fondo para la Transición Energética y Aprovechamiento Sustentable).

As with the 2007 ENCC, the PECC generated controversy. Greenpeace Mexico was disappointed that the public review process led to less stringent targets. For example, the original version targeted 6.6 million hectares for forestry activities, while the revised programme adjusted the land area to 2.95 million hectares. This amount was considered inadequate by Greenpeace to reach substantive mitigation (Greenpeace Mexico 2009). Other environmental NGOs argued that Mexico lacked the institutional capacity to meet the 2050 reduction goal. The Mexican Federation of Chambers of Commerce (Confederación de Cámaras Industriales de los Estados Unidos Mexicanos, CONCAMIN) criticized the GDP growth rates needed to reach PECC emissions goals. The PECC estimates an annual GDP growth rate of 3.5 per cent, while Jaime Williams, the president of CONCAMIN's energy commission, projects at minimum a GDP growth rate between 5 and 7 per cent to meet Mexico's development needs. Under the CONCAMIN scenario, energy intensity would have to decline by 0.7 per cent annually until 2050 to reach PECC targets, a very aggressive goal (Williams 2010).

Calderón's administration formalized the ENCC and the PECC in the 2012 General Law on Climate Change. The law cements the institutional structure for addressing the climate change challenge in Mexico via an inter-ministerial commission, establishes channels of communication between levels of government and between the government and the private sector and civil society, creates a GHG emissions registry and market, and sets goals to combat desertification and enhance electricity generation from renewable sources (Kraemer 2012). Calderón's administration also spearheaded other regulatory initiatives related to energy. In 2008, the government enacted the Law for the Promotion and Development of Biofuels (Ley para la Promocion y Desarrollo de Bioenergeticos) and the Law for the Use of Renewable Energy and Financing the Energy Transition (Ley para el Aprovechamiento de Energías Renovables y el Financiamiento de la Transición Energética). Both establish the regulatory frameworks to govern biofuels and renewable energy development, in relation to Pemex and CFE, the state-owned corporations that run the oil and electricity sectors in Mexico. Both are semi-independent organizations operating under the purview of SENER. Under the biofuels law, SENER was assigned responsibility for market development while SEMARNAT was tasked with evaluating the environmental impact of biofuels production, storage, transportation, distribution and marketing. The law is less specific regarding incentives to possible market entrants (Felix n.d.). The renewable energy law assigns regulatory responsibility to SENER and the Energy Regulation Commission (Comision de Regulacion de Energia, CRE) (Ecofys & Climate Analytics 2012, p. 78).

A third development in climate politics during Calderón's administration was the devolution of climate activities from the federal to state and local levels. Both the ENCC and the PECC shifted some responsibility onto states to develop climate plans. In addition, the new mayor of Mexico City, Marcelo Ebrard, made greening the city a central element of his administration. Also, elected in 2006 for a six-year term, Ebrard launched the fifteen-year Green Plan (Plan Verde) in August 2007. Among its objectives are land conservation, housing and public spaces, water supply and sanitation, transportation and mobility, air pollution, waste management and recycling, and the Climate Action Programme (SMA 2008; Mexico City Experience 2011). The latter sought to effect a 7 million tonne reduction in GHGs between 2008 and 2012. In August 2008, Ebrard announced that the city not only met but exceeded its goals, having reduced GHG emissions by 7.7 megatonnes. The Green Plan builds on a history of environmental concern in Mexico City, centred on local air pollution (Di Sbroiavacca & Girardin 2000). Ebrard's achievements have been recognized internationally. He became chairman of the World Mayors Council on Climate Change in 2009. In the lead up to COP16 in 2010, Mexico City hosted the World Mayors Summit on Climate, at which the organization launched the Global Cities Covenant on Climate, or the 'Mexico City Pact'. This voluntary initiative commits signatory cities to action on GHG reduction, climate adaptation, reporting to a climate action registry and inter-city cooperation (Mexico City 2010).

The Peña Nieto Administration, 2012–2018

The election of Enrique Peña Nieto in August 2012 put into question the initiatives of his predecessor. Peña Nieto, a member of the Institutional Revolutionary Party (Partido Revolucionario Institucional, PRI), which controlled the Mexican presidency continuously from 1924 to 1994, will focus on energy development as a central goal of his administration. In this, he is not different from Calderón, whose administration, for example, oversaw continued exploration of onshore and offshore assets in the Gulf of Mexico (EOE 2010). Like most of his predecessors, Peña Nieto has promised to expand oil and gas production in Mexico, by facilitating more private investment in the energy sector. However, unlike Calderón, he has not simultaneously endorsed the need for GHG mitigation and green development. Rather his focus is expected to be on delivering on a campaign promise of increased economic growth for Mexico. Analysts also expect a greater emphasis on domestic rather than international issues from the Peña Nieto administration. Unlike his predecessor, Peña Nieto will not seek a leadership role for Mexico in the international climate negotiations (Teixeira 2012).

News Coverage of Climate Change

The previous sections provide an overview of the evolution of Mexican climate politics at both the international and domestic levels. A content analysis of news coverage of climate change in *Reforma*, the leading mainstream prestige newspaper in Mexico City, offers additional insight into the particular issues that animated climate policy debates in Mexico.[3] The topics of debate that generated most coverage were the link between climate change and extreme weather events and the viability of alternative energy investments. The controversy about both topics speaks to the role of climate impacts in making the case for climate change and the importance of fossil based energy to Mexico's economic development.

Initially, newspaper coverage of climate change was quite limited. Between 1996 and 2006, *Reforma* published on average 71 such articles per year. Coverage was lowest in 1996, with 19 articles, and highest in 2005 with 164 articles. However, 2007 proved to be a watershed year. That year, *Reforma* published 691 articles that included the words 'climate change', 'global warming', 'greenhouse gas*', 'Kyoto Protocol' and/or 'IPCC'. The increased coverage continued in 2008 and 2009, with 571 and 542 articles, respectively. The jump in articles focused on climate change in 2007 is explained by newsworthy events at the international and domestic levels. At the international level, the Nobel Peace Prize was awarded to the IPCC and to Al Gore. Earlier that year, the IPCC had released its Fourth Assessment Report, which stated with 'very high confidence that the globally averaged net effect of human activities since 1750 has been one of warming' (IPCC 2007, p. 37). Al Gore received the prize for his climate change educational effort centred on the documentary *An Inconvenient Truth*. COP13 in December of 2007 also raised the political prominence of the climate issue across the developing world, because the focus of negotiation was on a successor agreement to the Kyoto Protocol that would include developing countries. At the domestic level, newly elected President Calderón presented his National Strategy for Climate Change. There were also storms and flooding on Mexico's Gulf Coast. The state of Tabasco alone is mentioned in 5 per cent of articles published in 2007. Finally, Mexico City's new mayor, Marcelo Ebrard, launched the fifteen-year plan to green Mexico City, including a climate action programme to reduce CO_2 emissions.

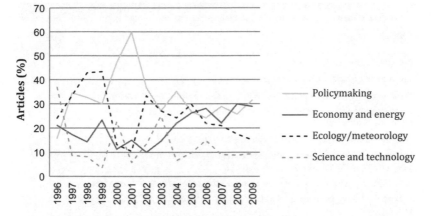

Figure 9.2 News coverage of climate change by article content, *Reforma*, 1996–2009

The majority of climate change news coverage in Mexico falls into one of four broad topical categories: ecology and meteorology, science and technology, policymaking, and economy and energy (figure 9.2).[4] Articles focused on policymaking consistently constituted around 30 per cent of total coverage in the period studied. The fraction of articles focused on ecology and meteorology and on science and technology declined between 1996 and 2009 from approximately half in the early to mid-1990s to just under 30 per cent in 2007, 2008 and 2009. This decline was matched by an increase in articles focused on economic and energy issues.

Much of the newspaper coverage is simply reporting on international and local events and policy developments. However, news coverage also highlights issues causing political controversy. Just under 25 per cent of the *Reforma* articles focused on topics that generated public debate. Such topics ranged from the appropriate role for nuclear energy in addressing climate change to the links between climate change and poverty (table 9.2). Most of the issues that generated some public debate in Mexico fall in two categories: issues related to climate science and impacts and issues of climate change mitigation and energy policy. Both foci reflect Mexico's structural circumstances and the history of Mexico's engagement in global environmental politics.

Climate Science and Impacts

When climate change was first identified as an issue of global concern, policymakers looked to the international community's successful effort to address the hole in the ozone layer as a possible template for addressing climate change. Many of the policy experts involved in the Montreal Protocol negotiations in the late 1980s shifted their attention to climate change in the early 1990s (Agrawala 1999).

Table 9.2 Topics of public debate, *Reforma*, 1996–2009

Topic	Articles (number)
Climate science and impacts	
Are weather events linked to climate change?	221
Is climate change impacting water scarcity, disease burdens, biodiversity?	66
Is climate change linked to poverty? Is it affecting the economy, mainly agriculture, already?	51
Is deforestation a major cause of climate change?	43
Is climate change happening?/Is climate change an anthropogenic phenomenon?/What constitutes evidence?	38
Does Mexico have enough climate change science/expertise/information?	21
Is climate change producing climate refugees in Mexico or other parts of the world?	7
Mitigation and energy policy	
Should Mexico actively invest in alternative energy sources, including biofuels/ethanol?	102
Has the Mexican government done enough to tackle climate change?	40
Should developed countries take more responsibility for climate change?	30
Is it cost effective to make climate change policies a priority?	30
What is the role of transport in causing and mitigating climate change?	29
Is Mexico adopting contradictory measures regarding emissions?	28
Has the CDM been effective in Mexico? Have the projects been implemented effectively?	24
Are industry and businesses aware of climate change challenges? Are they doing something?	23
Are a new vision and lifestyle the solution to climate change?	10
Is nuclear energy a feasible/good alternative against climate change?	9
By what percentage should Mexico reduce GHG emissions?	8

Mexico had a particular reputational stake in the ozone issue. Mario Molina, an atmospheric chemist who earned his bachelor's degree in chemical engineering from UNAM, was awarded the 1995 Nobel Prize in Chemistry for research that highlighted the effect of chlorine atoms on the ozone layer in the upper atmosphere. A postdoctoral fellow when conducting the research, Molina and his advisor Sherman Rowland became vocal advocates for banning the production and release of chlorofluorocarbons. Molina is the only Mexican scientist to have won a Nobel Prize (Molina 1995). The climate science community in Mexico was inspired by Molina's leadership and hoped to emulate in the climate arena the work he had accomplished in the ozone arena. Moreover, Molina himself has continued to be an active contributor to climate policy debates, both in Mexico and internationally.

Molina's legacy has shaped debates over climate science in Mexico. Unlike in the United States, where the focus of controversy is on the validity of climate change and the link to human activity (Boykoff 2007), Mexico's scientific and policy communities accept the findings of the IPCC. In the fourteen-year period from 1996 to 2009, only 38 articles in *Reforma* asked whether climate change is happening and whether it is an anthropogenic phenomenon. In contrast, over 200 articles spoke to the link between climate change and extreme weather events. This link is often made in media coverage as a way of making present in people's daily lives an issue which often seems remote in time and space. Moreover, it offers editors a way to link climate change to a newsworthy event. Finally, linking climate change and extreme weather has entered the standard rhetoric of politicians, who evoke images of possible future disasters to lobby for resources. Tabasco has been the site of multiple floods, which the state's governor, Andrés Granier, vocally links to climate change. Leading Mexican climate scientists, including Carlos Gay and Victor Magaña, are careful to challenge such explanations in the media. From a scientific standpoint, it is not possible to establish a direct causal link between global climate change and a specific local weather event.

Alongside extreme weather, newspaper articles focused on the wider range of climate impacts. Policy communities and the public have been actively interested in understanding Mexico's vulnerabilities to climate change. Vulnerability was one of the three focal areas of the CSP initiated in 1994 (Gay Garcia 2000). Each national communication to the UNFCCC includes a section on impacts. Vulnerability studies highlight concerns about water scarcity, effects on agriculture, and forest and biodiversity loss (Government of Mexico 2009a). Vulnerability concerns covered in *Reforma* include extreme weather, water scarcity, food production, health impacts, damage to ecosystems, and climate refugees.

Mitigation and Energy Policy

Climate change news coverage in Mexico has also been animated by questions about mitigation and energy policy. The prominence of energy issues reflects Mexico's history as an oil economy. Mexico is the eighth-largest oil producer in the world (Helman 2012), and oil currently accounts for 30 per cent of government revenue and 10 per cent of Mexico's export earnings, down from a record high of 67 per cent in 1980 (Di Sbroiavacca & Girardin 2000; Halpern 2001). Moreover, growth in Mexico's GHG emissions is mostly the product of energy-intensive economic development. Approximately 60 per cent of Mexico's GHG emissions are attributable to the energy sector; the balance comes from deforestation and changes in land use (Government of Mexico 2006). Mexico's efforts to reduce GHG emissions need to be understood in this broader context. Energy development has continued unabated, despite progress in climate policy and regulation. Some news coverage has focused on this apparent inconsistency.

During Calderón's term, twenty-eight articles in *Reforma* focused on contradictory measures related to energy and climate.

Re-envisioning Mexico's energy future raises questions about alternatives to oil, the effectiveness and cost effectiveness of such investments, and the role of industry in mitigating climate change. The greatest opportunities for large-scale reductions in Mexico's GHG emissions come from structural changes in the energy sector. Three factors are driving a decrease in the fuel oil percentage of Mexico's energy consumption. First, oil production in Mexico peaked in the mid-2000s and has since been on the decline. Revised estimates of oil reserves keep shortening the reserves/production ratio. Analysts attribute this decline to insufficient investment in new exploration and infrastructure improvements. Pemex lacks capital because it pays most of its profits into federal coffers. Second, oil exports are increasing due to high oil prices, reducing availability for domestic use. Third, government policies have incentivized cleaner fuels and increased efficiency (Belausteguigoitia & Lopez-Bassols 1999; Di Sbroiavacca & Girardin 2000; EIA 2007; Government of Mexico 2006).

Alternatives to fossil fuels include biofuels (particularly in the transport sector), solar and wind energy, and nuclear energy. The expansion of nuclear energy has not been a politically popular alternative. The Laguna Verde plant, Mexico's only nuclear power plant, mobilized a national environmental movement when it was built in the late 1980s. The expansion of biofuels received most attention in the press, alongside investments in wind and solar (102 articles). Both became topics of public debate because of the biofuel and renewable energy laws passed in 2008. Biofuels generated additional controversy because of the link between expanding biofuel acreage and increased food prices. As a result, investment has focused on feedstocks that do not compete for arable land or impact food production (Tournemille 2009).

News coverage of renewables and biofuels also intersects with public debates about the CDM, which in Mexico is only a partial success story. Globally, it ranks fifth in the number of CDM projects initiated, behind China, India, Brazil and Vietnam, and fifth in issued carbon credits, behind China, India, Brazil and South Korea. Mexico's CDM activities have yielded almost 16 million tonnes of CO_2 equivalent reductions to date. However, most of Mexico's projects cluster in one sector: biogas capture from feedlots. CDM opportunities have not been exploited by the same range of industries in Mexico as in other emerging economies (Fenhann 2012). Pemex's CDM experience may account for the limited interest shown by major industrial corporations. Pemex actively pursued CDM opportunities in the early 2000s. However, many Pemex projects were rejected by the CDM Executive Board and the mechanism did not yield the benefits expected by Pemex managers (Pemex 2006).

Despite the CDM's limited success, the Mexican private sector has made some progress in addressing climate change, mostly following the example of Pemex. Standing apart from most developing country oil companies, Pemex embraced a proactive approach to climate change and, in 2001, initiated an internal emissions trading system, pledging to reduce CO_2 emissions from its facilities by 1 per cent by the end of the year (Pemex 2002). Environmental Defense (ED), an environmental NGO based in Washington, DC, provided expert advice and technical support to Pemex, and the company has joined the ED Partnership for Climate Action (PCA), a collaboration among large firms like British Petroleum, Shell International, DuPont and Alcan which are committed to reducing their GHG emissions (Pulver 2007). Pemex was also among the twelve initial participants in Mexico's GHG Programme (Programa GEI México), under which participating companies compile corporate GHG inventories – the necessary precursor to emissions reductions. The programme is jointly coordinated by SEMARNAT, the World Resources Institute (WRI) and the World Business Council for Sustainable Development (WBCSD), and counts over 150 participating corporations in Mexico. To date, the corporate GHG inventories account for approximately 140 million tonnes of CO_2 equivalent, or 76 per cent of all GHG emissions from industrial processes (Programa GEI Mexico 2010; WRI 2006).

Conclusion

Mexico's status as a climate leader among developing countries is apparent. It is the only developing country to have legislated a long-term GHG reduction target. This commitment reflects a history of active engagement on climate change at the international and domestic levels. In addition, Mexico's climate policy community has accepted some responsibility for mitigating global climate change. These achievements are laudable. It can therefore come as a surprise that assessments of policy implementation and tangible progress in low carbon development in Mexico are critical. For example, Climate Action Tracker, a website that evaluates the emissions reduction commitments and climate policy actions of various countries, grades Mexico's performance at mostly Gs, on a scale from A (consistent with low carbon development) to G (no or very limited policies) (Ecofys & Climate Analytics 2012).

Looking to the future, Mexico's key challenge lies in translating its aspirational climate policies into tangible outcomes. There is some reason for optimism. First, at a local government level, Mexico City has been successful in both developing and implementing a climate action plan that exceeded its emissions reductions goals. One of the largest cities in the world, the Mexico City metropolitan area accounts for almost 20 per cent of Mexico's population. Second, Mexico's climate engagement has always been multi-sectoral. Although implementation lags, most ministries in the federal government have been engaged in domestic climate policy discussions since the mid-1990s. This history of engagement provides the groundwork for more tangible commitments. Third, the decline in Mexican oil production creates an opening for alternative energy strategies.

A primary obstacle to progress on implementation of climate policy in Mexico has been the reliance on executive action and the stop-and-go policymaking introduced by presidential elections. Several Mexican presidents have prioritized climate issues, but not until the end of their administrations. President Calderón broke this pattern, but even the National Strategy on Climate Change written under his purview extended only to 2014, two years past the end of his term. Likewise, Mexico's General Law on Climate Change was passed a few months before the election of President Peña Nieto, and he is unlikely to carry forward the climate agenda of his predecessor or to prioritize climate issues during his time in office. Building long-term climate policy momentum will require the development of bases of support for climate action beyond the federal government.

Notes

1 Some of the material presented in this section draws on a previous publication. For a more detailed discussion of Mexican climate politics between 1988 to 2008, please see Pulver (2009).
2 Over the period discussed in this chapter, Mexico's Ministry of the Environment has undergone several name changes. The current federal environment agency, SEMARNAT, was established in 1994 as the Secretaría de Medio Ambiente, Recursos Naturales, y Pesca (SEMARNAP). Prior to 1994, environmental issues were under the purview of the Ministry of Urban Development and Ecology (SEDUE), established in 1982. In 1992, SEDUE was transformed into the Ministry of Social Development (Secretaría de Desarollo Social, SEDESOL). For clarity, this chapter refers to Mexico's Ministry of the Environment as SEMARNAT.
3 Articles from *Reforma* were collected over the period from January 1996 to December 2009. The full-text article database was assembled from a variety of sources, including the news databases LexisNexis and Factiva and *Reforma*'s web archive (*Reforma* articles from 1996–2004).
4 This coding scheme was developed by the COMPON (Climate Policy Networks) project. For more information, please see www.compon.org.

References

Agrawala, S. (1999). Early science-policy interactions in climate change: lessons from the Advisory Group on Greenhouse Gases. *Global Environmental Change* 9(2).
Belausteguigoitia, J. C & I. Lopez-Bassols (1999). Mexico's policies and programs that affect climate change. In J. Goldemberg and W. Reid (eds.) *Promoting Development While Limiting Greenhouse Gas Emissions*. New York, NY: UN Development Programme and World Resources Institute.
Benioff, R., E. Ness & J. Hirst (1997). *National Climate Change Action Plans: Interim Report for Developing and Transition Countries*. Washington, DC: US Country Studies Program.

Black, R. (2012). Inside Mexico's climate revolution. *BBC News – Science and Environment* 20 April.

Boykoff, M. (2007). From convergence to contention: United States mass media representations of anthropogenic climate change science. *Transactions of the Institute of British Geographers* 32(4).

CAT (2012). *Mexico: Climate Action Tracker (CAT)*. Available at: http://climateaction-tracker.org/countries/mexico.html.

CCA/CEC (2001). *México y el Incipiente Mercado de Emisiones de Carbono*. Mexico City: Comisión para la Cooperación Ambiental.

CCC Newsdesk (2007). *Latin America Special Report: Mexico's Flimsy Raft of Climate Change Measures*. 16 August. Available at: htttp://www.climatechangecorp.com/content.asp?ContentID=4897.

CICC (2006). *Towards a National Climate Change Strategy*. Mexico City: Interministerial Commission on Climate Change, SEMARNAT.

CICC (2007). *National Strategy on Climate Change: Mexico*. Mexico City: Interministerial Commission on Climate Change, SEMARNAT.

CICC (2009). *Programa Especial de Cambio Climatico 2009–2012*. Mexico City: SEMARNAT.

Di Sbroiavacca, N. & L. Osvaldo Girardin (2000). Mexico. In B. Biagini (ed.) *Confronting Climate Change: Economic Priorities and Climate Protection in Developing Nations*. Washington, DC: National Environmental Trust.

Ecofys & Climate Analytics (2012). *Climate Action Tracker Mexico*. Potsdam: Climate Analytics.

EIA (2007). *Country Analysis Briefs: Mexico*. Energy Information Administration 2007. Available at: htttp://www.eia.doe.gov/cabs/Mexico/Full.html.

EOE (2010). Energy Profile of Mexico. In *Encyclopedia of the Earth 2010*. Available at: http://www.eoearth.org/article/Energy_profile_of_Mexico.

EU (2010). *EU/LAC Lima Summit, 16–17 May 2010*. Available at: http://eeas.europa.eu/lac/lima/index_en.htm.

Felix, R. (n.d.). Assessing the impact of Mexico's biofuels law. *Biomass Magazine*. Available at: http://biomassmagazine.com/articles/1678/assessing-the-impact-of-mexico's-biofuels-law.

Fenhann, J. (2012). *The CDM Pipeline*. Excel Database. UNEP Risø Centre 2012. Available at: http://cd4cdm.org.

Gay Garcia, C. (1994). Propuesta de Programa Nacional sobre Cambio Climático Global. In C. Gay Garcia, L. G. R. Suarez, M. Imaz, C. Conde & O. Sanchez (eds.) *Primer Taller de Estudio de País: México Ante el Cambio Climático, 18–22 April 1994 Cuernavaca*. Mexico City: Instituto Nacional de Ecología.

Gay Garcia, C. (ed.) (2000). *México: Una Visión Hacia el Siglo XXI – El Cambio Climático en México*. Mexico City: UNAM Programa Universitario de Medio Ambiente.

Government of Mexico (1997). *First National Communication under Framework Convention on Climate Change*. Mexico City: Secretaría de Medio Ambiente, Recursos Naturales, y Pescas.

Government of Mexico (2001). *Second National Communication under Framework Convention on Climate Change*. Mexico City: Secretaría de Medio Ambiente y Recursos Naturales.

Government of Mexico (2006). *Third National Communication under Framework Convention on Climate Change*. Mexico City: Secretaría de Medio Ambiente y Recursos Naturales.

Government of Mexico (2008). *Ideas and Proposals on the Elements Contained in Paragraph 1 of the Bali Action Plan.* Submission to AWG-LCA. Bonn: UNFCCC.

Government of Mexico (2009a). *Fourth National Communication under Framework Convention on Climate Change.* Mexico City: Secretaría de Medio Ambiente y Recursos Naturales.

Government of Mexico (2009b). *The Economics of Climate Change in Mexico.* Mexico City: SHCP and SEMARNAT.

Government of Mexico (2010). *COP16/CMP16 Cancun Mexico November 29th–December 10th 2010.* Available at: http://cc2010.mx/en.

Greenpeace Mexico (2009). *Comentarios al Programa Especial de Cambio Climático 2008–2012.* Press release. Mexico City: Greenpeace.

Halpern, J. (2001). Energy. In M. Giugale, O. Lafourcade & V. Nguyen (eds.) *Mexico: A comprehensive Development Agenda for the New Era.* Washington, DC: World Bank.

Helman, C. (2012). The world's biggest oil companies. *Forbes* 16 July.

IPCC (2007). *Climate Change 2007: Synthesis Report.* Geneva: Intergovernmental Panel on Climate Change.

Kraemer, S. (2012). *Mexico Emulates Neighbor California with 35% Clean Climate Law.* Cleantechnica.com, 15 April. Available at: http://cleantechnica.com/2012/04/15/mexico-emulates-neighbor-california-with-35-clean-climate-law.

Mexico City (2010). *Mexico City Pact: Global Cities Covenant on Climate Change 2010.* Available at: http://www.mexicocitypact.org.

Mexico City Experience (2011). *10 Highlights of Mexico City's Climate Action Program 2011.* Available at: http://www.mexicocityexperience.com/green_living.

Mintzer, I. M. & J. A. Leonard (eds.) (1994). *Negotiating Climate Change: The Inside Story of the Rio Convention.* Cambridge: Cambridge University Press and Stockholm Environment Institute.

Molina, M. (1995). *The Nobel Prize in Chemistry 1995.* Available at: http://www.nobelprize.org/nobel_prizes/chemistry/laureates/1995/molina-autobio.html.

Office of the President of the Government of Mexico (2007). *Plan Nacional de Desarrollo, 2007–2012.* Mexico City: Office of the President.

Pemex (2002). *Safety, Health, and Environment Report 2001.* Mexico City: Petróleos Mexicanos.

Pemex (2006). *Safety, Health, and Environment Report 2005.* Mexico City: Petróleos Mexicanos.

Programa GEI Mexico (2010). *Mexico GHG Program.* Programa GEI Mexico, 6 November 2010. Available at: http://www.geimexico.org.

Pulver, S. (2007). Importing environmentalism: explaining Petroleos Mexicanos' proactive climate policy. *Studies in Comparative International Development* 42(3/4).

Pulver, S. (2009). Climate change politics in Mexico. In H. Selin & S. VanDeveer (eds.) *Changing Climates in North American Politics.* Cambridge, MA: MIT Press.

Quadri, G. (2000). *Climate Change: Mexico and the Kyoto Flexibility Mechanisms.* Mexico City: Comisión de Estudios del Sector Privado para el Desarrollo Sustentable.

Ramos-Mane, C. & R. Benioff (1995). *Interim Report on Climate Change Country Studies.* Washington, DC: US Country Studies Program.

SEMARNAP (1998). *México ante el Cambio Climático.* Mexico City: Secretaría de Medio Ambiente, Recursos Naturales, y Pescas.

SEMARNAT (2006). *Dirección General Adjunta para Proyectos de Cambio Climático.* Available at: http://portal.semarnat.gob.mx/semarnat.

SENER (1998). *Climate Change and the Energy Sector*. Mexico City: Secretaría de Energía, Subsecretaría de Políticas y Desarrollo de Energéticos, Dirección General de Política y Desarrollo Energético.

SMA (2008). *Mexico City Climate Action Program*. Mexico City: Secretaria del Medio Ambiente, Gobierno del Distrito Federal.

Teixeira, M. (2012). Mexico's climate law to face challenge under new president. *Reuters.com* 24 July.

Tournemille, H. (2009). *Mexico Pushes Ethanol as a Means to Reduce Pollution*. Energy Boom 2009. Available at: http://www.energyboom.com/biofuels/mexico-pushes-ethanol-means-reduce-pollution.

Tudela, F., S. Gupta & V. Peeva (2003). *Institutional Capacity and Climate Actions: Case Studies on Mexico (by F. Tudela), India (by S. Gupta) and Bulgaria (by V. Peeva)*. Paris: Organization for Economic Cooperation and Development.

UNEP (2010). *Welcome to the UNEP Climate Pledges Site*. 23 November 2010. Available at: http://www.unep.org/climatepledges/Default.aspx?pid=1.

UNFCCC (2012a). *GHG Data from UNFCCC 2012*. Available at: http://unfccc.int/di/DetailedByParty.do.

UNFCCC (2012b). *Status of Ratification of the Kyoto Protocol*. Climate Change Secretariat 2012. Available at: http://unfccc.int/kyoto_protocol/status_of_ratification/items/2613.php.

Vance, E. (2012). Mexico passes climate-change law. *Nature: News & Comment* 20 April.

West, J. J., P. Osnaya, I. Laguna, J. Martinez & A. Fernandez Bremauntz (2004). Co-control of urban air pollutants and greenhouse gases in Mexico City. *Environmental Science and Technology* 38(13).

Williams, J. (2010). *Linea Base de Emisiones Nacional*. Paper presented at Competividad y Cambio Climatica, 17 June, Monterrey, Mexico.

World Bank (2012). *Data: Climate Change 2012*. Available at: http://data.worldbank.org/topic/climate-change.

WRI (2006). *Mexican Industry Takes Voluntary Action Against Climate Change; Government Gives Public Recognition*. Mexico City: World Resources Institute. Available at: http://www.wri.org/press/2007/10/mexican-industry-takes-voluntary-action-against-climate-change-government-gives-public.

Wynn, G. (2008). Mexico say to set climate targets, cap and trade. *Reuters Canada* 11 December.

PART III

AFRICA

10

Resources and Revenues: The Political Economy of Climate Initiatives in Egypt

Jeannie Sowers

Introduction

EGYPT'S summers are hot, and the hottest days have been getting warmer since the early 1970s, according to available temperature records. According to the Egyptian Meteorological Authority, mean maximum air temperatures increased .34 °C per decade, while mean minimum air temperatures increased .31 °C per decade between 1961 and 2000 (EEAA 2010b, p. 5). The number of days marked by haze, humidity, turbidity, sandstorms and intense air pollution episodes has also increased over the same time period (EEAA 2010b, p. xvii). These changes are only one of the many demands imposed on the inhabitants of Egypt by human-induced climate change. For Egypt, as for the Middle East and North Africa (MENA) as a whole, the effects of anthropogenic climate change have already produced tangible, adverse and disproportionate impacts (Sowers & Weinthal 2010).

Egypt is particularly vulnerable to the effects of anthropogenic climate change. It is largely dependent on one major source of renewable water resources, the Nile; the vast majority of its 82 million inhabitants (as of 2012) live in the densely settled delta and coastal areas; and most of its national territory is located in arid and hyper-arid zones. Egypt, like many developing countries, is thus particularly vulnerable to effects of anthropogenic climate change, although its contribution to global greenhouse gas (GHG) emissions is negligible compared to industrialized high emitters in Europe, North America and Asia (whether calculated in historical, per capita or annual terms). Egypt's carbon footprint is dwarfed by consumption in industrialized countries, in both aggregate and per capita terms, and similarly lags well behind those of the oil-exporting countries nearby in the Persian Gulf, whose fossil fuel exports are an essential pillar of high carbon consumption around the globe. We would therefore expect Egypt, to the extent that it takes action on global climate change at all, to focus its scarce funds and expertise on adaptation measures to reduce vulnerability to climate impacts. Instead, Egypt's climate initiatives,

199

begun in the 1990s, initially focused on mitigation measures rather than adaptation.

This emphasis derived largely from the financial incentives and reporting requirements for developing countries provided by the UN Framework Convention for Climate Change (UNFCCC) and the Kyoto Protocol, including the Clean Development Mechanism (CDM). Since the UNFCCC and the Kyoto Protocol originally focused on mitigation, and provided funds and expertise for developing countries to take part, Egypt's initial forays into climate governance consisted of conducting national GHG emissions inventories and identifying mitigation opportunities. With the advent of the CDM, Egypt successfully financed a number of fuel switching and infrastructure investment projects that had long been considered by central government ministries in industry, water and electricity. As international institutions and conventions have shifted towards dealing with the now-inevitable effects of human-induced climate change, so too have expert networks in Egypt worked to document the impacts of climate change and to convince policymakers to undertake adaptation measures. Egypt's small but growing cadre of environmental scientists has also highlighted how existing policies and infrastructure investments can serve both developmental and climate-proofing purposes.

The other important factor shaping Egypt's approach to climate change governance has been the significant role of the energy sector in the local political economy. The changing contours of Egypt's energy sector have driven many of the policy changes that are classified as 'climate mitigation' by external observers. Dominated by state-owned firms that partner with multinationals in a variety of downstream and upstream ventures, the energy sector helps pay the government's escalating bills for social subsidies (including fuel subsidies) and public sector wages. The Egyptian state has faced a steady decline in external revenue since the 1980s, and has thus long struggled with a structural fiscal crisis (Soliman 2011). The revenues from the export of oil and, more recently, natural gas are thus a much-needed source of rent. The government's emerging interest in renewable energy – namely, wind farms and concentrated solar power projects – is largely due to predicted declines in oil and gas exports and the resulting search for new sources of export revenue.

Meanwhile, those most in need of climate adaptation measures – poor farmers in rural areas, coastal residents, and poor residents of informal urban areas and villages – found little political consideration under the Mubarak regime. During the 2000s, however, Egypt's environmental scientists increasingly highlighted the importance of adaptation issues in the water and agricultural sectors and in Egypt's coastal areas, through their research and participation in regional and international forums. It is unclear whether the ongoing rewriting of the political game as a result of the 2011 uprising will strengthen the political clout of Egypt's small farmers and informal residents, or whether they will be forced to continue to cope on their own.

Climate Initiatives and Donor Aid

Ferguson (1994) argued that in many developing countries, state agencies and interventions by international donors have fused into a 'development apparatus'. The networks of experts and consultants that staff this apparatus typically approach challenges of development and environment as technocratic issues, to be tackled by implementing discrete projects, building institutional capacity and mobilizing professional expertise. Social contestation, community mobilization and interest group bargaining play little role in what Ferguson termed 'the anti-politics machine'. While the discourse of development has since changed, to invoke routinely notions of participatory consultation with local communities, 'end-users' and women, the actual conduct of projects, particularly those involving large-scale infrastructure in the energy and water sectors, has not kept pace with rhetorical commitments.

As I document elsewhere (Sowers 2013), official environmental initiatives in Egypt are typically undertaken by 'managerial networks' comprised of technocrats, environmental scientists and consultants working within a particular environmental policy domain. These networks coalesce around successive state-donor projects, located within enclaves of institutional reform established within or alongside existing central ministries. Egypt's managerial networks thus have extensive experience in seeking opportunities for external aid, and often play highly visible roles in regional institutions and international conventions.

Since the 1970s, international donors have funded a variety of infrastructure and policy reform agendas in Egypt, with the United States Agency for International Development (USAID) by far the largest player. USAID's outsized role in external funding was the product of Egypt's normalization of relations with Israel through the US-sponsored Camp David Accords, signed in 1978. Since then, external aid as a proportion of Egypt's gross domestic product (GDP) has steadily declined, as it has for all developing countries (Soliman 2011, p. 49). However, out of a shrinking pie for international aid, Egypt has fared relatively well in attracting environmental assistance. Egypt was the second largest recipient of international environmental aid during the 1980s, receiving a total of US$2.2 billion (Hicks et al. 2008, p. 61). During the 1990s, it was the seventh largest recipient of worldwide environmental aid, with an inflow of US$3.2 billion (Hicks et al. 2008, p. 62). The vast majority of this aid was targeted to investments in 'hard' infrastructure, such as expansions and improvements to irrigation systems, potable water treatment plants and sewage treatment plants. This emphasis on infrastructural improvements, as we shall see, continues to dominate Egypt's approach to climate impacts such as sea level rise.

A similar pattern of expert network engagement with external financing has driven Egypt's climate change initiatives. Egypt ratified

Table 10.1 Egypt: climate change policy initiatives, 1992–2011

Initiative	Year	Lead governmental agency and/or international funder
Egypt signs UNFCCC; Climate Change Unit established within EEAA as national focal point	1992	EEAA
Egypt ratifies UNFCCC	1994	UNFCCC enters into force in 1995
Building capacity for Egypt to respond to UNFCCC communications obligations	1995–2001	Funded by GEF; implemented by EEAA and UNDP Egypt
Egypt signs Kyoto Protocol and submits First National Communication to UNFCCC	1999	EEAA
National Committee on Climate Change established; inter-ministerial committee	Established 1997; restructured 2007	Headed by minister of state for environmental affairs
Egypt ratifies Kyoto Protocol and establishes a high-level committee to serve as designated authority for the CDM	2005	National Committee on Climate Change
Second National Communication to the UNFCCC	2010	Climate Change Central Department, EEAA and UNDP
Climate Change Risk Management Programme	2008–11	Joint project of GEF/UNDP, EEAA and Ministry of Irrigation and Water Resources
Egypt NEEDS for UNFCCC	2010	Climate Change Central Department, EEAA and UNDP

CDM = Clean Development Mechanism; EEAA = Egyptian Environmental Affairs Agency; GEF = Global Environmental Facility; NEEDS = National Environment, Economic and Development Study; UNDP = Unitwed Nations Development Programme; UNFCC = United Nations Framework Convention on Climate Change.

Sources: EEAA (1999a, 1999b, 2010a, 2010b); EEAA website (http://www.eeaa.gov.eg)

the UNFCCC in 1994 and signed the Kyoto Protocol in 1999. It therefore became eligible for donor assistance in preparing national reports and needs assessments established under the Protocol (see table 10.1). These were produced largely by local consultants, financed by international donors, and under the rubric of a newly established Climate Change Unit within the Egyptian Environmental Affairs Agency (EEAA). The principal results were GHG emissions inventories conducted in accordance with scientific standards set out by the Intergovernmental Panel on Climate Change (IPCC). It is noteworthy that while Egypt completed two national communications, as suggested under the UNFCCC, it did not prepare a National Adaptation Programme of Action (NAPA). NAPA plans were designed to fund urgent and immediate climate-related needs in least developed countries; other developing countries were encouraged to use the framework to help identify and prioritize critical areas for adaptation financing. Egypt's central government ministries already had extensive investment plans prepared in the water, agriculture and energy sectors for consideration by donors and foreign investors. Additional work on adaptation requirements emerged in a 2010 needs assessment study (EEAA 2010c).

The Energy Sector

The energy sector is key to understanding not only trends in Egypt's GHG emissions but also some of the most important actors in Egypt's political economy. Egypt's two principal energy sources are petroleum products and natural gas. The companies that extract, process and distribute fossil fuels – the state-owned petroleum and electricity companies, multinational energy firms, and public–private consortiums in refining and secondary industries – hold a privileged position in governmental planning and in state budgeting. Specifically, Egypt's energy sector is comprised of what one analyst termed 'two state-owned supply complexes', one serving gas and petroleum under the Ministry of Petroleum and one focused on electricity under the Ministry of Electricity (Suding 2011, p. 4441). Both are formally organized as holding companies, that is, state-owned joint stock companies. The Egyptian General Petroleum Company under the Ministry of Petroleum holds shares in approximately sixty joint ventures with multinationals, and both supply complexes own 'numerous public sector companies active in upstream and downstream activities, generation, transmission, and distribution, and also services' (ibid.). Multinational involvement in oil and gas production is organized via production sharing agreements with state-owned firms (Mabro 2006, p. 3), while other energy-related activities are often carried out as joint ventures between multinational and Egyptian firms. Since multinationals are needed for their investment dollars and technical expertise, the Egyptian government is structurally disadvantaged in negotiating contracts with multinational firms (Mabro 2006).

In 2010, the energy sector accounted for 46 per cent of Egypt's total GHG emissions, a figure that included fuel combustion for power generation and fugitive emissions from oil production. The remaining GHG emissions came from agriculture (16 per cent), transport (14 per cent), industrial processes (14 per cent) and the waste sector, which includes emissions from incineration, uncontrolled burning and release of landfill gases, at 9 per cent (EEAA 2010c). Egypt, like many developing countries, faces a rapidly rising domestic demand for power, with 11 per cent annual increases in 2011 and 2012 (Leila 2012).

This growth in demand is not only the result of increasing population growth, rising standards of living, or more demand for air conditioning in the face of warming temperatures and heat waves, although all these are drivers. Instead, energy subsidies also play a role. The government sets prices for electricity and fossil fuels below world market prices to encourage domestic industries and protect urban consumers. The Egyptian government extends subsidies to virtually all energy users, from households to power stations. The goal, notes Mabro (2006, p. 11), is to 'make electricity, goods produced by industry and retailed by merchants, transport fares, services, and so on, available to consumers at affordable prices'. Egypt is, of course, not exceptional in encouraging the rapid extraction of fossil fuel resources by the present generation; direct and indirect US fossil fuel subsidies are estimated to range from US$10 billion to US$52 billion annually, not including either health or environmental costs (Oil Change International 2012). The enormous range of these estimates attests to one of the central problems of energy governance seen around the world: the lack of consistent, transparent and credible reporting of indirect fossil fuel subsidies.

Egypt's fuel subsidies have long been criticized by the World Bank and local environmental experts. Cash outlays in the annual state budget are estimated to reach slightly more than US$4 billion (Mabro 2006, p. 9). The economic costs of the subsidy, however, are much higher. Under production sharing agreements, the Egyptian state-owned oil and gas firms purchase guaranteed shares of multinational production at world prices and then re-sell oil and gas on the domestic market at significantly lower administered prices. Some analysts estimate that this may almost double the cost of domestic energy subsidies to the Egyptian government (ibid., p. 10). In addition to the direct fiscal burden, supplying cheap energy to industry, transport and agriculture inhibits energy efficiency and conservation. Cost savings are not necessarily passed on to consumers in markets characterized by significant market concentration and cartels, as is the case for most of Egypt's industrial products (ibid., p. 11).

Nowhere have the pricing incentives been more evident than in Egypt's natural gas sector. During the 1990s, significant reserves of natural gas were discovered, estimated at 68.48 trillion cubic feet of proven gas reserves (Mabro 2011; BP 2009). For the Egyptian government, faced with declining oil production, the extraction, distribution and processing of natural gas (into secondary industries such as petrochemicals and fertilizers) offered new avenues to raise revenues. By pricing Egyptian gas below world prices, the government encouraged rapid investment by multinationals in natural gas infrastructure and in downstream industrial activities, such as fertilizer production. In addition, to conserve petroleum for export, the ministries of petroleum and electricity began an official policy of switching domestic fuel supplies for industrial, transport and residential use from petroleum to natural gas. The result was that natural gas combustion increased by 174 per cent between 1990 and 2000, while consumption of liquid petroleum products increased only 13 per cent (EEAA 2010b, p. 28).

The GHG emissions inventories undertaken as part of the First and Second National Communications to the UNFCCC show the importance of energy-intensive industrial production in Egypt's GHG emissions. Between 1990 and 2000, GHG emissions increased from 116.6 to 193.3 million tonnes of CO_2 equivalent. From 2000 to 2010, estimated total emissions increased to 318.2 million tonnes of CO_2 equivalent. Between 1990 and 2000, industrial processes were the fastest growing component of total GHG emissions, increasing from 9 to 14 per cent of total GHG emissions (EEAA 2010b, pp. 27–31). While population increased by about 10 million persons, GDP more than doubled, from £E34.12 billion to £E68.34 billion during the same period (EEAA 2010b).

While the production of lime, cement, and iron and steel dominate Egypt's industrial GHG emissions, the most rapid increases in emissions during the 2000s were in the sectors of nitric acid and ammonia, used in fertilizers. These increased 220–fold over the decade (EEAA 2010b, p. 29). The cement industry, which, like fertilizers, increasingly relied on natural gas as an input, showed a 129 per cent increase over the decade (ibid.). As Egypt's Second National Communication to the UNFCCC noted, 'current Egyptian exports are dominated by natural resource-based and low-technology products. In this context, high fossil fuel consuming industries and associated energy-intensive products are the primary growing industries and their impact on GHG emissions in Egypt will be felt in the near future' (EEAA 2010b, p. 16).

Some political economists have long argued that Egypt shares several structural features with other 'rentier states' in the region, even though the contribution of export revenues from fossil fuels to the state budget is far less than in the oil exporting countries of the Gulf. Conventionally, rentier states earn a significant proportion of domestic revenues from external sources rather than through domestic taxation. External rents accumulate from the sale of natural resources, worker remittances, foreign aid, and transit fees for strategic waterways, pipelines and other infrastructures. Because such external flows accrue directly to the state, many scholars have argued that rentier states have few incentives to develop robust mechanisms of fiscal accountability. Political elites and state officials face great temptations to spend such revenues in ways that inhibit long-term economic innovation and productivity. Rents are often used to sustain financing of patronage networks, large-scale infrastructure projects and domestic subsidies (Waterbury 1993; Lowi 2009; Luong & Weinthal 2010).

Although Egypt has formally pursued expansion of market-driven capitalism since the late 1970s, during the 2000s an increased share of GDP came from profits in the energy and industrial sectors as well as from state spending on subsidies (EEAA 2010b, p. 10). The petroleum and gas sectors remain the most attractive to foreign private investors; in 2008, foreign direct investment (FDI) in the petroleum and gas sector was US$2.8 billion, or 70 per cent of Egypt's total FDI inflows (Suding 2011, p. 4431). Growth in the energy sector fuelled an expanding share of the state-owned sector in total GDP. Despite a decade of intensified privatization, which shrank the role of the state-owned sector in most economic activities, the percentage of total GDP produced by the petroleum sector went from 5 per cent to 16 per cent, while the state-owned portion of the petroleum sector increased from 5.8 per cent to 13.3 per cent of total GDP between 1997/8 and 2006/7 (ibid.).

The recent, rapid exploitation of significant natural gas reserves has thus reinforced the structural position of large state authorities and multinational energy firms in Egypt's political economy. Investment flows in the energy sector have not solved the basic financial quandary facing the Egyptian government. As it has for several decades, the Egyptian government faces a growing wage and subsidy bill combined with insufficient government revenues, despite attempting to introduce various forms of taxation.

Climate 'Mitigation' and the Clean Development Mechanism

Egypt's portfolio of projects under the Kyoto Protocol's CDM illustrates how the political economy of the domestic fossil fuel sector shapes Egypt's climate initiatives. As of May 2012, Egypt had a total of 104 CDM projects registered, approved or accepted, or in the pipeline for approval (EEAA 2012). The CDM was designed to allow firms and government agencies from Annex I countries (i.e. industrialized countries) to undertake investments in developing countries as a way to meet their carbon reduction commitments at lower cost than in their home countries. Two immediate challenges are apparent, however. The first is whether it is meaningful for investment decisions by multinationals, with globalized supply chains, markets and management, to be 'credited' towards reducing carbon emissions in specific national accounts. Second, these investments are supposed to be in addition to, or distinct from, investment decisions that firms and developed countries would have undertaken in the absence of the CDM. The difficulties in establishing such distinctions, and monitoring them for accuracy and implementation success, have been well documented by scholars (see e.g. Repetto 2001).

The single largest category of CDM projects in Egypt is fuel switching in industrial processes (EEAA 2012). Fuel switching projects – that is, substituting a less carbon-intensive energy source – are eligible, under certain conditions, for participation in the CDM. In Egypt's national communications to the UNFCCC, the government identified fuel switching in local industry from heavy, low quality fuel oils (e.g. *mazut*) to natural gas as one of the most important national mitigation priorities (EEAA 1999a; EEAA 2010b). Natural gas produces roughly 30 per cent less carbon dioxide than petroleum per unit of heat generated; as importantly, the use of gas in transport and industry produces fewer small particulates and other pollutants, improving urban air quality. The claim that fuel switching constitutes mitigation of GHG emissions, however, highlights some of the problems endemic in conducting emissions inventories on a national basis. Domestic fuel switching reduces Egypt's GHG emissions, but does not actually reduce global GHG emissions, since the petroleum 'saved' at home is simply exported for consumption in Europe, the US and Asia.

Most of the beneficiaries targeted for fuel switching in Egypt's CDM projects are large state-owned or partially privatized firms. These were often the same firms that Egyptian officials had put forward in earlier requests for donor pollution abatement funding during the 1980s and 1990s. Thus, CDM projects continued a long-standing pattern in Egypt in which international donors focus environmental assistance on the most polluting and largest firms, which are typically state-owned or quasi-privatized firms (Sowers 2013, ch. 3). CDM funding thus served the same constituencies as earlier pollution control abatement funds. Many of these firms arguably have the financial resources to undertake fuel switching and pollution abatement measures. Yet historically these firms have delayed compliance with local environmental regulations, using their dominant position in domestic markets and, for state-owned enterprises, their role in providing captive revenues to the state budget to bargain with regulatory authorities (Sowers 2013, ch 3). Thus, such firms have generally been under insufficient *political* pressure from governmental authorities to make necessary investments in pollution control and energy efficiency (ibid.).

In addition, CDM funding may well be replacing traditional bilateral sources of environmental aid in Egypt rather than supplementing them. Environmental aid to Egypt shifted during the 2000s from bilateral donors to multilateral funding pools, such as the CDM and the GEF (Sowers 2013). An increasing proportion of donor-funded environmental initiatives is thus undertaken under the rubric of global environmental problems, like climate change, rather than pressing problems of local public services and pollution control.

The Renewable Energy Sector

Approved renewable energy projects in Egypt's CDM portfolio also show the dominance of donor funded projects or state-owned/military enterprises. Numerically, renewable energy projects constitute a small proportion of CDM funding to Egypt; Egypt has only 14 projects in renewable energy out of 104 total CDM projects (EEAA 2012). The wind sector has thus far attracted the most investment, with 8 CDM projects devoted to wind energy production. As shown in table 10.2, wind energy has occupied a prominent place in Egypt's limited renewable energy initiatives. A wind atlas, funded by the Danish aid agency Danida and the Egyptian government, was completed in 2005, and identified Egypt's Gulf of Suez coast as the area with the most

Table 10.2 Developments in Egypt's renewable energy sector, 1982–date

Initiative	Year	Governmental authorities	Comments
NREA established	1982	Ministry of Electricity	
Wind atlas undertaken: assessment of wind resources for energy production	1998–2005	Risø DTU, NREA and Egyptian Meteorological Authority	Funded by Danida and Egyptian government; focused on desert and coastal areas
National Energy Efficiency Strategy	2001 completed	National Energy Efficiency Council (inter-ministerial committee) formed	Project of USAID's Egyptian Environmental Policy Program, conducted with Bechtel
Z'afarāna Wind Farm; phased construction begins	2001– ongoing	Supported by donor funds from Germany, Denmark and Spain	By 2010, total installed capacity was 550 MW
Organization for Energy Planning dissolved	2006		Reduced data availability and reliability regarding energy (Suding 2011)
Egypt's Strategy for Energy Supply and Use	2007	Supreme Council on Energy formally revived, headed by prime minister, but with no staff, no institutional autonomy and no agenda-setting capacity	Adds nuclear energy to Egypt's energy planning, although EEAA 2010a notes that nuclear energy is not a cost effective mitigation measure (p. 8)
MENA Regional Center for Renewable Energy and Energy Efficiency established	2009	Ministry of Electricity; proposal to create national energy efficiency agency defeated	Egypt commits to 20% renewables by 2020, with 12% projected from wind farms
Gulf El-Zayt wind farm	2009	World Bank assists with first stage of international tender	Developers will build, own and operate under 20-year, government-guaranteed power purchase agreement
Suez wind farm	February 2010	NREA and UAE's Masdar company	Plans for 200 MW wind farm near Suez on eastern side
World Bank approves ££1.2 billion to Egypt for wind energy	August 2010	World Bank	Includes ££800 million from Clean Technology Fund; first loan to MENA from the fund
Egypt announces tender for grid swap with Saudi Arabia during peak hours	April 2011	Egyptian Electricity Holding Company and Saudi Electricity Company	

MENA = Middle East and North Africa; MW = megawatt; NEEDS = National Environment, Economic and Development Study; NREA = New and Renewable Energy Authority; UAE = United Arab Emirates; USAID = United States Agency for International Development.

Sources: EEAA (2010a, 2010b); Global Wind Energy Council website (http://www.gwec.net/index.php?id=122)

consistently high wind speeds (Mortensen et al. 2005). All of Egypt's wind projects, linked into an integrated wind grid, have thus been located in this area, concentrated around Z'afarāna.

Of the eight wind projects approved or accepted under the CDM, six were joint ventures between Egypt's New and Renewable Energy Authority (NREA) (part of the Ministry of Electricity established in 1982), the donor agencies of Japan, Denmark, Spain and Germany, and the Italian electricity/renewable energy producer Italgen. The only wind farm to be undertaken entirely under Egyptian ownership was a project under the large state-owned military complex, the Arab Organization for Industrialization (AOI). While most of the components for wind energy have been imported, a private wind turbine assembly factory was founded in 2008, Elsewedy for Wind Energy Generation (SWEG).

The same winds that drive turbines along the Gulf of Suez also facilitate bird migration from Africa to Europe, helping hundreds of thousands of migratory soaring birds make their transcontinental journeys back and forth in spring and autumn. Egyptian ornithologists have identified a number of areas around the Gulf of Suez that serve as crucial areas for many species of migratory birds, including several of Egypt's internationally important bird areas (IBAs) as designated by Birdlife International (Baha al-Din, n.d.). In apt illustration of how renewable energy initiatives have been divorced from broader environmental concerns, Egypt's small, active community of bird experts has repeatedly argued that no adequate impact assessments were undertaken to estimate avian mortalities or disruption in flight patterns from the construction of large-scale wind farms along the western Gulf of Suez.

In the field of solar energy production, a similar constellation of donors, state- and military-owned firms and a few private investors is apparent. As in wind energy, oversight by the environmental agency and environmental experts is lacking. Egypt's Ministry of Electricity and Energy lists the handful of local companies that are planning to be involved in solar energy production on its website (Ministry of Electricity and Energy 2010). Among these is the Arab–British Dynamics Company (ABD), founded in 1978 as a joint venture by British Aerospace and the AOI, owned by the military, as noted above. With 1,517 workers, the AOI is involved in producing defence systems, vehicle spare parts and medical parts, and now intends to move into renewable energy projects. Alongside this 'old' military firm is a much smaller private venture. The Egyptian Solar Energy System Company, located in the new industrial Sixth of October City, with thirty-six employees, is the local manufacturer of solar boilers and flat plate collectors for multinational firms.

Egypt has an ideal solar profile for the extensive use of decentralized solar systems, particularly household water heaters, yet little governmental effort has been exerted towards disseminating or subsidizing decentralized, small-scale, readily available solar technologies.

Instead, in line with the existing political economy of energy production, the Egyptian government and donors such as the World Bank are exploring possibilities for large-scale solar arrays in the MENA that would concentrate and convert solar energy to thermal energy and then electricity for export to Europe (see e.g. World Bank 2011). Emerging state interest in concentrated solar power in Egypt is thus driven by considerations familiar from oil and natural gas: if the initial capital costs can be met, solar power could be a significant source of export revenue for the government (ibid.).

The most ambitious and well-known of these initiatives is the DESERTEC proposal, which envisions an integrated European–MENA electricity grid in which solar power generation serves as a primary source of energy (Mason 2009). A regional power grid is already emerging, as Egypt exports electricity through connected grids to Jordan and Libya, and has finalized plans for a grid connection to Tunisia that would allow Egypt to export electricity onwards to Europe (EEAA 2010a, p. 28). Egypt has also continued to plan to build a grid with Saudi Arabia to swap electricity at peak load times (Kraemer 2011). Egypt, however, lags behind Morocco and Tunisia on moving ahead with concentrated solar power; both of those countries have already awarded the Spanish firms Cobra and Abener tenders for the construction and operation of concentrated solar power projects.

Adaptation Initiatives

As analysed above, Egypt's climate initiatives initially focused more on mitigation than adaptation. Drivers of this policy response include the opportunities presented by the CDM as well as broader governmental priorities in the energy and industrial sectors. In addition, CDM projects are relatively easy for the government to undertake, in that they involve a limited number of stakeholders. In contrast, undertaking robust adaptation measures involves much greater challenges in terms of mobilizing state capacity and building social trust, in order to assess differential vulnerabilities and devise appropriate measures accordingly (Sowers et al. 2010).

Egypt's Second National Communication on Climate Change began to identify, in general terms, adaptation challenges in terms of expected impacts, costs and recommended measures in the water and agricultural sectors, with some attention to safeguarding coastlines, the tourism sector, housing and roads, and public health. Some of these proposed measures are within the capacities of the Egyptian government or voluntary organizations to undertake, while others seem unlikely to be politically salient or adequately implemented.

As Agrawala et al. (2004, p. 15) have emphasized, climate impacts on the Nile and the coastal zones affect the welfare of the country as a whole, because Egypt's population and economic activities are centred on these areas. Agrawala et al. qualitatively ranked the severity of climate impacts in terms of certainty of impact, timing of impact, severity of impact, and importance of the resources for the Egyptian economy (ibid., p. 16). Under this ranking, coastal resources and water resources were the most adversely affected.

The Nile Basin and its sub-catchments are highly sensitive to changes in temperature and rainfall (Zereini & Hötzl, 2009; Beyene et al. 2010; EEAA 2010b, p. 74). Several climate and non-climate factors will thus impact Egypt's share of Nile flows. These include highly variable and uncertain effects on rainfall regimes in upstream states; higher temperatures and higher rates of evapotranspiration; greater demand for water and hydropower in upstream states; and official and unaccounted for abstractions in upstream states (Conway & Hulme 1996; EEAA 2010b). In the coastal zones, renewable shallow aquifers on the northern coast will be adversely affected by expected decreases in precipitation and increasing salinity from rising sea levels, delta subsidence and seawater intrusion. In addition, rainfall regimes in the eastern Mediterranean are widely predicted to shift northwards (Evans 2009), which in turn will affect coastal agriculture and aquifer recharge.

Using historical data from tide gauges, scientists with the Coastal Research Institute in Alexandria have calculated rates of land subsidence along selected locations of the Nile Delta between 1925 and 2000. Sea levels increased 1.0 mm per year at Al-Burullus, 1.6 mm per year at Alexandria and 2.3 mm per year at Port Said, relative to land levels (Frihy 2003). These increases result from a combination of sea level rise and land subsidence of the Delta, deprived of nourishment from Nile deposits with the creation of barrages and large dams (Stanley & Warne 1998). Egyptian scientists have also modelled the amount of land likely to be affected and have begun to enumerate the socioeconomic costs (El Raey 2008). Costs include not only those directly linked to population relocation but also much more widespread effects on livelihoods and income from displacements in agriculture, tourism, services and industry.

After impacts on water resources, the agricultural sector is widely viewed as the most vulnerable to climate change. Since agricultural production in Egypt relies on irrigation, changes in Nile flows or coastal aquifers have directly adverse impacts on agricultural production. Increased temperatures also bring a host of challenges to Egyptian cultivators. Under all of the IPCC's Special Report on Emissions Scenarios for climate change, seasonal crop-water requirements for all major crops increase by between 5 and 13 per cent (Attaher & Medany 2008). Many crops are already cultivated at the extremes of their tolerances to heat and to water and soil salinity; increasing temperature is expected to lower yields and shift cultivation patterns (Eid et al. 2007). Yields of major crops, including wheat, rice, maize, soybeans and barley, are expected to decrease significantly with higher temperatures (EEAA 2010b, p. 77) The incidence of pests and disease is also expected to increase with higher temperatures, in part from increased intensity and frequency of heat waves, sandstorms and dust storms (ibid., p. 88).

Egypt's Second National Communication to the IPCC made a preliminary case that climate impacts are likely to contribute to the spread of vector-borne diseases in Egypt. While Egypt has launched widespread public health campaigns to eradicate malaria and limit the spread of the parasitic disease schistosomiasis (carried by snails in irrigation channels), the distribution of hosts and vectors may well shift with temperature increases (EEAA 2010b, p. 94). Lymphatic filariasis is endemic in the Nile Delta, thanks to a widespread mosquito species; higher temperatures may well result in more mosquitoes and human exposure. Rift Valley fever is also spread by mosquitoes and is amplified by transmission through cattle and sheep; a severe outbreak in the Nile Delta in 1977/8 suggests possible future epidemics with temperature increase (ibid.).

The Political Feasibility of Proactive Adaptation

Given Egypt's topography, limited water resources, and settlement patterns, climate change thus imposes significant threats to human security. Egyptian communities and authorities have long had to deal with the problems of scarce water, an arid climate and vulnerable coastal areas. As a result, a number of institutions and policy communities are in place that could, theoretically, respond to some of the most important climate impacts. Yet a significant caveat is in order in the light of what we know about prior governmental interventions in Egypt's water, housing and environmental sectors.

As David Sims has masterfully shown for the enormous urban agglomeration of Greater Cairo (according to the 2006 census, the city then housed 11.6 million people) some of the key features that make the city function as well as it does developed in spite of state planning and interventions. Cairo is one of the most densely populated mega-cities in the world, expanding primarily through informal processes of housing and construction. This density facilitates the (often belated) provision of sanitation and water and the use of public transport. Small and medium enterprise activity has likewise clustered in and around Greater Cairo, providing income and employment. In contrast, the government's planned 'new cities' are characterized by 'empty lots, stalled construction, huge empty concessions, and skeletal subdivisions' (Sims 2010, p. 193). Formal government planning and infrastructure provision have long been biased towards providing for the middle and upper classes, even as the welfare rhetoric of the government remains populist (Dorman 2007). This trend has become more evident in recent decades, as economic reforms opened up new avenues of wealth creation for the political elite.

In the absence of more adequate governmental intervention, some adaptation measures will be 'forced' – that is, consist of informal and communal responses to changing conditions. Just as the dynamics of urbanization have been largely governed by informal processes of land conversion and housing construction, agricultural adaptation will include informal measures to cope with salinization and sea level rise. In some areas of the Delta, farmers have already dug deeper wells or shifted to crops and crop varieties that can better tolerate salinity. While Sims emphasized the positive externalities of private and informal adaptive responses for Cairo, the negative externalities of these specific adaptations in the water sector are well known, and include over-extraction of coastal aquifers and accelerated seawater intrusion. The official NEEDS study submitted by the Egyptian government in 2010 requested project financing to monitor and analyse climate impacts in agriculture, but no mention was made of mobilizing financing to support community initiatives or social insurance to address increased climate risks for small-scale agricultural producers.

More effective, proactive adaptation strategies are more taxing in terms of state capacities and often require social trust to gain adequate information about local level needs and environmental impacts. Egypt's record on adaptation to sea level rise illustrates this point. There are a number of possible policy responses to safeguard parts of the Delta from sea level rise and to facilitate changes in economic activities to accommodate such a rise. These range from simple, low cost measures such as beach nourishment and building artificial dunes to more complex policy initiatives such as integrated coastal zone management and supporting changes in livelihoods and land use, such as shifting from agriculture to aquaculture (Agrawala et al. 2004, pp. 31–2).

There is substantial support for several of these policies from some local scientists and officials in Egypt's coastal cities. Conducting small-scale (100 person) surveys of 'stakeholders' in the coastal cities of Alexandria and Port Said, El-Raey et al. (1999) showed that the majority of those interviewed were well aware of the problem of sea level rise, with 86 per cent of respondents in Port Said and almost all in Alexandria indicating awareness of the issue (cited in Agrawala et al. 2004, pp. 32–6). The surveys also revealed that there was strong support for pursuing such policy measures as integrated coastal zone management and low cost physical interventions, including beach nourishment and building breakwaters.

Governmental interventions to date, however, have focused largely on building more costly forms of 'hard' infrastructure, such as sea-walls and dykes, which cover only a small portion of the vulnerable areas (Fanos et al. 1995). Egypt's 2010 climate NEEDS study conducted under the UNFCCC estimated that approximately 80 per cent of the 250 kilometre coastline would require such protection, costing approximately US$2 million (EEAA 2010a, p. 24). Existing infrastructural investments in coastal protection have been made without reference to climate change per se, but to cope with beach erosion and expansion of road, port and tourism infrastructures. These projects provide revenue to construction firms in the public and private sectors, including the military, and require little or no coordination between public institutions and affected communities or business interests. Precisely for these reasons, central ministries view such projects as attractive policy choices, while more sophisticated policy interventions, such as coastal zone management, have not yet been seriously undertaken.

Conclusion

As explored in this chapter, climate governance in Egypt has been largely driven by two factors. The UNFCCC and the CDM provided a set of reporting requirements and financial incentives for networks of local experts and a few governmental authorities to engage in climate-related initiatives. These initiatives identified trends in Egypt's GHG emissions, mapped out vulnerable geographical areas and economic sectors, and put forward requests for external funding. Adaptation planning has begun to play a larger role in Egypt's climate governance as climate impacts become more evident, but this planning is still very limited.

Even more important in setting Egypt's climate agenda, however, has been the ownership structure and composition of the energy sector, and government policies towards the energy sector. State-owned supply complexes control the production of oil and natural gas, relying on partnerships with multinational firms to provide expertise and competitive technologies; fuel exports are an important source of hard currency for the state. This 'public–private symbiosis' is just as evident in Egypt's industrial sectors that rely on low priced fossil fuels for competitive production, such as cement, steel, petrochemicals and fertilizers. The result is a systematic bias towards large-scale production and distribution of energy and electricity, including emerging state and donor interest in renewable energy, such as wind and concentrated solar power. Ironically, given Egypt's solar profile, low cost, small-scale, decentralized applications might go some way towards meeting household and community needs for energy.

The extraordinary mass uprising of 2011, and the upsurge in popular protest that both preceded and followed the deposing of President Mubarak, have politicized some of these features of the energy sector. The export of 'cheap' natural gas and the siting of new industrial export facilities became lightning rods for political debate. As a result, post-Mubarak governments raised export prices for gas to Jordan and cancelled the gas contract for Israel following repeated attacks on the natural gas infrastructure in Sinai. Newly elected President Mohamed Mursi announced in the summer of 2012 that the government would begin to restructure fuel subsidies, though it retreated from implementing these reforms shortly thereafter.

The political transition under way in Egypt will thus exert contradictory pressures on climate initiatives. Policy initiatives that
combine 'climate proofing' with immediate and concrete benefits
(such as preservation of beaches or the provision of salt-tolerant
crop varieties) may find new constituencies and be pursued more
vigorously. Measures such as lifting fuel subsidies, however, will face
populist and electoral counterpressures, particularly in the absence
of functioning, targeted systems of welfare provision. The need to
address water shortages, power cuts and crop failures will take on
more urgency than in the past (see e.g. Leila 2012). In lieu of adequate
state policies, localized, 'forced' and informal adaptation measures
are likely to remain significant as climate impacts translate into tangible losses in livelihoods and incomes.

References

Agrawala, S., A. Moehner, M. El-Raey, D. Conway, M. van Aalst, M. Hagenstad
& J. Smith (2004). *Development and Climate Change in Egypt: Focus on Coastal
Resources and the Nile*. Paris: Environmental Directorate, Organization for
Economic Cooperation and Development.

Attaher, S. M. & M. A. Medany (2008). Analysis of crop water use efficiencies in
Egypt under climate change. In *Proceedings of Natural Resources and Sustainable
Development*. Minoufiya: Sadat Academy of Environmental Science.

Baha el Din, S. M. (n.d.). *Important Bird Areas in Africa and Associated Islands*. Available at: http://www.birdlife.org/datazone/userfiles/file/IBAs/AfricaCntryPDFs/
Egypt.pdf.

Beyene, T., D. P. Lettenmaier & P. Kabat (2010). Hydrologic impacts of climate
change on the Nile River basin: implications of the 2007 IPCC scenarios.
Climatic Change 100: 433–461.

BP (2009). *Statistical Review of World Energy*. June. Available at: www.bp.com/
statisticalreview.

Conway, D. & M. Hulme (1996). The impacts of climate variability and climate
change in the Nile Basin on future water resources in Egypt. *Water Resources
Development* 12(3).

Dorman, W. J. (2007). *The Politics of Neglect: The Egyptian State in Cairo, 1974–1998*.
PhD thesis, University of London.

EEAA (1999a). *Initial National Communication on Climate Change, Prepared for the
UNFCCC*. Cairo: Egyptian Environmental Affairs Agency.

EEAA (1999b). *National Action Plan of Climate Change*. Cairo: Egyptian Environmental Affairs Agency.

EEAA (2010a). *Egypt National Environmental, Economic, and Development Study
(NEEDS) for Climate Change, Prepared for the United Nations Framework Convention
on Climate Change (UNFCCC)*. Cairo: Egyptian Environmental Affairs Agency.

EEAA (2010b). *Second National Communication of Egypt, Submitted to the United
Nations Framework Convention on Climate Change (UNFCCC)*. Cairo: Egyptian
Environmental Affairs Agency.

EEAA (2010c). *Estimated GHG Inventory in Egypt*. Available at: http://www.eeaa.
gov.eg/english/reports/CC/Estimated%20GHG%20Inventory%20in%20Egypt.
pdf.

EEAA (2012). *Egyptian CDM Project Portfolio (Updated May 2012)*. Available at:

http://www.eeaa.gov.eg/english/reports/CC/doc/Total%20CDM%20Project%20
Portofolio%20Public%20May%202012.pdf.

Eid, H., S. M. El-Marsafawy & S. A. Ouda (2007). *Assessing the Economic Impacts of Climate Change on Agriculture in Egypt*. Policy Research Working Paper. Washington, DC: World Bank.

El Raey, M. (2008). *Impact of Climate Change on the Nile Delta Region*. Paper presented at the Climate Change in Egypt conference, Cairo, 11 November.

El Raey, M., Kh. Kewidar & M. El Hattab (1999). Adaptation to the impacts of sea-level rise in Egypt. *Climate Research* 12: 117–28.

Evans, J. P. (2009). Global warming impact on the dominant precipitation process in the Middle East. *Theoretical and Applied Climatology* 99(3–4).

Fanos, A. M., A. A. Khafagy & R. G. Dean (1995). Protective works on the Nile Delta coast. *Journal of Coastal Research* 11(2):516–28.

Ferguson, J. (1994). *The Anti-Politics Machine*. Minneapolis, MN: University of Minnesota Press.

Frihy, O. (2003). The Nile Delta–Alexandria coast: vulnerability to sea-level rise, consequences, and adaptation. *Mitigation and Adaptation Strategies for Global Change* 8.

Hicks, R. L., B. C. Parks, J. Timmons Roberts & M. J. Tierney (2008). *Greening Aid? Understanding the Environmental Impact of Development Assistance*. Oxford: Oxford University Press.

IPCC (2007). *Impacts, Adaptation, and Vulnerability: Contribution of the Working Group II to the Fourth Assessment Report of the IPCC*, eds. M. L. Parry, O. F. Canziani, J. P. Palutikof, P. J. van der Linden & C. D. Hanson. Cambridge: Cambridge University Press.

Kraemer, S. (2011). Post-revolution Egypt restarts planned peak load swap with Saudis. *Green Prophet* 1 April.

Leila, R. (2012). Power to the people? *Al Ahram Weekly*, 25–31 July. Available at: http://weekly.ahram.org.eg/2012/1108/eg5.htm.

Lowi, M. (2009). *Oil Wealth and the Poverty of Politics: Algeria Compared*. Cambridge: Cambridge University Press.

Luong, P. J. & E. Weinthal (2010). *Oil is Not a Curse*. Cambridge: Cambridge University Press.

Mabro, R. (2006). Egypt's oil and gas: some crucial issues. *Egyptian Center for Economic Studies, Distinguished Lecture Series* 25, pp. 1–39.

Mabro, R. (2011). The oil/gas reserves problem. In S. Elmusa (ed.) *The Burden of Resources: Oil and Water in the Gulf and the Nile Basin. Cairo Papers in Social Science* 30(4), pp. 141–50.

Mason, M. (2009). Conclusion: towards a renewable energy transition in the Middle East and North Africa. In M. Mason and A. Mor (eds.) *Renewable Energy in the Middle East: Enhancing Security Through Regional Cooperation*. Dordrecht: Springer.

Ministry of Electricity and Energy (2010). *New and Renewable Energy Companies*. Available at: http://www.moee.gov.eg/english/EgyComp-EN/fr_renewable. htm.

Mortensen, N. G., U. Said Said & J. Badger (2005). *Wind Atlas for Egypt*. Available at: http://www.windatlas.dk/egypt/download/wind%20atlas%20for%20egypt%20 paper%20(menarec3).pdf.

Oil Change International (2012). *Low Hanging Fruit: Fossil Fuel Subsidies, Climate Finance, and Sustainable Development*. Washington, DC: Heinrich Boll Stiftung.

Available at: http://priceofoil.org/2012/06/14/report-low-hanging-fruit-fossil-fuel-subsidies-climate-finance-and-sustainable-development.

Repetto, R. (2001). The Clean Development Mechanism: institutional breakthrough or institutional nightmare? *Policy Sciences* 34(3/4).

Sims, D. (2010). *Understanding Cairo: The Logic of a City Out of Control*. Cairo: American University in Cairo Press.

Soliman, S. (2011). *The Autumn of Dictatorship: Fiscal Crisis and Political Change in Egypt*, trans. P. Daniel. Stanford, CA: Stanford University Press, 2011.

Sowers, J. (2013). *Environmental Politics in Egypt: Activists, Experts and the State*. Routledge Studies in Middle Eastern Politics. New York, NY: Routledge.

Sowers, J. & E. Weinthal (2010). *Climate Change Adaptation in the Middle East and North Africa: Challenges and Opportunities*. Dubai Initiative Working Paper. Belfer Center for Science and International Affairs, Harvard Kennedy School.

Sowers, J., A. Vengosh & E. Weinthal (2010). Climate change, water resources, and the politics of adaptation in the Middle East and North Africa. *Climatic Change* 104 (3–4): 599–627.

Stanley, D. J. & A. Warne (1998). Nile Delta in its destruction phase. *Journal of Coastal Research* 14(3).

Suding, P. H. (2011). Struggling between resources-based and sustainable development schemes: an analysis of Egypt's recent energy policy. *Energy Policy* 39: 4431–44.

Waterbury, J. (1993). *Exposed to Innumerable Delusions: Public Enterprise and State Power in Egypt, India, Mexico, and Turkey*. Cambridge: Cambridge University Press.

World Bank (2011). *Middle East and North Region Assessment of the Local Manufacturing Potential for Concentrated Solar Power (CSP) Projects*. Available at: http://arabworld.worldbank.org/content/dam/awi/pdf/CSP_MENA__report_17_Jan2011.pdf.

Zereini, F. & H. Hötzl (eds.) (2009). *Climatic Changes and Water Resources in the Middle East and North Africa*. Berlin: Springer.

11

Ethiopia's Path to a Climate-Resilient Green Economy

David Held, Charles Roger and Eva-Maria Nag

Introduction

OVER the past several years, climate change has risen up the Ethiopian government's official agenda. Internationally, the country has become much more engaged in the United Nations Framework Convention on Climate Change (UNFCCC) negotiations. Ethiopian delegates have been more active than in the past, and the late prime minister, Meles Zenawi, became an international spokesperson on the impacts of climate change in Africa before his passing in 2012. At Copenhagen in 2009, he led the African Group of Negotiators and helped to advance a common African position in the negotiations, calling for a fair, effective and accountable system of global climate governance. Domestically, awareness of the problem of climate change has increased among officials from nearly all ministries and levels of government. Ethiopia's newest economic development framework, the Growth and Transformation Plan (GTP), also now recognizes climate change as a cross-cutting development issue that risks compromising the considerable developmental gains the country has achieved since the end of its civil war in 1991. The GTP boldly states that the formulation and implementation of an effective response to climate change is a 'dictate of Ethiopia's survival' (MOFED 2010a, p. 77).

On its own, this new sense of urgency in Ethiopia represents a quite dramatic reversal from past trends. Climate change once used to warrant little to no mention by officials outside the country's main UNFCCC and Clean Development Mechanism (CDM) focal points. Adaptation and mitigation policies and programmes were underdeveloped, at best. Yet, since Copenhagen, Ethiopia has set a number of bold climate change targets as well. Furthermore, it has initiated a policymaking process to elaborate and implement a strategy for meeting them. The greater priority given to the task of mounting a more ambitious response is widely regarded as a positive development by global civil society groups and international donor agencies, as well as journalists, academics and non-governmental organizations (NGOs) within Ethiopia. Of course, important challenges and questions remain; although a number of climate-related policies and programmes are currently being implemented, the country's new approach to climate governance remains more of a promise than a reality on the ground at present. But, given that the issue had been so low on the government's political agenda until quite recently, it is important to ask: what factors have underpinned this sudden shift? This is the question that this chapter investigates.

In what follows, we first discuss Ethiopia's contribution to global warming and the effects that climatic changes are likely to have on the country. We then track the evolution of Ethiopia's climate change policymaking in detail, showing how it has developed at both the international and domestic levels since the early 1990s. The two levels, we suggest, are intimately related, with the former very much laying the basis for the latter. In a third section, we explore the underlying political and economic factors that have produced this shift. We argue that the country's top political leadership rather than civil society or the business community has been the main initiator of change. It has been motivated, in part, by a growing sense of Ethiopia's vulnerability. Perhaps more importantly though, the change has been a product of Ethiopia's move towards global and regional leadership in the UNFCCC, which helped raise domestic ambitions; of the appearance of new policy concepts that provided inspiration and shifted ideas about the trade-offs between emissions abatement and economic growth; and of a growing perception of opportunities for tapping into international sources of climate finance that could facilitate domestic economic objectives.

Climate Change and Ethiopia

Ethiopia's priorities in relation to climate change are clearly geared towards reducing the country's vulnerability; that is, towards adaptation. The country has made only a marginal contribution to global greenhouse gas (GHG) emissions. In 2000, the country produced just 0.2 per cent of all global GHG emissions, ranking as the 63rd largest emitter in absolute terms and the 171st in per capita terms.[1] The average Ethiopian is responsible for around one tonne of CO_2 per year. In the future, according to the 'business-as-usual' scenario outlined by the government, GHG emissions in Ethiopia will increase from roughly 150 megatonnes (Mt) CO_2, at present, to as much as 400 Mt CO_2 by 2030 (FDRE 2011). This will be mainly the result of the growth of agriculture, especially commercial farming and husbandry, and deforestation, which is influenced by the expansion of croplands and population growth. Yet despite this expected rise in emissions, Ethiopia would remain a very minor producer of GHGs by global standards.

At the same time, a growing number of studies show that Ethiopia is likely to be one of the countries most severely affected by climate change. Its high vulnerability is derived from the fact that its economy and the livelihoods of most Ethiopians are extremely dependent on agriculture. While the service and industrial sectors have grown in recent years, agriculture continues to account for nearly half of the country's gross domestic product (GDP), more than 85 per cent of its export revenues and roughly 80 per cent of employment (Yesuf et al. 2008). Further, although there is a growing trend towards modernized commercial farming, the majority of Ethiopia's agricultural production continues to rely heavily on natural rainfall to feed crops. Indeed, irrigated agriculture accounts for only 1 per cent of the total cultivated land (Yesuf et al. 2008). Changes in temperature and the timing, distribution and intensity of rainfall, therefore, have the potential to affect the mainstay of Ethiopia's economy deeply.

Ethiopia has, of course, historically suffered from extreme weather events (World Bank 2010, pp. xvi–xxvi). Droughts of different degrees of intensity affect the country almost every year, with significant impacts on agricultural production. Since the start of the 1980s there have been at least seven serious droughts. Five resulted in widespread famine. Drought-induced losses in the hard-hit north-east from 1998 to 2000, for example, were estimated at around US$266 per household, an amount greater than the annual average income of roughly three-quarters of the households in the region (Carter et al. 2006). At the other extreme, flooding has also affected Ethiopia on a regular basis. At least six major floods have occurred in different parts of the country since 1980, causing significant damage to communications infrastructure, roads, and public and privately owned property (World Bank 2010). Both droughts and flooding are expected to be exacerbated by future climate changes, with corresponding negative impacts upon agriculture, incomes and food security.

According to the United Nations Development Programme (UNDP), average temperatures in Ethiopia have already increased by about 1.3 °C since 1960 (UNDP 2008). The most recent estimates predict that this upward trend will continue. The mid-range emissions scenario of the Intergovernmental Panel on Climate Change (IPCC), for instance, suggests that temperatures in Ethiopia are expected to increase by 0.9–1.1 °C by 2030, 1.7–2.1 °C by 2050 and 2.7–3.4 °C by 2080 (NMA 2007). The number of 'hot' days and nights relative to seasonal averages between 1970 and 1999 is expected to rise by 26–69 per cent and 34–87 per cent, respectively, by 2090, with the fastest increases occurring during the country's wet season (UNDP 2008). As a result, droughts will become more frequent and intense. Indeed, in its list of the twelve countries most at risk from drought due to climate change, the World Bank placed Ethiopia in second place, behind only Malawi (World Bank 2009). The Bank expects Ethiopia's agricultural sector to be affected seriously by climate changes. It anticipates that changes in rainfall and temperatures will shorten the maturity periods of crops and decrease crop yields. Food deficits are expected to become more common. The IPCC also predicts that rising temperatures could lead to a steady expansion of malaria to the presently unaffected highland areas, where much of the Ethiopian population resides (IPCC 2007). The incidence of a number of other diseases, including livestock diseases, is anticipated to increase as well (Aklilu 2010). Finally, in addition to these serious impacts on livelihoods, agriculture and health, climate change will increase desertification, contract pastoral zones, affect forest growth patterns and result in major changes in wildlife patterns (NMA 2007).

Already, the Ethiopian government estimates that climate change results in economic losses equivalent to 2 to 6 per cent of GDP each year (MOFED 2010b). But the cumulative economy-wide impact of future climatic changes is predicted to be especially severe. One study estimates that, by negatively affecting agricultural production as well as production in related parts of its economy, climate change may reduce Ethiopia's expected GDP by about 10 per cent in upcoming decades (Mideska 2009). The same study forecasts that climate change will lead to heightened inequality according to the Gini coefficient by about 20 per cent. Similarly, the World Bank estimates that GDP is likely to be at least 2 per cent below its baseline level in each decade up to 2050, with possible deviations of up to 10 per cent or more in the last three decades of that period (World Bank 2010). Finally, the Stern Review has stated that climate change may reduce average GDP growth by around 38 per cent and increase poverty by as much as 25 per cent (Stern 2007).

Thus, on the one hand, even in the best (and increasingly less likely) global warming scenarios, Ethiopia will bear the physical brunt of climate change, making adaptation an objective priority. On the other hand, even in the worst scenarios, it will remain a comparatively small emitter of GHGs, at least in the short to medium term, which means that abatement of its emissions is a less urgent concern. Yet, interestingly, it is mitigation rather than adaptation that has become the hallmark of Ethiopia's climate governance strategy, as discussed below.

The Evolution of Climate Change Policymaking in Ethiopia

Despite strong evidence of negative impacts and the urgent need for adaptation, Ethiopia's coordination of climate change policy at both the domestic and international levels was relatively limited until about 2009. While the Council of Ministers recognized the need for an effective response to global warming as far back as 1997, including several policy recommendations for responding to climate change in the Environmental Policy of Ethiopia that was adopted in that year, the issue failed to become a high priority concern. Climate change policymaking, such as it was, remained fragmented and largely confined to a few sectoral agencies and ministries which were expressly concerned with environmental or climate-related issues. According to most observers, the efforts made by these bodies were generally disappointing, as they were chronically under-resourced departments with relatively little capacity for national implementation, regulation or inter-ministerial coordination. However, as climate change became a greater concern throughout Africa in the late 2000s, the Ethiopian government began to develop a more proactive response. This began haltingly after the launch of the Bali Plan of Action in 2007, but took off after the Fifteenth Conference of the Parties (COP15) in Copenhagen. The country first became much more involved in the global negotiations than before, with Meles Zenawi playing a key role in Copenhagen negotiations. It then began to develop a much more substantial domestic approach as well. Tracking this evolution in Ethiopia's international and domestic climate policymaking is the objective of this section.

Early Efforts

The foundations of domestic environmental policymaking in Ethiopia, including climate change policymaking, can be traced back to the development of the Conservation Strategy of Ethiopia (CSE) which began in 1989. Initially an undertaking of the Office of the National Committee for Central Planning (known as the Ministry of Planning and Economic Development after 1991, the Ministry of Economic Development and Cooperation after 1995, and the Ministry of Finance and Economic Development [MOFED] after merging with the Ministry of Finance in 2001), the CSE started as a major initiative which aimed to develop environmental and sustainability policies across all sectors and levels of government. After several years, however, responsibility for developing Ethiopia's environmental policies and coordination of its environmental programmes was given first to the newly established but short-lived Ministry of Natural Resources Development and Environmental Protection in 1992, and then, in 1995, to an independent institutional arm of the Ethiopian government, the Environmental Protection Authority (EPA), which operates under the aegis of the Council of Ministers. This gradual shift away from the Ministry of Planning, a central policymaking and regulatory body, to institutions exclusively dedicated to natural resource management and environmental protection occurred partially in response to recommendations by the CSE itself. But the shift in responsibility was also related to the sidelining of the CSE process, which was slowly being divorced from the main concerns and policymaking processes of the bodies responsible for economic planning. As responsibility for the environment was delegated to sectoral institutions, it became more and more difficult to make environmental concerns felt at the highest levels of government.

The Environmental Policy of Ethiopia, one of the critical outputs of the CSE process, was adopted by the Council of Ministers in 1997, as mentioned above. Among other things, this formally established the goal of creating a climate monitoring programme and taking action on climate change. Yet these goals were vaguely defined and relatively few steps were actually taken. Almost no specific policies or strategies were elaborated, and few programmes or projects were implemented beyond those that were directly supported and promoted by international public and private donor agencies or domestic civil society organizations. Instead, the government's response to climate change was limited to conducting research assessing the country's adaptation and technological needs in cooperation with several external organizations. The low priority given to climate policymaking became especially apparent when climate change considerations failed to be included in any substantial way in the Plan for Accelerated and Sustained Development for Ending Poverty (PASDEP), which was adopted as the national economic development framework for Ethiopia in 2006. The PASDEP was widely criticized by both global and local civil society organizations for failing to 'mainstream' climate change into Ethiopia's major development plans (PANE 2009).

Diplomacy at the international level was similarly limited for most of the period since the early 1990s. The government participated in the climate change negotiations after the Rio Earth Summit in 1992, and its negotiators had been present at nearly all of the major COPs. It signed the UNFCCC in June 1992 and ratified the agreement in April 1994. Likewise, it ratified the Kyoto Protocol in April 2005, shortly after it came into force in February 2005. However, at least until COP13, Ethiopia's participation in and contribution to the global climate change negotiations was not commensurate with its size, vulnerability and important geopolitical position in Africa. In the main, it contributed to the negotiations as a member of the Group of 77 (G77) and the African Group, which were focused on ensuring that developing countries had few obligations and were given special access to funds and technology, and that developed countries fulfilled their obligation to take the lead in limiting their emissions to sustainable levels. But, rather than actively serving as a key coordinator or formulator of G77 policy or African common positions, its contribution was mainly to add its weight and stature passively to these groupings.

Indeed, Ethiopia dedicated few resources to the negotiations. From COP1 to COP14, the country rarely sent more than two negotiators to represent its interests, and occasionally sent only one or even none, as occurred during COP9 in 2003. Furthermore, while those that they did send were generally well versed in the issues, they typically did not have a strong base of support or the resources to contribute effectively to the negotiations. This combination of factors often led Ethiopian negotiators to take a 'defensive' position, forgoing novel or bold proposals that might turn out to be unacceptable back home

(Gray & Gupta 2003). In this respect, Ethiopia was not unique among African states. Most had not participated extensively in the negotiations either and took defensive positions as well. It was only COP12, in Nairobi in 2006, which saw a deepening and intensification of African participation; though at this point Ethiopia's role in both the COP and the regional preparatory process remained minimal. The result was that Ethiopia did not have a great impact upon the negotiations. It played a large role neither in the UNFCCC nor in regional climate change diplomacy, such as it was.

Instead, Ethiopia's main form of participation in the UNFCCC process consisted of the preparation of official UNFCCC documentation. Ethiopia released its Initial National Communication on Climate Change in June 2001 (NMA 2001). Its National Adaptation Programme of Action (NAPA) and its Climate Change Technology Needs Assessment (TNA) Report were both released in June 2007. All were produced with financial and technical assistance from the Global Environment Facility (GEF) and UNDP, and it is doubtful whether the documents would have been undertaken without this support. Only after the potential for receiving finances through the CDM became apparent, in 2006 and 2007, did Ethiopia begin to increase modestly its level of engagement in the UNFCCC process. Nevertheless, attempts actually to make use of the CDM in Ethiopia encountered difficulties as a result of insufficient institutional and technical capacity, low awareness and knowledge of CDM processes, unclear policies and a generally challenging operating environment (GTZ 2007). Effective use of the CDM was also hindered by the extremely onerous requirements for registering many of the kinds of projects that were most relevant for Ethiopia, namely land use and forestry projects, as well as their exclusion from the European Emissions Trading System. Thus far, only one CDM project has been successfully registered in Ethiopia: the Humbo Community-Based Natural Regeneration Project, a reforestation project that aims to restore 2,728 hectares of forest to sequester over 165,000 tonnes of CO_2 by 2017 (Dettman et al. 2008). The product of a collaboration between World Vision, the World Bank, the Ministry of Agriculture and Rural Development and the EPA, the Humbo Project was intended to serve as a blueprint for future CDM projects and a capacity building exercise, but more than anything it highlighted the pressing challenges that CDM projects have faced in Ethiopia (see e.g. the discussion in Dettman et al. 2008).

New Engagement at the International Level

Ethiopia was clearly a latecomer to the UNFCCC process in terms of the government's level of interest and participation. However, in a sudden reversal, its engagement increased considerably in the lead-up to COP15 in Copenhagen. Across Africa, participation in the global negotiations grew during COP12 in Nairobi, the so-called 'African COP'. Its goal was, quite explicitly, to attend to deep-seated concerns in both Africa and the wider developing world: increasing the priority given to adaptation in the negotiations and facilitating access to the CDM. African participation then took off (albeit from a low base), as the UNFCCC negotiations climbed up the international diplomatic agenda, especially after COP13, which initiated the Bali Plan of Action and the Ad Hoc Working Group on Long-Term Cooperative Action (AWG-LCA), which would spearhead negotiations on Nationally Appropriate Mitigation Actions (NAMAs) by developing states.

The Bali Plan raised the stakes at the global level for the developing world, promising new sources of funding for NAMAs and envisioning a new global agreement that would be concluded at Copenhagen. The opportunities and threats that this presented meant that there were much greater incentives for high level participation. In its twelfth session, held in Johannesburg in June 2008, the African Ministerial Conference on the Environment (AMCEN) underscored the need for Africa to participate strategically in the negotiations in order to ensure that its interests were adequately reflected in any future agreement. Ministers stressed the need for Africa to elaborate a common position on commitments to funding, the global agreement that the continent wanted from the international community, particularly from industrialized states, as well as the character, scale and scope of the actions that African countries would themselves be willing to take. In November 2008, prior to COP14 in Poznan, such a position was finalized at a preparatory meeting for the African Group of Negotiators and ministers of the environment. Known as the African Climate Platform to Copenhagen (or Algiers Platform), this established a basic negotiating framework and principles for the African Group in the Kyoto and AWG-LCA negotiations. It would be significantly updated and elaborated at subsequent meetings of the African Group as Copenhagen approached.

Following an update at the third special session of AMCEN in May 2009, the revised Platform was formally endorsed as the common position of Africa at the 13th Ordinary African Union (AU) Summit in Sirte, Libya, in July 2009. It was the first time that the AU clearly endorsed a common position ahead of a COP, and signalled the extent to which climate change and the UNFCCC negotiations had risen up the agendas of Africa's leaders. The AU also acceded to the UNFCCC and Kyoto Protocol at the same time. Perhaps most importantly, the AU Summit in Libya established the Conference of African Heads of State and Government on Climate Change (CAHOSCC). Intended to represent the highest level of African political leadership officially in the global negotiations, CAHOSCC included representation from eight states: Algeria, the Republic of the Congo, Ethiopia, Kenya, Mauritius, Mozambique, Nigeria and Uganda. It would also include the chairperson of the AU. Together, they would act as a kind of subcommittee of the many African leaders who would be attending the negotiations, approving the common position developed by the technical negotiators and negotiating on behalf of all of Africa's leaders in the ministerial level meetings. For Africa, this was a notable development that promised to raise international attention to the concerns of the region further, building upon the growing level of participation that had taken place since Nairobi. But for Ethiopia it was a turning point, as Meles Zenawi was chosen to be the official chair.

The prime minister's nomination transformed Ethiopia from a marginal participant to a key player in the UNFCCC process almost overnight. The size of its national delegation increased from three persons in 2006 at COP12 in next-door Nairobi to forty-seven persons at Copenhagen three years later. This level of participation was also roughly maintained at COP16 in Cancun and COP17 in Durban, where Ethiopia's delegation reached a total of thirty-four and fifty-six persons respectively. Beyond sheer numbers, however, Ethiopian negotiators were more fully engaged in the preparations for developing an African common position and contributed in a more substantive manner to the UNFCCC negotiations. As the chair of CAHOSCC, Meles Zenawi played a notable role in the negotiation of finances for developing countries at Copenhagen. He proposed, for instance, that US$50 billion be provided for developing countries by 2015, US$10 billion in 'fast-start' financing, and at least US$100 billion by 2020, with 50 per cent of those funds earmarked for especially vulnerable countries, such as African and small island developing states (see Vidal 2009). He also proposed that developing countries be given significant control over how the funds would be allocated, and called for a panel to be established in order to monitor the delivery of the financial pledges made by the industrialized world.

The prime minister's leadership of CAHOSCC was not without controversy. According to many observers, while his proposals were pragmatic and accorded with offers made by the United Kingdom and the European Union, they departed significantly from the level of funds requested by the G77 and even the technical negotiators of the African Group in the AWG-LCA, who had earlier called for at least US$400 billion of fast-start financing (Vidal 2009). Several African ministers, negotiators and NGOs roundly dismissed Zenawi's proposals, although they were publicly lauded by many others, from Nicholas Stern to the then French president Nicolas Sarkozy. Zenawi's term as the chair of CAHOSCC was nevertheless renewed by the AU. And, at the request of UN Secretary General Ban Ki-Moon, he also became co-chair of the High-Level Advisory Group on Climate Change Financing, which would study various alternatives for monitoring and delivering the financial pledges made by developed states at Copenhagen.

A New Domestic Approach

The new level of Ethiopian engagement in the international negotiations was followed by some major changes in the government's domestic approach to climate change. Immediately after Copenhagen, the EPA was designated as the new UNFCCC focal point (formerly, the National Meteorology Agency [NMA] played this role) and was mandated by the prime minister to coordinate a national response to climate change. One of the first actions it took was to put together Ethiopia's NAMA submission. With backing from the Prime Minister's Office, the EPA initiated a consultation process with the main ministries in Ethiopia to discern the kinds of actions that were already in the pipeline or under study that could count as NAMAs and demonstrate Ethiopia's response to climate change. A list of seventy-five mitigation projects and plans categorized into seven broad groups was compiled and quickly submitted to the UNFCCC in January 2010. The NAMA submission was significant in so far as it offered further evidence of Ethiopia's growing involvement with the UNFCCC and reaffirmed Ethiopia's support for the Copenhagen Accord. However, it was equally a reflection of the poor state of domestic climate policy-making within the country. It was hastily put together, contained no quantitative targets and provided few estimates of the benefits of the various projects that were identified. It was, therefore, a much weaker and not very credible kind of proposal compared to those offered by some other developing states (Brazil, China, etc.; see the introduction to this volume), which had offered more precise targets and/or quantitatively specified the effects of the actions they planned to take.

The drawbacks of Ethiopia's NAMA nevertheless prompted the government to draw up a more detailed climate change plan which would demonstrate a level of commitment more commensurate with the proactive role that it had taken in the UNFCCC negotiations. The EPA was already doing so to some extent, drawing up several concept notes on climate policy as mandated by the prime minister. But, shortly after the submission of the NAMA, Meles Zenawi also called upon the Ethiopian Development Research Institute (EDRI) to conduct a thorough investigation of what was needed to mitigate and adapt to climate change in the country. EDRI, a think-tank with ministerial status whose executive director, Newai Gebre-Ab, served as the prime minister's chief economic advisor, was a significant repository of economic expertise. At the time, though, it did not have enough experts with sufficient experience conducting detailed studies on the scale required. EDRI therefore approached the Global Green Growth Institute (GGGI) for assistance, a South Korean organization that had recently started to partner with governments in order to help with the development of low carbon growth strategies and projects, as well as implementation and capacity building (for more on GGGI see chapter 5 by Jae-Seung Lee in this volume). GGGI would help, initially, by undertaking an analysis of opportunities for 'green growth' in the country.

When GGGI finally reported to the government the results of its study, it suggested that there was in fact significant potential for reducing emissions while maintaining high levels of growth in Ethiopia. The country was already investing heavily in hydropower, and could help to provide clean energy for much of the region. There was also potential for increasing the cultivation of biofuels. Transportation infrastructure could be upgraded to reduce emissions. And so on. Further, all of this could be done while increasing access to energy, scaling up industry, attracting climate finances, and reducing the burden of spending precious foreign exchange on fossil fuels. The message was enthusiastically received by the government, and would have a major impact on subsequent planning. Climate change considerations began to be included in the discussion documents that started to emerge from the inter-ministerial consultative process designed to develop Ethiopia's new economic development framework (the GTP) that was just being orchestrated by MOFED. The work being done in EDRI (with GGGI) was also merged with that being undertaken at the EPA through the creation, in late 2010, of a Ministerial Steering Committee under the authority of the Council of Ministers in order to oversee the development of Ethiopia's official climate change strategy. With Newai Gebre-Ab as the chair, the Ministerial Committee comprised the heads of the EPA and NMA and ministers from MOFED, the Ministry of Agriculture and Rural Development (MOARD), the Ministry of Water and Energy (MOWE), the Ministry of Trade and Industry (MOTI) and the Ministry of Transport and Communication (MOTC). A Technical Committee, chaired by the deputy director of the EPA, Dessalegn Mesfin, would assist the Ministerial Committee, and was itself divided into several working groups that focused on particular sectors or issues. Together, these two groups were responsible for designing the policies and institutional arrangements necessary for putting Ethiopia on the path to becoming a 'climate-resilient green economy', or CRGE.

The creation of the Ministerial Steering Committee marked the first time that a major cross-sectoral policymaking body had been convened in Ethiopia with the explicit purpose of developing a national response to climate change, establishing responsibilities across sectors, and creating the overall administrative structure necessary for their implementation on a national scale. By all accounts, coordination among the ministries in the Steering Committee remained relatively fragmented and suffered from the fact that many ministries did not yet have the expertise and administrative capacity that were required for sufficiently identifying their specific needs. Further, it was criticized by local civil society groups for excluding their input in the policymaking process. However, as an initiative largely originating from within the Prime Minister's Office, the Ministerial Steering Committee was notable for its high political status, and for its already quite substantial ability to stimulate climate change awareness and planning in all the major ministries.

The growing prominence of the issue of climate change, and the fruits of the planning already undertaken, were clearly in evidence when the country finally released the GTP in late 2010 (see MOFED 2010b). The GTP outlined the economic development strategy that would guide the country over the 2011–15 period, and it set out twenty-two targets specifically focused on climate change, addressing both mitigation and adaptation. These included increasing the amount of energy produced from renewable sources by 8,000 megawatts (MW), raising sales of ethanol and biodiesel by 35 million litres, and expanding the area covered by forests by 25,000 km^2. Perhaps most notably, it established a long-term target of making the Ethiopian economy 'carbon free' by 2025. In order to achieve these objectives, the GTP called for the identification of key infrastructure which was highly vulnerable to climate change, and for appropriate adaptive measures to be put in place. It identified a need for strengthening the capacity of all levels of government for implementing these measures, for the development and implementation of regional climate change plans and laws, and for national systems for facilitating the work of NGOs, shifting the economy towards a low carbon pathway, and enhancing access to global finances.

In contrast with the country's previous economic development framework (the PASDEP), which had been criticized for not taking climate change issues into account, the GTP therefore established a number of significant goals for responding to climate change. Yet it ultimately failed to lay out the specific strategies for meeting them. Instead, these would be developed in a more detailed CRGE strategy document that would sit alongside the GTP, fleshing out the country's approach. The actual drafting of Ethiopia's CRGE strategy took place between February and July of 2011 under the supervision of the Ministerial Committee. Interestingly, this was mainly done not by staff in the EPA or EDRI, but by a group of consultants from McKinsey & Company in collaboration with GGGI and a variety of local experts from government, civil society and academia who were recruited to provide inputs on specific issues, such as forestry or agriculture. The draft was then circulated to various ministries for comment, and after incorporating their feedback between August and October the final CRGE strategy document (FDRE 2011) was presented at COP17 in Durban. There, it attracted a great deal of attention as an example of African leadership on climate change and was widely reported on.

The document itself sets out a roadmap for realizing Ethiopia's ambition of becoming a 'green economy front-runner' (FDRE 2011, p. 1). In keeping with the GTP, it identifies two pillars of Ethiopia's approach: moving towards a 'green economy' by way of NAMAs and creating 'climate resilience' through an Ethiopian Programme of Adaptation to Climate Change (EPACC). The first pillar, which was based on a comprehensive analysis of potential low cost/high value actions, involved identifying around sixty initiatives that could form the basis for green growth. Four, in particular, were highlighted for 'fast track implementation': developing hydropower; promoting low carbon cooking technologies; efficiency improvements in Ethiopia's livestock value chain; and Reducing Emissions from Deforestation and Forest Degradation (REDD). These initiatives formed the basis of a CRGE Investment Package, which would then attract funding through a CRGE Facility – essentially a multi-donor trust fund. The second pillar of Ethiopia's strategy – the EPACC – followed a more bottom-up approach. Following a blueprint set out in a draft EPACC document, each regional government within the country was obliged to develop its own adaptation plan, in collaboration with the EPA, key stakeholders and a range of donors. Each regional government and sectoral ministry would then be responsible for implementing its own plan. The various plans would also be incorporated into a single climate resilience strategy that would guide efforts by the central government to fill gaps in local implementation capacity, although this process remains incomplete at the time of writing.

To what extent has Ethiopia's CRGE strategy been implemented? Unfortunately, this is difficult to assess at present; because of data limitations we cannot yet track success in terms of emissions reductions, projects or programmes implemented, or funds attracted. Perhaps the most notable step thus far has been the development and reform of relevant institutions. For example, the Ministerial Steering Committee responsible for the development of the CRGE strategy has been delegated the task of overseeing its implementation. It is now a permanent institution within the government acting under the aegis of the Environmental Council, which is chaired by the prime minister. CRGE desks, responsible for communicating and coordinating activities with the Steering Committee, are also now a feature of nearly all the relevant ministries. Most promisingly, the CRGE Facility has been established by MOFED with the assistance of UNDP, while Norway and the United Kingdom have already reportedly expressed interest in contributing funds. The CRGE Facility is, effectively, the linchpin of Ethiopia's climate governance strategy, which is heavily dependent on channelling international funding for successful implementation. Its stationing within MOFED, which now has responsibility with the EPA for attracting funding for the sixty-plus CRGE initiatives, is a positive sign of the government's seriousness about this new endeavour. However, how it will perform in upcoming years and its ultimate impact remain to be seen.

Explaining the Emergence of Ethiopia's CRGE Strategy

Though we cannot yet effectively gauge its success, the development of Ethiopia's CRGE initiative and the country's much greater level of engagement in the international negotiations nevertheless represented a notable and quite sudden reversal of past trends. For years, climate change had been relatively neglected by the central government beyond the EPA and NMA, the main CDM and UNFCCC focal points. The issue had hardly figured in the country's previous economic development framework, the PASDEP. Further, the costs of governing climate change were believed to be significant; Ethiopia needed to focus on more pressing issues such as economic development and poverty reduction, not reducing its emissions. If anything, the country needed to focus on reducing its vulnerability. Yet after Copenhagen both mitigation and adaptation apparently shot up the government agenda. What factors and agents underpinned this move after such an extended period of inactivity? More than anything else, we argue that the change in Ethiopia's approach was driven by its leadership, especially Meles Zenawi, who set in motion the process leading to the creation of the country's NAMAs and CRGE strategy in the months after he led Africa in the global negotiations. International and domestic civil society groups, while active and more organized on the issue of climate change in the period preceding Copenhagen, generally followed the government's lead. They had criticized the government's failure to 'mainstream' climate change in the PASDEP. But the main role they played was helping to shape at the margin a process initiated at the highest levels of government. The business community, likewise, was not a major force for change, and, although no survey data exists, awareness of climate change among the wider public was believed to be quite low. According to most observers, it increased only after the government's high level participation in the negotiations. Thus, electoral incentives were not a major force influencing the decision to act in the first place. The government's move was motivated by other factors.

In part, the government's reversal was a product of its growing awareness of Ethiopia's vulnerability to climatic changes. The Stern Review of 2006, for example, had identified Africa as the region that would be most severely affected by climate change. Ethiopia, in particular, was expected to be especially hard hit, and the Horn of Africa was highlighted for the way in which climate change would be likely to lead to adverse effects on regional security dynamics. The following year, the Stern Review's findings were reinforced by the IPCC's Fourth Assessment Report. It similarly revealed the extent to which Africa would be negatively impacted. Ethiopia's NAPA was completed in 2007 as well, providing a comprehensive assessment of the country's vulnerability and the kinds of measures needed to adapt successfully. Therefore, the scientific understanding of climate change in Ethiopia had improved towards the end of the decade. The consequences of climate change were predicted to be dire, and urgent action was needed to forestall the worst of them. However, Meles Zenawi's reversal could also be attributed to three further factors, which are discussed in the remainder of this section: first, opportunities for displaying regional and global leadership, which would raise domestic ambitions; second, the emergence of policy concepts that provided inspiration and changed the government's evaluation of the costs and benefits of mitigating climate change; and relatedly, third, a perception of growing opportunities for attracting financing and aid that would facilitate the achievement of Ethiopia's ambitious developmental goals.

Copenhagen was expected to be a major event that would be well attended by heads of state and well covered by the global media. It would mark the culmination of the round of negotiations initiated in Bali and was slated to produce a new 'global deal'. Industrialized states would renew their commitments under Kyoto, and the newly elected president, Barack Obama, had promised much more significant action by the United States. Developing countries were anticipated to play a more important role as well, specifying NAMAs and suitable monitoring, reporting and verification measures. They would, in return, receive financial support from industrialized states. As a result, climate change had become one of the most visible issues on the global agenda in the years leading up to Copenhagen. It had gained a great deal of attention among African leaders, too. They had been prompted to play a more direct role in the negotiations, as discussed earlier. In this context, chairing CAHOSCC (and, later, co-chairing the UN Advisory Group on Climate Change Financing) presented a significant opportunity for the government. First, it would allow Meles Zenawi to assume a prestigious leadership position among African states and to play a powerful brokering role between them and other major players, with significant potential for receiving side-payments for taking certain positions. Second, it would place him at the centre of the high level UNFCCC negotiations, where he could present a more positive image of Ethiopia at a time when his regime had been subject to mounting international criticism, particularly following the elections in 2005 and 2008.

This helps explain why Ethiopia became much more engaged at the international level than it had been in the past; Copenhagen offered an opportunity for playing a key role in an historic round of negotiations and improving the government's reputation. However, leadership in the international negotiations and within Africa also helped to spur action domestically by encouraging the submission of NAMAs to the UNFCCC Secretariat. In contrast with past trends, a number of other non-Annex I states – China, Brazil, South Africa and so on – had offered quite substantial voluntary commitments to manage climate change before, during and immediately after Copenhagen. With Zenawi serving as the chair of CAHOSCC, it therefore appeared appropriate for Ethiopia to take a more proactive stance as well, particularly when domestic climate policymaking was in such a dismal state. Putting together a NAMA submission was a relatively quick, low cost (though, as noted above, not very credible) way of appearing to do this, since it would mainly adumbrate actions already planned or under consideration which dovetailed with a climate agenda. Many could, without too much change, be portrayed as action on climate change, largely because of the emphasis that the country had already placed on the expansion of hydroelectric power and other renewable sources of energy.

Around the same time, however, ideational support for greater action also came from the policy concept of 'green growth' that had been put forward by states such as South Korea, which Ethiopia had long looked up to as a developmental role model (see Altenburg 2010). The concept had proliferated among developing and developed states, as well as international organizations, to a remarkable extent since its appearance in 2008 (Blaxekjær 2012), and it had an important influence on Ethiopia. Indeed, the 'green growth' policy concept would provide direct inspiration for Ethiopia's CRGE strategy through the government's partnership with Korea's GGGI, which EDRI had approached for support when it began to conduct research on climate mitigation and adaptation strategies after Copenhagen. GGGI conducted analyses on the behalf of EDRI in order to identify opportunities for meeting Ethiopia's economic objectives while at the same time reducing the emissions that this would be likely to entail. Its findings then motivated the government to create the Ministerial Steering Committee which would oversee the development of a climate governance strategy, with GGGI's support, by prompting a shift in its evaluation of the costs and benefits of abating emissions in the country. As a result of GGGI's work, it was now thought that the trade-off between economic growth and mitigation of climate change was less harsh than previously supposed. An innovative climate change plan could actually help to facilitate the country's twin economic goals of sustaining high rates of economic growth and reducing poverty.

Finally, the growth of international public and private climate finances would also influence Ethiopia's decision to develop a serious climate change strategy, since these funds could potentially help to fill an important funding gap that the country faced. Building on the country's impressive accomplishments since the end of its civil war in 1991, the GTP had set out an ambitious goal of maintaining an average annual GDP growth rate of 11 per cent from 2011 to 2015. Doing so would require a range of large-scale investments in agriculture, industry, hydroelectric facilities and other infrastructure projects. Yet, as the GTP noted, domestic savings in Ethiopia would be far from sufficient. The amount of foreign direct investment and economic assistance predicted for upcoming years was also expected to fall short. Some key projects, such as the government's major hydroelectric project, the massive 'Renaissance' Dam, had even been declined international funding from the World Bank and other international financial institutions because of inadequate environmental impact assessments. Faced with these constraints, then, tapping into the international sources of public and private climate finance that had grown (or had been promised) around the time of Copenhagen appeared increasingly attractive, offering an additional stream of money for meeting the government's economic goals.

The CRGE strategy could facilitate access to these new sources of funding that had been opening up by (re)framing and 'upgrading' many of the critical investments needed for sustaining a high rate of economic growth as part of an ambitious domestic response to climate change. Moving first among low income states, setting highly demanding mitigation targets and couching its actions in the newly prominent rhetoric of 'green growth' would help attract investors and donors to the various CRGE initiatives. Investment in or aid for CRGE initiatives could be portrayed not only as profitable enterprise or as a contribution to economic development but as participation in a major effort to limit emissions and adapt to global warming in a large developing state. The elaboration of sixty CRGE initiatives would provide a menu for potential investors and donors to make informed choices from. The careful documentation of their value as a function of cost and emissions abatement would allow specific mitigation figures to be attached to individual investments and projects. Finally, the establishment of a Climate Facility would offer a central, streamlined conduit for receiving, administering and transparently monitoring the use of funds. The elaboration of a serious climate change strategy would therefore facilitate Ethiopia's economic objectives by creating incentives and propitious conditions for public and private climate financing.

Conclusion

Ethiopia's approach to climate change has evolved in a remarkable fashion. The issue once used to warrant little to no mention by those in the government outside of the NMA and EPA. It was all but absent from the country's approach to development; the PASDEP, the country's previous economic development framework, was widely criticized for its failure to take into account climate change considerations. Policies and programmes, if they existed at all, were underdeveloped. Likewise, involvement in the international negotiations was minimal. This was the status quo for most of the twenty years after the Earth Summit in 1992. However, after Copenhagen, Ethiopia's level of engagement, both in the international negotiations and domestically, increased considerably. Climate change now occupies a much more central place in the GTP; an ambitious carbon neutral target has been set for 2025; a CRGE strategy has been developed; and there are institutions officially responsible for its implementation. Although some have been critical of the lofty goals set out in the CRGE strategy, its appearance undoubtedly represents a positive move. The policymaking process has led to some serious thinking about climate change in regional governments, ministries and departments that had rarely, if ever, done so.

As we have attempted to show, the decision to elaborate a coherent strategy for governing climate change coincided with a growing awareness and scientific understanding of Ethiopia's vulnerability. Yet it has mainly been a by-product of the new leadership role Ethiopia played in the UNFCCC; new ideas, norms and information; and a new perception of the gains that could be accrued by accessing international sources of climate finance. The decision was taken as a result of (1) the government's view that articulating a more ambitious response was 'appropriate' given the country's new position as a leader in the international negotiations; (2) the influence of new transnational actors like GGGI, which provided credible new information about the trade-offs between curbing emissions and economic growth; and (3) the emergence of new sources of climate finance which could facilitate domestic economic objectives.

Nevertheless, the character of the CRGE strategy also leads to questions about the sustainability of the changes that have taken place which deserve to be noted by way of conclusion. Ethiopia's carbon neutral target is extremely ambitious. However, the strategy that the country has elaborated for meeting it means that success will be a function of both international and domestic developments. First, the strategy crucially depends on attracting and mobilizing international climate finances. Ethiopia has attempted to set itself up to be a good recipient of public and private funds by drawing up its own detailed set of CRGE investments. Yet the ability to attract funds to CRGE initiatives is not simply a matter of creating a conducive domestic environment. Ultimately, the strategy's success turns on whether or not such funds are actually supplied. So far, private climate financing has grown impressively, but public funds have yet to materialize on the scale that has been promised by industrialized states (CPI 2011). Furthermore, many international institutions have already proven reluctant to fund some of the key projects that the CRGE strategy calls for – namely, large hydropower projects – when insufficient attention has been given to ancillary environmental and social impacts; and it is not clear that reframing these projects as NAMAs will change this. The risk is, therefore, that if funds do not appear on the levels hoped for, Ethiopia's ambitious climate agenda may be undermined.

Second, while the government has started the process of establishing the institutions necessary for successfully implementing the CRGE strategy, much remains to be done, according to most observers. The institutions responsible for attracting and administering funds at the highest level of government – the Ministerial Steering Committee, the EPA and MOFED – appear to be increasingly well positioned to do so. However, success also depends on the ability of other ministries and local governments to implement the CRGE initiatives (and regional adaptation plans). Some, like MOWE, already appear to have considerable capacity for carrying out the kinds of large infrastructure projects that the CRGE strategy calls for. However, others have so far proven unable to create the requisite capabilities. MOARD, for instance, has yet to establish the kind of sustainable land management systems that are necessary for implementing REDD projects – one of the four CRGE initiatives designated for 'fast track implementation' – and close observers have expressed scepticism about the potential for change in this area. The difficulties experienced in setting up reforestation projects under the CDM offer a potent reminder of the tremendous challenges that have been encountered in this field, even when financial incentives and significant international assistance are available. Thus, Ethiopia's CRGE strategy still requires many demanding domestic institutional reforms before its success is assured.

Notes

The research upon which this study is based is primarily derived from semi-structured interviews with a range of stakeholders and observers in Addis Ababa that were conducted in April and May 2011. Those interviewed included officials from several relevant ministries, individuals from civil society groups that have closely followed climate change issues for some time, and a number of academics, journalists and diplomatic officials. All are to be thanked for contributing their time, and, of course, none can be held responsible for any of the conclusions reached in this paper. Charles would also like to thank the Horn of Africa Regional Environment Centre (HoAREC) of Addis Ababa University for kindly hosting him as a Visiting Fellow in 2012.

1 The year 2000 is the most recent for which there is comprehensive data on Ethiopian emissions, including land use change and forestry (LUCF) emissions and GHGs other than CO_2.

References

Aklilu, N. (2010). *Toddling to Cope with Climate Change: The Case of Ethiopia*. Paper prepared for the 2nd UNITAR-Yale Conference on Environmental Governance and Democracy, 17–19 September, New Haven, CT. Available at: http://confer ence.unitar.org/yale/sites/conference.unitar.org.yale/files/Paper_Aklilu.pdf.

Altenburg, T. (2010). *Industrial Policy in Ethiopia*. German Development Institute Discussion Paper 2/2010. Available at: http://www.die-gdi.de/CMS-Homepage/ openwebcms3.nsf/(ynDK_contentByKey)/ANES-843GXA/$FILE/DP%202.2010. pdf.

Blaxekjær, L. (2012). *The Emergence and Spread of the Green Growth Policy Concept*. Paper prepared for the Earth System Governance Conference, Lund University, 18–20 April. Available at: http://www.lund2012.earthsystemgovernance.org/ LC2012–paper370.pdf.

Carter, M., P. Little, T. Mogues & W. Negatu (2006). *Shocks, Sensitivity and Resilience: Tracking the Economic Impacts of Environmental Disaster on Assets in Ethiopia and Honduras*. DSGD Discussion Papers 32, International Food Policy Research Institute.

CPI (2011). *The Landscape of Climate Finance*. October. Available at: http://climate policyinitiative.org/wp-content/uploads/2011/10/The-Landscape-of-Climate-Fi nance-120120.pdf.

Dettman, P., T. Rinaudo & A. Tofu (2008). Case study: the Humbo Community-Based Natural Regeneration Project, Ethiopia. In C. Streck, R. O'Sullivan, T. Janson-Smith & R. Tarasofsky (eds.) *Climate Change and Forests: Emerging Policy and Market Opportunities*. London: Chatham House.

FDRE (2011). *Ethiopia's Climate-Resilient Green Economy: Green Economy Strategy*. Available at: http://www.epa.gov.et/Download/Climate/Ethiopia's%20Climate-Resilient%20Green%20economy%20strategy.pdf.

Gray, K. & J. Gupta (2003). The United Nations climate change regime and

Africa. In B. Chaytor & K. R. Gray (eds.) *International Law and Policy in Africa*. London: Kluwer.

GTZ (2007). *The Clean Development Mechanism in Relation to Energy East Africa: Status Quo, Obstacles and Recommendations*. Regional Energy Advisor Platform, East Africa.

IPCC (2007). *Climate Change 2007: Impacts, Adaptation and Vulnerability*. Contribution of Working Group II to the Fourth Assessment Report of the Intergovernmental Panel on Climate Change, eds. M. L. Parry, O. F. Canziani, J. P. Palutikof, P. J. van der Linden & C. E. Hanson. Cambridge: Cambridge University Press.

Mideska, T. (2010). Economic and distributional impacts of climate change: the case of Ethiopia. *Global Environmental Change* 20.

MOFED (2010a). *Growth and Transformation Plan 2010/11–2014/15: September Draft*. Addis Ababa: Ministry of Finance and Economic Development.

MOFED (2010b). *Growth and Transformation Plan 2010/11–2014/15. Vol. 1: Main Text*. Addis Ababa: Ministry of Finance and Economic Development.

NMA (2001). *Initial National Communication of Ethiopia to the UNFCCC*. Addis Ababa: National Meteorological Agency.

NMA (2007). *Climate Change National Adaptation Programme of Action (NAPA) of Ethiopia*. Addis Ababa: National Meteorological Agency.

PANE (2009). *The Impact of Climate Change on Millennium Development Goals (MDGs) and Plan for Accelerated and Sustained Development to End Poverty (PASDEP) Implementation in Ethiopia*. Addis Ababa: Poverty Action Network of Civil Society Organizations in Ethiopia.

Stern, N. (2007). *The Economics of Climate Change: The Stern Review*. Cambridge: Cambridge University Press.

UNDP (2008). *UNDP Climate Change Country Profiles: Ethiopia*. Available at: http://country profiles.geog.ox.ac.uk/UNDP_reports/Ethiopia/Ethiopia.lowres.report.pdf.

Vidal, J. (2009). Copenhagen: head of African bloc calls on poorer nations to compromise on climate funding. *Guardian*, 16 December.

World Bank (2009). *Convenient Solutions to an Inconvenient Truth: Eco-System Based Approaches to Climate Change*. Available at: http://siteresources.worldbank.org/ENVIRONMENT/Resources/ESW_EcosystemBasedApp.pdf.

World Bank (2010). *Ethiopia: Economics of Adaptation to Climate Change*. Washington, DC: World Bank.

Yesuf, M., S. Di Falco, T. Deressa, C. Ringler & G. Kohlin (2008). *The Impact of Climate Change and Adaptation on Food Production in Low-Income Countries: Evidence from the Nile Basin, Ethiopia*. IFPRI Discussion Paper No. 828. Available at: http://www.ifpri.org/publication/impact-climate-change-and-adaptation-food-production-low-income-countries.

12
Reducing Climate Change Vulnerability in Mozambique: From Policy to Practice

Angus Hervey and Jessica Blythe

Introduction

MOZAMBIQUE is regularly identified as one of the countries that will suffer the worst effects of future changes to the earth's climate as a result of human-led activities. This extreme vulnerability is due to a number of physical factors, such as Mozambique's geographic location, its long coastline and its position at the confluence of several major river basins in southern Africa, as well as the extensive area of its land that lies below sea level, its high temperatures, aridity and infertile soils. These factors are further exacerbated by the country's extreme levels of poverty, the high dependence of most of its citizens on natural resources, and a lack of existing infrastructure and government capacity to support adaptation. At the same time, Mozambique bears little responsibility for its predicament. Its national production of greenhouse gases (GHGs) is the lowest in southern Africa, and one of the lowest in the world. Total annual emissions are 1.93 megatonnes (Mt) of CO_2, just 0.006 per cent of the world total. Annual per capita emissions are 0.09 tonnes, which is 10 per cent of the African average and just 2 per cent of the world average. In this sense, Mozambique represents one of the clearest examples of how climate change will affect those that have the least responsibility for it, and offers a compelling case for those arguing that developed countries have a moral obligation to help developing countries deal with the effects of their actions.

In this chapter, we develop an account of the evolution of climate change-related policy in Mozambique since the early 1990s, concentrating on the interplay of interests, ideas and institutions. Our argument is that concern about the country's vulnerability to climate change and, in particular, about vulnerability to the increased likelihood of extreme weather events has been the key driver shaping initial policy responses. However, in spite of a strong consensus in favour of the need for action and the incorporation of adaptation priorities into critical areas of policy, the implementation of adaptation measures has thus far been held hostage to political competition, differing discourses around vulnerability and top-down processes that have largely excluded civil society organizations, communities and vulnerable voices from the conversation. This chapter therefore offers one explanation for a problem common to many developing countries: the apparent disconnect between political commitment on measures to reduce the impact of climate change on the one hand, and actual policy outcomes on the other.

The first section examines Mozambique's vulnerability to climate change in greater detail. Much of that vulnerability is due to the likelihood that extreme events such as cyclones, floods and droughts will increase in both intensity and frequency in the future. The potential costs to the country are high, with estimates suggesting economic losses of between 4 and 14 per cent of gross domestic product (GDP) over the next few decades. This makes adaptation, and particularly disaster preparedness, a key policy priority for the government. In the second section we describe the various actors with roles and responsibilities for climate change. We show how their interaction has affected the way in which both government policies and donor programmes relating to climate change adaptation have been implemented. We also show how events such as the 2000 and 2007 floods demonstrate the evolution of government policy in response to the increased number and severity of natural disasters. Next, we explore how international climate change programmes have been translated via networks and negotiation into actions that have important impacts upon vulnerable communities. Finally, we argue that while the intention and broad scope of Mozambique's climate change adaptation and disaster response policies are quite good, implementation has been difficult because of political competition and differences in aims and intentions on the part of both government and multilateral and bilateral donors.

Mozambique's Vulnerability to Climate Change

Awareness about the nature of the threat that climate change poses to Mozambique has existed since at least the early 1990s, when researchers such as Downing (1991), Goldenman (1990), Magadza (1994) and McGregor (1994) first began highlighting its potential impacts on factors such as food security and water availability. In 1995, Mozambique ratified the United Nations Framework Convention on Climate Change (UNFCCC), and as one of the conditions began preparations for an initial national communication with information on GHG emissions, mitigation options, climate change vulnerability and adaptation options. Further signals about the severity of climate change threats were also provided by the 1997 Intergovernmental Panel on Climate Change (IPCC) special report on *The Regional Impacts of Climate Change*, which concluded that 'the African continent is particularly vulnerable to the impacts of climate change because of factors such as widespread poverty, recurrent droughts, inequitable land distribution and overdependence on rain-fed agriculture' (IPCC 1997, p. 7). However, it was only really in the 2000s, and especially in the last years of the first decade, that the true magnitude of Mozambique's vulnerability became apparent. The definitive work in this regard was a study on the *Impacts of Climate Change on Disaster Risk in Mozambique*, conducted between May 2008 and January 2009 by the National Institute for Disaster Management (INGC) and funded by the Danish International Development Agency (DANIDA), the United Nations Development Programme (UNDP) and the German Agency for International Cooperation (GIZ).

The main purpose of the study was to understand how the climate of Mozambique may already be changing and how it may be expected to change in the future. The study combined the best available research with a range of new studies utilizing the most current and widespread weather data, and employing four different national and global climate change scenarios. It reported changes in the seasonal climate of Mozambique between 1960 and 2005, and presented future scenarios focusing on the mid-century (2046–65) and late century (2080–100). The findings were sobering. For a start, the report showed that natural disasters such as droughts, floods and tropical cyclones – the main threats to Mozambique – have increased in both intensity and frequency in recent years. Of the fifteen tropical cyclones and storms that entered the Mozambique Channel and made landfall in the period between 1980 and 2007, for example, only four occurred in the period running from 1980 to 1993, whilst the other eleven occurred in the later period running from 1994 to 2007.

A severe drought between 1991 and 1993 also affected 1.32 million people throughout the country, and major droughts have subsequently occurred every year between 2000 and 2006, thanks largely to decreased rainfall, especially in the southern and central provinces. As Ribeiro & Chauque (2010) point out, the prevalence of these is striking; while southern Mozambique has always suffered from occasional droughts, it has never been afflicted by droughts for seven years in a row. Likewise with flooding: central Mozambique has always suffered from floods in the Zambezi Basin, with a big flood event occurring about every fifteen years, but with major floods in 2000, 2001 and 2007 there have been growing concerns about the frequency of flooding (World Food Programme 2009). Overall, between 1996 and 2006, 50 per cent more people were affected by natural disasters than in the previous decade, and the number of people killed more than tripled (Artur & Hillhorst 2012).

According to the INGC report, these disasters are likely to increase in both frequency and intensity in the future thanks to higher temperatures, rising sea levels, less rainfall and changes in water flows from the major river systems. Overall, it is expected that the risk of flooding in river basins and flood plains will increase notably in the south, whereas the coastal areas of the central zone will be heavily impacted by more intense cyclones and rising sea levels. Some of these changes are already happening: between 1960 and 2005 significant upward trends in temperatures were found over most of the country. In central Mozambique, increases of up to 1.6 °C have occurred, and approximately 1.1 °C in the north. Heat waves increased in duration by an average of 9 days, and the number of hot nights and hot days has increased over the whole of the country. During the same period, the start of the rainfall season has been delayed by an average of 10 days, and by up to 45 days in some locations (INGC 2009). Estimates for future temperature rises predict an increase of 2.5 °C to 3 °C by 2050 and as much as 5 °C to 6 °C by the end of the century. In general, the climate is expected to become more extreme, with drought spells becoming hotter and longer, and precipitation becoming more unpredictable, increasing risks of crop failure, drought, flooding and uncontrolled fires.

Rising sea levels will also have a noticeable effect on the 2,700-km Mozambican coastline. Between 1960 and 2001, sea levels rose by 2–3 mm per year. Under a scenario of low and gradual sea level rise (i.e. about 30 cm) by 2100, coastal set-back in Mozambique will be approximately 30 m; high level and non-linear scenarios predicting sea rise of 5 m by 2100 will result in the permanent inundation of the coast and the low lying areas behind it, with a coastal set-back of approximately 500 m. According to Dasgupta et al. (2009), Mozambique could experience an incremental impact loss of 3,268 km² of land area (over 40 per cent of the coastal total), affecting more than half of the population living in these areas. Economic costs to the country will also be high. A World Bank (2010) report estimates total damage due to sea level rise at between US$8.9 and US$11.2 million per year in the 2010s. By the 2040s, costs could rise to between US$31.6 and US$87.0 million per year. The report also estimates that between 44,000 and 90,000 migrants will be forced to leave their dwellings due to flooding and land area lost to erosion by 2020. This number grows to 916,000 displaced persons by the 2040s.

Following the IPCC's working definition, vulnerability is usually thought of not only as a function of the magnitude and duration of exposure to physical changes and the degree to which systems are affected by those changes, but also in terms of adaptive capacity, that is, the system's ability to withstand or recover from that exposure (IPCC 2001). This means that vulnerability can also be defined in terms of the ability of individuals and social groupings to respond to, recover from and adapt to any external stress placed on their livelihoods and well-being (Kelly & Adger 2000). Social class, gender, ethnicity, age group, income, health status and citizenship thus all influence people's vulnerability. The poor are particularly vulnerable because of their higher reliance on natural resources, and their limited means for recovering from disasters, which can often act as a 'push-back' into poverty, creating a vicious circle of increasing vulnerability to climate change. Climate change is thus also an 'underlying cause of poverty' in that it triggers – or worsens – a wide range of immediate and intermediate causes of poverty (Ehrhart & Twena 2006).

In this regard, Mozambique is particularly ill suited to deal with the aforementioned threats. In spite of sustained economic growth since the end of its civil war in 1992 and a number of successes in improving access to education and reducing infant mortality, it remains the poorest country in southern Africa. Over half the population lives in absolute poverty and two out of five children under the age of five suffer from malnutrition.

Agriculture is the main livelihood activity for 80 per cent of the population, most of whom (96 per cent) farm small plots of less than 2 ha with minimal inputs and primarily for subsistence purposes (Batidizirai et al. 2006). Only marginal surpluses are sold in local markets. These smallholders account for 90 per cent of the total area of land under cultivation (Census 2010). They are also particularly vulnerable to climate change. Key crops such as maize, sorghum, cassava and beans all face production risks due to increasingly unpredictable weather, heat stress, increases in carbon dioxide concentrations, which will decrease the protein content of vegetation, and rising rates of evapotranspiration, which will increase pressure on water supplies (Ehrhart & Twena 2006). The World Bank (2010), for example, predicts an average reduction on yields of 2.05 per cent across all crops in all regions by 2050. The zones most affected by loss of suitable area will generally be those that already struggle with the impacts of irregular and extreme climate events. These include the mixed arid and semi-arid systems in Gaza and semi-arid systems in parts of northern Inhambane and south of Tete, the coastal regions of the southern and central southern zones, and many of the drier zones of major river systems like the Limpopo, Save and Zambezi. Salt water intrusion along the coast due to reduced river flows is also expected, impacting negatively on agricultural land and productivity, especially in the Zambezi, Limpopo and Save estuaries (INGC 2009). Households with livelihoods dependent on livestock will also be affected, particularly by drought (lack of pasture and water) and changes in the prevalence of (vector-borne) livestock diseases (IPCC 2001; MICOA 2003, p. 35).

The other livelihood activity which will be severely affected is fishing. Coastal areas are home to around 12 million people and the oceans are the main source of livelihood for approximately 334,000 individuals (Hoguane et al. 2012). Increasing floods, droughts and the severity and frequency of tropical cyclones will worsen their vulnerability. Cyclones disrupt fishing activities and destroy household and community assets such as gear, boats and houses. Increasing severity and frequency of storms also leads to fewer days at sea and increased risk of accidents for resource-poor fishers who rely on small, man-powered boats, and are ill equipped for storms in the open ocean (Gillet et al. 2003). In addition, subsistence livelihood activities can exacerbate climate-related stress on coastal systems, compounding social vulnerability to climate change. For example, erosion rates in the northern region of Mozambique are less intense since the area is protected by coral reefs, which form a nearly continuous barrier between the open ocean and the coast. However, these reefs are under heavy pressure from intense extractive activities such as over-fishing (MICOA 2007).

Research by Ehrhart & Twena (2006), Birmingham et al. (1997) and Shapiro et al. (1999), among others, shows that climate change is also likely to have an effect on health in Mozambique. This is predicted to occur both directly, through increased injuries, deaths and disease associated with extreme events, and indirectly, via changes in water quality, air quality, food availability and quality, and the range, frequency and severity of diseases. Floods, for example, are usually associated with epidemics of diarrhoea and cholera, and have led to higher transmission rates of malaria (WHO 1999; IPCC 2001). Climate change will also place additional stress on those households living with HIV/AIDS by, amongst other things, challenging livelihoods and reducing the nutritional value of crops.

In 2010, a year after the release of the INGC report, the World Bank conducted a study estimating the potential costs of climate change to the Mozambican economy over the next 50–100 years. The report revealed that GDP is likely to fall by between 4 and 14 per cent by 2050, with worst-case estimates suggesting total costs of US$7.5 billion, or US$400 million annually. The report also revealed that while livelihood activities will certainly be affected, it is flooding and the damage it causes to transportation infrastructure that are likely to dominate overall welfare losses. This is because of the high ratio of unpaved to paved roads, and high reliance on these roads to connect urban centres to outlying and rural communities. Unfortunately, these are the same roads that are impacted to the greatest extent by climate change, with changes in precipitation patterns accounting for around 80 per cent of total road degradation. Increases in temperature will also have an impact, accounting for around 30 per cent of maintenance issues with paved roads. As the temperature increases due to climate change, if roads are not maintained, significant cracking and degradation will occur, resulting in a reduced life span and the need for more frequent repaving (World Bank 2010).

Domestic Roles, Responses and Policies

Because of its extreme vulnerability to climate change, Mozambique has begun to implement a range of innovative policies focusing on increasing climate resilience, though climate mitigation has taken a back seat to policies focusing on climate adaptation. Following the 2001 and 2007 floods in particular, Mozambique gained international attention and became the locus of a number of bilateral and multilateral climate change preparedness and adaptation programmes.

The government has realized that disaster preparedness must be included in its planning, and national legislation suggests that there is a growing awareness of climate change issues and efforts to mainstream them into domestic policies and programmes. However, climate change planning is still a relatively new issue and has yet to be fully integrated across government institutions and policies. Policy implementation has also been hampered by obstacles, especially competition between domestic ministries, misalignment between climate change policy and budget allocations, and mistrust between national political parties. This section explores these issues by looking at the evolution of domestic climate change policies in Mozambique, the existing government roles and responses, and the challenges constraining effective climate change action.

During the last half century, Mozambique has experienced several major periods of socio-economic change. The colonial period, of about 500 years, came to a close when the Front for the Liberation of Mozambique (FRELIMO) initiated an armed campaign for independence against Portuguese authorities in 1964. After more than a decade of conflict and increasing anti-colonial pressure in mainland Portugal, the colonial war ended in 1975 and FRELIMO established an independent, socialist state. Shortly following independence, a civil war erupted between the ruling, socialist FRELIMO and the anti-communist Mozambique National Resistance (RENAMO). The civil war led to widespread migration, destruction of infrastructure and economic collapse. Then, in 1992, both parties signed a peace agreement and Mozambique transitioned from a centrally planned economy to a free market state under the rule of the FRELIMO party.

From the beginning, environmental protection was one of the key issues considered by the new government. The 1990 Constitution acknowledged that socio-economic development relies on the preservation of the environment. The National Environment Commission (CNA) was established in 1992 and participated in the UN Conference on Environment and Development in Brazil. Two years later, the CNA established the basis for the creation of a Ministry for the Coordination of Environmental Affairs (MICOA), the body responsible for the implementation of the UNFCCC, and on 25 August 1995 Mozambique ratified the Convention (MICOA 2003). MICOA was officially established the same year and from its inception has taken the leading role on climate change policy in Mozambique. Another key player is the INGC, a unit within the Ministry of State Administration. The INGC is responsible for disaster preparedness and response and has received international praise for its early incorporation of climate change into its programmes and planning. The INGC was one of very few developing country participants to take part in the World Conference on Disaster Reduction in Japan. Other ministries and government bodies with a significant stake in climate change policy include the Ministry of Agriculture (MINAG), which takes responsibility for almost all national resource management, and the National

Meteorological Institute (INAM), which is responsible for collecting weather data and providing early storm warnings in the country.

In many countries, climate change policymaking is relatively new and is generally confined to ministries associated with environmental sustainability or disaster risk reduction. Yet there is increasing emphasis on mainstreaming climate change into national plans, with the aim of moving the issue from peripheral environmental ministries to the agendas of ministries responsible for central planning and economic development. In this regard, Mozambique has made good efforts to integrate climate change across government departments. The Ministry for Planning and Development (MPD), for example, has begun to play a leading role in trying to integrate climate change into policy planning in Mozambique. Moreover, national policies for the management of water resources under climate change acknowledge that successful implementation will require coordinated efforts from the Ministry for State Administration, Ministry of Science and Technology, Ministry of Education and Culture, Ministry of Defence and Ministry of Fisheries, among others (MICOA 2007). The Ministry of Public Works and Housing is also working on a pilot project for increasing the climate resilience of unpaved roads (Government of Mozambique 2011a). Finally, while Mozambique has not yet incorporated climate change planning into social protection programmes, discussions between the Ministry of Women and Social Welfare, the Ministry of Finance and the World Bank on how to integrate climate change into social protection planning are currently ongoing (Macaringue 2010).

Since the early 1990s, therefore, Mozambique has developed a broadly favourable domestic climate change policy framework. The Poverty Reduction Action Plan (PARP) 2011–14 is Mozambique's national strategy for poverty reduction.[1] It describes macroeconomic, structural and social policies to address three priorities: (1) enhancing productivity of agriculture and fisheries, the sectors which provide income and employment for the largest proportion of rural households; (2) promotion of employment; and (3) human and social development. Given Mozambique's high incidence of poverty, the plan understandably focuses on measures for poverty reduction and economic growth, while discussions of climate change are of secondary importance. Nevertheless, the PARP integrates climate change into the three central objectives. In order to boost fisheries and agricultural productivity, for example, the PARP states the need to 'establish, train and equip local risk management committees in areas prone to natural disasters or vulnerable to climate change' (Government of Mozambique 2011a, p. 18). The PARP declares that expansion of infrastructure, such as the building and rehabilitation of water resources, must take into account the country's vulnerability to natural disasters and climate change. Moreover, the PARP includes national strategies for both climate change mitigation (especially through reduction of emissions from deforestation, promotion of

245

reforestation and the development of carbon stocks) and adaptation (primarily centred on disaster risk response). Thus, several important climate change considerations are included for the first time in a national poverty reduction strategy paper.

Climate change mainstreaming is also evident in other domestic policies. The Five-Year Plan (PQG) 2010–14 is Mozambique's overarching plan to guide government activities in the country. The focus of the PQG is broader than that of the PARP. It aims to reduce poverty, improve social development and foster key economic sectors including agriculture, fisheries, minerals, tourism and transport. The PQG integrates climate change and disaster risk reduction into two objectives: (1) to reduce loss of life and property due to disasters and reduce vulnerability to hunger and water scarcity in drought prone areas, and (2) to enhance dissemination of information on disaster prevention and mitigation in local communities. The PQG also includes strategies for the fight against erosion and drought and for the conservation of biodiversity. The National Adaptation Programme of Action (NAPA) was prepared by the MICOA for submission to the UNFCCC in 2007. The NAPA, which was developed through a review of existing data and a participatory assessment of vulnerability to climate change, is a critical policy document that identifies the country's most urgent adaptation priorities. According to the NAPA, Mozambique's four most urgent adaptation priorities are (1) strengthening early warning systems, (2) strengthening the capacity of agricultural producers to cope with climate change, (3) reduction of climate change impacts along the coastal zone, and (4) improved water resource management under climate change (MICOA 2007). The Government of Mozambique has also demonstrated strong commitment to the integration of climate change and gender planning (Ribeiro & Chauque 2010). As a vivid example, in 2010, the Government of Mozambique approved the Gender, Environment and Climate Change Strategy and Action Plan, with the aim of ensuring equality between women and men to access and control natural resources and technologies for climate change adaptation and mitigation. Finally, the Oceanography Department at the University of Eduardo Mondlane is undertaking a number of technical pilot studies in coastal areas on developing alternative energy sources for the drying and freezing of fish, small-scale water desalinization plants and small aquaculture projects. Unfortunately, several obstacles constrain the public sector's ability to implement their climate change programmes effectively.

Competition between ministries for control of climate change planning, a lag between promised and available climate change funding, and pervasive political mistrust create tensions which plague domestic climate change action. We discuss each of these problems in the remainder of this section. First, since the establishment of the UNFCCC, the magnitude and availability of global climate funding have risen rapidly, particularly for developing countries. This increased funding has sparked competition between national institutions over leading roles and control of resources in Mozambique. MICOA, for example, has traditionally taken the leading role on climate policy. However, the MPD has also recently claimed that climate change is more of a developmental problem than an environmental problem, creating tension between the two ministries (Artur & Hilhorst 2012). Moreover, thanks to the laudable response of the INGC to the 2001 flooding many international agencies are choosing to work with it rather than MICOA (Artur & Hilhorst 2012).

Second, international consensus indicates that climate change impacts will require urgent adaptation actions in developing countries; yet, while much has been promised, substantial funding has yet to be secured, creating a gap between adaptation planning and implementation (Osman-Elasha & Downing 2007; Cabral & Francisco 2008). For example, while environmental priorities from the PARP II were featured in the NAPA and the INGC's master plan, these activities are highly dependent on the availability of funding. The INGC has stated that funding is one of the major constraints in operationalizing their plan (Macaringue 2010). In addition, only one of four adaptation priorities identified in Mozambique's NAPA has been approved for funding, and where funding has been secured, the national government has had very little authority over its allocation (Huq 2011). In Mozambique, NAPA teams expressed deep concerns regarding the funding of adaptation projects and described available funding opportunities as 'either insufficient or difficult to access' (Osman-Elasha & Downing 2007, p. 22). Lack of funding and limited national ownership of climate change funding will constrain Mozambique's capacity to respond to their most critical climate risks.

A third issue, which has the potential to damage climate change policies and actions in Mozambique, is the growing tension between FRELIMO and the newly formed Democratic Movement of Mozambique (MDM). Since independence in 1975, Mozambique has been ruled by FRELIMO. The party has successfully led Mozambique through its fight for independence, through the civil war and from socialism to a free market economy. It has demonstrated a remarkable ability to transform and has developed strong partnerships with the international donor community. However, FRELIMO has also won every poll since multiparty elections began in 1994, and in 2009 anti-MDM election manipulations were cited as the main cause for a temporary donor strike (Chambote & Shankland 2011). Two years later, Beira, governed by MDM's David Simango, was identified by the Pilot Programme for Climate Resilience (PPCR) as the most appropriate city for climate resilience investment. Beira is Mozambique's second largest city, it is a key centre of economic activity, and it is highly vulnerable to sea level rise and damage from tropical cyclones (Government of Mozambique 2011b). Yet FRELIMO was reluctant to approve the investment of several million dollars' worth of climate investment in Beira because it is an MDM stronghold (Chambote & Shankland 2011). After much negotiation, the final report for Phase 1 of the PPCR lists both Beira and Nacala, the latter governed by FRELIMO's Chale Ossufo, as the selected cities for climate resilient investment. This type of political tension has the potential to derail climate change planning, resulting in less efficient climate change actions for vulnerable populations.

Despite these challenges, the general consensus amongst researchers and donors is that Mozambique has made discernible improvements to national climate change policies in recent years. Climate change has been, more or less, mainstreamed across multiple government sectors and is no longer confined to peripheral ministries. In addition, priorities related to national policies on poverty reduction have been integrated into policies focusing solely on climate change and vice versa. One area where these improvements are clearly visible is in the government's response to natural disasters.

The Government's Evolving Response to Natural Disasters

Arguably, the most significant transformation to climate change-related policy in Mozambique has come about as a direct result of the country's most serious natural disaster of the last few decades. Between December 1999 and March 2000, record breaking rains occurred in the southern parts of the country, triggering the worst flooding ever recorded in Mozambique. The rainfall was associated with twelve meteorological systems, namely cyclones and tropical storms, left 800 people dead and half a million people living along the main branch of the Limpopo homeless. The UN World Food Programme reported that Mozambique lost at least one third of its staple food, maize, and 80 per cent of its cattle. Total losses were estimated at US$428 million, about 20 per cent of Mozambique's GDP for that year (World Bank 2000). With limited resources to respond to an event of this magnitude, the government of Mozambique was forced to seek international assistance of over US$160 million (World Bank 2000).

The floods exposed serious weaknesses in the Mozambican government's capacity to respond to natural disasters, as well as a lack of coordination between international response teams and domestic institutions that reduced response efficiency. For example, Matsimbe (2003) reported dozens of abandoned boreholes which had been constructed by international donors without consultation with local governments and in inappropriate locations. National challenges were compounded by local inexperience: in the Buzi district, flood warnings were issued 48 hours prior to flooding, yet local communities did not take the warnings seriously because of fairly regular small-scale flooding and a lack of understanding of the magnitude of the 2000 flood (Matsimbe 2003).

As a result, the government developed a new strategy to ensure a better response to future events. This involved strengthening the three national institutions for disaster management, namely the National Board for the Coordination of Disaster Management (CCGC), the Technical Council for Disaster Management (CTGC) and the INGC. The government invested in early response systems and flood resilient buildings, such as elevated grain storage (Patt & Schröter 2008). In addition, in 2001, the government approved the Law of Disaster Management, which aimed at improving strategies for disaster prevention and reducing state and community vulnerability to disasters (Matsimbe 2003). International donor support was also critical for building national disaster management capacity. Donors helped fund the employment and training of 285 staff and equipped a national headquarters and regional offices to support disaster management at central, regional and local levels (Stal 2011). The German government, for example, contributed two million euros for disaster preparedness, seconded several technical staff to the INGC, and paid for a number of projects, including equipping emergency response centres, training and simulation exercises.

Seven years later, these investments were put to the test. In December 2006, heavy rains in southern Africa caused the Cahora Bassa Dam to overflow, and by February 2007 the banks of the Zambezi had ruptured. Water flow peaked at 10,404 m^3/s, higher than during the 2000 flood, and resulted in widespread flooding affecting nearly all areas along the Zambezi. This time, the government of Mozambique was more prepared. In October 2006, when weather forecasts predicted heavy rains, the government disbursed US$5 million for early response (Artur & Hilhorst 2012). By February, the government declared a red alert and ordered the evacuation of people in the Zambezi flood plains. Significant improvements in the government's response were evident from the human impact. In the 2000 floods, 800 people were killed and over 5 million people were affected. In 2007, no lives were lost and only 163,000 people were affected (INGC 2007). Clearly, national and international investments in improving early response systems, increasing coordination between international and domestic institutions and integration of disaster response mechanisms into domestic planning significantly improved the government's capacity to respond to natural disasters.

Despite these improvements, though, several challenges still constrained flood response. Artur & Hilhorst (2012) have argued that the government's resettlement programme was driven by an underlying and long-standing desire to 'modernize' local communities, sometimes against their will, by moving them to settlements with cement houses, modern infrastructure and agriculture, rather than solely by flood response. Additionally, national strategies are still largely based on macro-scale disaster management, with a limited focus on increasing communities' own capacities to prepare for and respond to disasters. A challenge for future policy planning will, therefore, be to include the integration of climate change and disaster preparedness across institutional scales.

International Climate Change Programmes in Mozambique

International climate change programmes in Mozambique are predominantly designed to respond to the country's high climate vulnerability. Mozambique has acknowledged and adheres to a number of international initiatives aimed at ensuring environmental sustainability. These include the Vienna Convention on the protection of the ozone layer; the UNFCCC; the Kyoto Protocol (as a non-Annex I party); the Montreal Protocol and its respective London and Copenhagen amendments; the Convention on Biological Diversity (CBD); the Nairobi Convention for the protection, management and development of the East African marine and coastal areas; and the Basel Convention on the control of transborder movements of dangerous residuals and their elimination. In the UNFCCC negotiations, the country's position has, unsurprisingly, been determined primarily by concerns about its vulnerability. The country's negotiators have consistently called for the renewal of the Kyoto Protocol, arguing that its expiry in December 2012 means the end of the primary instrument that the world has to oblige developed countries to finance measures of adaptation. Mozambique has also called for technical assistance for adaptation, such as scholarships and training for experts; support for research activities; support for public awareness activities; knowledge transfer via participation of national experts in regional and international activities; and support for monitoring and the processing of existing data for research activities (MICOA 2007). Besides taking a national position at the negotiations, Mozambique also participates as a member the African Group. The African position argues that global warming should be kept below a 1.5 °C temperature increase by the end of the century; that developed and emerging countries (China, India, Brazil, etc.) should agree to reduce their emissions massively; and that the international community should provide financing and technical support to help African countries to adapt to the impact of climate change because their economies are fragile (UNDP 2011).

In 2003, as part of its commitment to the convention, Mozambique submitted its Initial National Communication (INC) to the UNFCCC. The document was prepared by MICOA and it presents an inventory of national sources of GHG emissions, provides an assessment of vulnerability and adaptation to climate change impacts and suggests policy options for raising public awareness. The INC identifies agriculture, forests, water resources and coastal areas, infrastructure, health and fishing as the sectors most vulnerable to climate change (MICOA 2003). It includes strategies to reduce vulnerability to the impacts of inundation of low coastal areas and coastal erosion, of reduced availability of fresh water and of reduced agricultural production. The INC argues that successful climate change adaptation measures will require the integration of environmental issues with development efforts. Because of Mozambique's low GHG emissions, high incidence of poverty and weak institutional capacity, the INC focuses on reducing vulnerability and increasing adaptive capacity as opposed to efforts to mitigate GHG emissions.

Since the early 2000s, a number of multilateral and bilateral programmes aimed at reducing climate vulnerability and increasing adaptive capacity have also been initiated in Mozambique. The PPCR, for instance, was approved in November 2008. It is a multilateral project financed through the World Bank, the African Development Bank and the International Finance Corporation that is being implemented domestically via the MPD and MICOA. The PPCR aims to demonstrate ways in which climate risk and resilience can be integrated into national planning and implementation (Government of Mozambique 2011b). The project is designed to be country driven, build on the NAPA and produce relevant climate knowledge that may be scaled up to enhance national climate change resilience.

The Africa Adaptation Programme (AAP) is an ongoing regional programme that seeks to enhance the adaptive capacity of vulnerable African countries by supporting climate change adaptation mainstreaming into national policy, development and investment frameworks. AAP is funded by the Japanese government, managed by the UNDP and implemented in Mozambique in partnership with the INGC and MICOA. The AAP aims to enhance domestic capacity to utilize current scientific climate change knowledge in planning, budgeting and implementation strategies. To date, the project has resulted in several positive outcomes, including the development of a climate change risk analysis matrix, a decisions support system for the Zambezi and training of several INAM technicians in overseas workshops. However, institutional structures related to the UNDP's internal procedures and national procurement rules have delayed assessment, implementation, completion and dissemination of proposed programme objectives. And in Mozambique, weak technical skills and limited climate change awareness also present obstacles for climate change adaptation mainstreaming in the country.

Between 2008 and 2010, the UNDP also managed the Joint Programme on Environmental Mainstreaming and Adaptation to Climate Change in Mozambique. This three year programme aimed to enhance government capacity to integrate climate change into policies and development plans as well as to strengthen community coping mechanisms, particularly through livelihood diversification. Thus, rather than working at a national scale, this programme focused on the Chicualacuala district in the Limpopo Basin, an area prone to floods and droughts. Activities included roof reinforcement against wind, adoption of drought resilient crops and strengthening of early warning systems. Other climate change programmes in Mozambique include the Joint Programme on Strengthening Disaster Risk Reduction and Emergency Preparedness, convened by the UNDP and focusing on risk reduction on a broad national level. The Coping with Drought and Climate Change project, funded by the Global Environmental Facility, MICOA and Samaritan's Purse, focuses on coping with the negative impacts of drought in a number of pilot sites. Adaptation in the Coastal Zones of Mozambique, run by the Global Environment Facility, aims to develop coastal community capacity to manage climate change through mainstreaming, pilot demonstrations on coastal erosion mitigation and improved knowledge management.

In 2011, the government of Mozambique launched a Strategic Environmental Assessment (SEA) along the national coast. This ongoing assessment involves extensive data collection in order to produce baseline assessments which will inform land use decision-making and planning at local, provincial and national levels in coastal zones in order to ensure that environmental considerations are integrated into development plans. Finally, other climate change projects in Mozambique include Climate Change Dare (United Nations Environment Programme [UNEP] and UNDP), which includes a project on erosion in Xai-Xai, and a World Wide Fund for Nature project, which focuses on increasing community resilience to climate change in conservation areas.

Beyond Rhetoric: The Challenges of Operationalizing Climate Change Programmes in Mozambique

Climate change policy is translated into practice via complex negotiations and there is no linear path between policy objectives and resulting actions. Rather, multilateral and bilateral donors, politicians, local chiefs and communities translate climate change policy to meet a variety of needs and objectives. Research suggests that the successes and failures of climate change policies may depend more on these negotiations than on the availability of appropriate policies, technologies or funding (Artur & Hilhorst 2012). It is thus critical to explore these negotiations, to identify where tensions arise and to understand how programme rhetoric is translated into actions that affect the lives of vulnerable people. Here, we explore the misalignment between climate discourse emphasizing national ownership and the priority given to multilateral development banks to implement climate change policy in Mozambique. Next, we outline how multiple, and sometimes conflicting, stakeholder interpretations of climate change hinder effective climate change action. Finally, we highlight the tension between a policy emphasis on broad participation and the exclusion of vulnerable social groups from climate change planning.

National ownership is often identified as a core principle for successful climate change adaptation programmes, yet researchers are beginning to question whether calls for national ownership necessarily translate into practices which reflect those objectives (Chambote & Shankland 2011). The case of the PPCR in Mozambique provides a clear example of the potential disconnect between policy rhetoric and the realities of implementation. Like many other climate change programmes, the PPCR emphasizes the importance of national ownership (Government of Mozambique 2011b). As the first phase of the programme began, the government of Mozambique indicated that MICOA should be the leading ministry for the implementation of the PPCR. The World Bank, on the other hand, suggested that MPD should be the leading ministry. The World Bank had already established a management unit in the MPD and argued that the MPD would be more consistent with the PPCR goal of integrating climate change planning into national development planning (Chambote & Shankland 2011). After a period of negotiation, representatives from both government ministries were chosen to work with a non-Mozambican coordinator, who was appointed by the World Bank and worked out of country (Chambote & Shankland 2011). Thus, despite the commitment to national ownership outlined in the PPCR policy, implementation was largely driven in a 'top-down' fashion according to World Bank priorities, negating claims for national ownership.

Partnerships between stakeholders with widely different perceptions of climate risks can also obscure successful climate change adaptation. International donors, national governments, nongovernmental organizations (NGOs) and local residents vary in their conceptualization of climate change, in the way they frame it and, thus, in the way they plan to adapt to the impacts of climate change. For example, the INGC frames climate change as a technical issue requiring data collection and modelling, while NGOs and local farmers' associations emphasize the linkages between climate change, poverty and livelihoods (Chambote & Shankland 2011). By contrast, multilateral agencies, such as the World Bank, take a managerial approach, identifying rapid disbursement of funds as a critical component for successful climate change planning and action (Chambote & Shankland 2011). In an analysis of the resettlement programmes in Mozambique following the 2007 flooding, Artur & Hillhorst (2012) found that effective adaptation was hampered by conflicting perceptions of climate change. International donors were promoting 'living with floods', while the national government attempted to integrate resettlement into a longer, politically motivated tradition of resettlement. Local interpretations of natural disasters ranged from acts of God to the will of ancestors to witchcraft. These contradictions complicate effective collaboration towards the goal of reducing climate vulnerability.

Last, while most climate change policies in Mozambique stress the importance of socially inclusive processes, vulnerable groups, such as women, youth and local communities, have been largely excluded from planning and implementation processes thus far. Civil society organizations were scarcely included in the first phase of the PPCR. When local groups were invited to participate in workshops and planning, they reported feeling that their attendance was required only as proof of the participatory process and that most decisions had already been made by more powerful stakeholders (Chambote & Shankland 2011). This is problematic since international experience underlines the importance of participatory planning in climate change programming to ensure that resources are used effectively and reach the vulnerable people who are targeted (Huq 2011). Moreover, when local populations are excluded from climate risk planning, it can lead to basic policy failures. In Mozambique, exclusion of farmers from flood risk planning surrounding the Limpopo resulted in misaligned perceptions of flood risk and a failed resettlement programme (Patt & Schröter 2008). Patt & Schröter (2008) argue that simply telling people that climate risks are increasing, and that they should respond in particular ways, does not work. These experiences highlight the need for active dialogue across stakeholder groups, as a necessary condition for successful climate change planning and policy implementation.

Conclusion

Because of Mozambique's high vulnerability and low capacity to respond to climate change, understanding and strengthening Mozambique's policy response is critical right now. Since Mozambique is one of the poorest countries in the world and one of the lowest emitters of GHGs, climate policies are primarily aimed at reducing the impact of climate change on the most vulnerable. Adaptation, in short, has taken priority over mitigation. Up to this point, the Mozambican government, with the assistance of international donors, has done a good job of mainstreaming climate change and integrating climate policies into national development policies. The government has performed exceptionally well in the area of disaster management, as evidenced by the massive improvements to flood response visible between the 2000 and 2007 floods.

As this chapter has made clear, however, while Mozambique has developed a strong policy framework for adapting to climate change, what is needed now is action that puts the policies that have been developed into practice. This is an area which has proved far more contentious, since climate change policy has had to be translated into practice via complex negotiation between stakeholders at multiple scales. In Mozambique, these stakeholders include not only the government and citizens, but also a number of international actors. It has become apparent that improving trust and collaboration within and between government institutions is critical to climate change mainstreaming. Further, international emphasis on national ownership and broad participation has to move beyond 'paper' commitments to actual engagement. Past experience has shown that calling for multi-stakeholder engagement is not enough; when less powerful partners, such as civil society, are effectively excluded from the processes the implementation of policies will fail. Therefore, adequate time and resources must be allocated to ensure that claims for country owner-ship can acquire some substance.

As the other case studies in this book show, policy responses to climate change are complex, and need to be sensitive to country-specific social, ecological, economic and political processes that shape interventions. Mozambique is no exception – and past practice has shown that climate change policies and actions are shaped by differ-ent interests and by competition, power dynamics and conflicting interpretations of climate risks. There are clear signs that existing policies are good and that the government's response to the kinds of natural disasters which are likely to increase in the future has been progressive and steadily improving. Given the country's high vulner-ability, and the obvious economic and political advantages of putting adaptation measures in place, there are good grounds to believe these policies will be translated into real actions that will help to improve the lives of vulnerable people in Mozambique.

Note

1 The PARP is equivalent to Poverty Reduction Strategy Papers in other least developed countries.

References

Artur, L. & D. Hilhorst (2012). Everyday realities of climate change adaptation in Mozambique. *Global Environmental Change* 22.

Batidzirai, B., A. P. Faaij & E. M. W. Smeets (2006). Biomass and bioenergy supply from Mozambique. *Energy for Sustainable Development* 10(1).

Birmingham, M. E., L. A. Lee, M. Ntakibirora, F. Bizimana & M. S. Deming (1997). A household survey of dysentery in Burundi: implications for the current pandemic in sub-Saharan Africa. *Bulletin of the World Health Organization* 75(1).

Cabral, L. & D. Francisco (2008). *Environmental Institutions, Public Expenditures and the Role for Development Partners.* Mozambique Case Study, Overseas Development Institute. Available at: http://www.odi.org.uk/sites/odi.org.uk/files/odi-assets/publications-opinion-files/4657.pdf.

Chambote, R. & A. Shankland (2011). *Understanding the Political Economy of Low Carbon and Climate Resilient Development: Mozambique Case Study Report.* Brighton: Institute of Development Studies.

Dasgupta, S., B. Laplante, C. Meisner, D. Wheeler & J. Yan (2009). The impact of sea level rise on developing countries: a comparative analysis. *Climatic Change* 93(3).

Downing, T. E. (1991). Vulnerability to hunger in Africa: a climate change per-spective. *Global Environmental Change* 1(5).

Ehrhart, C. & M. Twena (2006). *Climate Change and Poverty in Mozambique: Realities and Response Options for CARE.* Background Report. Geneva: CARE International.

Gillet, N. P., F. W. Zwiers, A. J. Waeve & P. A. Stott (2003). Detection of human influence on sea-level pressure. *Nature* 422.

Goldenman, G. (1990). Adapting to climate change: a study of international rivers and their legal arrangements. *Ecology* 17.

Government of Mozambique (2011a). *Poverty Reduction Action Plan (PARP) 2011–2014*. Available at: http://www.imf.org/external/pubs/ft/scr/2011/cr11132.pdf.

Government of Mozambique (2011b). *Strategic Program for Climate Resilience*. Available at: https://www.climateinvestmentfunds.org/cif/sites/climateinvest mentfunds.org/files/PPCR%206%20SPCR%20Mozambique.pdf.

Hoguane, A. M. E. da Lucia Cuamba & T. Gammelsrød (2012). The influence of rainfall on tropical coastal artisanal fisheries: a case study of Northern Mozambique. *Journal of Integrated Coastal Zone Management* 12(4).

Huq, S. (2011). *Adaptation: Resources Now to Plan and Implement*. London: International Institute for Environment and Development.

INGC (2009). *INGC Climate Change Report: Study on the Impacts of Climate Change on Disaster Risk in Mozambique*. Synthesis Report, eds. B. Van Logchem & R. Brito. Available at: http://www.undp.org.mz/en/Publications/Other-Publications/ INGC-Climate-Change-Report-Study-on-the-Impact-of-Climate-Change-on-Disaster-Risk-in-Mozambique.-Synthesis-report.-INGC-2009.

IPCC (1997). *The Regional Impacts of Climate Change: An Assessment of Vulnerability*. Cambridge: Cambridge University Press.

IPCC (2001). *Climate Change 2001: Impacts, Adaptations and Vulnerability*. Contribution of Working Group II to the Third Assessment Report of the Intergovernmental Panel on Climate Change. Cambridge University Press, Cambridge.

Kelly, P. M. & W. N. Adger (2000). Theory and practice in assessing vulnerability to climate change and facilitating adaptation. *Climatic Change* 47(4).

Macaringue, J. (2010). *Mozambique: Country Level Literature Review*. Africa Climate Change Resilience Alliance. Available at: http://community.eldis. org/.59d669a7/Mozambique%20ACCRA%20lit%20review.pdf.

Magadza, C. H. D. (1994). Climate change: some likely multiple impacts in Southern Africa. *Food Policy* 19(2).

Matsimbe, Z. (2003). *The Role of Local Institutions in Reducing Vulnerability to Recurrent Natural Disasters and in Sustainable Livelihoods Development*. Available at: http://www.fao.org/docrep/007/ae079e/ae079e00.htm.

McGregor, J. (1994). Climate change and involuntary migration: implications for food security. *Food Policy* 19(2).

MICOA (2003). *Mozambique Initial National Communication under UN Framework Convention on Climate Change*. Available at: http://unfccc.int/resource/docs/natc/ moznc1.pdf.

MICOA (2007). *National Adaptation Programme of Action*. Available at: http:// unfccc.int/resource/docs/napa/moz01.pdf.

Osman-Elasha, B. & T. E. Downing (2007). *Lessons Learned in Preparing National Adaptation Programmes of Action in Eastern and Southern Africa*. Oxford: European Capacity Building Initiative.

Patt, A. G. & D. Schröter (2008). Perceptions of climate risk in Mozambique: implications for the success of adaptation strategies. *Global Environmental Change* 18.

Ribeiro, N. & A. Chauque (2010). *Gender and Climate Change: A Case Study of Mozambique*. Heinrich Böll Stiftung, South Africa. Available at: http://www. za.boell.org/downloads/Mozambique.pdf.

Shapiro, R. L., M. R. Otieno, P. M. Adcock, P. A. Phillips-Howard, W. A. Hawley, L. Kumar & P. Waiyaki (1999). Transmission of epidemic *Vibrio cholerae* 01 in rural western Kenya associated with drinking water from Lake Victoria: an environmental reservoir of cholera? *American Journal of Tropical Medicine and Hygiene* 60

Stal, M. (2011). Flooding and relocation: the Zambezi River valley in Mozambique. *International Migration* 49.

UNDP (2011). *Mozambique Prepares to the Global Climate Negotiations COP17/CMP7 in Durban*. Available at: http://www.undp.org.mz/en/content/pdf/2839.

WHO (1999). *The World Health Report 1999: Making a Difference*. Geneva: World Health Organization.

World Bank (2000). *A Preliminary Assessment of Damage from the Flood and Cyclone Emergency of February–March 2000*. Washington, DC: World Bank.

World Bank (2010). *Economics of Adaptation to Climate Change: Mozambique Country Study*. Washington, DC: World Bank Group.

World Food Programme (2009). *A Report from the Office of Evaluation: Full Report of the Evaluation of the Mozambique Country Programme 10446.0 (2007–2009)*. Rome: World Food Programme.

13

Reaching the Crossroads: The Development of Climate Governance in South Africa

Lesley Masters

Introduction

SOUTH Africa is particularly vulnerable to the effects of climate change. Already classed as semi-arid, the country faces the threat of increased drought in the west, particularly in the Western and Northern Cape provinces, while the east coast of KwaZulu-Natal is threatened by the growing frequency and intensity of flooding (DEA 2011a). Recognizing the country's vulnerability and the impact of climate change on the country's social and economic development, post-apartheid South Africa has adopted a visible role within the international climate change negotiations. Pretoria has been a vocal defender of developing countries through the loose political grouping of BASIC countries (Brazil, South Africa, India and China), as a prominent member of the Africa Group, and as part of the Group of 77 (G77)/China coalition. As a signatory of the United Nations Framework Convention on Climate Change (UNFCCC), South Africa has also sought to demonstrate its own commitment to mitigating climate change as a 'responsible international citizen' (DIRCO 2011, p. 10). Most recently, it has done so by committing to a 34 per cent reduction in emissions (compared to 'business-as-usual') by 2020 and to a 42 per cent reduction by 2025 at the Fifteenth Conference of the Parties (COP15) in Copenhagen.

As a developing country that ranks among the top twenty global emitters of greenhouse gases (GHGs), meeting this target presents a significant challenge. To achieve it, the government has introduced a number of new climate change policies and initiatives, which are reviewed in what follows. However, as this chapter argues, major obstacles have been encountered as the government has tried to develop a cohesive approach to climate governance. Indeed, South Africa has reached a crossroads. On the one hand, the government has set several ambitious targets and there has been a good deal of progress towards developing climate change policies. Yet, on the other hand, there is still considerable distance to be covered before there is any likelihood of actually meeting the government's lofty goals. The question, then, is: why has the government set such ambitious policies while only limited efforts have been made to implement them? In order to unpack the disconnect between what government has rhetorically committed to in terms of reducing the country's GHG emissions and the lack of a sustained approach to climate governance, this chapter begins by setting out the domestic context in which climate change policymaking has occurred. It highlights the implications of South Africa's apartheid past as well as its future developmental trajectory, in which the government is likely to face growing demands (and regular protests) for 'service delivery' and for job creation in an economy that is becoming more – not less – dependent on fossil fuels. What becomes apparent from this overview is that South Africa's approach to climate change is heavily conditioned by an emphasis on fossil fuel-dependent development and economic growth. Balancing the goal of reducing emissions with that of economic development has proved particularly challenging.

The second part of this chapter then provides an overview of the rapid evolution of climate policies and initiatives since 2000. It reveals that an increasingly confusing 'mosaic' of policies and programmes across a number of different sectors has emerged over time as the government has responded to domestic and international forces. By and large, these remain fragmented and do not amount to a coherent strategy for governing climate change. If considered in isolation – that is, as individual policy positions – these initiatives may be viewed as 'progressive'. Yet, if they are considered together, it is clear that they remain distinct 'parts' of a climate change strategy and do not coalesce into a coherent whole. The final section then considers the role that international actors, domestic political leadership, the private sector and civil society have played in shaping South Africa's approach towards climate change. It is argued that while these 'players' have increasingly pushed for a more ambitious response over time, competing interests and priorities among them have led to disagreements over the content and character of policies, and to inconsistencies in the country's overarching approach to the climate.

Energy and Climate Change in South Africa: The Domestic Context

This section highlights the context in which current climate change policy decisions are made in South Africa. The factors it identifies form the structure within which policymakers act, thereby shaping the decisions that they make. The most important factors to consider are the country's significant dependence upon coal and other fossil fuels for the production of energy, and the government's priorities in relation to questions of economic inequality and the future prospects for social and economic development, which have been heavily influenced by the country's past history of racial discrimination under apartheid. In what follows, each of these important aspects of the South African context and their relation to climate change decision-making are discussed.

South Africa, first of all, has an energy intensive economy, with many large energy consuming industries, such as the mineral extractive, chemical and petrochemical industries, which together contribute a significant share of economic growth (Jooste et al. 2009). The country's energy mix is dominated by coal, which contributes 65.7 per cent of the country's total primary energy supply. The next largest components of South Africa's energy supply are oil (21.6 per cent), renewable energy and waste energy (7.6 per cent), gas (2.8 per cent) and nuclear (1.9 per cent) (DOE 2010, p. 21). This coal-intensive energy production structure, which includes a focus on coal-to-liquid (CTL) technology, is largely a legacy of the country's apartheid past, which forced the government to focus on ensuring security of supply as it became increasingly isolated internationally. South Africa's abundant coal reserves and distorted prices for migrant labour made coal a relatively 'cheap' source of energy for supporting the industrial sector (Davidson 2006, p. 6; Durning 1990, pp. 21–4). It also meant that the country became a major contributor to global stocks of GHGs.

South Africa is not only highly reliant on fossil fuels at present, however; it is becoming increasingly dependent on them because of other legacies of apartheid, especially significant inequality in access to electricity. Under apartheid, the minority white population and big business had generally good access to energy, while the disenfranchised majority black population remained reliant on traditional energy sources, such as paraffin and biomass. Due to this history of inequality, the new (in 1994) democratically elected government made the issue of energy access a top priority. This motivated, for instance, the post-apartheid government's electrification programme, which led to the electrification of 2.4 million new households between 1991 and 1997 (DME 1998, p. 5). The government also developed an electricity initiative that provided a free basic electricity quota of 50 kWh per household to support parts of the population that remained 'energy poor'. The problem is that this large-scale expansion of energy and use of subsidies supports inefficient energy use, and heavily depends on coal-fired power stations, which contribute a significant share of the country's GHG emissions. Programmes such as these have demonstrated the centrality of coal in South Africa's current and future energy mix. Further, they make the government particularly sensitive to any schemes that might increase the price of energy for poorer consumers. Thus, despite its commitment to curbing emissions, the government has consistently emphasized the primacy of coal for the near future. Recent years have even seen growing coal mining in the Waterberg region, the reinstating of mothballed power stations and the building of the new coal-burning power stations, Medupi and Kusile, which will be the amongst the largest in the world.

The Evolution of Climate Change Policies in South Africa

South Africa's apartheid legacy not only gave rise to significant dependence on coal for energy, it also left a legacy of socio-economic inequality that has considerably shaped the government's priorities. As a result, economic growth, job creation and poverty alleviation have been central concerns since the country's successful transition to democracy. This section shows that while there has been increased awareness of the problem of climate change across all parts of the government, giving rise to an evolving 'mosaic' of climate policies and initiatives (shown in figure 13.1), these have not yet translated into a coherent strategy. The section does so by examining a number of climate policies elaborated by the Department of Environment (DEA) since the early 1990s, as well as key policies related to climate change established by the Department of Energy (DOE).

Initial Developments: South Africa's Early Climate Policies

Climate policy was slow to develop in post-apartheid South Africa. Following the transition to democracy, as indicated above, the government largely focused on departmental reform, restructuring parts of the government, and developing policies that would address the immediate economic and developmental concerns that had arisen from the inequalities and injustices of the past.

1992	Earth Summit
1993	South Africa signs the UNFCCC
1997	South Africa ratifies the UNFCCC
1998	White Paper on the Energy Policy of the Republic of South Africa
2000	South Africa's Initial National Communication under the UNFCCC
2003	Integrated Energy Plan (March); White Paper on Renewable Energy (November)
2004	A National Climate Change Response Strategy
2007	The Long Term Mitigation Scenarios (October); ANC Policy Resolution on Climate Change (December)
2009	National Climate Change Summit (March); National Renewable Energy Summit (March); Copenhagen Commitment (December)
2010	Nationally Appropriate Mitigation Action Submission (January); Green Economy Summit (May); National Climate Change Response Green Paper (November); Discussion Document on Carbon Tax (December)
2011	Integrated Resource Plan for Electricity (March); National Climate Change Response White Paper (October); Green Economy Accord (November); Second National Communication to the UNFCCC (November); COP17 in Durban (November/December)
2012	National Planning Commission's National Plan

Table 13.1 Timeline of climate change policies and initiatives in South Africa, 1992–2012

Although South Africa ratified the UNFCCC and actively participated in the international negotiations, climate change did not receive a great deal of attention in the new government. The issue was, instead, incorporated into broader environmental considerations. The early post-apartheid period saw the African National Congress (ANC), along with the South African Communist Party (SACP) and the South African National Civic Organization (SANCO), bringing stakeholders together to discuss the development of policies aimed at protecting the environment. Central to the outcome of these discussions was the need to demonstrate links between the environment and human welfare (Schreiner 1995, p. 3). This bridging of environmental and socio-economic developmental concerns was essential for making environmental issues relevant to the black majority, which generally regarded environmental protection as primarily about 'nature conservation', and considered abstract issues such as climate change to be the preserve of the white elite (Leck et al. 2011, p. 66).

Thus, it took some time before climate change would rise up the government's agenda. The development of policies specifically focused on climate change only really began to gather momentum during the early 2000s, largely driven by the former Department of Environment and Tourism (DEAT) under the leadership of Marthinus van Schalkwyk. As minister for DEAT, van Schalkwyk adopted a prominent position in the international climate change negotiations by calling for greater commitments from developed countries, particularly from the US. Domestically, van Schalkwyk also oversaw the development of the National Climate Change Response Strategy and the Long Term Mitigation Scenarios (LTMS), which he himself described as 'progressive, ambitious and far-reaching' initiatives (Benton 2008). Nevertheless, although there may have been 'progressive and ambitious' elements within each of these climate initiatives, neither actually amounted to very much in practice.

The first of these – the National Climate Change Response Strategy – was released in 2004 (DEAT 2004). Coordinated by DEAT, the Response Strategy drew on contributions from a number of selected stakeholders, including representatives from the public utility Eskom, academic institutions, research organizations and individual experts. It provided an initial outline of the government's approach to climate governance, highlighting the importance of creating adequate institutional arrangements and singling out the leadership role of DEAT, though it also recognized that other government departments would need to play important roles. In certain respects, it was quite progressive in the plans it set out for dealing with climate change, including those related to adaptation, mitigation, education, institutional arrangements and legislation. Yet it also clearly explained that – as a non-Annex I country – economic and social development remained paramount in South Africa.

Indeed, despite the government's rhetoric, it actually adopted a quite conservative approach towards climate change. Many of the more ambitious elements of the country's Response Strategy were hindered or diluted by the government's cautious approach towards fossil fuel-based energy, which was deemed essential to maintaining South Africa's international competitiveness and furthering domestic developmental priorities. The Response Strategy was also severely affected by major shortfalls in climate change awareness and understanding within other parts of the government. Finally, although the Response Strategy identified priority areas such as sustainable development, adaptation, energy, education and capacity development, the document failed to set out precise targets or timeframes for implementation. Indeed, although eleven overarching objectives were listed for addressing national climate change priorities, there was no indication of when they were to be achieved and how achievement should be measured or monitored.

The LTMS, released by DEAT in 2007, had been commissioned by the Cabinet and was aimed at informing the country's long-term climate policymaking effort by setting out the costs of different GHG reduction scenarios. The first, 'Growth without Constraints', acted as a reference for the others, highlighting the implications of taking no actions to mitigate emissions while growing at a rate of between 3 and 6 per cent per annum. This scenario assumed that growth would be achieved primarily using fossil fuels, with renewable sources of energy comprising only a small share of the country's energy profile. The result, it was calculated, would be a quadrupling of the country's emissions. The second scenario, 'Required by Science', set out what would be required for South Africa to reduce emissions by approximately 30 to 40 per cent from 2003 levels by 2050 (DEAT 2007, p. 9). Realizing this scenario, it was argued, would require making much greater use of renewable and nuclear technologies, increasing energy efficiency, and improving emissions standards. Other scenarios then fell in between these two.

While the LTMS provided more information about the likely costs of addressing climate change than the initial Response Strategy, it remained a contested initiative. One of the major problems was that the LTMS gave significant attention to the use of nuclear power as a means of mitigation. This led civil society groups, such as Earthlife and the Coalition Against Nuclear Energy (CANE), to question the viability (and desirability) of the scenarios for meeting South Africa's mitigation commitments. Their critique was based, to a great extent, on the linkages between the continued use of fossil fuels and the harmful side-effects of nuclear generation processes. The government's ability to support a nuclear energy programme was also subsequently called into question when financing was withdrawn for the government-supported Pebble Bed Modular Reactor (PBMR) project and the government halted plans for a second nuclear power plant (the first being the Koeberg nuclear power station in the Western Cape). Thus, while the LTMS played an important role in policy discussions by outlining the costs of various paths, it was never revised or updated as the government's focus turned towards the development of a white paper on climate change in the years after, which would formalize South Africa's approach towards climate change.

Towards a White Paper on Climate Change

South Africa played an increasingly visible role throughout the early period of the UNFCCC negotiations. Yet, as a result of the limited domestic efforts that had been undertaken to cut emissions, as well as the country's rising status as a major emitter, Pretoria encountered growing pressure from the international community to demonstrate its commitment to mitigating emissions. As one of the BASIC countries, and a developing country with significant GHG emissions, South Africa saw calls from both the industrialized countries and groups such as the small island developing states (SIDS) and least developed countries (LDCs) to undertake legally binding reductions. Under the Copenhagen Accord, Pretoria responded by committing to a Nationally Appropriate Mitigation Action (NAMA) of achieving a reduction of GHG emissions of 34 per cent by 2020 and 42 per cent by 2025. However, this seemingly ambitious NAMA was not backed up by any real climate policies for meeting it. The development of a white paper on climate change was meant to show the world that South Africa could, in the words of Edna Molewa, 'walk the walk' (Naidoo 2011a). Yet it got off to a slow start. Led by the DEAT, the process of developing such a policy document on climate change actually began in 2008, when Minister van Schalkwyk announced a plan to host a national climate change summit that would include representatives from government, the private sector and civil society. At this event, which took place in March 2009, over 600 individuals gathered in Midrand to set out their positions on the development of a climate change framework in South Africa and the country's approach to the UNFCCC negotiations. It proved to be a significant venue for facilitating dialogue between government and key stakeholders. However, the green paper (DEA 2010) that followed lacked adequate timelines and targets, as well as a clear division of responsibilities for implementation among the various government departments (Parliamentary Monitoring Group 2011).

As a result of the lack of confidence in the green paper on the part of stakeholders from both civil society (global and local) and the private sector, South Africa remained under pressure to release a national climate change policy ahead of COP17. Thus, after further consultations through stakeholder workshops and public comment sessions on draft text, a final National Climate Change Response white paper was released in October 2011, just one month prior to the Durban negotiations. The white paper outlined the government's 'vision for an effective climate change response and the long-term transition to a climate-resilient, equitable and internationally competitive lower-carbon economy and society' (DEA 2011b, p. 10). Unlike the green paper and the Response Strategy, the white paper set out actions for addressing adaptation and mitigation, as well as specific targets and timeframes. In addition, recognizing the urgency of responding to climate change, the white paper also identified a number of 'Near-term Priority Flagship Programmes' in public works, water conservation, renewable energy, energy efficiency, transport, waste management, and carbon capture and sequestration (CCS).

The development of the white paper signalled South Africa's formal commitment to meeting the initial emissions reduction targets set out in the LTMS and the country's NAMA submission under the Copenhagen Accord. As the white paper noted, South Africa had an international obligation to draft, update and implement policies to mitigate emissions as well as to establish a GHG inventory. As a significant emitter of GHGs seeking to play the role of a 'responsible global citizen ... with moral as well as legal obligations under the UNFCCC' (DEA 2011b, p. 24), the white paper provided the institutional framework for mounting an effective response. Like the Response Strategy, however, it continued to emphasize economic competitiveness and economic growth to a considerable extent (DEA 2011b, p. 10). This, it was believed, was essential for bringing on board key domestic constituencies; the government needed to assure stakeholders, particularly those in the private sector, that economic growth and climate governance would be mutually reinforcing. The problem was that, in the South African case, this was especially difficult: more often than not, economic considerations simply led to the watering down of ambitious climate policies, as is discussed below.

At Cross-Purposes? Energy and Climate Policy

With energy identified as a key element in any effort to address South Africa's growing GHG emissions, linking energy and climate policy is essential for forming a coherent climate change strategy. Yet two different departments have traditionally governed each of these areas, and they have had difficulty coordinating policy positions. While the DEA assumes the central role in climate change policy, it is the DOE that is the lead department on renewable energy and energy management. The latter's major strategic documents include the Integrated Energy Plan (DME 2003a), the White Paper on Renewable Energy (DME 2003b), and the Integrated Resource Plan (DOE 2011). But, with the DOE's mandate focused primarily on ensuring energy security, climate change has been poorly integrated into them. For instance, while the aim of the Integrated Energy Plan was to 'balance energy demand with supply resources in concert with safety, health and environmental considerations' (DME 2003a, p. 5), it emphasized how South Africa will continue to rely on coal for at least a further two decades. It also pointed to the importance of developing the country's own oil and gas deposits, as well as increasing the number of oil refineries. Any discussion of the linkages between energy and climate change was restricted to ensuring 'environmental considerations in energy supply' (DME 2003a, p. 4).

With renewable energy options increasingly singled out for their role in mitigating emissions, supporting job creation, and moving towards a green economy (ANC 2007), the expectation both from within the renewable energy sector and from climate lobby groups was that renewable energy options would be pursued more vigorously. Nevertheless, since the release of the white paper on Renewable Energy, a 2003 supplement to South Africa's Energy Policy of 1998, there has not been significant momentum for expanding the share of renewable energy sources in South Africa's energy mix. Although the white paper highlights the role of renewable energy for supporting the country's sustainable development and energy security goals, setting a target of 10,000 GWh in South Africa's total energy consumption by 2013, in practice there has been little progress in terms of implementation. Of the targeted 10,000 GWh, equivalent to a 4 per cent contribution towards energy consumption by 2013, only 4 per cent of the 4 per cent target had been achieved by 2009 (Sonjica 2009).

In 2009, a renewable energy stakeholder summit was convened in Centurion to discuss the future of renewable energy in South Africa. Hosted by the Department of Minerals and Energy (DME), the aim of the summit was to review the progress made since the white paper's release. The discussion highlighted the slow progress in implementation as well as the numerous barriers to the inclusion of renewable energy within the country's prevailing energy mix, including 'inadequate legal and regulatory frameworks, inadequate research and development, limited funding instruments, low electricity tariffs, lack of technical capacity and lack of clarity on the appropriate level of national ambition' (DME 2009, pp. 3–4). The elaboration of a revised version of the paper based upon this review is still in progress with ongoing deliberations over the target, the sources of renewable energy that should be included, and the potential for feed-in tariffs for independent power producers. The problem is that climate change considerations have so far remained marginal within South Africa's renewable energy policy dialogues. Few efforts have been made to ensure that the new renewable energy policies cohere with the goals set out in the Climate Change Response White Paper.

Growing Climate Consciousness?

Despite a lack of coherence in South Africa's energy and climate policies, as well as poor implementation of the former, a number of other developments in international and domestic policymaking seem to have signalled a growing level of concern about the climate within the government. Internationally, Pretoria has aligned with other developing countries in pursuing sources of finance that are new, additional, significantly scaled up and predictable. For South Africa, in particular, addressing climate change hinges on the country's ability to access such support. Thus, the country has been active in negotiating financing for adaptation, with the minister in the presidency, Trevor Manuel, involved in shaping negotiations on finances as a member of the High-Level Advisory Group on Climate Change Finance. As part of the National Planning Commission within the Presidency, Manuel has also been responsible for the National Plan – South Africa's long-term economic strategy – that was released in 2012, which includes a chapter on 'ensuring environmental sustainability and an equitable transition to a low carbon economy'. This affirms the need to move towards a sustainable, climate resilient and low carbon economy by 2030, while maintaining the country's international competitiveness. The Plan highlights the linkages between development concerns and climate change through an approach that emphasizes environmental sustainability, climate change resilience, skills development and the use of market mechanisms for mitigating GHG emissions (NPC 2012).

In addition to the National Plan, the focus on highlighting the socio-economic development potential of climate change policy can be seen in several subsequent initiatives. The Departments of Environment, Economic Development, Science and Technology as well as Trade and Industry, for instance, hosted the 2010 Green Economy Summit in Sandton, Johannesburg. The summit provided a platform for a broad cross-section of stakeholders to discuss the prospects and implications of a green economy for South Africa. In its final statement, the summit resolved to develop a 'green economy' plan, understanding the green economy as a system of economic activities related to the production, distribution and consumption of goods and services that result in improved human well-being over the long term, while not exposing future generations to significant environmental risks or ecological scarcities (DEA et al. 2010, p. 5). The final Green Economy Accord was officially launched by the Department for Economic Development at COP17, and was widely supported as a major effort to align climate change policies with economic growth and job creation. It set an ambitious target of creating five million new 'green' jobs by 2020, and called for the introduction of solar water heaters and the localization of their production, renewable energy and energy efficiency projects, biofuels, clean coal, transport and electrification projects.

Not all were as well received. Other climate policies proposed around the same time encountered resistance from the public. At the end of 2010, for instance, the National Treasury indicated that it might introduce a R75 per tonne of CO_2 carbon tax on major emitters. The discussion document that was circulated focused on the economics of climate change and technical designs for a carbon tax aimed at avoiding a significant impact on low income households and international competitiveness. The initiative could certainly be deemed 'progressive', yet was criticized by both civil society and business groups alike. Several civil society groups expressed concern about whether tax revenues would be put towards environmental uses, while business pointed to the impact that the carbon tax would have on international competitiveness (van der Merwe 2011). South Africa's power utility, Eskom, also indicated that the tax on carbon emissions set out in the government's discussion documents would force it to push the additional costs onto consumers, many of whom are quite poor.

As this section highlights, many standalone policies – those set out in white papers on climate change and renewable energy, and the Green Economy Accord, for instance – can be considered progressive steps from a developing country confronting significant socio-economic and development inequalities. Yet they do not always align and are, at times, even conflicting. As the discussion above also indicates, economic growth continues to be the overriding priority for the government. Emphasizing this has been important for making climate change policies palatable to the private sector and wider public, but has also often simply led to the subordination of real environmental considerations. The sum of the parts has also not produced a greater whole in terms of climate governance. The DOE has initiated policies that are only loosely coordinated with those elaborated by the DEA. Unfortunately, there have been few efforts to rectify this situation. In recent years, the Inter-Ministerial Committee on Climate Change (IMCCC) and the Intergovernmental Committee on Climate Change (IGCCC) have both been mandated with the cross-sectoral coordination of climate policy at a national level. In effect, however, neither organization has managed to provide an inclusive platform for climate change.

The Players: Competing Interests and Influence

The section above discussed the challenges that South Africa has encountered as it has attempted to establish a coherent approach to climate governance across government departments. This section highlights the role that individual actors have played in shaping the development of South Africa's approach towards climate change. In the first instance, the role of the international milieu needs to be highlighted. A key driver in the development of South Africa's own approach to climate change has been the country's position as a signatory of the climate change convention and its role within the international climate change negotiations. As a signatory of the UNFCCC and the Kyoto Protocol (as a non-Annex I country), South Africa has been compelled to fulfil its international legal obligations. These have included the submission of national communications on climate change under Article 12 of the convention; the development and implementation of policies concerning the mitigation of its emissions; and monitoring arrangements for reporting to the UNFCCC the steps it has taken in addressing GHG emissions (DEA 2011b, p. 9). These have generated action, in the first instance, by raising the importance of the issue across relevant arms of the government and creating constituencies determined to see obligations fulfilled.

Second, South Africa's own role in the international climate change negotiations has added impetus to the country's climate policy development. In line with South Africa's foreign policy position of acting as a 'responsible international citizen', the climate change discourse within the country has increasingly revolved around the country's moral obligation of pursuing a legally binding agreement. As a result, the country has been pursuing a role as a 'bridge builder', with the aim of bringing together developed and developing countries to reach a common consensus within the climate change negotiations (note here the similarities between South Africa and South Korea in this respect; see chapter 5 by Jae-Seung Lee in this volume). As hosts of the Durban negotiations (COP17), South Africa sought to build on its position as a bridge builder by demonstrating its commitment to reducing GHG emission through the development of its own climate policies. By doing so, South Africa managed to achieve a diplomatic victory with the Durban Platform for Enhanced Action, and commitments by all parties to move towards binding emission cuts by 2020, even though this was resisted by South Africa's BASIC partners (Masters 2011).

Thus, the international environment, combined with South Africa's foreign policy goals, has been an important driver of South Africa's climate policies. However, the government's approach has also been conditioned by the preferences and actions of domestic actors. It has not simply been a product of international pressures. Indeed, as Robert Putnam (1988) has explained in his work on two-level games, it is at the national level that domestic groups seek to push government decision-making in the direction of their preferences. The rest of this section therefore considers in greater detail the role of political leadership by the governing party in championing the development of climate governance. Initially, attention given to climate change by the ANC allowed the issue to rise up the political agenda. In addition to the ANC and key figures within its leadership, however, both the private sector and civil society groups have actively sought to shape the governance of climate change in South Africa, with varying degrees of success. Business interests, in particular, have occupied a prominent position in climate change debates, though mainly as critics of the government's stance. Civil society, on the other hand, has generally been supportive, but, by contrast, has had more mixed results in terms of its ability to engage with decision-makers and frame policy. Interaction between the government and civil society groups has not been sustained or inclusive, and, as such, civil society groups have seen widely varying degrees of success in shaping climate governance at the domestic level.

Climate Governance and Political Leadership

With so many competing priorities and interests at the domestic level, political leadership plays a particularly important part in keeping climate change concerns on the agenda. And, within South Africa, understanding the policy positions of the ANC is crucial. As the majority party in the tripartite alliance, and with the lines increasingly blurred between the party and the state, its positions feed directly into those of the state. While broader environmental concerns have always received some attention within the ANC's policy discussions, climate change received particular attention with the release of a Climate Change Resolution at the ANC's 52nd National Conference held in Polokwane Limpopo, in 2007. Concern about climate change within the party came increasingly to the fore following growing recognition of the impact of climate change on the most vulnerable countries and the potential to address environmental degradation, job creation and poverty alleviation simultaneously, especially after the release of the *Stern Review* and the IPCC's Fourth Assessment Report (Stern 2006; IPCC 2007). The 'ANC's vision', the Resolution stated, was 'to embrace a transformative environmentalism based upon the idea of sustainable development, which is built upon the inter-connection of environmental, social and economic justice' (ANC 2007). Climate change concerns also rose up the ANC's political agenda as the government sought to play a role as a bridge builder between developed and developing countries positions, as discussed above. This reflected the ANC's emerging perception of South Africa's growing role in the international system, its desire to increase the country's diplomatic clout and reputation, and the ANC's own experience of democratic transition, which forced the government to try to bring divergent positions together to arrive at an acceptable solution for all parties.

The inclusion of climate change concerns within the ANC policy resolutions increased political support for the development of climate policies considerably, paving the way for the developments discussed in the previous section. Yet, to a considerable extent, it has been the government's overriding focus on growth and its efforts to ensure that climate change policies are, above all, compatible with economic development that have given rise to discrepancies between policy and practice in the country. For instance, while President Zuma publicly committed South Africa to reducing carbon emissions, he has also expressed support for expanding the CTL process in South Africa, which would dramatically increase the use of coal for energy production in the country. The Zuma administration's emphasis on escalating infrastructure development, likewise, continues to be tied to fossil fuels. It has, for example, strongly supported the building of a major crude oil refinery, the Mthombo project by PetroSA, and the building of the enormous Medupi and Kusile coal-burning power stations, which presently underpin the government's energy strategy (de Bruyn 2010). Similarly, Ebrahim Patel, the economics and development minister, has emphasized the ongoing importance of coal in South Africa's future development, noting that '[w]e cannot abandon coal as coal contributes to the relatively low electricity prices we have' (Patel 2011). South Africa's minister of finance, Pravin Gordhan, has also highlighted the country's continued dependence on coal. In a piece written for the *Washington Post* he noted that to 'sustain the growth rates we need to create jobs, we have no choice but to build new generating capacity – relying on what, for now, remains our most abundant and affordable energy source: coal' (Creamer Media Reporter 2010). Even the environmental minister, Edna Molewa, when confronted with questions concerning the continued construction of the Medupi and Kusile power stations, has indicated that South Africa 'could not do without coal' (Naidoo 2011b).

In addition to South Africa's political leadership, both the private sector and civil society have played roles in the development of climate governance. Yet, as the next sections also demonstrate, there have been major disagreements over the precise character of South Africa's policies and this has further contributed to the government's fragmented response.

The Business of Climate Change

With big business's central position in the national economy, private sector interests have been able to assume a prominent role in national debates on climate change and within South Africa's own negotiating team in the UNFCCC. Indeed, this was evident in the inclusion of big business interests as part of South Africa's delegation at the Bonn talks in 2011 (Earthlife Africa and GroundWork 2011). This close collaboration led to an agreement between the DEA and business groups to work together in addressing mitigation, although this was under the provision that any targets established would not hamper economic development (Prinsloo 2011). Yet, while there have been businesses that have sought to include climate change considerations in their investment strategies, such as those participating in the Carbon Disclosure Project, Anglogold Ashanti (which has created a number of energy efficiency programmes) and Sasol (which has been engaged in biofuel research), big business has generally been slow to adopt some of the more progressive elements of the government's policy, hampering implementation. The slow uptake of the government's climate initiatives is due, in part, to the private sector's active resistance to what is perceived to be an ever-growing set of policy initiatives and structures that risk high compliance burdens and increased operating costs. It is also due, as Yaw Afrane-Okese from the National Business Initiative noted (Anon. 2009), to the absence of clear and coherent policy frameworks for companies to measure emissions and set targets for carbon reductions.

In general, therefore, the private sector has been particularly cautious in its approach towards climate change. Many of South Africa's energy intensive industries (the mineral and chemical industries, especially) have been opposed to the adoption of binding mitigation targets. At South Africa's national climate change summit, for instance, the Energy Reality Group (comprising a group of scientists, engineers and economists from major corporations) released a statement cautioning against adopting emissions reduction targets because of the high cost of mitigation measures for South Africa's development (Energy Reality Group 2009). The Energy Intensive User Group (EIUG) reiterated this position. With respect to the government's carbon tax, for example, the EIUG has sought to emphasize the tax's potentially adverse impacts on businesses, job creation and growth. In a similar vein, in public hearings related to the green paper (discussed above), the petroleum company Engen noted that any international commitment to reduce emissions or the adoption of 'stringent targets' could lead to 'South Africa being prejudiced against [sic] its competitors' (Parliamentary Monitoring Group 2011). Thus, many of the country's energy intensive companies have advocated more conservative targets for addressing GHG emissions than the government has sought. While there have been some positive developments among some companies in addressing climate change and some who have supported the government's renewable energy policies, in the main there has not been a major drive from within the private sector to see the government's policy initiatives implemented.

Civil Society and Climate Change Policy

Since the country's struggle against apartheid, South Africa has had a particularly active civil society. In the context of climate change, in particular, its civil society includes a diverse group of large transnational organizations, such as the World Wide Fund for Nature (WWF) and Greenpeace, and more community based organizations, such as the Rural Women's Assembly (RWA). However, these civil society groups have had mixed results in terms of their engagement with policy development and decision-making on the issue of climate change. In the case of the development of both the green paper and white paper on climate change, the DEA sought to engage all stakeholders through summits, stakeholder meetings and regional consultation workshops. Channels were created for civil society to engage in the development of climate policies. In some instances, this allowed groups to have a large impact on the shape of climate policies and positions. For instance, opposition from civil society, particularly from organized groups such as Earthlife Africa and CANE to the use of nuclear energy as a viable strategy for responding to climate change, led to the exclusion of nuclear power from the white paper (DEA 2011b).

In other instances, however, certain civil society groups have had much less input into South Africa's approach towards climate governance. Indeed, despite the emphasis on engagement through consultations, this has not always translated into participation for all groups. Often, the means of communication have not been well suited to ensuring engagement by some of the most vulnerable groups in society; for instance, those who may not have access to computers. In other instances, participants in the creation of the LTMS and the Climate Change Response Strategy were selectively chosen from particular groups. In his critique of the LTMS, David Hallowes (2008) has claimed that participation was 'skewed to current dominant economic players in terms of representation'. Civil society groups have also frequently found themselves at a disadvantage relative to business interests. Unlike big business, which tends to be better funded and more organized, South African civil society groups have not been able to arrive at a coordinated strategy for engaging the government. This became especially apparent in the preparations for the civil society event that ran parallel to COP17, as deep divisions emerged among the parties organizing it (Hargreaves 2012).

In sum, while there is a complex array of proactive civil society actors within South Africa pushing the government to adopt more stringent policies and implementing them accordingly, it has generally been larger groups, such as the WWF, that have occupied a more central position in the climate change debates. Although smaller groups representing disadvantaged parts of the population have had an impact at times, their voice has largely been neglected. This has, to some extent, hindered the overall impact of civil society, and raised important questions about the accountability and fairness of the policymaking process.

Conclusion

In addressing the question of why climate change governance has been slow to develop in South Africa, this chapter has considered three key issues: (1) the historic context shaping the country's approach towards climate change; (2) the evolution of climate policy; and (3) the role of competing interests and stakeholder positions in defining climate governance. South Africa's history of apartheid gave rise to inequalities along racial lines, including inequalities in terms of access to energy, as well as growing dependence upon coal for the production of energy as a result of the government's efforts to ensure energy security. Following the advent of democracy, the government largely focused on addressing the inequalities of the past. Thus, while South Africa was engaged in international climate change negotiations, the government remained preoccupied with its internal transformation during the 1990s. Domestically, climate change was relatively neglected.

In the early 2000s, however, attention was increasingly given to questions of climate change, mirroring its rising importance on the international agenda. The ANC also became more proactive on the issue, largely as a result of new information about the country's vulnerability and its recent foreign policy ambitions. Yet, as this chapter has argued, although there has been greater domestic recognition of the impact of climate change and the need for mitigation, with many policy documents making reference to climate change, this has not translated into a coherent approach to climate governance. The emphasis in South Africa's climate policies remains firmly on maintaining its economic competitiveness and addressing economic growth and development priorities. This emphasis has been important for bringing on board business interests in the country, which have traditionally been opposed to stringent climate policies. But it has also had the effect of diverting real attention away from effective climate governance. Furthermore, efforts to support a cross-sectoral approach to climate change have seen limited success. Structures such as the IGCCC and the NCCC have tended to exclude important departmental players.

In order to explain these outcomes, this chapter has highlighted the role of various actors involved in the policy process. Climate change remains an issue deeply affected by political, private sector and civil society interests. In combination with international pressures, the government's ambitions in the UNFCCC negotiations and in support of its role as a 'responsible international citizen' have been the primary drivers of climate policy. However, actual implementation has encountered obstacles at the domestic level as a result of the cautious and occasionally oppositional stance on climate change initiatives taken by the private sector, and difficulties in ensuring stakeholder participation across civil society groups. South Africa has, therefore, reached a crossroads. While there has been some progress in terms of policy development and stakeholder engagement, there is still a long way to go before the 'mosaic' of standalone initiatives discussed in this chapter adds up to a coherent approach towards climate governance.

Acknowledgements

I would like to thank Charles Roger and his colleagues for all their help and invaluable insights on earlier drafts of this chapter.

References

ANC (2007). *52nd National Conference: Climate Change Resolution*. Available at: http://www.anc.org.za/show.php?id=2536#climate.

Anon. (2009). *Putting the Brake on Climate Change*. Available at: http://www.joburg.org.za/index.php?option=com_content&task=view&id=2563&Itemid=168.

Benton, S. (2008). SA adopts 'bold' climate change policy. *South Africa.info*. Available at: http://www.southafrica.info/about/sustainable/climate-300708.htm.

Creamer Media Reporter (2010). Gordhan defends Eskom's World Bank loan in *Washington Post* column. *Engineering News*. Available at: http://www.engineeringnews.co.za/article/gordhan-defends-eskoms-world-bank-loan-in-washington-post-column-2010-03-24.

Davidson, O. (2006). Energy policy. In H. Winkler (ed.) *Energy Policies for Sustainable Development in South Africa: Options for the Future*. Cape Town: Energy Research Centre, University of Cape Town.

DEA (2010). *National Climate Change Response Green Paper*. Pretoria: Department of

Environmental Affairs. Available at: http://us-cdn.creamermedia.co.za/assets/articles/attachments/30766_climate_change_greenpaper.pdf.

DEA (2011a). *South Africa's Second National Communication under the United Nations Framework Convention on Climate Change.* Available at: http://unfccc.int/resource/docs/natc/snc_south_africa_.pdf.

DEA (2011b). *National Climate Change Response White Paper.* Available at: http://rava.qsens.net/themes/theme_emissions/111012nccr-whitepaper.pdf.

DEA, DED, DST, DTI, SACN & SALGA (2010). *Green Economy Summit: Summit Report.* Available at: http://www.environment.gov.za/sites/default/files/docs/greene_conomy_summit.pdf.

DEAT (2004). *A National Climate Change Response Strategy.* Pretoria: Department of Environmental Affairs and Tourism. Available at: http://unfccc.int/files/meetings/seminar/application/pdf/sem_sup3_south_africa.pdf.

DEAT (2007). *Long Term Mitigation Scenarios: Scenario Document.* Pretoria: Department of Environment Affairs and Tourism.

deBruyn, C. (2010). Coega refinery to save SA R12,6bn/y in energy costs – Zuma. *Engineering News.* Available at: http://www.engineeringnews.co.za/article/coega-refinery-to-save-sa-r126bny-in-energy-costs-zuma-2010-10-14.

DIRCO (2011). *Building a Better World: The Diplomacy of Ubuntu.* White Paper on South Africa's Foreign Policy. Available at: http://www.info.gov.za/view/DownloadFileAction?id=149749.

DME (1998). *White Paper on the Energy Policy of the Republic of South Africa.* Available at: http://www.info.gov.za/whitepapers/1998/energywp98.htm.

DME (2003a). *Integrated Energy Plan for the Republic of South Africa.* Available at: http://www.info.gov.za/view/DownloadFileAction?id=124574.

DME (2003b). *White Paper on Renewable Energy.* Pretoria: Department of Minerals and Energy. Available at http://unfccc.int/files/meetings/seminar/application/pdf/scm_sup1_south_africa.pdf.

DME (2009). *Renewable Energy Summit 2009: Summit Resolutions.* Available at: http://www.cityenergy.org.za/files/resources/re/RE%20summit%20Resolution%2008042009%20final.pdf.

DOE (2010). *South African Energy Synopsis 2010.* Available at: http://www.energy.gov.za/files/media/explained/2010/South_African_Energy_Synopsis_2010.pdf.

DOE (2011). *Integrated Resource Plan for Electricity 2010–2030.* Pretoria: Department of Energy. Available at: http://www.doe-irp.co.za.

Durning, A. B. (1990). *Apartheid's Environmental Toll.* Worldwatch Paper 95. Worldwatch Institute.

Earthlife Africa and GroundWork (2011). South Africa's high carbon emission negotiators, UNFCCC failing. *GroundWork* 15 June. Available at: http://www.groundwork.org.za/Press%20Releases/15june2011.html.

Energy Reality Group (2009). *Statement for the National Climate Change Summit.* Available at: http://www.ccsummit2009.co.za/Downloads/Media/ERG_Climate_Change_Summit_Statement.pdf.

Hallowes, D. (2008). *A Critical Appraisal of the LTMS.* Prepared for the Sustainable Energy and Climate Change Project (SECCP) of Earthlife Africa, Johannesburg. Available at: http://www.earthlife.org.za/wordpress/wp-content/uploads/2008/12/ltms-final-web.pdf.

Hargreaves, S. (2012). *COP 17 and Civil Society: The Centre Did Not Hold.* Occasional Paper No. 64. Pretoria: Institute for Global Dialogue.

IPCC (2007). *Climate Change 2007: Synthesis Report*. Contribution of Working Groups I, II and III to the Fourth Assessment Report of the Intergovernmental Panel on Climate Change, eds. R. K. Pachauri & A. Reisinger. Available at: http://www.ipcc.ch/pdf/assessment-report/ar4/syr/ar4_syr_frontmatter.pdf.

Jooste, M., H. Winkler, D. van Seventer & T. P. Truong (2009). *The Effect of Response Measures to Climate Change on South Africa's Economy and Trade*. Energy Research Centre, Cape Town. Available at: http://www.erc.uct.ac.za/Research/publications/09Joosteetal-Response_Measures.pdf.

Leck, H., C. Sutherland, D. Scott & G. Oelofse (2011). Social and cultural barriers to adaptation implementation. In L. Masters & L. Duff (eds.) *Overcoming Barriers to Climate Change Adaptation Implementation in Southern Africa*. Pretoria: Africa Institute of South Africa.

Masters, L. (2011). *Building Bridges: South Africa as Hosts of the UNFCCC Climate Change Negotiations, Durban 2011*. COP 17: South Africa and the Road to Durban 2011. Pretoria: Institute for Global Dialogue.

Naidoo, B. (2011a). Policy shows SA ready to take action on climate change. *Engineering News*. Available at: http://www.engineeringnews.co.za/article/policy-shows-sa-ready-to-take-action-on-climate-change-2011-11-04.

Naidoo, B. (2011b). SA not backing away from its GHG reduction targets – minister. *Engineering News*. Available at: http://www.engineeringnews.co.za/article/sa-not-backing-away-from-its-ghg-reduction-targets-minister-2011-11-08.

NPC (2012). *Ensuring Environmental Sustainability and an Equitable Transition to a Low-Carbon Economy: The National Development Plan*. Available at: http://www.npconline.co.za/MediaLib/Downloads/Home/Tabs/NDP%202030-CH5-Environmental%20sustainability.pdf.

Parliamentary Monitoring Group (2011). *National Climate Change Response Policy Green Paper 2010: Public Hearings Day 3*. Available at: http://www.pmg.org.za/report/20110309-climate-change-green-paper-2010-public-hearings.

Patel, E. (2011). Coal to remain vital: Patel. *Times Live*. Available at: http://www.timeslive.co.za/local/2011/11/08/coal-to-remain-vital-patel.

Prinsloo, L. (2011). Business engaging with government on climate change. *Engineering News*. Available at: http://www.engineeringnews.co.za/article/sa-business-engaging-with-government-on-climate-change-2011-08-10.

Putnam, R. D. (1988). Diplomacy and domestic politics: The logic of the two-level game. *International Organization* 42(3).

Schreiner, B. (1995). A Popular Guide to Environmental Reconstruction and Development. Ottawa: IDRC.

Sonjica, B. (2009). Speech by Ms Buyelwa Sonjica, MP, Minister of Minerals and Energy at the Renewable Energy Summit: Swan Lake Conference Centre, Centurion, Gauteng. Available at: http://www.info.gov.za/speeches/2009/09032311151001.htm.

Stern, N. (2006). *Stern Review on the Economics of Climate Change*. London: HM Treasury. Available at: http://webarchive.nationalarchives.gov.uk/+/http:/www.hm-treasury.gov.uk/sternreview_index.htm.

van der Merwe, C. (2011). Budget could set green-economy tone. *Engineering News* 18 February. Available at: http://www.engineeringnews.co.za/print-version/greener-budget-2011-02-18.

Index

Note: abbreviations used in the index are explained on pp. xiii–xix.

277

Index

Index

Index